COMPUTER BOOK SERIES FROM IDG

The Internet For Dummies, 2nd Edition

If you don't have time to read the book, here are some Internet essentials

Cheat Sheet

W9-APF-038

IDG BOOKS

® Copyright © 1994 IDG Books Worldwide. All rights reserved.
Cheat Sheet $2.95 value. Item 222-8.
For more information about IDG Books, call
1-800-762-2974 or 415-312-0650

Fill in Your Important Internet Information Here

Your e-mail address: _____@_____

Your Internet host name: _____

Your Internet host number: _____ . _____ . _____ . _____

Electronic mail (Chapter 7-10)

Your mail program:

❏ mail ❏ elm ❏ pine ❏ Eudora

(Fill these in for your mail program)

To do this	Type this
Read new mail	_____
Delete a message	_____
Save a message	_____
Reply to message	_____
Forward a message	_____
Leave mail	q or Q or x

To send to	With this address	Use this address
AOL	Jim Smith	jimsmith@aol.com
Delphi	jsmith	jsmith@delphi.com
Easylink	3141592	3141592@eln.attmail.com
GEnie	J.SMITH7	J.SMITH7@genie.geis.com
MCI Mail	555-2468	5552468@mcimail.com
	Jim Smith	jim_smith@mcimail.com
CompuServe	7123,4567	7123.4567@compuserve.com
BITNET	user@node	user@node.bitnit *or* user % node.bitnet@cunyvm.cuny.edu
Fido	Mary Smith 1:2/3.4	mary.smith@p4.f3.n2.z1.fidonet.org
Sprintmail and other X.400 systems, See Chapter 9		

Usenet news (Chapters 11-12)

Fill these in for your news program:

Your news program: ❏ rn ❏ trn ❏ nn ❏ tin ❏ trumpet

To do this	Type this
Read next message	space
Skip this message	n
Skip all related messages permanently	k
Save message to file	sfilename
Respond to author	r or R
Respond to the world	f or F
Leave news	q or ___ (may have to type 2 or 3 times)

Command to send new news items: ❏ Pnews ❏ :post ❏ Other ___

Logging into another system (Chapter 14)

Type: **telnet** *hostname*
or **rlogin** *hostname*

Your telnet escape:
❏ Ctrl/] ❏ Window Menu
❏ Other ___
After escape, type **quit** to leave telnet

Your rlogin escape:
❏ Enter ~ . Enter
❏ Other ___

. . . For Dummies: #1 Computer Book Series for Beginners

COMPUTER
BOOK SERIES
FROM IDG

The Internet For Dummies, 2nd Edition

Cheat Sheet

File copying: ftp and rcp

Type: **ftp** *hostname*

If you don't have an account there, use anonymous as the login name and use your e-mail address as the password.

To do this	Type this
List current directory	dir
List another directory	dir *dirname*
Change directory	cd *dirname*
Prepare to copy text	ascii
Prepare to copy non-text	binary or image
Retrieve a file	get *filename*
Retrieve many files	mget *file1 file2...*
Store a file	put *filename*
Store many files	put *file1 file2...*
Delete remote file	del *filename*
Leave FTP	quit

To copy from other machines where you have an account:

```
rcp hostname:remotefile localfile
```

To copy to other machines where you have an account:

```
rcp localfile hostname:remote file
```

Finding files by name: Archie (Chapter 19)

Telnet: telnet to_____
(See Chapter 19)

By e-mail: mail to archie@_____
(See Chapter 19)

Mail or type: prog *nametomatch*

With a local Archie program, type:
archie *nametomatch*, and then use FTP to retrieve files.

Finding data through menus: Gopher (Chapter 20)

Access via: ❑ local command_____

❑ telnet to_____

To do this	Type this
Move to menu item	line number or ↑ and ↓
Select item	Enter or →
Next page of menu	+
Previous page of menu	-
Search menu for string	/*string*
Previous menu	u or
Go to main menu	m (in menu, not in item)
Mail item to you	m (at end of item, not in menu)
Save item as file	s (not if telnet)
Print item	p (not if telnet)
Leave Gopher	qqq
Download item	D (in menu, not in item)

Text Search: WAIS (Chapter 21)

Access to WAIS:

❑ Gopher menu ❑ Local client called_____
❑ via WWW

Don't try to telnet; see Chapter 21

Hypertext: WWW (Chapter 22)

Access via: ❑ local client program ❑ telnet to_____

Choosing an item: ❑ type number ❑ mouse click
❑ move cursor, then Enter

Get help on other commands: ?

Search indexed data:_____

Leave WWW: q or quit

. . . For Dummies: #1 Computer Book Series for Beginners

™

References for the Rest of Us

COMPUTER BOOK SERIES FROM IDG

Are you intimidated and confused by computers? Do you find that traditional manuals are overloaded with technical details you'll never use? Do your friends and family always call you to fix simple problems on their PCs? Then the ... *For Dummies™* computer book series from IDG is for you.

... *For Dummies* books are written for those frustrated computer users who know they aren't really dumb but find that PC hardware, software, and indeed the unique vocabulary of computing make them feel helpless. ... *For Dummies* books use a lighthearted approach, a down-to-earth style, and even cartoons and humorous icons to diffuse computer novices' fears and build their confidence. Lighthearted but not lightweight, these books are a perfect survival guide to anyone forced to use a computer.

> *"I like my copy so much I told friends; now they bought copies."*
>
> **Irene C., Orwell, Ohio**

> *"Quick, concise, nontechnical, and humorous."*
>
> **Jay A., Elburn, IL**

> *"Thanks, I needed this book. Now I can sleep at night."*
>
> **Robin F., British Columbia, Canada**

Already, hundreds of thousands of satisfied readers agree. They have made ... *For Dummies* books the #1 introductory level computer book series and have written asking for more. So if you're looking for the most fun and easy way to learn about computers, look to ... *For Dummies* books to give you a helping hand.

IDG BOOKS

THE INTERNET FOR DUMMIES™

2ND EDITION

THE INTERNET FOR DUMMIES™
2ND EDITION

**by John R. Levine
and Carol Baroudi**

Foreword by Paul McCloskey
Executive Editor of *Federal Computer Week*

IDG
BOOKS

IDG Books Worldwide, Inc.
An International Data Group Company

Foster City, CA ♦ Chicago, IL ♦ Indianapolis, IN ♦ Braintree, MA ♦ Dallas, TX

The Internet For Dummies™, 2nd Edition

Published by

IDG Books Worldwide, Inc.

An International Data Group Company

919 E. Hillsdale Blvd.

Suite 400

Foster City, CA 94404

Text and art copyright © 1994 by IDG Books Worldwide, Inc. All rights reserved. No part of this book, including interior design, cover design, and icons, may be reproduced or transmitted in any form, by any means (electronic, photocopying, recording or others) without the prior written permission of the publisher.

Library of Congress Catalog Card No.: 94-78897

ISBN: 1-56884-222-8

Printed in the United States of America

10 9 8 7 6 5 4

2A/SY/RS/ZU

Distributed in the United States by IDG Books Worldwide, Inc.

Distributed by Macmillan Canada for Canada; by Computer Technical Books for the Caribbean Basin; by Contemporanea de Ediciones for Venezuela; by Distribuidora Cuspide for Argentina; by CITEC for Brazil; by Ediciones ZETA S.C.R. Ltda. for Peru; by Editorial Limusa SA for Mexico; by Transworld Publishers Limited in the United Kingdom and Europe; by Al-Maiman Publishers & Distributors for Saudi Arabia; by Simron Pty. Ltd. for South Africa; by IDG Communications (HK) Ltd. for Hong Kong; by Toppan Company Ltd. for Japan; by Addison Wesley Publishing Company for Korea; by Longman Singapore Publishers Ltd. for Singapore, Malaysia, Thailand and Indonesia; by Unalis Corporation for Taiwan; by WS Computer Publishing Company, Inc. for the Philippines; by WoodsLane Pty. Ltd. for Australia; by WoodsLane Enterprises Ltd. for New Zealand.

For general information on IDG Books in the U.S., including information on discounts and premiums, contact IDG Books at 800-434-3422 or 415-655-3000.

For information on where to purchase IDG Books outside the U.S., contact IDG Books International at 415-655-3021 or fax 415-655-3295.

For information on translations, contact Marc Jeffrey Mikulich, Director, Foreign & Subsidiary Rights, at IDG Books Worldwide, at 415-655-3018 or fax 415-655-3295.

For sales inquiries and special prices for bulk quantities, write to the address above or call IDG Books Worldwide at 415-655-3000.

For information on using IDG Books in the classroom, or ordering examination copies, contact Jim Kelly at 800-434-2086.

Trademarks: Windows is a registered trademark of Microsoft Corporation. All brand names and product names used in this book are trademarks, registered trademarks, or trade names of their respective holders. IDG Books Worldwide is not associated with any product or vendor mentioned in this book.

Limit of Liability/Disclaimer of Warranty: The author and publisher have used their best efforts in preparing this book. IDG Books Worldwide, Inc., International Data Group, Inc., and the author make no representation or warranties with respect to the accuracy or completeness of the contents of this book and specifically disclaim any implied warranties of merchantability or fitness for any particular purpose and shall in no event be liable for any loss of profit or any other commercial damage, including but not limited to special, incidental, consequential, or other damages.

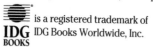 is a registered trademark of IDG Books Worldwide, Inc.

About the Authors

John Levine was a member of a computer club in high school — before high school students, or even high schools, *had* computers. He came in contact with Theodor H. Nelson, author of *Computer Lib* and inventor of hypertext, who fostered the idea that computers should not be taken seriously and that everyone can and should understand and use computers.

John wrote his first program on an IBM 1130 (a computer roughly as powerful as your typical modern digital wristwatch, only harder to use) in 1967. He became an official system administrator of a networked computer at Yale in 1975. He started working part-time (for a computer company, of course) in 1977, and has been in and out of the computer and network biz ever since. He got his company put on USENET (see Chapter 11) early enough that it appears in a 1982 *Byte* magazine article, which included a map of USENET sites.

He used to spend most of his time writing software, but now he mostly writes books (including *UNIX For Dummies* and *MORE Internet for Dummies,* published by IDG Books Worldwide) because it's more fun. He also teaches some computer courses, publishes and edits an incredibly technoid magazine called *The Journal of C Language Translation,* and moderates a Usenet newsgroup. He holds a B.A. and a Ph.D in Computer Science from Yale University, but please don't hold that against him.

Carol Baroudi met her first computer in college at Colgate University in 1971. Her first encounter with electronic communication was in the form of *send ttys,* an ancient form of terminal warfare.

She taught programming and helped design a computer science curriculum but majored in Spanish Literature. For the past ten years, she's been writing about computer software, including various electronic mail packages.

She firmly believes that computers should be easy and fun to use but are no substitute for real life.

ABOUT IDG BOOKS WORLDWIDE

VIII

WINNER
*Eighth Annual
Computer Press
Awards ≥ 1992*

IX

WINNER
*Ninth Annual
Computer Press
Awards ≥ 1993*

IDG BOOKS

Welcome to the world of IDG Books Worldwide.

IDG Books Worldwide, Inc. is a subsidiary of International Data Group, the world's largest publisher of computer-related information and the leading global provider of information services on information technology. IDG was founded more than 25 years ago and now employs more than 7,000 people worldwide. IDG publishes more than 220 computer publications in 65 countries (see listing below). More than fifty million people read one or more IDG publications each month.

Launched in 1990, IDG Books Worldwide is today the #1 publisher of best-selling computer books in the United States. We are proud to have received 3 awards from the Computer Press Association in recognition of editorial excellence, and our best-selling *...For Dummies*™ series has more than 12 million copies in print with translations in 25 languages. IDG Books, through a recent joint venture with IDG's Hi-Tech Beijing, became the first U.S. publisher to publish a computer book in the People's Republic of China. In record time, IDG Books has become the first choice for millions of readers around the world who want to learn how to better manage their businesses.

Our mission is simple: Every IDG book is designed to bring extra value and skill-building instructions to the reader. Our books are written by experts who understand and care about our readers. The knowledge base of our editorial staff comes from years of experience in publishing, education, and journalism — experience which we use to produce books for the '90s. In short, we care about books, so we attract the best people. We devote special attention to details such as audience, interior design, use of icons, and illustrations. And because we use an efficient process of authoring, editing, and desktop publishing our books electronically, we can spend more time ensuring superior content and spend less time on the technicalities of making books.

You can count on our commitment to deliver high-quality books at competitive prices on topics consumers want to read about. At IDG, we value quality, and we have been delivering quality for more than 25 years. You'll find no better book on a subject than an IDG book.

John J. Kilcullen

John Kilcullen
President and CEO
IDG Books Worldwide, Inc.

IDG Books Worldwide, Inc. is a subsidiary of International Data Group, the world's largest publisher of computer-related information and the leading global provider of information services on information technology. International Data Group publishes over 220 computer publications in 65 countries. More than fifty million people read one or more International Data Group publications each month. The officers are Patrick J. McGovern, Founder and Board Chairman; Kelly Conlin, President; Jim Casella, Chief Operating Officer. International Data Group's publications include: **ARGENTINA'S** Computerworld Argentina, Infoworld Argentina; **AUSTRALIA'S** Computerworld Australia, Computer Living, Australian PC World, Australian Macworld, Network World, Mobile Business Australia, Publish!, Reseller, IDG Sources; **AUSTRIA'S** Computerwelt Oesterreich, PC Test; **BELGIUM'S** Data News (CW); **BOLIVIA'S** Computerworld; **BRAZIL'S** Computerworld, Connections, Game Power, Mundo Unix, PC World, Publish, Super Game; **BULGARIA'S** Computerworld Bulgaria, PC & Mac World Bulgaria, Network World Bulgaria; **CANADA'S** CIO Canada, Computerworld Canada, InfoCanada, Network World Canada, Reseller; **CHILE'S** Computerworld Chile, Informatica; **COLOMBIA'S** Computerworld Colombia, PC World; **COSTA RICA'S** PC World; **CZECH REPUBLIC'S** Computerworld, Elektronika, PC World; **DENMARK'S** Communications World, Computerworld Danmark, Computerworld Focus, Macintosh Produktkatalog, Macworld Danmark, PC World Danmark, PC Produktguide, Tech World, Windows World; **ECUADOR'S** PC World Ecuador; **EGYPT'S** Computerworld (CW) Middle East, PC World Middle East; **FINLAND'S** MikroPC, Tietoviikko, Tietoverkko; **FRANCE'S** Distributique, GOLDEN MAC, InfoPC, Le Guide du Monde Informatique, Le Monde Informatique, Telecoms & Reseaux; **GERMANY'S** Computerwoche, Computerwoche Focus, Computerwoche Extra, Electronic Entertainment, Gamepro, Information Management, Macwelt, Netzwelt, PC Welt, Publish, Publish; **GREECE'S** Publish & Macworld; **HONG KONG'S** Computerworld Hong Kong, PC World Hong Kong; **HUNGARY'S** Computerworld SZT, PC World; **INDIA'S** Computers & Communications; **INDONESIA'S** Info Komputer; **IRELAND'S** ComputerScope; **ISRAEL'S** Beyond Windows, Computerworld Israel, Multimedia, PC World Israel; **ITALY'S** Computerworld Italia, Lotus Magazine, Macworld Italia, Networking Italia, PC Shopping Italy, PC World Italia; **JAPAN'S** Computerworld Today, Information Systems World, Macworld Japan, Nikkei Personal Computing, SunWorld Japan, Windows World; **KENYA'S** East African Computer News; **KOREA'S** Computerworld Korea, Macworld Korea, PC World Korea; **LATIN AMERICA'S** GamePro; **MALAYSIA'S** Computerworld Malaysia, PC World Malaysia; **MEXICO'S** Compu Edicion, Compu Manufactura, Computacion/Punto de Venta, Computerworld Mexico, MacWorld, Mundo Unix, PC World, Windows; **THE NETHERLANDS'** Computer! Totaal, Computable (CW), LAN Magazine, Lotus Magazine, MacWorld; **NEW ZEALAND'S** Computer Buyer, Computerworld New Zealand, Network World, New Zealand PC World; **NIGERIA'S** PC World Africa; **NORWAY'S** Computerworld Norge, Lotusworld Norge, Macworld Norge, Maxi Data, Networld, PC World Ekspress, PC World Nettverk, PC World Norge, PC World's Produktguide, Publish& Multimedia World, Student Data, Unix World, Windowsworld; **PAKISTAN'S** PC World Pakistan; **PANAMA'S** PC World Panama; **PERU'S** Computerworld Peru, PC World; **PEOPLE'S REPUBLIC OF CHINA'S** China Computerworld, China Infoworld, China PC Info Magazine, Computer Fan, PC World China, Electronics International, Electronics Today/Multimedia World, Electronic Product World, China Network World, Software World Magazine, Telecom Product World, **PHILIPPINES'** Computerworld Philippines, PC Digest (PCW); **POLAND'S** Computerworld Poland, Computerworld Special Report, Networld, PC World/Komputer, Sunworld; **PORTUGAL'S** Cerebro/PC World, Correio Informatico/Computerworld, MacIn; **ROMANIA'S** Computerworld, PC World, Telecom Romania; **RUSSIA'S** Computerworld-Moscow, Mir - PK (PCW), Sety (Networks); **SINGAPORE'S** Computerworld Southeast Asia, PC World Singapore; **SLOVENIA'S** Monitor Magazine; **SOUTH AFRICA'S** Computer Mail (CIO),Computing S.A.,Network World S.A., Software World; **SPAIN'S** Advanced Systems, Amiga World, Computerworld Espana, Communicaciones World, Macworld Espana, NeXTWORLD, Super Juegos Magazine (GamePro), PC World Espana, Publish; **SWEDEN'S** Attack, ComputerSweden, Corporate Computing, Macworld, Mikrodatorn, Natverk & Kommunikation, PC World, CAP & Design, Datalngenjoren, Maxi Data,Windows World; **SWITZERLAND'S** Computerworld Schweiz, Macworld Schweiz, PC Tip; **TAIWAN'S** Computerworld Taiwan, PC World Taiwan; **THAILAND'S** Thai Computerworld; **TURKEY'S** Computerworld Monitor, Macworld Turkiye, PC World Turkiye; **UKRAINE'S** Computerworld, Computers+Software Magazine; **UNITED KINGDOM'S** Computing / Computerworld, Connexion/Network World, Lotus Magazine, Macworld, Open Computing/Sunworld; **URAGUAY'S** PC World Uraguay; **UNITED STATES'** Advanced Systems, AmigaWorld, Cable in the Classroom, CD Review, CIO, Computerworld, Computerworld Client/Server Journal, Digital Video, DOS World, Electronic Entertainment Magazine (E2), Federal Computer Week, Game Hits, GamePro, IDG Books, Infoworld, Laser Event, Macworld, Maximize, Multimedia World, Network World, PC Letter, PC World, Publish, SWATPro, Video Event; **VENEZUELA'S** Computerworld Venezuela, PC World; **VIETNAM'S** PC World Vietnam.
11/16/94

Acknowledgments

John would like to thank Lydia Spitzer for putting up with him while he wrote this, particularly when he should have been out sailing with her. Sophie, who knows who she is, was patient too, and kept his feet warm.

Many of the tables in *The Internet For Dummies,* 2nd Edition were adapted from material provided gratis by people on the Internet. The list of countries with Internet connections in the Appendix was written by Professor Larry Landweber. The lists of newsgroups in Chapter 12 were condensed from master lists maintained by David Lawrence. The information on DOS and Windows TCP/IP packages in Chapter 28 was adapted from a list maintained by C. J. Sacksteder at the Pennsylvania State University.

John particularly thanks his editors at IDG, Mary Bednarek and Diane Steele, for believing him when he said he was finishing the first edition of this book, despite considerable evidence to the contrary. Carol thanks them too and feels blessed to be in such fine company.

Carol would also like to thank Joshua Reinhold whose spirit and good cheer lighten every day, and all those who've helped us come this far.

And special thanks to IDG editors Corbin Collins and Becky Whitney, who kept all the bits and pieces of this project running smoothly. Thanks also to Tamara Castleman, Andy Cummings, Shawn MacLaren, and Erik Dafforn for pitching in to tie up loose ends.

Thanks also to Dennis Cox, Jim Moody, and Paul McCloskey for providing some additional perspectives. And, of course, thanks to all the incredible production staff at IDG Books Worldwide in Indianapolis. (And thanks to IndyNet for appearing just in time.)

(The publisher would like to give special thanks to Patrick J. McGovern, without whom this book would not have been possible.)

Credits

Executive Vice President, Strategic Product Planning & Research
David Solomon

Editorial Director
Diane Graves Steele

Acquisitions Editor
Megg Bonar

Brand Manager
Judith A. Taylor

Editorial Managers
Tracy L. Barr
Sandra Blackthorn

Editorial Assistants
Tamara S. Castleman
Stacey Holden Prince
Kevin Spencer

Acquisitions Assistant
Suki Gear

Production Director
Beth Jenkins

Project Coordinator
Cindy L. Phipps

Pre-Press Coordinator
Steve Peake

Project Editor
Corbin Collins

Editor
Rebecca A. Whitney

Technical Reviewer
Dennis Cox

Production Staff
Tony Augsburger
J. Tyler Connor
Drew R. Moore
Mark Owens
Laura Puranen
Dwight Ramsey
Patricia R. Reynolds
Gina Scott

Proofreader
Henry Lazarek

Indexer
Sherry Massey

Cover Design
Kavish + Kavish

Contents at a Glance

Cartoons at a Glance
By Rich Tennant

"I THINK WHAT WE LIKE MOST ABOUT IT IS ITS TRANSPARENCY IN THE SYSTEM."

page 165

"NO SIR, THIS ISN'T A DATING SERVICE. THEY INTRODUCE PEOPLE THROUGH A COMPUTER SO THEY CAN TALK TO EACH OTHER IN PERSON. WE INTRODUCE PEOPLE IN PERSON SO THEY CAN TALK TO EACH OTHER THROUGH A COMPUTER."

page 73

"I think this answers our question—no, it's not a good idea to try to download the entire Internet at one time."

page 231

"WELL, I NEVER THOUGHT I'D SEE THE DAY I COULD SAY I TELNETTED TO A BRAZILIAN HOST, THEN USED THE WORLD WIDE WEB TO GET A GOPHER MENU, ONLY TO FIND OUT I HAVE TO ANONYMOUS FTP."

page 323

"HOW SHOULD I KNOW WHY THEY TOOK IT OFF THE LIST? MAYBE THERE JUST WEREN'T ENOUGH MEMBERS TO SUPPORT AN 'AIREDALES FOR ELVIS' NEWSGROUP."

page 5

"I DON'T THINK OUR NEWEST NETWORK CONFIGURATION IS GOING TO WORK. ALL OF OUR TRANSMISSIONS FROM OHIO SEEM TO BE COMING IN OVER MY ELECTRIC PENCIL SHARPENER."

page 289

Table of Contents

Foreword

 year ago I was the original Internet Dummy.

Although I had been covering technology in one form or another for 10 years as a journalist, I considered most computers to be typewriters on steroids. I just needed a good text editor, about 15 megabytes of storage, and a push-button phone.

Also, I thought most of my office mates who actually did bury their heads in their personal computers were the newsroom equivalents of heating and air conditioning engineers. I had better things to do than marvel about "personal productivity tools" or "spreadsheet performance." Computing in a bubble, I thought.

Then while I was on vacation, a colleague ran some telephone wire into the back of my computer, loaded a communications package, and left me a note about how to launch the operation.

Readers, that note is now framed in my office. Eventually, that telephone wire led to the Internet and the single most amazing, entertaining, and educational experience of my career.

Quite simply, the Internet has revolutionized the way I interact with the outside world, altered my work habits, and burst the bubble around my PC. It has also challenged my thinking about the future of personal communications technology. And I believe that sooner — rather than later — those changes will be mapped onto society as a whole.

Consider this: My $1,000 PC is now a personal broadcasting station that reaches more people than the CBS affiliate in Washington D.C. I can get more local viewers with a single e-mail posting to the Internet than Sally Jessy Raphael can get in a sweeps month.

Or this: I'm going to send this piece to my editor for about a sixtieth of a cent — it will take roughly a sixth of a second. (Memo to the Letter Carriers Union: Invest in night schools, *now*.)

Or this: When Vice President Al Gore released his proposal for the National Information Infrastructure, his personal vision for the Information Superhighway, it was zapped to my e-mail box that very morning, courtesy of an Internet group I belong to that is interested in such matters. (Hey *Washington Post*! POOF! You're a newsletter!)

I've also had some amazing interactions on the Internet, the implications of which I am still trying to figure out. For instance, a few months ago I was logged on to the Internet's equivalent of a live on-line forum in which two other people were present. Now that's not so unusual, considering the popularity of similar forums running on the dressier, private on-line services. But then one of them handed me a photograph. Actually, it was a little more complicated than that — given the hardware and software being used, I had to execute some commands, download the file, and stomp on it a few times — but that is essentially what happened. Instead of exchanging text messages, we swapped graphics.

Although it was a simple transaction, given that I was in Washington, D.C., and the other two people possibly in Wheaton, Illinois, and Durban, South Africa, it was an amazing interaction. Wait until baseball card collectors get ahold of that one.

But that is one of the joys of the Internet. Its constantly evolving set of applications is being driven not so much by software developers but by its users, all crowding around, talking, and trying out new things.

And while the Internet has turned around the way I interact with the outside world, it has also made me more keen about the technology on my end of the wall jack. Those little pieces of software that make my personal computer more of a convenience have a whole new power and meaning when attached to the two million computers on the Internet.

I now run short digital motion pictures on my PC. The software and the graphics are tucked away in their proper places on the Internet. My PC is humming with software — Indiana Jones never saw more icons. My home and office are now wired together. And I no longer discredit the office PC tinkerers; I just urge them to get on the Internet.

I therefore urge you to read John Levine's *The Internet For Dummies,* 2nd Edition. It will guide you with patience and a refreshing sense of humor through the sometimes daunting job of getting going on the net. But you will be rewarded. And the rest is up to your imagination.

Paul McCloskey
Executive Editor
Federal Computer Week

Introduction

. . . .

*W*elcome to *The Internet For Dummies,* 2nd Edition! There are lots of books available about the Internet, but most of them assume that you have a degree in computer science, would love to learn every strange and useless wart of the Internet, and enjoy memorizing unpronounceable commands and options. We hope this book is different.

Instead, this book describes what you actually do to become an *Internaut* (someone who navigates the Internet with skill) — how to get started, what commands you actually need, and when to give up and go for help. And we describe it in plain old English.

About This Book

This book is designed to be used when you can't figure out what to do next. We don't flatter ourselves that you are interested enough in the Internet to sit down and read the whole thing (although it should be a fine book for the bathroom). When you run into a problem using the Internet ("Hmm . . . I thought I typed a command that would log into another computer, but it didn't respond with any message..."), just dip into the book long enough to solve your problem.

Pertinent sections include:

- ✔ What the Internet is
- ✔ Communicating with electronic mail
- ✔ Using other computers on the Net
- ✔ Moving files and other data around
- ✔ Ways to find useful stuff on the Internet
- ✔ Common mistakes and how to correct them
- ✔ Where to find services and software to get onto the Internet

How to Use This Book

Use this book as a reference. Look up your topic or command in the Table of Contents or the Index, which refers you to the part of the book in which we describe what to do and perhaps define a few terms (if absolutely necessary).

When you have to type something, it appears in the book like this:

```
cryptic command to type
```

Type it in, just as it appears. Use the same capitalization we do — many systems care very deeply about CAPITAL and small letters. Then press the Enter or Return key. The book tells you what should happen when you give each command and what your options are.

You'll find chapters that list error messages that you may run into as well as common user mistakes. You may want to peruse the latter topic (Chapters 23 and 24) in order to avoid these mistakes before they happen.

Who Are You?

In writing the book, we assumed that

- ✔ You have or would like to have access to the Internet.
- ✔ You want to get some work done with it.
- ✔ Someone has set up your system so that you can use your computer to get to the Internet without running cables, installing satellite dishes, or the like.
- ✔ You are not interested in becoming the world's next great Internet expert.

How This Book Is Organized

This book has six parts. The parts stand on their own — you can start reading wherever you like, but you should at least skim Part I first to get acquainted with some unavoidable Internet jargon.

Here are the parts of the book and what they contain:

Part I: Getting onto the Internet

This part discusses what the Internet is and why it's interesting (at least why we think it's interesting). There's also figuring out whether your computer is on the net, which is not as obvious as it sounds, and some vital Internet terminology you'll need for the rest of the book.

Part II: Mail and Gossip

In this part, you learn how to exchange electronic mail with people down the hall or on other continents and how to use electronic mailing lists to keep in touch with people of like interests. You learn about using Usenet news to keep in touch even better, and there are even some suggestions for checking out the thousands of topics that Usenet addresses.

Part III: Instant Gratification

Here you learn how to log into other computers, how to retrieve useful files from computers around the world, and how to figure out what to do with the files once you've got them.

Part IV: Finding Stuff on the Net

This part tells you about four extremely cool programs that help you find useful stuff among the millions (no kidding) of computers on the Net.

Part V: The Part of Tens

This part is a compendium of ready references and useful facts (which implies, we suppose, that the other chapters are full of useless facts, but we hope not).

Part VI: Resource Reference

In this part, you learn where to find providers of Internet connections, purveyors of useful Internet software — commercial, shareware, and free — and where to learn more.

Icons Used in This Book

This icon lets you know that some particularly nerdy, technoid information is coming up, so that you can skip it if you want (on the other hand, you might want to read it).

This icon indicates that a nifty little shortcut or time-saver is explained.

Watch out below — time to duck and run for cover!

This icon alerts you to particularly juicy information related to locating something or someone on the Net.

What Now?

That's all you need to know to get started. Whenever you hit a snag using the Internet, just look up the problem in the Table of Contents or Index of this book. You'll either have the problem solved in a flash or you'll know whether you need to find some expert help.

Because the Internet has been evolving for over 20 years, largely under the influence of some extremely nerdy people, it was not designed to be particularly easy for normal people to use. So don't feel bad if you have to look up a number of topics before you feel comfortable using the Internet. After all, most computer users never have to face anything as complex as the Internet.

Feedback, Please

If you want to contact us, please feel free to do so in care of

IDG Books Worldwide
7260 Shadeland Station, Suite 100
Indianapolis, IN 46256

Or, even better, send Internet e-mail (see Chapters 7 through 10) to Internet For Dummies Central at internet@dummies.com.

Part I
Getting onto the Internet

The 5th Wave   By Rich Tennant

"HOW SHOULD I KNOW WHY THEY TOOK IT OFF THE LIST? MAYBE THERE JUST WEREN'T ENOUGH MEMBERS TO SUPPORT AN 'AIREDALES FOR ELVIS' NEWSGROUP."

In this part . . .

The Internet is a big and happening place. But it's full of computers, so nothing there is quite as simple as it should be. First we take a look at what the Internet is, how it got that way, and how to figure out where your computer stands in relation to the Net. Then we see some of the gruesome details involved in getting various kinds of computers onto the net.

Chapter 1

What Is the Internet? Why?

· ·

· ·

What Is the Internet?

The Internet — also known as the net — is the world's largest computer network. "And what is a network?" you may ask. Even if you already know, you may want to read the next couple of paragraphs to make sure that we're speaking the same language.

A computer network is basically a bunch of computers hooked together somehow. (Here in the world of computers, we like these crisp, precise definitions.) In concept, it's sort of like a radio or TV network that connects a bunch of radio or TV stations so that they can share the latest episode of "The Simpsons."

But don't take the analogy too far. TV networks send the same information to all the stations at the same time (what's called *broadcast* networking, for obvious reasons); in computer networks, though, each particular message is usually routed to a particular computer. Unlike TV networks, computer networks are invariably two-way, so that when computer A sends a message to computer B, B can send a reply back to A.

Some computer networks consist of a central computer and a bunch of remote stations that report to it — a central airline-reservation computer, for example, with thousands of terminals at airports and travel agencies. Others, including the Internet, are more egalitarian and permit any computer on the network to communicate with any other.

So, as we were saying, the Internet is the world's largest computer network. "So what?" you're probably saying. "I once saw the world's largest turnip on TV, and it didn't look very interesting — and I bet that it didn't taste so great either." Well, with networks, unlike vegetables, size counts for a lot because the larger a network is, the more stuff it has to offer.

Actually, the Internet isn't really a network — it's a network of networks, all freely exchanging information. The networks range from the big and formal, like the corporate networks at AT&T, Digital Equipment Corporation, and Hewlett-Packard to the small and informal, like the one in John Levine's attic (with a couple of old PCs bought through the *Want Advertiser*), and everything in between. College and university networks have long been part of the Internet, and now high schools and elementary schools are joining up too. As of August 1994, more than 20,000 networks on every continent connecting more than 3 million computers were part of the Internet, with 1,000 new networks and 100,000 computers per month being added.

You can think of the Internet as being two things:

✔ The people who use it

✔ The information that resides in it

Why Do I Care?

If you use a telephone, write letters, or do any kind of research, or if you are interested in what other people may have to say about darned near any topic in the whole wide world, the Internet can radically alter your whole world view. People of all ages, colors, creeds, and countries freely share ideas, stories, data, and opinions on the net.

A Few Real-Life Stories

Seventh-grade students in San Diego use the Internet to exchange letters and stories with kids in Israel. Partly it's just for fun and to make friends in a foreign country, but a sober academic study reported that when kids have a real audience for their stuff, they write better. (Big surprise.)

In some parts of the world, the Internet is the fastest and most reliable way to move information. During the 1991 Soviet coup, for example, a tiny Internet provider called RELCOM, which had a link to Finland and through there to the rest of the Internet world, found itself as the only reliable path to get reports in and out of Moscow because telephones were shut off and newspapers weren't being published. RELCOM members sent out stories that would have been in newspapers, statements from Boris Yeltsin (hand-delivered by friends), and their personal observations from downtown Moscow.

Medical researchers around the world use the Internet to maintain databases of rapidly changing data.

The Internet has more-prosaic uses too. Here are some from our personal experience:

One day John's wife wanted to find patterns to make a 1960s-era military shirt. (A friend had an old shirt he loved from his days in the army, but it was running out of places on which to sew patches.) So John asked the net to help. The net has several running discussions on military topics and one on historical costuming, so he sent out a message asking for help. Within one day, five different people responded by giving the addresses of pattern makers. Most of them said that they would be happy to offer tips and advice if we ran into trouble.

The Internet is its own best source of software. Whenever we hear about a new service (such as the ones described in Chapters 19, 20, 21, and 22), it usually takes only a few minutes to find software for one of our computers (a 386 laptop running Windows), download it, and start it up. Even better, nearly all the software available on the Internet is free.

The Internet has local and regional parts as well. When John wanted to sell a trusty but tired minivan, a note on the Internet in a local for-sale area found a buyer within two days.

The Internet and You

We've established that the Internet is large and, for some people, useful. What does this mean for real people?

Anybody can access it?

The Internet is probably the most open network in the world. Thousands of computers provide facilities that are available to anyone who has net access. This situation is unusual — *most* networks are very restrictive in what they allow users to do and require specific arrangements and passwords for each service. Although a few pay services exist (and undoubtedly more will be added), the vast majority of Internet services are free for the taking, once you are connected. If you don't already have access to the Internet through your company, your school, or John's attic, you'll probably have to pay for access to the Internet by using an Internet access provider. We talk about providers in Chapter 2.

Every continent?

Some skeptical readers, after reading the claim that the Internet spans every continent, may point out that Antarctica is a continent, even though its population consists largely of penguins, who, as far as we know, are not interested in computer networks. Does the Internet go there? It does. A few machines at the Scott Base on McMurdo Sound in Antarctica are on the net, connected by radio link to New Zealand. The base at the South Pole is supposed to have a link to the U.S., but it doesn't publish its electronic address.

At this writing, the largest Internet-free land mass in the world appears to be Bali, or maybe Java. (Greenland got on the Internet in 1992.)

Politically, socially, religiously correct

The final unusual thing about the Internet is that it is what one might call *socially unstratified*. That is, one computer is no better than any other, and no person is any better than any other. Who you are on the net depends solely on how you present yourself through your keyboard. If what you say makes you sound like an intelligent, interesting person, then that's who you are. It doesn't matter how old you are or what you look like or whether you're a student, a business executive, or a construction worker. Physical disabilities don't matter either — one of the authors of this book corresponds with several people who are blind or deaf. If they hadn't felt like telling, we never would have known. Famous people are in the net community too, some favorably and some unfavorably, but they got that way through their own efforts.

What's in It for Me?

The Internet's facilities are provided through a large set of different services. There's hardly room to give a complete list here (indeed, a complete list would fill several books larger than this one), but some examples follow to encourage you to keep reading:

Electronic mail (e-mail): This is certainly the most widely used service — you can exchange e-mail with millions of people all over the world. And people use e-mail for anything they might use paper mail or the telephone for: gossip, recipes, rumors, love letters — you name it. (We hear that some people even use it for stuff related to work.) Electronic *mailing lists* enable you to join in group discussions and meet people over the net. *Mail servers* (programs that respond to e-mail messages) let you retrieve all sorts of information. See Chapters 7, 8, and 10 for details.

On-line conversation: You can "talk" in real time to other users anywhere on the net. Although on-line conversation is pretty pointless for someone down the hall, it's great for quick chats with people on other continents, particularly when one party or the other isn't a native English speaker (typing a foreign language is easier and clearer than speaking it).

Information retrieval: Zillions of computers have files of information that are free for the taking. The files range from U.S. Supreme Court decisions and library card catalogs to texts of old books, digitized pictures (*nearly* all of them suitable for family audiences), and an enormous variety of software, from games to operating systems. Many of the tools discussed in this book help you make sense of the mountain of information available on the net and figure out what is available where. As mentioned in the Introduction, you'll see a Navigate icon here and there — this icon points to places in the book that help you navigate the net.

Bulletin boards: A system called *Usenet* is an enormous, distributed, on-line bulletin board with about 100 million characters of messages in more than 4,000 different topic groups flowing daily. Topics range from nerdy computer stuff to hobbies such as cycling and knitting to endless political arguments to just plain silliness. The most widely read Usenet group is one that features selected jokes, most of which are pretty funny.

Games and gossip: A game called *MUD (Multi-User Dungeon)* can easily absorb all your waking hours — in it, you can challenge other players who can be anywhere in the world. *Internet Relay Chat (IRC)* is a party line over which you can have more or less interesting conversations with other users all over the place. IRC seems to be mostly frequented by bored college students, but you never know whom you'll encounter.

Where Did the Internet Come From?

The ancestor of the Internet was the ARPANET, a project started by the Department of Defense (DOD) in 1969, both as an experiment in reliable networking and to link DOD and military research contractors, including the large number of universities doing military-funded research. (*ARPA* stands for *Advanced Research Projects Administration,* the branch of Defense in charge of handing out grant money. For enhanced confusion, the agency is now known as *DARPA* — the added *D* is for *Defense,* just in case there was any doubt where the money was coming from.) The ARPANET started small and connected three computers in California with one in Utah, but it quickly grew to span the continent.

Can the Internet really resist enemy attack?

It looks that way. During the Gulf War in 1991, the U.S. military had considerable trouble knocking out the Iraqi command network. It turned out that the Iraqis were using commercially available network routers with standard Internet routing and recovery technology. In other words, dynamic rerouting really worked. It's nice to know that dynamic rerouting works, although perhaps this was not the most opportune way to find out.

The reliable networking part involved *dynamic rerouting.* If one of the network links were to become disrupted by enemy attack, the traffic on it could automatically be rerouted to other links. Fortunately, the net rarely has come under enemy attack. But an errant backhoe cutting a cable is just as much of a threat, so it's important for the net to be backhoe-resistant.

The ARPANET was wildly successful, and every university in the country wanted to sign up. This success meant that the ARPANET began getting hard to manage, particularly with the large and growing number of university sites on it. So it was broken into two parts: MILNET, which had the military sites, and the new, smaller ARPANET, which had the nonmilitary sites. The two networks remained connected, however, thanks to a technical scheme called *IP (Internet Protocol),* which enabled traffic to be routed from one network to another as necessary. All the networks connected by IP in the Internet speak IP, so they all can exchange messages.

Although there were only two networks at that time, IP was designed to allow for tens of thousands of networks. An unusual fact about the IP design is that every computer on an IP network is, in principle, just as capable as any other, so any machine can communicate with any other machine. (This communication scheme may seem obvious, but at the time, most networks consisted of a small number of enormous central computers and a great deal of remote *terminals,* which could communicate only with the central systems, not with other terminals.)

Meanwhile, back in the classroom

Beginning around 1980, university computing was moving from a small number of large *time-sharing* machines, each of which served hundreds of simultaneous users, to a large number of smaller desktop *workstations* for individual users. Because users had gotten used to the advantages of time-sharing systems, such as shared directories of files and e-mail, they wanted to keep those same facilities on their workstations. (They were perfectly happy to leave behind the disadvantages of time-shared systems. A sage once said, "The best thing about a workstation is that it's no faster in the middle of the night.")

Most of the new workstations ran a variety of UNIX, a popular (and, for universities, nearly free) kind of operating software that had been developed at AT&T and the University of California at Berkeley. The people at Berkeley were big fans of computer networking, so their version of UNIX included all the software necessary to hook up to a network. Workstation manufacturers began to include the necessary network hardware also, so all you had to do to get a working network was to string the cable to connect the workstations, something that universities could do for cheap because they usually could get students to do it.

Then, rather than have one or two computers to attach to the ARPANET, a site would have hundreds. What's more, each workstation was considerably faster than an entire 1970s multiuser system, so that one workstation could generate enough network traffic to swamp the ARPANET, which was getting creakier by the minute. Something had to give.

Enter the National Science Foundation

The next event was that the National Science Foundation (NSF) decided to set up five *supercomputer* centers for research use. (A supercomputer is a really fast computer with a hefty price, like $10 million apiece.) The NSF figured that it would fund a few supercomputers, let researchers from all over the country use the ARPANET to send their programs to be supercomputed, and then send back the results.

The plan to use the ARPANET didn't work out for a variety of reasons, some technical, some political. So the NSF, never shy about establishing a new political empire, built its own, much faster network to connect the supercomputing centers: the NSFNET. Then it arranged to set up a bunch of regional networks to connect the users in each region, with the NSFNET connecting all the regional networks.

The NSFNET worked like a charm. In fact, by 1990 so much "business" had moved from the ARPANET to the NSFNET that, after nearly 20 years, the ARPANET had outlived its usefulness and was shut down. The supercomputer centers the NSFNET was supposed to support turned out to be not successful: Some of the supercomputers didn't work, and the ones that did were so expensive to use that most potential customers decided that a few high-performance workstations would serve their needs just as well. Fortunately, by the time it became clear that the supercomputers were on the way out, the NSFNET had become so entrenched in the Internet that it lived on without its original purpose. By 1994, several large commercial Internet networks had grown up within the Internet, some run by large, familiar organizations such as IBM and Sprint, and others by such specialist Internet companies as Performance Systems International (always known as PSI) and Alternet. And now, as we write, the NSFNET is being wound down, and its traffic taken over by commercial networks.

The NSFNET permitted traffic related only to research and education, but the independent, commercial IP network services can be used for other kinds of traffic. The commercial networks connect to the regional networks just like the NSFNET does, and they provide direct connections for customers. Chapter 27 has a list of these services.

IP networks have appeared in many countries, either sponsored by the local telephone company (usually also the local post office) or run by independent national or regional providers. Nearly all of them are connected directly or indirectly to some U.S. network, meaning that they can exchange traffic with each other.

The national network

In 1991, then-Senator Al Gore decided that for the United States to continue to be a competitive, with-it, first-world kind of country, we should have really great computing and networks. He sponsored the High-Performance Computing Act of 1991, which is supposed to hook up all researchers, universities, primary schools, government agencies — you name it — into one big, happy and very fast (100 times faster than the primary Internet links are now) network called the National Research and Education Network, or NREN.

Considerable political wrangling has since ensued, as lots of different organizations have attempted to belly up to the trough to get part of the lucrative business of building this network. At the moment, the main concrete progress toward the NREN is that the NSFNET is now officially the interim NREN. The NREN doubtless will be built eventually; equally doubtless, it will take longer and cost more than anyone cares to admit.

What this means for you is debatable. Many people find the prospect of a network brought to them by the same people who run the post office and Amtrak to be underwhelming, and it is certainly true that fast commercial networks, which are already under construction, will appear long before the NREN arrives. On the other hand, if you are in an impoverished part of the educational establishment, such as a public elementary school, the NREN is supposed to hook you up to the same resources as the big guys — and the reports trickling in from the field say that getting Internet access in the K-12 world is pretty exciting.

Chapter 2

Connecting to the Internet: The Basics

· ·

In This Chapter

▶ Getting to the Internet

▶ Service providers, on-line services, and bulletin boards

▶ Getting on and off the Information Superhighway

· ·

Which Way to the Internet?

"Great," you say, "but how do I get to the Internet?" Well, depending on your lifestyle, including your job or your school, checking out the Internet can be trivially easy or moderately difficult. If you want to make it really difficult, that's an option too. Here we assume that you want the easiest, most straightforward, commonly available approaches.

In the best case, you may have the Internet literally under your fingertips and not know it. In the worst case, you have never seen a computer in your life. If you've never seen or played with a computer, we highly recommend finding a friend who has one to show you the basics. Here in Cambridge, Massachusetts (a world center of geekdom where your authors happen to live), our very own public library has implemented a pilot program providing free Internet access. We're hoping that it will be a great hit and quickly adopted by other enterprising resource centers. When you read about the World Wide Web and other Internet facilities, you'll wonder why they haven't done so already. (The answer, of course, is money. A commercial Internet provider sponsored our library connection partly for publicity and partly to test its new Internet-via-cable-TV system.)

How Can I Tell If I'm on the Internet?

If you have access to a computer or a computer terminal, you *may* already be on the Internet. Here are some ways to check:

- ✔ If you have an account with an on-line service such as CompuServe, GEnie, or MCI Mail, you can use the service's e-mail system to exchange messages with anyone on the Internet. Some on-line services, notably Delphi and America Online, also provide other, more interactive Internet services.

- ✔ If you use a bulletin board system (BBS) that exchanges messages with other BBSs, you can exchange e-mail with the Internet.

- ✔ If your company or school has an internal e-mail system, it may also be connected to the Internet. Ask a local mail expert.

- ✔ If your company or school has a local network, it may be connected directly or indirectly to the Internet, for mail or a wider variety of services. Networks of UNIX workstations usually use the same networking conventions that the Internet does, so that connection is technically easy. Networks of PCs or Macs often use different conventions, so a *gateway* is necessary to translate.

OK, Really, How Do I Get on the Internet?

You've looked all over the place: You have no network cables, at least none that connect to the outside world, no networked mail services, no shared bulletin boards — what do you do?

One approach (the "geek" or "deranged" approach) is to run network cables — held in place by duct tape, of course — all over your house, climb up on the roof, put up radio antennas, and fill up the attic with humming boxes full of routers and subnets and packet driver NDIS shims and heaven knows what else. This approach can be made to work (John did it, in fact), but if you were the kind of geek who liked to do that sort of thing, you probably wouldn't be reading this book.

The other approach, the "normal" approach, is to use a computer, a modem , and a phone line to dial into an Internet service where the geeks have already set things up for you. You run a normal terminal program on your computer — something like CrossTalk or ProComm or Macterminal — and then use your modem to call in the same way you would call into CompuServe or your local computer bulletin board. John has done that too, at the beach even. (He was on vacation and ran out of duct tape.)

If that last paragraph caused you to start sweating, pause here while we play catch-up in Jargon Land. If that last paragraph caused you no anxiety, you can skip ahead.

Modems ho!

A modem is a nifty little device that enables data from one computer to travel to another computer by using ordinary telephone lines. This cute little (or maybe not so little if it's older) box goes between your computer and your phone line and between the phone line and the computer on the other end. Modems are built-in to some computers, so if you're not sure whether one is in your computer, ask. The bad news about modems is that they come with lots of different switches and settings. The good news is that most modems are set up with appropriate default settings, and you probably can get going without much difficulty.

If you need to buy a modem, find the cheapest fax modem that runs at 14,400 bps, currently the fastest usable speed — you can pay more for things that go faster, but that speed isn't really passed on to you by using your ordinary phone line just now. Make sure that your modem comes with some communications software (most do now) that's appropriate for the computer and version of operating system you're using. And make sure that whoever's selling it to you gives you the correct cable for your computer. If you want to find out more about modems, check out Tina Rathbone's book *Modems For Dummies,* published by IDG Books Worldwide.

Normal terminal program (is that contagious?)

To go along with your modem, you need some software to be able to use other people's computers. Much of this software is called "terminal emulation" software because it makes your computer look like just another terminal on that remote computer. *Modems For Dummies* describes this software and how to get it up and running on your computer.

What's an Internet service provider?

The Internet is out there with tons of exciting things to do, people to meet, jokes to read. But unless you already have access to it through a friend or school or work, you have to *get* access to it before it does you any good. The folks who provide access to the Internet (generally for a fee) are called Internet service providers or Internet access providers. Having no access to the Internet is sort of like having a telephone that isn't connected to anything.

You can use lots of Internet services, and more appear every month. See Chapter 27 for a long list of them. If your city has a *freenet* (they're listed at the end of Chapter 27), try that first because it's free, gives you a taste of what the Internet has to offer, and is interesting in its own right.

Failing that, see whether any commercial providers are in your own city (they're listed in the first part of Chaper 27) and check them out. You'll probably find that if you use the Internet at all, you'll be on-line for long periods, so it's nice if both the service itself and the voice help line are a local phone call away.

If there's no local provider, try Delphi (listed in Chapter 15), which provides Internet service nationally. Delphi usually gives you five free introductory hours on-line so that you can see how you like it.

The Internet, on-line services, and bulletin boards

If you're like most people, these terms sound sort of the same. Indeed, many are used interchangeably. Many are used incorrectly. And the definitions and distinctions are blurring even as we speak. We think that it's useful, however, to get a sense of what they are and how they are different so that when you begin to put your foot in the water, it's the water you had in mind.

On-line, in-flight, on-board services

On-line services are services provided to you by a computer or computers interactively. They include but are not limited to computerized banking, shopping, dating, entertainment, and study. *Note:* They may or may not have anything to do with the Internet. For many years, these types of major on-line service providers, such as CompuServe, existed independently of the Internet. They allowed users to exchange electronic mail among other CompuServe users but failed to reach out to touch anyone else. Now most of these services *do* provide e-mail access beyond their insulated client base. This is a far cry, however, from real, live Internet access and capability.

For lots of information about on-line services and what they have to offer, see Tina Rathbone's *Modems For Dummies.* Stay tuned here for the scoop on the Internet. And this may not be an either/or choice for you. You may want certain on-line services, certain bulletin-board access, *and* certain Internet capability. We're just here to help you try to sort it all out.

Bulletin boards (BBS, BBSs, BS, BSO)

Electronic bulletin board systems (abbreviated as BBS, or BBSs for plural) provide on-line services generally on a smaller scale and often with a particular focus. We say *generally* because Usenet, a bulletin board that's part of the Internet's offerings, can in no manner be considered small or of limited focus. Chapter 11 tells you all about Usenet. Anyway, bulletin board systems are often local, often very cheap, and sometimes even free to callers. They might provide e-mail, chatting (on-line conversations with other users), forums about special interests, games, ads, and lots, lots more. We have found bulletin board users to be very friendly and welcoming to newcomers. The downside is that because they may not have much funding, they can be flaky at times, and you don't have much recourse in tracking down problems.

Local bulletin boards offer people a new way to meet. After you have established a pal on the board, you don't have to leave him or her there. Many bulletin-board regulars find fun and interesting things to do together that have nothing to do with computers.

In the name of mixing business with pleasure, one of the authors of this book has been investigating a local bulletin board called Connections. It sports a matchmaking service, chat channels, links to the Internet for worldwide chatting, games, horoscopes, and much more. For a free introductory trial period, use your modem to dial 617-332-3200.

A couple of hints: First, BBS users don't use their real names. Just like CB radio users, bulletin board users generally use such handles as Pecos Bill, Annie Oakley, Athena, or Silver. Think of it as a chance to create a new identity. Second, BBS junkies develop their own jargon to add to the milieu, in part to reflect tone or other responses, such as <grin> and <chuckle>.

BS stands for bachelor of *science* (really!), and BSO stands for the Boston Symphony Orchestra.

As far as we know, there is absolutely no truth to the rumor that 12-step programs are already dealing with bulletin board addiction. We do believe, however, that if such a service were provided anonymously on-line, it would have many takers. Arguably, it's not terribly different being glued to your computer than it is to your TV, but at least your computer can put you in touch with other (we hope) still real people and expand your world view in a non-Hollywood-style adventure. (Hollywood style is available, complete with commercials, from many on-line services. But we here in the land of the raw and relatively unadorned Internet still cherish direct, commercial-free communication.)

On and Off the Information Superhighway

There's a first time for everything and if it's the information superhighway you're looking for, just buckle up. If the computer you use is connected to a network, you're probably familiar with such terms as *user ID,* or *login name.* If you're not, here's the scoop.

The Internet, as we keep saying, is really a network of networks. And each of those networks is composed of a bunch of computers hooked together. Now, not even in your wildest imagination did you suppose that everyone really had access to *everything,* did you? And you probably don't want everyone to have access to everything you do, either. The schemes that have been put in place to protect what needs protecting and to allow the allowable all fall under the general category of *security.*

Although security issues may not be your primary concern, you really do need to know about a few concepts.

Would you sign in please?

Not so different from that prehistoric TV show "What's My Line," service providers of all sorts want to know who's on the system. To track usage, users are given an account, sort of like a bank account. The account has your name and a secret password associated with it.

Your account name may also be called your user ID, or your login or logon name. Your name must be unique within the bounds of the system you are using.

Your password, just like those associated with bank teller-machine cards, should not be a common word or something easily guessed. (For best results, include both numbers and letters so that a hacker using a dictionary-based program won't find your password listed.) You don't want strangers using your account, and your password is really your only protection.

Please don't touch the crystal!

After you begin exploring the Internet, you can find yourself in many far-off and not-so-far-off lands on many strange computers. Those computers have information that's available to every Sally and Sam, but usually the computers are used for lots of other things also. Those other things are none of your business (nor ours, for that matter).

To protect information from the voyeuristic, the ignorant, and the vile, an elaborate scheme of permissions is used. *Permissions,* also known as *access control,* are what determine who can do what to what. What? Permissions are assigned to files and directories and determine who can access each file and directory and in what way. Levels of permission include *no access,* which in some cases means that you can't even see a file or directory; *read,* permission to read the file or directory; *write,* permission to write to or delete the file or directory; and *execute,* permission to run a program file. In traveling around from system to system, you no doubt will find information protected by some of these permissions.

Many of the computers you travel to on the net are UNIX systems. For more information about UNIX permissions and the commands that display and change them, see *UNIX For Dummies* by John R. Levine and Margaret Levine Young (published by IDG Books Worldwide).

If you have information on a networked system, you probably want to protect it in the same way. Although you can screen out ordinary users, remember that system administrators and sometimes clever hackers can override permissions. If you have something of an extremely personal nature that you feel compelled to leave on the net, encode it. See Chapter 17 for information about encoding files.

How to get off

After you've gotten yourself on the Internet, you're inevitably placed in the position of having to get off. There are more and less graceful ways of getting off. And depending on how far you've gone, there are potentially layers of systems to exit from.

If you use a modem to dial in, you can always hang up the phone from your terminal program. However, a cleaner, more polite way to leave is to say good-bye to everyone to whom you've said hello. The problem is that not all computers say good-bye in the same language. This section shows a few commonly used exit sequences. If none of them works, try typing **help** to see whether the system has any clues for you. If you can't get help, use your terminal program to hang up the phone and don't feel too guilty about it.

The most common exit sequences include the following:

✔ **Exit**

✔ **Ctrl-D** (popular on always excessively terse UNIX systems)

✔ **Logout**

✔ **Bye**

If you use the `telnet` command (see Chapter 14), you may have signed on to systems other than the one you originally dialed in to. Remember that you have to exit from all the systems you have signed on to. You aren't really out until you've exited from your original Internet service provider. You may at that point begin to see random characters generated across your screen while your modem listens to an empty line. Or the modem will more likely hang up by itself with a satisfying click. Whew!

If your computer is connected directly to the Internet by way of a network cable, you cannot just hang up the phone, because there's no phone to hang up. You have to exit from all the systems you've accessed in order to get back to your home environment. In the worst case, if you're on a PC or a Mac, you can always reboot your system. If you're in a UNIX environment, pressing Ctrl-D enough times usually does the trick.

Chapter 3

Starting Off, If You're a PC User

· ·

In This Chapter

▶ PCs versus the Internet

▶ Too many ways to get hooked up

▶ Why PCs have trouble receiving e-mail

· ·

PCs versus the Internet

If you have a PC you use for work or study or fun or whatever, and you want to connect to the Internet, you have a fair amount to choose from. In this chapter, we assume that you're running DOS or Windows; if you're running UNIX, look in the next chapter. When we refer to PCs, we mean PCs running DOS or Windows. We also assume that you have read Chapter 1 and Chapter 2 and know that you're not already connected to the net. For most stand-alone PC users (we mean folks who have only one computer — you normal, nongeek types), we think that buying a modem and communications software as described in Chapter 2 is the way to go. If you're intent on making your life more difficult, read on.

On larger computers, hooking up to the Internet is a relatively straightforward task. You pay an unconscionable amount of money to your software vendor, they send you the network software that goes with your system, your hired expert installs it, and after no more than six months or so of finger-pointing and arguing with tech support, your hookup works.

With PCs, however, life is not so simple. Dozens of different Internet-compatible network packages are available, ranging from flaky (and sometimes shaky) shareware to slick commercial stuff (and vice versa, of course). Even worse, you can hook up your PC to the Internet in about four fundamentally different ways.

We presume that you have better things to do than to install your own Internet software and have a local expert utter the magic incantations that are necessary to install the network software. (Well, even if you *don't* have better things to do, there's no way we could give instructions for more than one or two of those packages, and you just *know* that neither one would be the package you use.)

So in this chapter, we look at the different ways in which you can hook up a PC to the Internet and the advantages and disadvantages of each way. Chapter 28 has a list of most of the currently available PC packages for hooking up to the Internet. Your best bet is to use one for which a local expert can help you get set up.

These software packages for hooking up to the Internet are based on the *TCP/IP protocol,* which is techspeak for the system that networks use to communicate with each other. You learn most of what you need to know about TCP/IP in Chapter 6, so if you're interested in the lingo, turn to that chapter for some background information.

Through a Gateway Dimly

The first question is whether your PC has a *native* connection to the Internet or whether it goes through some other type of network. If it has a native connection, your PC runs network software that handles the TCP/IP network protocols the Internet uses.

The alternative is that your PC is running another kind of network software (most often Novell's Netware) and is attached to a gateway system that speaks Netware on one side and TCP/IP on the other. To add to the confusion, it's also possible to load up both TCP/IP *and* some other kind of network software on the same PC and run them on the same physical network cables at the same time.

The pros and cons are described in the following list:

✔ If you already have a large Netware network, your system manager can load up a single Netware gateway that all the other PCs on the network can use. If each PC is to run TCP/IP itself, your network manager has to load TCP/IP on each PC, which is a great deal more work.

✔ TCP/IP works better in heterogeneous networks — that is, networks made up of lots of different kinds of computers. As far as TCP/IP is concerned, the only difference between a $10 million Cray supercomputer and a $900 PC is that the Cray is a little faster. Novell Netware is great on networks of PCs and less great on other kinds of computers because Netware at this point works on far fewer kinds of computers than TCP/IP does.

✔ Depending on the particular gateway you use, you may not be able to do everything through a Netware gateway that you can do through native TCP/IP.

SLIP-ing an Ethereal Token

Assume that your PC runs TCP/IP by itself and not by way of another kind of network. The next question is: How is it connected to the rest of the net? The three major choices are Ethernet, Token Ring, and serial lines (the last uses schemes we discuss later in this chapter, which are called SLIP and PPP).

Through the ether

The most common way to hook up PCs to networks is with *Ethernet,* a kind of network that is fast and cheap but limited to a total distance of less than a mile. (For larger networks, a person can hook together several Ethernet networks by using devices called *bridges* and *routers,* but that's a complication we can ignore. See Chapter 6 if you care.)

The three main varieties of Ethernet are known as *thicknet, thinnet* (or *cheapernet*), and *twisted pair.* Your classic Ethernet is half-inch-thick yellow cable (that you rarely see because it's all hidden in the wall or ceiling), shown in Figure 3-1. Your computer is connected to the Ethernet by a different kind of cable known as a *drop cable,* which is about the same size as Ethernet but is usually gray. The business end of the drop cable attaches to your computer by way of a plug with 15 pins and a clever little slide latch.

Figure 3-1:
Thick
Ethernet
cable
(thicknet)

If your computer uses thicknet and it suddenly develops network forgetfulness, the most likely problem is that the clever little latch has let go. Plug it back in and see whether you can slide the latch more firmly.

Fire at the wall

Even if your PC runs native TCP/IP software, if you're in a large organization that has (not altogether unreasonable) concerns about confidential company secrets leaking out by way of the Internet, a *firewall* system placed between the company network and the outside world may limit outside access to the internal network.

The firewall is connected to both the internal network and the external network, so any traffic between the two must go through the firewall. Special programming on the firewall limits which kinds of connections can be made between the inside and outside and who can make them.

In practice, therefore, you can use any Internet service that is available within the company, but for outside services you're limited by what can pass through the firewall system. Most standard outside services, such as logging in to remote computers or copying files from one computer to another, should be available, although the procedures may be somewhat more complicated than what's described here.

You often have to log in to the firewall system first and from there get to the outside. It's usually impossible for anyone outside the company to get access to systems or services on the inside network (that's what the firewall is for). Except for the most paranoid of organizations, electronic mail flows unimpeded in both directions.

Finally, keep in mind that you probably have to get authorization to use the firewall system before you can use *any* outside service other than mail services.

Classic thick Ethernet was intended for organizations that plan years ahead and arrange to expensively prewire all their offices for network connections. Real organizations aren't usually like that. They have a few PCs and want to wire them up without ripping all the walls apart. They need thinnet (cheapernet). Thinnet is thin, flexible, and black (see Figure 3-2). It resembles cable-television cable (although it's not quite the same). The connection to the computer is a little T-shaped connector that plugs in directly to a matching connector on the back of the computer.

Figure 3-2:
Thin
Ethernet
(also called
thinnet,
cheapernet,
or 10base2)

Cheapernet is quite unforgiving. In particular, the T connector must be plugged in directly to the computer. You can't put the T on the floor and run a connecting cable to the computer, not even an inch-long stub, because it just won't work. You should also remember that if you break the cable, everyone's connection to the network stops working. (It may seem reasonable to think that computers on the same side of the break could continue to talk to each other, but they can't. If you want to know why not, just corner someone who has a degree in electrical engineering and ask.)

The third kind of Ethernet cabling is twisted-pair, which is the same kind of wiring telephones use (see Figure 3-3). Most offices have tons of spare phone wire in the walls already, and even if they don't, it's by far the cheapest kind of wire to string. So twisted-pair Ethernet is pretty much the only kind used in new installations. A wire that looks much like a phone wire with the familiar phone jack (see Figure 3-4) plugs in to the back of your computer. Each computer has its own, separate wire back to a central connection box called a *hub* — which is usually stashed in a closet somewhere — so if you unplug your computer, you won't affect anyone else's. As long as you don't physically mangle the wire, twisted pair is pretty foolproof.

Figure 3-3:
Twisted pair
Ethernet
cable (also
called
10baseT)

Figure 3-4:
Twisted pair
jack (almost
like a phone
jack)

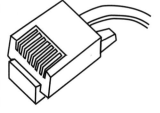

A token of our esteem

A few years back, IBM decided that because every other computer manufacturer in the world was using Ethernet, it would avoid the heartache of excessive compatibility by coming up with its own network called *Token Ring*. Furious technical debates raged on about the relative merits of Ethernet and Token Ring, which we can summarize by saying that the differences are 95 percent political. Token Ring uses a clever rectangular connector that has the advantage over many versions of Ethernet in that it comes unplugged only when you want it to.

SLIP sliding away

One place where the Internet's TCP/IP network protocol definitely wins over other brands of networks is at the low end. All you need in order to set up a TCP/IP connection is the lowly serial port your PC already has. It's not as fast as an Ethernet connection — but it's not as expensive either. You can run a wire directly to another computer nearby, or you can use a modem and a phone line and dial a computer somewhere else.

One extra complication of using a serial connection is that two incompatible software schemes are used. One is called *SLIP (Serial Line IP)* and the other is *PPP (Point-to-Point Protocol)*. Which one you use depends on which kind of system you're connecting to — you use what they use.

If you're using a modem and a phone line, you want to use the fastest modem you can get. The standard, cheap, 2400 bps (bits per second) modems seem pretty fast when you're dialed up to an on-line service such as CompuServe, but these modems are painfully slow on the Internet. Faster 9600 and 14,400 bps modems are now available and are quite adequate. (Modem weenies call these last two kinds V.32 and V.32bis, where *bis* is French for "and a half." Ask for them by name at your computer store, and they'll think you're an expert.)

SLIP really works and can make your computer a full-fledged player on the Internet. For example, John wrote this chapter holed up in a cottage on a sandbar at the New Jersey shore, using a laptop computer with his modem dialed in by way of SLIP to an Internet-connected system on the mainland that let him do anything on the net — such as retrieve data from computers in Australia — that he can do back at his office plugged in to the Ethernet (just a little slower).

Getting SLIP or PPP configured correctly is a pain in the neck that involves phone numbers, login names, passwords, and everything else required to log in to a remote system over the phone, *on top of* the usual network configuration problems. Before you take your computer to the beach, try plugging it in to a spare phone line at the office and dialing in to make sure that its SLIP configuration is working. Then, when you find that it's not, you have your office network guru on hand to figure out what's wrong.

Is Windows Really Cooler Than DOS?

We're still undecided about Windows in general, but when it comes to TCP/IP, Windows wins hands-down over DOS for two reasons. The first is aesthetic. Most DOS TCP/IP applications are straightforward ports of the UNIX originals — which means that they use a line-at-a-time interface, like the DOS command language or — perish the thought — EDLIN, the old DOS text editor. (*Nothing's* as bad as EDLIN.) If you want to know more about the UNIX background for the Internet, see Chapter 4 for plenty of details.

Windows network applications, on the other hand, have all the spiffy bells and whistles you expect from all Windows applications. In many cases, this makes them much easier to use. For example, when you're using FTP — the program that copies files from one computer to another — most Windows versions let you pick the files to copy by clicking on filenames in a list in a window, whereas the DOS versions make you type the filenames yourself.

The other reason Windows works better is that it allows *multitasking,* which is computerese for *running several programs at a time.* Under Windows, you can have several network applications running at one time in different windows. You can even have terminal sessions in different windows that are logged in to several computers *at the same time* while you simply click among them. A few DOS versions of TCP/IP (such as the shareware program KA9Q) offer multitasking, but none as conveniently as Windows does.

See Chapter 28 for a list of DOS and Windows TCP/IP packages.

At Your Service — Not

In one important way, PCs are not really full-blown members of the Internet. Every Internet application uses the client/server model, in which part of the application, the *client,* runs on your computer, and the other part, the *server,* runs on a remote computer that has the resources you want to use. (Client/server is the hot, new thing in mainframe computing, but the Internet and its predecessors have been using the concept since at least 1969. They didn't know how advanced they were — they just wanted to get the job done.)

DOS computers are not really full-blown members of the Internet. To be frank, PCs make fine clients but rather inferior servers. DOS and Windows are simply not the best environments for servers. Suppose that you want to make some resource available on the Internet, such as a bunch of files for people to retrieve. You put them all in a common place and then start a server program that waits for client programs to contact it and ask it to do something. But because DOS runs only one program at a time, if you start the server program, the PC cannot do anything else.

Sometimes that's OK — compared to some of the alternatives, a single dedicated computer is a cheap way to provide a service — but it's not really great if it's the same PC you need to use to get your work done. Even under Windows, which is designed to allow multiple programs to run at a time, servers don't work all that well — largely because most nonnetwork programs tend to hog the computer when you run them and don't give the server any time to serve its clients.

Note: The following discussion of mail trouble applies only to users of native Internet mail (sometimes known as SMTP mail). If you have a different mail system — one that uses a gateway to the Internet — from the point of view of other Internet systems, all your mail is sent and received by the gateway, and the following doesn't apply.

(Some software packages help you figure out what's happening to your mail. Mail Check, from Baranof Software, 479 Washington Street, Brighton, MA 02135, supports most electronic-mail packages.)

"But," you say, "I don't *need* to publish files. I just want to use resources elsewhere on the Internet. I don't need to run any servers." That's almost but not quite true. The biggest problem with not having servers occurs when you receive electronic mail. Internet e-mail considers the *sender* to be the client, and the *recipient,* the server.

Here's the scenario and its complications:

The sender's machine tries to contact the recipient's machine to deliver a message. If the recipient's machine doesn't have a mail server running, the sender's machine tries a few more times but eventually gives up. If your mail program doesn't happen to be running at the moment the sender tries to send you something, the message may not get delivered.

Reality: If you have correspondents in different time zones, they may well send you mail in the middle of the night when your computer is turned off.

Fortunately, a work-around solution exists for this problem. Your system manager can (and probably already has) arranged to have your mail received on a larger computer that runs 24 hours a day. When you want to read your mail, your mail program contacts that computer and downloads any waiting mail. The usual downloading scheme is known as *Post Office Protocol,* or *POP.* (A bunch of versions exist; the current ones are *POP2* and *POP3.*)

With any luck, all this works automatically, but it's worth remembering that although POP is common on PCs, it's not the way the rest of the net handles its mail. In particular, it means that the machine that sends your mail (your PC) is different from the one that receives your mail (the larger one), a situation that has been known to foul up some automated mail robots (see Chapter 10). If that turns out to be a problem for you, your system manager can probably make your mail *appear* to be sent and received by the same system.

WINSOCK? Like at an airport?

No, WINSOCK is short for *Win*dows *Sock*ets. It's like this: Every DOS version of TCP/IP consists of two parts. One part is the application programs you use to access various services over the Internet. The other part is a common library of network functions that all the network applications use. In each case, the vendor documented the functions in the library so that third parties could write applications of their own that worked with the vendor's TCP/IP package.

Unfortunately, each vendor's functions are slightly different in the details, even though functionally they do the same thing, so applications that work with one don't work with another. Some of the vendors boast that they have compatibility libraries for four or five other vendors so that programs that expect to use the other vendors' libraries will work. (It's like the situation with electrical appliances in Europe: The power is all the same, but the plugs are all different. So if you bring an English sewing machine to France, you can't use it unless you can find an adapter plug.)

In 1991, all the network vendors were gearing up to produce Windows TCP/IP packages. One day a bunch of them got together at a trade show and thrashed out a common, standard set of functions for Windows TCP/IP applications based on the Sockets library that most versions of UNIX use. Every TCP/IP vendor (even Microsoft, which has a TCP/IP version for Windows NT and one in the works for Windows 4.0) quickly agreed to support this Windows Sockets library, or WINSOCK.

In practice, therefore, after a few compatibility bugs were shaken out (which as of mid-1994 is pretty much done), any Windows TCP/IP application you find that uses WINSOCK — whether it's commercial, shareware, or free — should work with any Windows TCP/IP networking package. In the annals of software development, this degree of a priori compatibility is virtually unprecedented, so let's hope that it's a harbinger of things to come.

Chapter 4

Starting Off, If You're a UNIX User

● ●

In This Chapter

▶ UNIX network facilities

▶ UNIX-specific facilities

▶ Networked files

▶ Electronic mail

▶ The yellow plague

● ●

*M*ost UNIX systems come with Internet software either as part of the standard package or as an add-on from the same vendor who supplies the UNIX operating system. For those who don't — or who do but aren't directly connected to the Internet — all UNIX systems come with an old but serviceable package called UUCP. UUCP (the UNIX to UNIX CoPy program) uses ordinary modems and phone lines to handle e-mail and network news (see Chapter 9 for more info).

Your Usual UNIX Network Stuff

If you're using a UNIX workstation, it definitely includes Internet software. The main question is whether you're attached to the Internet directly, indirectly, or (horror of horrors) not at all. To be sure that you have Internet software loaded, try typing this command:

```
telnet localhost
```

You should get a login prompt shortly (in a few seconds) from your own computer. Log in as yourself and then log out. So far, so good. If it says something like telnet: not found, you're using one of the few remaining UNIX systems with no network software. Bummer. (You still may be able to send and receive e-mail by way of UUCP.)

You can also check for the trappings of networking: Is a network cable attached to the back of your computer? (See Chapter 3 for a rundown of popular network cable types.) When you print something, does it appear on a printer attached to a different computer? That's a sure sign that a network is active. Can you send electronic mail to people on other computers? Again, that's a sure sign.

Help! I'm Trapped in a Local Network!

Even assuming that your network software is all tuned up and your computer is attached to a network (usually with an Ethernet cable hanging out the back), the question remains whether it's attached to the net or just to some local machines. This important detail has nothing to do with the setup of your computer but rather whether the local network to which your computer is attached is in turn attached to the Internet.

Probably the easiest way to check is to see whether you can contact well-known Internet sites. Try to *telnet* (log in as a terminal) to `rs.internic.net`, the Network Information Center for the domestic part of the Internet, by typing this line:

```
telnet rs.internic.net
```

If it says `Connected` and you see messages from the NIC telling you what's available, you win — you're on the net. (Type **exit** to make the NIC disconnect.)

If not, either your network isn't directly attached to the Internet or you have some other connection problem — you will have to ask a local guru for advice. Again, even if your network isn't attached directly to the Internet, you may still be able to exchange mail with people on the net.

For Your Convenience, We've Done Everything Twice

UNIX supports the two most traditional Internet services: telnet, for logging in to a remote host, and FTP, for copying files to and from a remote host. The UNIX network facilities were written by a bunch of college students, however, and they couldn't leave well enough alone. They invented a second set of similar (but different) programs with names beginning with *r* that are useful primarily only between UNIX systems:

✔ **rlogin:** Almost but not quite like telnet

✔ **rsh:** Runs one command at a time on remote machines

✔ **rcp:** Sort of resembles FTP

Each of these *r* programs has its own advantages and is worth learning about. The main advantage they all share is that you can arrange things on machines on which you have accounts so that you can log in from one to another and copy stuff among them without having to enter your username and password every time you want to do something.

We discuss the *r* commands in the same chapters with their generic non-UNIX equivalents. You can find rlogin and rsh in Chapter 14 and rcp in Chapter 16.

My Files Are Where?

Another network feature particularly common to UNIX systems is NFS (Network File System), originally released by Sun Microsystems but now commonly available from most UNIX vendors. NFS lets you treat disk files and directories that are present on one computer as though they were on another computer. In particular, this means that many of the files that seem to be on your computer may actually be on a machine down the hall. This situation normally doesn't make much practical difference unless the network or the other computer breaks, and then your computer comes to a screeching halt in much the same way as it would if you unplugged a disk drive attached directly to the computer.

Fortunately, NFS picks up pretty reliably where it left off when the network or other computer gets fixed. A legendary tale is told of a program on a workstation that waited patiently while the computer with its NFS files broke and was taken apart and shipped back to the vendor. A replacement system eventually arrived, so the new server was assembled, reloaded from the backup tapes, and restarted. Then the program, which by then had been waiting for about six months, continued.

Stupid NFS Tricks

Although NFS originally was written for UNIX systems, versions of NFS also exist for lots of other kinds of computers ranging from Macs and PCs to IBM mainframes. These versions allow for flexible file-sharing. While this book was written, for example, the files with the text and graphics resided on a UNIX system, but the MS-DOS and Windows examples were run on a networked PC. Then the screen shots were saved, by way of NFS, in files back on the UNIX host.

If you use a bunch of different kinds of computers, NFS is often the only work-able way to hook them all together because it runs on a much wider variety of computers than does any other file-sharing system.

NFS is based on a pair of standard Internet communication protocols called *UDP/IP*. (Chapter 6 explains what these protocols are, but it's not important now.) If your machine uses NFS, therefore, you can in principle use NFS files that are anywhere on the Internet, as long as the host on which the files live grants you permission to access them.

If your computer and the one on which the files live are connected by a fast enough network, you can use files many miles away just as though they were local. Remote network links are usually considerably (often about 100 times) slower than local networks are, which means that you can get the impression of a very s-l-o-o-o-o-w disk.

For use as regular file storage, slow remote NFS is hopeless unless you are a total masochist. As a way to browse and retrieve files from an archive, however, NFS can be okay. Many systems that have large file archives allow anyone to access their disks by way of NFS (for reading, not for writing — they're not totally stupid). Because public archive systems can have hundreds of directo-ries and thousands of files, mounting a remote system's disk by way of NFS lets you use familiar directory and file commands to look at them.

Yes, it takes a while to list directories, read files, and so on, but it would take a while whether you used NFS or FTP (the standard remote-file program, de-scribed in Chapter 16). When you find a file or group of files you like, copy them to a faster disk if you plan to use them much.

Some UNIX systems, namely SunOS if it's configured correctly, mount remote NFS systems automatically. Many do not, however. Ask your system administra-tor to help you.

Playing Post Office

All UNIX systems come with at least a rudimentary mail system, and most have pretty good mailers. You can at least mail stuff to other users on your local system and those on the local network. If you're on the Internet, you can send mail to any other user on the Internet. Even if you're not directly on the net, you may still be able to send and receive mail to and from other systems by way of other intermediary systems.

The connector *is* the network, unfortunately

If you try all this stuff and still get no network response, a surprisingly common problem is that your workstation has come unplugged from the network. The three kinds of Ethernet cable are known as thicknet, thinnet, and unshielded twisted pair (UTP). You can see pictures of these cable types in Chapter 3.

The original thicknet uses a cable about as big around as one of your fingers. The connector at the end of the cable attaches to the computer by way of a large, flat connector that has a clever slide latch. The latch's only disadvantage is that it doesn't work very well. It often comes loose and the plug falls out. If this is your problem, just plug the cable back in.

Thinnet (also known as cheapernet because the cable is indeed much cheaper than thick Ethernet) is a much thinner cable — the same size as cable-TV cable. It uses what are known in the network biz as BNC connectors, which twist and latch quite reliably. The main problem with thinnet is that if several computers are attached by thinnet cable, the cable must physically come all the way to the computer where there is a T-shaped connector with the BNC jack. With this setup, there usually are two cables — one to the computer and one from the computer.

Because this arrangement looks untidy, some people try to clean things up by putting a section of cable between the T and the computer. For boring reasons that have to do with the laws of physics, doing so introduces so much electrical noise into the network that all communication can come to a screeching halt. So don't do that.

If your computer happens to be the last one on its cable, one cable will lead to the usual T connector, which is plugged in to the back of the computer, and a little terminator plug will be on the other end of the T. That's okay.

A few sites have a clever setup with a special cable from the wall to the computer that combines both the to and from cables in one physical cable leading to a BNC plug with the T hidden in molded plastic. That setup is okay too (and very tidy), although it's so expensive that it's not widely used.

UTP uses plain telephone wire and a connector similar to but larger than a telephone plug that actually works, so you're less likely to run into trouble with it. Because phone wire is so much cheaper and easier to use than are thicknet or thinnet, you may reasonably ask why they didn't use it in the first place. The folks who designed Ethernet in the early 1980s didn't realize that it would work. Oh, well.

If you are one of the few sites that has a Token Ring network, you may be interested in knowing that Token Ring networks use a sturdy connector that isn't likely to give you any trouble unless you kick it hard. If the token connector comes out, you must reboot your computer after plugging it back in, because the computer must perform a special initialization sequence to get back on the ring.

Several large Internet sites, such as UUNET and PSI, provide network mail connectivity for hundreds (if not thousands) of dial-in systems, and many smaller systems provide mail forwarding on a more or less formal basis. (See Chapter 27 for a list of some of these systems.)

The easiest way to tell whether you can send and receive Internet e-mail is to try it (see Chapter 7 for details).

Because so many different mailers are on UNIX systems, it is hard to give general-purpose directions that will work on any of them. Our examples use *elm,* which is probably the most widely used UNIX mailer (it works, and it's free). If you use another mail system, such as *mail* or *mh,* you have to inquire locally for instructions. Fortunately, almost all the UNIX mailers use the same mailbox format, so no matter which mailer various people use, the mail still gets through.

The Yellow Plague

The final network concept UNIX users need to know about is the Network Information System (NIS). NIS used to be called Yellow Pages until someone pointed out that the name is a trademark of the local phone company in some countries. Many NIS commands still begin with the letters *yp,* however.

When a company or department has a bunch of workstations, the most convenient way to set them up is to have them all share files by way of NFS and to give all users accounts on all machines so that they act like a large shared system. (This setup mimics the central time-sharing systems that were popular in the 1970s, which now are generally considered hopelessly obsolete. Hmm.)

The practical aspects of keeping all the workstations' administrative information in sync, however, was a nightmare. Each system has a password file that lists valid users, a mail names file that lists mail users and mailing lists, and a set of *mount points* (directories in which remote files can be referenced). In a cluster of 50 workstations, when the system manager added a new user, that user had to be added to 50 password files, 50 mail files, and so on, and the chances of getting everything right was close to nil. System administrators were tearing out what little hair they had left.

NIS solves much of this problem by putting nearly all the administrative data in one place controlled by NIS, and all the workstations consult NIS rather than their private files. When a new user arrives, the administrator has only to add the user to the shared NIS database, which instantly makes all the workstations available to the new user.

This capability is great in principle, and in practice it works pretty well. Occasionally, however, the NIS databases can get out of sync. (After the administrator updates the master files, a clumsy set of commands is necessary to regenerate the NIS database, and it's easy to make a mistake.) When the NIS gets out of sync, it can cause some extremely peculiar results. Also, the design of NIS makes it possible to create some embarrassing security holes — a minor annoyance if the computers are accessible to only a small group of trustworthy users but potentially disastrous if any of the millions of users on the Internet can break in.

NIS and Mail

One thing NIS does is to centralize e-mail sorting. Each user's electronic mailbox resides on a *home* machine. It usually is the same machine generally used for day-to-day work, but it doesn't have to be. NIS centralizes the mail-addressing database, so even though a user has accounts on every machine in the group (courtesy of NIS), mail is automatically routed to the mailbox on the user's home machine. No matter which machine a user happens to be using, she can read mail from her mailbox and send mail to both users in the group and elsewhere.

This capability can cause some peculiar-looking mail addresses in mail that comes from users on NIS systems. Suppose that a company has 26 workstations, named in alphabetical order. You would begin with `aaron.yoyodyne.com`, for example, and then go to `bertha.yoyodyne.com`, and on through the alphabet until you finally get to `zelda.yoyodyne.com`. Depending on which machine a user happens to be sitting in front of, the return address on e-mail messages may be `lauren@aaron.yoyodyne.com`, `lauren@bertha.yoyodyne.com`, or any of the others.

If you are responding to mail from a user in this type of group, how do you know which machine to send it to? The answer, fortunately, is that it doesn't matter. Send it to any of them. If the machine you choose happens not to be the user's home machine, it automatically forwards the mail to the home machine. This extra forwarding step adds about an extra half-second to the time it takes to deliver a mail message but is otherwise invisible. (If having your e-mail arrive half a second late is an issue, you have bigger problems than NIS.)

SLIP sliding away

Ideally, you want your computer attached to the net by the fastest and most reliable connection available. Realistically, you take what you can get. Sometimes the best you can get is a regular ol' dial-up modem. The Internet community fortunately has had plenty of impoverished users, and plenty of support for networking is available on a shoestring.

The two main techniques for working by way of a dial-up phone link are called SLIP (Serial Line Internet Protocol) and PPP (Point-to-Point Protocol). (You can forget these names.) In the fanciest SLIP and PPP setups, your computer automatically dials its net neighbor and logs in whenever there is network traffic to send, and then it hangs up after a minute or two of inactivity. More typically, though, you have to do the logging in your-

self by using programs with names like *slattach*.

Little consistency exists in the way SLIP and PPP are started up; guru assistance is often needed. Don't forget to say thank you when you receive assistance, because SLIP and PPP are fragile enough that expert help is almost always necessary from time to time.

You may wonder what the difference is between SLIP and PPP. Technically, a considerable difference exists: SLIP is a network-layer protocol, and PPP is a link-level protocol. There are two practical differences: PPP is a little faster, and PPP can handle other kinds of networks, such as DECnet. If you're at a low-budget site doing one or the other, though, be grateful that you have any kind of network.

Chapter 5

Macs, VAX, and Other Cultists

● ●

● ●

A Few Words about Macintoshes

Just in case the hair on the back of your neck feels like it's being rubbed the wrong way, let us assure you that we aren't anti-Mac. As a matter of fact, one of the authors, the one who doesn't have a Ph.D., owns a Macintosh and is using it right now to write this very book. It's just that we couldn't resist the alliteration.

Macs, too (not to mention Mac users), have taken some time getting comfortable on the net. As users of a terrific graphical user interface, Mac users are often underwhelmed by UNIX offerings. As Mosaic becomes more popular as a net interface (see Chapter 22), this angst may dissipate.

To the Internet in a Mac-ly way

In terms of just getting connected to the Internet, Macs are very much like PCs. The simplest, easiest way to get on the Internet is to use a modem and communications software and an Internet access provider. We tell you all about that in Chapters 1 and 2. If you feel that your Macintosh point-and-click interface is indispensable, however, it might be worth it to you to connect to the net more directly, if more harriedly.

How hard can it be to get a Mac on the net? Everyone knows that Macs have great networking; just plug them in and they work. That's true as long as the only things you want to network to are other Macs. Getting Macs on the Internet is kind of a pain, partly because the built-in networking tends to get in the way.

SLIP-ing in the Mac way

One way to preserve your Mac view of the world while venturing into the Internet is to use a high-speed modem (no, 1200 and 2400 won't do), MacTCP, and a service provider with SLIP or PPP access. With SLIP (Serial Line Protocol) or PPP (Point-to-Point Protocol), your Mac can be directly connected to the Internet. MacTCP comes with Apple's System 7.5 and also comes with other Internet software packages. Configuring MacTCP is tricky, however, and the settings have to correspond with the service provider you choose. If possible, ask your service provider to configure your MacTCP or to talk you through it over the phone.

I thought I'd always be plug-compatible

Normally, when you plug Macs together, they communicate by using a built-in scheme called *AppleTalk*. So long as all you have are Macs and they're all physically close enough to connect by using standard Apple-type cable, AppleTalk works great. Over longer distances, AppleTalk doesn't work as well, and on most non-Mac machines, it doesn't work at all. But for a long time, AppleTalk was pretty much all that Apple Computer supported for Mac networking.

A few years back, Apple finally admitted that the Internet's TCP/IP (the Internet's own protocol — see Chapter 6 for more info on TCP/IP) was here to stay. (The original plan was for the entire rest of the world to convert to AppleTalk. Nice try, fellas.) So Apple wrote some standard low-level TCP/IP support that nearly all Mac Internet software now uses.

The support code is generally known as *MacTCP,* although its official product name is now *TCP/IP Connection for Macintosh* (see Chapter 28). The current version of MacTCP is 2.0.2, which is supposed to fix some serious problems in version 2.0. Older versions of MacTCP were sometimes bundled with network applications; that's no longer the case — you should bite the bullet and get an up-to-date copy, even if you have to pay for it.

Installing MacTCP is a little tricky; unless you are in the mood for a serious Mac Hack Attack, get a local Mac expert to do it and at the same time arrange for the network wiring.

MacTCP does two things for you: It appears as a Mac control panel that gives you some ability to adjust what it's doing, and it has some standardized internal libraries that network applications use so that multiple network applications can run without clobbering each other. In System 7, the applications can even run simultaneously.

What if I have to install this stuff myself?

The Internet itself offers some excellent advice about connecting your Mac to the net. If you already have net access, a MacTCP primer is available from FTP or Gopher (see Chapters 16 and 20) from site `spider.math.ilstu.edu`, under the name `/pub/mac/mac-tcp.txt`.

A four-part Mac communications *Frequently Asked Questions* note is posted monthly on the Usenet group `comp.sys.mac.comm`. It is available by way of FTP from `sumex-aim.stanford.edu` as `info-mac/report/comp-sys-mac-comm-faq.txt`. This note talks about all sorts of Mac communications, but the third part is mostly about TCP/IP networking.

For more on Macs and the Internet, see *The Internet For Macs For Dummies* by Charles Seiter (IDG Books, 1994). And for a complete discussion of Macintosh networking, see the *Macworld Networking Handbook* by Dave Kosiur and Nancy E. H. Jones (IDG Books, 1994 — look for the latest edition).

Hey, my MacTCP is locked!

If your Mac has been set up by someone else, you may find that you cannot make any changes on your MacTCP control panel because it's locked. That's probably good news because it means that whoever set it up went to the trouble to set and lock your MacTCP options.

The only way to unlock the control panel is with an administrator's version of MacTCP. If you have a problem, rather than try to steal the disk and fiddle with it yourself, find the administrator who set the lock and ask that person (politely, as always) to make any network changes you need.

Note that you have to unlock only to change network parameters. You do *not* have to unlock to use — or even to install — network applications.

Down the wire

Three network wiring options are available for your Mac:

- ✔ **LocalTalk or PhoneNet:** These use thin cable and small connectors.
- ✔ **Ethernet:** This option uses thick cable, thin cable-TV-like cable, or phone wire (see the discussions of Ethernet wiring in Chapter 3; Macs have the same Ethernet options as PCs do).
- ✔ **Token Ring:** This system uses thin cable and big, square connectors.

All three wiring options have their advantages and disadvantages, but the choice is usually obvious: You have to have whatever kind of network the other computers around you use so that you can talk to them.

If you have a LocalTalk network, most of the other computers on the network are also Macs, and you need a gateway box to connect you to the Internet TCP/IP world. If you have Ethernet or Token Ring, you can be on the same network with other computers. You may or may not need a gateway box.

Talking the talk

Unfortunately, far too many different ways exist to set up your Macintosh network. The reason is that there are two different network *protocols,* which are software conventions for communicating among computers, and three different kinds of network hardware.

The two most important protocols are the Internet's TCP/IP and Apple's AppleTalk.

The three kinds of hardware are as follows:

- ✔ LocalTalk (or PhoneNet, which works the same way)
- ✔ Ethernet (any of the three varieties)
- ✔ Token Ring

A Mac can handle AppleTalk on LocalTalk, Ethernet, or Token Ring. It can also handle TCP/IP on Ethernet or Token Ring. Okay so far? (If not, never mind — with luck, you won't need to know about this subject.)

AppleTalk has the advantage when you're using a Mac that it's well integrated into the rest of the Mac system. As soon as you turn on an AppleTalk connection, your Mac can *see* all the other AppleTalk resources on the network, such as printers, Mac file servers, and Novell AppleShare servers. AppleTalk can run on any of the kinds of hardware just mentioned. When your Mac sends AppleTalk by way of an Ethernet, that's known as *Ethertalk*. When it sends AppleTalk by way of a Token Ring, that's *Tokentalk*.

TCP/IP has the advantage that many other kinds of computers can handle it, including every computer on the Internet. When your Mac sends TCP/IP over an Ethernet or Token Ring, it's known as TCP/IP. (No cutesy names are needed on the Internet.) There's no provision for native TCP/IP on LocalTalk.

If you want your Mac to communicate with the Internet, therefore, your Mac *must* speak TCP/IP. But your Mac can send out a packet of Internet TCP/IP in two different ways:

  ✔ Wrap a layer of AppleTalk around it and send it out as an AppleTalk packet with the TCP/IP hidden inside (called *encapsulated* TCP/IP)

  ✔ Send it out as a regular *native* TCP/IP packet

In the former case, only other Macs that are running MacTCP and a few compatible gateway systems can understand it. In the latter case, any other TCP/IP system can immediately understand it.

In short, if your network uses Ethernet or Token Ring, you should set up your Mac to use native TCP/IP. (You set it that way on the MacTCP control panel.) This setup gives you maximum access to other TCP/IP systems, both Mac and non-Mac.

If you are using LocalTalk, on the other hand, you have to use encapsulated TCP/IP; if you want to connect to the outside Internet world, you need a gateway box that unwraps the encapsulated data and sends it along to the outside. Many different gateway boxes are available, including Shiva's FastPath, Cayman Systems' Gatorbox, Webster Computer Corporation's Multiport Gateway, and Compatible Systems' EtherRoute/TCP.

Incidentally, it is possible to send native TCP/IP and AppleTalk over the same cable — it often makes sense to communicate with other nearby Macs by using AppleTalk, and with the outside world by using TCP/IP, both running at the same time on your Mac.

Whaddaya mean, I'm not dynamic?

One exciting aspect of Mac TCP/IP networking (in the sense that it unavoidably generates excitement even though people would rather remain calm) is address assignment. Every computer on the Internet has a four-part numeric address similar to 127.85.46.9, which identifies it to other computers on the net.

Each Internet network is assigned a range of addresses for the computers on that network. The normal way to assign addresses to individual computers is to go around to each computer in the office and slap a sticker with an address on the computer. This process is called *static addressing* because the address stays with the computer permanently (or as permanently as anything in the computer biz can be).

If your Macs communicate with each other by using AppleTalk and are hooked to the outside world by using a gateway box, they use an alternative numbering scheme known as *dynamic addressing*. Rather than permanently assign an address to each Mac, the gateway box is given a pool of Internet addresses. Every time one of the Macs contacts the gateway box to get in touch with the outside world, the box assigns the Mac a free address from the pool. When the Mac is finished with its Internet application, the address goes back into the pool.

Dynamic addressing has a couple of advantages:

- There's no need for a system administrator to wander around the office with stickers and to have to come up with a new sticker every time someone gets a new Mac.

- You can get away with having fewer addresses than you have Macs.

Because the Internet is in the midst of a numbering crisis, if you have a thousand Macs in your organization, getting a thousand addresses is a major bureaucratic hassle. On the other hand, it's much easier to get 250 addresses (the size of chunk the Internet powers that be like to hand out). If you don't expect more than a quarter of your Macs to be using the Internet at one time, you can get by with 250 addresses for 1,000 Macs.

This formula applies equally on a smaller scale. If your organization has a bunch of departments, it probably will take its 250 addresses and divide them into eight subnets with 30 addresses each (a few addresses get lost to round-off and other reasons). So you may have a 50-Mac network with 30 addresses — same principle.

Dynamic addressing has one main disadvantage: The outside world cannot find any particular Mac. If you want to have a server that other people can use (a folder of public or semipublic files, for example), the Mac doing the serving must have a static address so that people on the outside can find it. It's possible to have mixed setups in which most Macs use dynamic addresses but some have fixed static addresses, so the servers can have static addresses and everyone else uses dynamic addresses.

Your network guru should have set up your addressing already, so you generally do not have to worry. If you want to provide some network service to friends on the outside, however, be sure that your server has a static address.

TECHNICAL STUFF

Help, I've bin hexed!

In the opinion of users of most other kinds of computers in the world, Macintoshes use strange kinds of files. Each Mac file contains two parts, called the data fork and the resource fork. The *data fork* contains the plain data of the file (text if it's a document, and the actual image if it's a GIF picture); the *resource fork* stores stuff related to the data, such as international settings, the page you were last editing, and voice annotations. Mac executable files consist almost entirely of resources.

Other kinds of computers don't handle these two-part files, so a bunch of ad hoc conventions have been developed (which folks in the computer biz call hacks or gross hacks). These conventions pack up Mac files so that they can be stored and transferred by other, inferior kinds of computers. The two main hacks are listed here:

✔ **MacBinary**: Simply takes the two parts of the files and (here's another technical computer term) gloms them together with a little bit of other info, such as the file's true name (most computers cannot handle names like `Second Draft of My Novel`), file type, and creation date. MacBinary then makes a simple one-part file that any computer can handle. If you see a file in an on-line archive whose name ends in .bin, it's a MacBinary.

✔ BinHex: Does the same thing as MacBinary and takes it one step further to produce a version of a file disguised as printable text characters. The reason it does this is that if you want to pass a file around as e-mail or as Usenet news (see Chapters 7 and 11), the file must look like text because that's all that mail and news handle. If you see a file whose name ends in .hqx, it's BinHex-ed. BinHex messages are easy to recognize because they all begin with the following line:

(This file must be converted with BinHex 4.0)

Several versions of BinHex have been created over the years, but the one that everyone uses is 4.0.

Lots of programs turn files into MacBinary or BinHex and back. Some of the network applications do it automatically, or you can use a stand-alone program such as StuffIt instead.

A discussion of the intricacies of Mac file-wrangling are beyond the scope of this book, so check out some of the Mac books from IDG Books Worldwide for the complete lowdown. Here are a few to get you started: *Macs For Dummies* (1992) by David Pogue; *Macworld Macintosh SECRETS* (1993), by David Pogue and Joseph Schorr; and *Macworld Complete Mac Handbook Plus CD* (1993) by Jim Heid.

Now that I have it, what do I do with it?

After you have MacTCP going, you can run a bunch of applications on top of it, which gives you access to all the network services discussed in this book (see Chapter 28 for sources). Some popular applications include the ones in this list:

✔**NCSA Telnet:** The most popular version of *telnet,* which is the application that lets you log in to other computers. This application is popular for two unbeatable reasons: It works well, and it's free. It also includes *FTP* (file-transfer protocol), the application that copies files from one computer to another, and both an FTP client that allows you to copy files to and from other computers and an FTP server that (if you turn it on) lets other people copy files to and from your computer.

NCSA Telnet happens to be one of the few Mac TCP/IP applications that doesn't require MacTCP, although it works with MacTCP if it's there. If you have a single Mac and a modem, NCSA may be all you need in order to get on the net. See Chapter 28 for more information.

✔ **COMET:** Another version of telnet, from Cornell. It includes an IBM 3270-style telnet, which you need to talk to many IBM mainframes.

✔ **SU-Mac/IP:** A full-featured package from Stanford with telnet, FTP, printing, and other goodies. It's available only to educational institutions.

✔ **Eudora:** A full-featured mail program. Versions through mid-1993 were free; now it's a commercial program from Qualcomm.

✔ **Newswatcher:** A Usenet newsreading program developed by Apple but available for free.

VAXen

One of the most popular kinds of minicomputers on the Internet circuit is the Digital VAX. For those of you who missed the minicomputer era, there was a time, peaking in the late 70s and early 80s, when the hottest technology in computers was being developed by companies such as Digital Equipment Corporation. They were radically different from the mainframe computers of IBM. They were easier to use and available on a smaller scale that made them affordable by small- and medium-size business. And Digital invested a great deal of equipment in higher education, providing many campuses with state-of-the-art computers. In a world full of personal computers and superpowered workstations, nobody's investing more in the world of proprietary software and architecture. However, there is a mountain of, how shall we say it, *installed base* — that is, a ton of people are already out there with VAXes who are very loyal users. For you who have found yourself at a DEC site, we provide the following attempt to connect you with the rest of the world.

You can run one of three different operating systems on a VAX: VMS, Ultrix, and OSF/1. The latter two systems are versions of UNIX, so you can find out about how to work with them in Chapter 4. VMS is different, so we talk about it a little here.

TECHNICAL STUFF

The Alpha state

Even the VAX lovers at DEC admit that the VAX is getting a little long in the tooth. (It was a brilliant design to take advantage of the kind of technology available in the mid 1970s. Unfortunately for DEC, it's no longer the mid-1970s.) So they started a huge project to come up with a super-duper new design that includes the latest 1990s computer design buzzwords, such as "RISC" and "scalable" and named the resulting family of computer chips "Alpha."

The Alpha is a fine chip, and the finest thing about it, from DEC's point of view, is that with only a small amount of conversion effort (well, small compared to transmuting lead into gold), it runs all the same software the VAX does. So for our purposes, everything we say about the VAX and in particular VAX VMS applies equally to Alpha VMS.

By and large, the VMS TCP/IP Internet network facilities are modeled after the UNIX ones. (Indeed, wherever possible, they borrowed the UNIX code and adapted it.) But VMS is different for a couple of reasons:

- ✔ There is no single dominant version of TCP/IP for VMS. About five versions exist, all from different vendors, and all provide slightly different services. Whoever runs your VMS machine will have chosen one of them already, so you have what you have. They all work perfectly well but have slightly different warts.

- ✔ VMS has its own native network (DECnet) and its own file-management system (RMS). In many places (notably mail), VMS assumes that when you talk about a network, you mean DECnet, and you have to say specifically that, no, you mean the Internet instead.

VMS Mail peculiarities

Most VMS shops use DEC's standard mail package or something compatible with it, or else the All-In-1 office-automation package. Normal mail addresses are taken to be DECnet addresses, so you have to say something special to mean Internet addresses. In DEC Mail, you usually say something like this:

```
MX%"elvis@ntw.org"
```

MX is a common, free, Internet mail gateway. Some people use IN% rather than MX%. (Contact a local expert to find out the exact incantation to use.)

If you're using a VMS system within Digital's own Easynet network, all Internet mail is routed through the DECnet host called DECWRL. To send to the Internet from a system on Easynet, you say the following:

```
nm%DECWRL::"elvis@ntw.org"
```

If you're using All-In-1, the address looks something like this:

```
elvis@ntw.org @Internet
```

Again, details vary depending on how your local network is set up, so ask a local expert. While you're asking, ask what your Internet e-mail address is because there are various ways to turn a DECnet address into an Internet address.

File peculiarities

One of the best or worst parts of VMS, depending on your point of view, is RMS, a fancy built-in file-management system. Unfortunately, the people who designed the Internet's FTP file-transfer program did not have VMS and in particular RMS in mind. (In fairness, FTP predates RMS by several years.) If you have a file full of plain ol' text, you can transfer it without trouble by using FTP. If, on the other hand, you have a nontext file of some sort, you're in minor trouble.

Don't bother to read the remainder of this section until you read Chapters 16 and 17 (on FTP). The information is here because it's about VMS.

If you want to transfer RMS files by using FTP, you have two basic choices:

✓ If the machine you're transferring to or from is also running VMS, with any luck they both have FTP programs that have been upgraded to know about RMS. Try entering **STRU VMS** or checking your FTP program's documentation for a command to transfer VMS-structured files. If such a command exists, and it works when you try it (the other end must cooperate in order for it to work), you're all set and can transfer without trouble any kind of file you want.

✓ The alternative is to hide the RMS file in a plain file and then transfer the plain file and unhide it on the other end. The usual hiding technique is to use the command **VMS BACKUP** to create a small backup file that contains your file (or files — there can be more than one) or else use **ZIP** to create an archive. Given a choice, ZIP probably creates a smaller (and therefore faster to copy) transfer file.

X Marks the Spot

One kind of computer terminal that has become popular in recent years is the *X terminal*, which is basically a stripped-down workstation running a single program, the graphical server for X Window System. X terminals invariably have a network connection to other nearby computers, so you log in to one or more of those computers to get your work done. But because the Internet is an egalitarian network, if the network to which your X terminal is connected is attached to the Internet, you can (in principle — see the next Tip) use X-compatible programs on any Internet host in the world.

Your typical X terminal has a telnet (see Chapter 14) application built in that you use to log in to a nearby computer. For anything beyond that initial long session, you use programs that open their own windows on your screen. Typically, you start a couple of *xterm* (the standard X remote terminal) windows logged in to nearby computers.

Many Internet services, such as Archie, Gopher, and WAIS (Chapters 19, 20, and 21, respectively) have X versions called, creatively, *xarchie, xgopher,* and *xwais*. You can use them and have their windows automatically appear on your terminal. Just be sure that you set your DISPLAY environment variable (or the equivalent on non-UNIX systems) to point at your screen. If your terminal is called x15.ntw.org, for example, you type one of the following lines in a telnet or xterm window before starting another X application:

```
setenv DISPLAY x15.ntw.org:0       (C shell)
DISPLAY=x15.ntw.org:0 ; export DISPLAY (Bourne or Korn shell)
```

The :0 is necessary to indicate that your terminal is supposed to use the first screen on your display. (Yes, we know that your display has only one screen, but computers, because they're stupid, don't know that.)

You also have to tell your X terminal that it's OK to allow X client applications on other computers to draw their windows on your screen. The details of that process vary by model of X terminal, but generally you have to add to the list of hosts allowed to use your screen the name of the computer on which the X application is running (probably the one you telnetted to in the first place).

Although you usually run X client programs only on nearby computers, in principle X applications anywhere in the Internet can draw their windows on your screen so that you can use them directly, even if they're running on a computer in, say, Slovenia. In practice, though, the connection to the other computer had better be very fast or else the application will be so sluggish that you won't want to use it.

We've run X clients in Wisconsin with windows on our screen in Massachusetts using a medium-speed link, and it worked, but we wouldn't want to use it every day because i-t w-a-s a-w-f-u-l-l-y s-l-l-o-o-o-w-w-w. (Perhaps if we had been in a more relaxed California frame of mind rather than in an overwrought Eastern one, or if we had worked while immersed in a vat of molasses so that we couldn't move our fingers or any other part of our bodies very fast, it would have been okay.)

If You've Gotten This Far, We Have No Idea What Kind of Computer You Have

Most computers connected directly to the Internet have network applications modeled after the UNIX versions that in turn were modeled after the DEC-20 originals, written more than 20 years ago. The commands described for FTP, telnet, and so on, therefore, work because the programmers who wrote your version of the programs used the same commands they were already used to using. Even if your versions use a window system or are otherwise souped up, you can probably recognize the originals underneath. Window versions of FTP, for example, tend to have menus and buttons with choices that, amazingly enough, match the commands in the command-oriented original.

As far as physical network connections go, pretty much the same set of choices exists for nearly all computers these days.

- ✔ If a local network connects computers in the same building, it almost certainly is some version of Ethernet or a Token Ring.

- ✔ If you have a forward-thinking and resource-rich employer, you may use the extremely fast network FDDI, but it's just like Ethernet, only faster.

- ✔ If you have a single computer, its connection to the outside is likely a modem and phone line, either dial-up or dedicated line to a network hub.

- ✔ If you're using a supercomputer or giant mainframe, it may have some sort of super-exotic, fiber-optic, broadband network gizmo. In that case, however, guards would probably arrest you if you tried to fiddle with the network connection, so it hardly matters which kind it is.

- ✔ The other possibility is that your computer doesn't have a network connection or software — just a modem and a terminal emulator. You can probably log in as a terminal to a time-shared system that has an Internet connection. In that case, it's the system you log in to rather than the computer you're using that determines which kind of software you have.

Chapter 6

How Does the Internet Work?

This chapter contains gruesome details about how the Internet sends data from one place to another. You can skip this entire chapter if you want. But don't, because we think that it's interesting. And besides, we've been telling you since Chapter 1 that this chapter tells you all about the famous TCP/IP, so you wouldn't want to waste it.

First We Get Organized

Okay, so the Internet has more than a million computers attached to it. How do you find the one you want? There are two ways (nobody said that this was going to be simple). Each machine on the net is identified by a *number* and a *name*. First we look at the numbers and then at the names.

An Executive Summary

The way the numbers and names are assigned on the Internet is, unavoidably, fairly technical. So here's the short version, in case you would rather save the full version for later.

  ✔ Each machine on the net (called a *host*) has a number assigned to identify it to other hosts, sort of like a phone number. The numbers are in four parts, such as 123.45.67.89. You should know the host number of the computer you use most, but otherwise you can forget about the numbers.

✔ Most hosts also have names, which are much easier to remember than numbers are. The names have multiple parts separated by dots (`chico.iecc.com`, for example, the name of our computer). Some hosts have more than one name, but it doesn't matter which of them you use.

✔ Complicated rules control how names and numbers are assigned. But because you're not likely to be doing any of the assigning, you don't really have to know what they are.

✔ Each network in the Internet has rules about what kinds of network traffic (e-mail, terminal sessions, and other connections) it allows. You should know the rules that apply to the network (or networks) you use to avoid getting the network managers mad at you.

What's in a Number?

Any computer of any kind, from the smallest to the largest, attached to the Internet is called a *host* (which must make us users parasites — *yuck*). Some hosts are giant mainframes or supercomputers that provide services to thousands of users; some are little workstations or PCs with one user; and some are specialized computers, like *routers,* which connect one network to another, or *terminal servers,* which let dumb terminals (or PCs running Procomm, Crosstalk, or the like) dial in and connect to other hosts. But from the Internet's point of view, they're all hosts.

Each machine is assigned a *host number,* which is sort of like a phone number. Being computers, the kind of numbers hosts like are 32-bit binary numbers. For example, our computer's number is

```
10001100101110100101000100000001
```

Hmmm. That's not very memorable. To make the number slightly easier to remember, it's broken up into four 8-bit groups, and then each group is translated into a decimal equivalent. So our computer's number turns into

```
140.186.81.1
```

which isn't much better, but it's at least possible for humans to remember for a minute or two.

How much should I care about these numbers?

By and large, you can get by without knowing any host numbers, because in most cases you use the much more memorable host *names* described later in this chapter. Occasionally, though, the naming scheme breaks down. In this case, having written down the following two numbers is helpful:

✔ The number of the computer you use

✔ The number of some other nearby computer to which you have access

The reason to know the second number is that if you can contact the second computer by number but not by name, you can reasonably conclude that the naming scheme has failed. If you can't contact it either way, it's more likely that the network, or at least your network connection, has failed, quite possibly because you inadvertently kicked a cable loose. Oops.

Networks have numbers too?

We're afraid so. Consider, for a moment, your phone number, which is something like 202-653-1800. In the phone number, the first six digits designate where the phone exchange is — in this case, Washington, D.C. The last four digits are a particular phone in that exchange. (Call it for a good time, by the way.)

Internet *host numbers* are also divided into two parts: The first part is the network number (remember that the Internet is composed of many different but interconnected networks), and the second part, the *local* part, is a host number on that particular network. In the case of our computer, 140.186.81.1 means network number 140.186, and local host number (on that network) 81.1. Sometimes, for added confusion, people write out network numbers in four parts by adding zeroes, like 140.186.0.0.

Because some networks have many more hosts on them than others do, networks are divided into three sizes: large, medium, and small. In large networks *(Class A)*, the first of the four numbers is the network number, and the last three are the local part. In medium networks *(Class B)*, the first two numbers are the network number, and the last two are the local part. In small networks *(Class C)*, the first three numbers are the network number, and the last is the local part.

The first of the four numbers tells you in which class the network is. Table 6-1 is a little table that summarizes classes and sizes.

Table 6-1	Network Numbers and Sizes		
Class	*First Number*	*Length of Net Number*	*Maximum Number of Hosts*
A	1 through 126	1	16,387,064
B	128 through 191	2	64,516
C	192 through 223	3	254

Great big organizations (or at least organizations that have a large number of computers) tend to have Class A networks. IBM has network 9, for example, and AT&T has network 12, so host number 9.12.34.56 would be at IBM, and 12.98.76.54 would be at AT&T. Medium-size organizations, including most universities, have Class B networks. Rutgers University has network 128.6, and Goldman Sachs (an investment broker that has to use a large number of computers to keep track of all the money it handles) has network 138.8. Class C networks are used by small organizations and sometimes small parts of large organizations. Network 192.65.175, for example, is used by a single IBM research lab. (Why don't they use the general IBM network number? Who knows?)

Some host and network numbers are reserved for special purposes. In particular, any number with a component of 0 or 255 (two numbers with great mystical significance to computers) is special and cannot be used as an actual host number. (This is a slight exaggeration, but it's close enough for most purposes.)

Multiple multiple numbers numbers

The final added confusion in host numbering is that some hosts have more than one number. The reason for this is quite simple: Some hosts are on more than one network, so they need a host number on each of the networks to which they are attached. If you need to contact a machine with multiple host numbers, it doesn't matter which of the numbers you use.

TECHNICAL STUFF

Subnets, supernets, super-duper nets . . . .

This discussion is extremely technoid. Don't say that we didn't warn you.

Frequently, an organization that has a single network number wants to set up its computers internally on multiple networks. All the computers in a single department, for example, are usually attached together on a single network, with some sort of connection linking together department networks. (Both administrative and technical reasons exist for this arrangement, but we don't bore you with them.) But adhering to the way the Internet was originally set up would mean that an outfit with 25 internal networks would have to get 25 different network numbers for them.

This was bad news for several reasons. It meant that every time a company set up a new internal network, it had to apply for a new network number. Even worse, the rest of the Internet world had to put that network number in their tables so that they knew how to route messages to it.

Clearly, something had to be done. That something is called a *subnet*. All that means is that one network can be divided into pieces called subnets. On a subnet, part of what would normally be the host number becomes part of the network number. In network 140.186, for example, the third number in the host number is the subnet number, so for machine 140.186.81.1, the subnet number is 140.186.81, and the host number is 1. This enables plenty of local networks to be installed (on our network, we currently use only 90 of the 254

possible subnets), and as far as the outside world is concerned, there's still only the single network 140.186 to worry about.

In practice, all but the smallest networks are subnetted. Also in practice, you almost never have to worry about subnets. When your computer is first attached to the network, the guru who installs it has to set its *subnet mask* to reflect correctly the current subnetting conventions. If the mask is wrong, you may have strange problems, such as being able to communicate with half your company's departments (such as the even-numbered ones but not the odd-numbered ones).

A few organizations have an opposite problem. They have too many computers for a Class C network, more than 254, but nowhere near enough to justify a Class B. (These days, the demand for network numbers is so great that it's practically impossible to get anything bigger than a Class C.) In this case, the organization can get a block of adjacent network numbers and treat part of the network number as a host number, a process called *supernetting*.

(The supernetted number is then invariably subnetted, an extra wart we won't even begin to consider.) Supernetting is currently uncommon but will become more widely used as more companies put a large number of computers on the Internet. As with subnetting, you don't have to worry about it unless someone screws up your system's configuration.

Name?

Normal people use names, not numbers, so in a rare bow to normality, Internet hosts are usually referred to by name, not by number. For example, the machine we have heretofore referred to as 140.186.81.1 is named chico. In the earliest days of the ARPANET, machines had simple one-part names, and there was a master list of names. The machine at Harvard was called HARVARD, and so on. But with a million machines on the net, it would be sort of hard to come up with different names for all of them.

To avoid a crisis of naming creativity, the solution was to go to multipart names, a scheme grandly known as the *Domain Name System* or *DNS.* Host names are a string of words (or at least wordlike things) separated by dots. In the multipart regime, chico's real name is CHICO.IECC.COM. (The naming scheme was evidently invented by people WHO LIKE TO SHOUT EVERYTHING IN CAPITAL LETTERS. Fortunately, the lowercase in host names is always taken to be equivalent to uppercase, and henceforth we avoid shouting and put the names in lowercase.)

Zones, domains, and all that

You have to decode an Internet name from right to left. This process may seem perverse, but it turns out in practice to be more convenient than the other way around, for the same reason we put surnames after first names. (In England, where they drive on the left, they write host names from left to right. Typical.)

The rightmost part of a name is called its *zone.* If we examine chico's full name, the rightmost part is com, which means that this is a *commercial* site (in the com zone), as opposed to educational, military, or some other kinds of zones we mention later in this chapter.

The next part of chico's name, iecc, is the name of the company, the Invincible Electric Calculator Company. (Yes, it's sometimes pronounced "yecch" — John should have picked a better abbreviation.) The part to the left of the company name is the particular machine within the company. This happens to be a rather small company with only five computers, so chico's friends, milton, tom, astrud, and xuxa, are known as milton.iecc.com, tom.iecc.com, astrud.iecc.com, and xuxa.iecc.com.

There really is a logic to the naming scheme we used. They're named after some favorite Brazilian singers. Chico is Chico Buarque, who's quite political. Tom (pronounced "tome") is Antonio Carlos "Tom" Jobim, who wrote "Girl from Ipanema," best known in the U.S. from a soda-pop ad 25 years ago. Milton is Milton Nasciemento, who's more lyrical and melodic. Xuxa is Xuxa, who's sort of a cross between Madonna and Mr. Rogers. And Astrud is Astrud Gilberto, known here for singing the original pre-soda-pop version of "Girl from Ipanema."

The host naming system is quite egalitarian. In it, `iecc.com`, a company with two employees, is right up there with `ibm.com`, a company with several hundred thousand employees. Larger organizations usually additionally subdivide machine names by site or department, so that a typical machine in the computer science department at Yale University is called `bulldog.cs.yale.edu`. Each organization can set up its names in any way it wants, although in practice, names with more than five components are rare, not to mention hard to remember and type.

If you type a simple host name with no dots, your local computer assumes that the rest of the name is the same as the computer you're currently using. So, if we're logged in to `milton` and want to contact `chico`, we can simply refer to `chico` and it assumes that we mean `chico.iecc.com`.

The Twilight Zone?

Name zones divide into two general categories: the three-letter kind and the two-letter kind. The three-letter zones are set up by type of organization. We have seen `com` for `commercial`. Table 6-2 lists the rest of them.

Table 6-2	Three-Letter Zone Names
Zone	**Meaning**
com	Commercial organizations
edu	Educational institutions
gov	Government bodies and departments
int	International organizations (mostly NATO at the moment)
mil	Military sites
net	Networking organizations
org	Anything else that doesn't fit elsewhere, such as professional societies

Within the United States, most Internet sites have names in one of the three-letter zones. Elsewhere, it's more common to use geographic names, which are discussed next.

Is there a complete list of host names anywhere?

No. In principle, it should be possible to go through all the various systems in which names are registered and enumerate them all. People used to try to do that, partly out of nosiness and partly out of an interest in collecting network statistics. They gave up when the net had grown to the point that the collection program ran for over a week and still hadn't finished.

Where's Vanuatu?

Two-letter zone names are organized geographically. Each zone corresponds to a country or Other Recognized Political Entity. There's an official international standard list of two-letter country codes, which is used almost but not quite unmodified as the list of two-letter zones. The country code for Canada is CA, so a site at York University in Canada is called `nexus.yorku.ca`. The network administrators in each country can assign names as they see fit. Some countries have organization-level subdivisions; a site at a university in Australia, for example, is called `sait.edu.au`. Others assign names more haphazardly.

In the United States, relatively few computers have names in the geographic U.S. zone, which is mostly organized by city and state. Because I.E.C.C. is in Cambridge, Massachusetts, `chico.iecc.com` used to be known as `iecc.cambridge.ma.us`. (John hadn't named it `chico` yet, because at the time, it was the only computer he had.) In the United States, the choice of geographic or organizational names is pretty arbitrary. If you have one or two machines, it's easier to get a geographic name. If you have more than that, it's easier to get an organizational name, which lets you administer names within your organization yourself. In recent months, the Internet powers that be have started to encourge more people to use the U.S. zone rather than the overcrowded `com` and `edu` zones, so you'll be seeing more .us addresses.

Table 6-3 lists some of the more common geographic zone names. A full table of geographic zones is in the Appendix.

Incidentally, Vanuatu is an island in the South Pacific formerly known as the Condominium of the New Hebrides. It was jointly administered by France and Britain; when you arrived, you had to state whether you wanted to be subject to French or British law. Now the stereophonic legal system is gone and they even have a limited dial-up Internet connection.

Table 6-3	Some Two-Letter Zone Names
Zone	*Country*
AU	Australia
AT	Austria (Republic of)
BE	Belgium (Kingdom of)
CA	Canada
CZ	Czech Republic
DE	Germany (Federal Republic of)
DK	Denmark (Kingdom of)
FI	Finland (Republic of)
FR	France (French Republic)
IN	India (Republic of)
IE	Ireland
IL	Israel (State of)
IT	Italy (Italian Republic)
JP	Japan
NL	Netherlands (Kingdom of the)
NO	Norway (Kingdom of)
RU	Russian Federation
SU	Former Soviet Union (officially obsolete but still in use)
ES	Spain (Kingdom of)
SE	Sweden (Kingdom of)
CH	Switzerland (Swiss Confederation)
TW	Taiwan, Province of China
UK	United Kingdom (official code is GB)
US	United States (United States of America)
VU	Vanuatu (Republic of)

Do you need a number to get a name?

No. It is quite possible to register a site as a *Mail Exchange,* or *MX,* site, meaning that it's not really on the net but that you can send electronic mail to it anyway. Many sites on other networks, including all sites on the FIDO hobbyist network, have MX names. For sending mail, you can treat an MX name the same way as any other name.

No other Internet services work for MX machines, though. If you try to reach them any other way, either the attempt will fail or you will reach a machine on the net that forwards mail for them. Most on-line and e-mail services, including CompuServe, MCI Mail, AT&T Mail, and Prodigy, are also MX'ed into the Internet. See Chapter 9 for more info.

Some other random zones

You might run into a few other zones and pseudozones. Even though the ARPANET has been officially dead for several years, a few sites still, for historical reasons, have names ending in *arpa*. And as for machines on the UUCP and BITNET networks, you occasionally see names ending in *uucp* and *bitnet*. These aren't real zones, and therefore names that use them aren't really valid host names, but many systems have arranged to treat these names as special cases and route mail to them anyway. Any BITNET or UUCP site can arrange to get itself a real host name, so *bitnet* and *uucp* names are heading for well-deserved oblivion.

Rules of Conduct

Various parts of the Internet have some relatively firm rules of conduct. Depending on which part of the net you are attached to, the rules may be more or less strict. The most restrictive rules are for the NSFNET (summarized in the following sidebar), which prohibits all commercial activity. As of mid-1994, the NSFNET was being phased out, in favor of letting the sites attached to it make arrangements with other commercial networks.

Regional networks have less-restrictive policies, and commercial networks are less restrictive still. All reserve the right to boot you off for malicious or destructive conduct. Be aware of the rules that apply to your site and be prepared to honor them.

Also keep in mind that even if you are on a less restrictive network, if you use a more restrictive one — for example, logging on to a machine at an educational institution that uses the NSFNET rules — you are subject to the most-restrictive rules of any network you use.

Why the Post Office Isn't Like the Phone Company

Enough of this administrative nonsense. Let's get back to the grotty details. What the Internet does, basically, is transmit data from one computer to another. How hard can that be? It's not that hard, but it is fairly complicated.

The most-familiar examples of information transfer in real life are the post office and the phone company. If you want to contact someone by telephone, you pick up the phone and dial the number. The phone company then arranges an electrical circuit from your phone to the phone you're calling. You and the other person gossip until you're done (or if it's a modem call, your computer and the other computer gossip until *they're* done) and then you hang up, at which point the phone company releases the circuit. Then you can call someone else. At any particular moment, you can have only one call in progress over a particular phone line. (Yeah, there's three-way calling, but that doesn't count.) This scheme is called *circuit switching* because a circuit is set up for the duration of the conversation. The Internet doesn't work this way, so forget it. (Don't entirely forget it; we come back to simulated circuit switching later.)

The NSFNET backbone services acceptable-use policy

The NSFNET supports research and education, primarily for schools and research institutions but also for commercial firms when they do the same sorts of things. Here's a summary of the policy:

- It's okay to use it to communicate with people on foreign networks.

- It's okay to use it for "professional development," scheduling academic conferences, society meetings, and the like.

- It's okay to use it for applying for and administering grants (not surprising because the NSF is the biggest grant maker around).

- New product announcements are okay; advertisements aren't.

- For-profit uses are forbidden except when they support a permitted use listed here.

- Extensive use for private or personal business is forbidden.

The other model is the post office. If you want to mail a package to someone, you write the recipient's address and your return address on it and mail it. The U.S. Postal Service doesn't have dedicated trucks from every post office to every other post office (they may be inefficient, but they're not *that* inefficient). Instead, the package is routed from your local post office to a central post office, where it's then loaded on a truck or a train headed in the right general direction and passed repeatedly from office to office until it gets to the recipient's post office, at which point the letter carrier delivers it to your door along with the rest of the day's mail.

The post office model is much closer to how the Internet works. Each time a host wants to send a message to another host, either the recipient is on a network to which the first host is directly connected (in which case it can send the message directly) or it's not. In that case, the sender sends the message to a host that can forward it. The forwarding host, which presumably is attached to at least one other network, in turn delivers the message directly if it can or passes it to yet another forwarding host. It's quite common for a message to pass through a dozen or more forwarders on its way from one part of the net to another.

You're probably wondering: *What kind of cretin would think that the post office is a better model than the phone company?*

Don't be led astray by the analogy. The main complaints people have about the post office are that it's slow and that it loses stuff. The Internet occasionally has both of these problems, but they're not as much of an issue as they are with paper mail. In the middle of a busy day, the net can indeed slow down, although the time a message takes to be delivered is still measured in seconds. Losing stuff turns out not to be a problem in practice, for reasons discussed later in this chapter.

All the World's a Packet

Now let's take our postal analogy a step further. Suppose that you have a close friend in the island nation of Papua New Guinea to whom you want to send a copy of the manuscript for your new and very long book. (Papua New Guinea doesn't have many bookstores.) Unfortunately, the manuscript weighs 15 pounds, and the limit on packages to Papua New Guinea is 1 pound. So you divide the manuscript into 15 pieces and on each package you write something like "PART 3 OF 15" and send them off. When the packages eventually arrive, probably not in the right order, your friend takes all the pieces, puts them back in order, and reads them.

The various networks on the Internet work in pretty much the same way: They pass data around in chunks called *packets,* each of which carries the addresses of its sender and its receiver (those host numbers we talked about earlier in this chapter). The maximum size of a packet varies from network to network, but it is usually between 200 and 2,000 *octets* (Internet-speak for *bytes* or *characters*). A typical size is 1,536 octets, which for some long-forgotten reason is the limit on an Ethernet network, the most popular kind of local network. Messages too large for a single packet have to be sent as several packets.

One advantage the Internet has over the post office is that when Internet software breaks a large package of data into smaller pieces, putting the pieces back together is no problem; but when the post office delivers something in small pieces, you are generally out of luck.

Defining the Internet Protocols

The set of conventions used to pass packets from one host to another is known as the *Internet Protocol,* or *IP.* (Catchy, huh? Actually, the network is named after the protocol, not the other way around.) The Internet, quite simply, is the collection of networks that pass packets to each other by using IP.

It's entirely possible to set up a network that uses IP but that isn't connected to the Internet. Many networks were set up that way in companies that wanted to take advantage of IP (which comes free with every UNIX workstation) but that weren't connected at all to the outside world or were connected only by a funky mail connection. In the past year or two, many of these disconnected networks have gotten hooked to the Internet. That's partly because the advantages of being on the net have increased and mostly because new commercial Internet vendors have made the cost of connection about a tenth of what it used to be.

Many other protocols are used in connection with IP. The two best known are *Transmission Control Protocol (TCP)* and *User Datagram Protocol (UDP).* TCP is so widely used that many people refer to *TCP/IP,* the combination of TCP and IP used by most Internet applications.

I'll Build a Gateway to Paradise

Three kinds of *things* (for lack of a better term) pass packets from one network to another: *bridges, routers,* and *gateways.* This section provides a quick run-down of the differences among them so that you can hold your own at nerd cocktail parties.

Bridges

A *bridge* connects two networks in a way that makes them appear to be a single, larger network. Bridges are used most commonly to connect two Ethernet local area networks. (An Ethernet physically consists of a long cable connecting all the machines on a network, and there is a limit on how long a single cable can be.) The bridge looks at all the packets flying by on each of the networks and when it sees a packet on one network destined for a host on the other, the bridge copies it over.

Ethernet host numbers (which, of course, are different from Internet host numbers) are assigned by the serial number of the Ethernet card rather than by network number, so the only way the bridge can tell what hosts are on which network is to build a large table listing which hosts are on each network, based on the return addresses on all the packets flying by on each network. It's a miracle that it works at all.

The good thing about bridges is that they work transparently — the hosts whose packets are being bridged don't have to be aware that a bridge is involved, and a single bridge can handle a bunch of different kinds of network traffic (such as Novell and Banyan in addition to IP) at the same time. The disadvantages of bridges are that they can connect only two networks of the same type and that bridging fast networks that are not physically next to each other is difficult.

Routers

A *router* connects two or more IP (that's the Internet Protocol) networks. The hosts on the networks have to be aware that a router is involved, but that's no problem for IP networks because one of the rules of IP is that all hosts have to be able to talk to routers.

- ✔ A good thing about routers is that they can attach physically different networks, such as a fast, local Ethernet to a slower, long-haul phone line.
- ✔ A bad thing about routers is that they move packets slower than bridges do because it requires more calculation to figure out how to route packets than it does to bridge them, particularly when the networks are of different speeds.

A fast network can deliver packets much faster than a slow network can take them away, causing network constipation, so the router has to be able to tell a sending host to talk slower.

Another problem is that routers are protocol-specific — that is, the way a host talks to an IP router is different from the way it talks to, say, a Novell or DECnet router. This problem is now addressed by the router equivalent of a Ginsu knife that slices and dices every which way and knows about routing every kind of network known to humankind. These days, all commercial routers can handle multiple protocols, usually at extra cost for each added protocol. Incidentally, this kind of router is usually pronounced "ROOter," because a "ROWter" is something you use in a woodworking shop (except in Australia.)

Routers: The good, the bad, and the really bad

One of the hot topics among Internet weenies these days is routing policy. The Internet is for the most part redundantly connected — that is, getting from one network to another can be accomplished in several ways. In the good old days, finding a route was relatively easy because the main goal was to find the shortest route to each known network. Only a handful of networks were around, so the routers (hosts that pass packets from one network to another) simply compared notes to figure out which one had the shortest route to where. If you wanted to be really fancy and if you had two equally fast routes to somewhere, you could monitor the amount of traffic on each route and send packets by the less busy route.

Things are no longer so simple. For starters, the number of networks a router has to be aware of is no longer a handful (unless you have extraordinarily large hands). More than 10,000 different networks are attached to the Internet, and more are added weekly. Furthermore, the speeds of communication lines have increased much more quickly than have the speeds of computers used for routing, enough that special hardware is needed to keep up with the networks that will be installed in the next few years.

Another issue is that there are now political in addition to technical distinctions among networks. The Commercial Internet Exchange (CIX), for example, has a router that handles traffic for only CIX members and their immediate customers. This means that some traffic can't be routed in the most direct way, if the traffic isn't appropriate for one of the networks on that route.

Another wart on the face of routing is that many organizations have *firewall* routers that pass only certain kinds of traffic. Typically, firewall routers allow incoming electronic mail but not incoming remote terminal sessions or file transfers, in an effort to keep out ill-mannered users looking for security holes (and if you have a large enough internal network, a hole will certainly be found somewhere).

Lots of technical papers are published about advanced new routing schemes, policies, or whatever. Fortunately, you as a user can ignore the issue because as long as routers eventually get your packets to the right place, it doesn't really matter how they do it.

Gateways

A *gateway* splices together two different kinds of protocols. If your network talks IP, for example, and someone else's network talks Novell or DECnet or SNA or one of the other dozen Leading Brands of Network, a gateway converts traffic from one set of protocols to another. Gateways are not only specific to particular protocols but also are application-specific, because the way you convert electronic mail from one network to the other is quite different from the way you convert a remote terminal session.

Mix-and-match terms

These terms are not cast in stone. The term *gateway* has often been used for what we here call a *router,* and things called *brouters* act like something halfway between a bridge and a router. Also keep in mind that all the differences among bridges, routers, and gateways are based on software, so in some cases it's quite possible to make the same pieces of hardware into a bridge, router, or gateway, depending on the software in use.

TCP: The Rocket-Powered Mailman

We have established that the Internet works just like the post office, in that it delivers hunks of data (packets) one at a time. So what do you do if you want to "have a conversation," such as logging in to a remote computer? Back to the postal analogy. Suppose that you're a chess player. Normal chess is played face-to-face with each player immediately responding to the other. Abnormal chess is sometimes played by mail with each player mailing moves to the other. These types of games can take months to complete. But what if your mail were delivered by someone with rocket shoes who zipped each move to the other player within a fraction of a second? That would be much more like normal chess.

TCP (Transmission Control Protocol) is that rocket-powered mailman. TCP provides what looks like a dedicated connection from one computer to another. Any data you send to the other computer is guaranteed to be delivered, in the same order it was sent, just as though a dedicated circuit were connected from one end to the other (the details of this process are explained in the next section). What TCP provides isn't really a circuit, in fact, it's just a great deal of IP packets, so what TCP provides is called a *virtual circuit.* But it's real enough for most purposes, which is why nearly every Internet application uses it.

TCP has to add a great deal of glop to each packet to do its magic, which makes TCP somewhat slower than the raw IP. A considerably less fancy protocol called UDP (User Datagram Protocol) doesn't make any promises about reliability, making do with whatever IP gives it, for the benefit of applications that want to roll their own reliability features or that can live with the flakiness. (In most cases, IP correctly delivers upward of 99 percent of all packets, even without TCP's help.)

Certify That Packet!

Make no mistake — the Internet shares with the U.S. Postal Service some inherent unreliability. The Postal Service has two schemes for ensuring that something is delivered: registered mail and return receipts. If you're mailing something of great intrinsic value, such as an original 45 RPM record of Bill Haley and the Comets' "Rock Around the Clock," you send it registered. When you mail something registered, the post-office clerk immediately puts it in a locked drawer. Each time the package is moved from one place to another, it's carefully logged and signed for all the way until the recipient signs for it. Registered mail is reliable but slow because of all the logging and signing. (Yeah, these days any sane person uses overnight express, but it turns out to be handled much like superfast registered mail: Electronically scanning the bar code on the package label logs the package's progress. But we digress.)

The other scheme is used for certified letters that don't have any intrinsic physical value but that contain an important message, typically a letter from your insurance company saying that it has canceled your insurance. These letters are sorted and handled normally until they are delivered, at which point the recipient signs a card that is mailed back to the sender. If the sender doesn't get the card back in a reasonable amount of time, it sends the letter again.

Different computer networks use either of these schemes. *X.25* networks (used in many commercial networks, such as Tymnet and Sprintnet) use the registered model, with each packet carefully accounted for. There's even a protocol called X.75 that is used to hand packets from one network to another very reliably. X.25 works okay, but it's slow for the same reason that registered mail is slow — there's all that logging and checking at each stage.

TCP/IP is much more like certified mail. As IP routes each packet through the network, it does what it can to deliver it, but if some problem arises or if the packet is garbled on a communication line, tough luck — IP just throws away the packet. TCP numbers each packet, and the TCP software on the two communicating hosts (but not on any intermediate hosts) track the packet numbers: Each tells the other what it has received and what it hasn't and resends anything that got lost.

This approach has two advantages over the X.25 approach. One is that the end-to-end approach is faster and fundamentally more reliable because it doesn't depend on all the intermediate hosts (between the sender and the recipients) doing everything correctly. The other is that it enables networks to be built much more cheaply because routers can be much dumber. A router for TCP/IP has to understand only IP, not TCP or any other higher-level protocol.

This means that for a small network, you can build a perfectly adequate router out of a small computer and a few network cards. All the Internet traffic to and from the network here at I.E.C.C., for example, passes through a router built from an old clone 286 PC, which cost only $300. Works fine.

Any Port in a Storm

The final topic in this survey of Internet geekspeak is *ports*. In postal terms, port numbers are sort of like apartment numbers. Suppose that you want to communicate with a particular host. Okay, you look up its host number and you send it some packets. But you have two problems here. One is that a typical host has lots of programs running that can be having simultaneous conversations with lots of other hosts, so you have to find some way to keep the different conversations separate. The other problem is that when you're contacting a host, you need some way of telling it what sort of conversation you want to have. Do you want to send some electronic mail? Transfer files? Log in?

Ports solve both these problems. Every program on a host that is engaged in a TCP or UDP conversation is assigned a *port number* to identify that conversation. Furthermore, a large set of low port numbers is reserved (sort of like low-numbered license plates) for particular well-known services. If you want to log in to a host by using the standard telnet service, for example, you contact port 23 because that's where the telnet server is.

Connections to *client programs* — programs that use remote services — are assigned arbitrary port numbers that are used only to distinguish one connection from another. Servers, on the other hand, use well-known port numbers so that the clients can find them. Several hundred well-known (well-known to Internet programming geeks, at least) port numbers are assigned. Hosts are under no obligation to support them all — just to use the correct number for those they support. Some of the well-known numbers are pretty stupid, such as port 1025 for network blackjack games; others are very specialized, such as port 188 for an implementation of the MUMPS database language. But they're there if you need them.

Usually you don't have to worry about port numbers, but in a few cases it's handy to know about them. When you want to use a conversational service on another computer, the usual technique is to use the telnet program to connect to port 23 on the remote computer and log in as a normal user. (See Chapter 14 for all the gory details.) But some services are provided on other ports.

A computer in Michigan offers a geography server (described in Chapter 15), for example, that lets you look up any place name or ZIP code in the U.S. If you telnet to that computer on the standard port 23, you get an invitation to log in as a regular user. This isn't very useful because you don't have any passwords for that computer. (If it makes you feel better, neither do we.) But if you telnet to port 3000 on the same computer, you're connected directly to the geography server. When you need to use a port other than the standard one to contact any service, that's noted in the service's description.

Two separate sets of port numbers exist: one for TCP and one for UDP. But all the well-known port numbers are assigned identically for both. TCP port 23 is telnet, for example, so UDP port 23 is also telnet for inattentive users who don't mind if some of their data gets lost.

ISO protocols: Trust us — they'll be great

The *International Organization for Standardization* (inexplicably known as *ISO*) for many years has been developing a set of communication protocols that was supposed to replace TCP/IP eventually. ISO is an enormous international consortium of standardization groups, so it probably will not come as a big surprise to hear that they move ahead at a rate that suggests that they are stapled to a somewhat arthritic snail.

A bunch of ISO standards are supposed to define various network protocols (we mentioned X.25 already), but they are in most cases slow, complex, and not well debugged (much like the group that is defining them), so nobody uses even the ones that exist unless they are forced to for political reasons. If someone tells you to forget all this unofficial and unsanctioned TCP/IP nonsense

because ISO protocols will replace them all, nod politely and pay no attention.

In fairness, the ISO's electronic-mail protocols have achieved moderate success. The mail-transfer standard is called X.400 and is used in some places as a gateway protocol between mail systems. (You can find out about sending mail to X.400 addresses in Chapter 9.) X.400 is in some ways better than Internet mail because you can use addresses similar to those you would use for real postal mail rather than often arbitrary login names, as is more common with Internet mail. The standard for name-lookup service X.500 is late and slow but looks to be widely adopted because the Internet has nothing like it. Mail is the *only* place, however, where ISO is getting much attention — their standards for file transfer and other applications seem to be dead on arrival.

If You're a Glutton for Punishment

Some of the readers of the first edition of this book sent us e-mail comments (which you too can do — see Chapter 7). To our astonishment, many of those readers not only read this entire chapter but also hounded us for more low-level details. In fairness to the more, er, normal readers, we haven't put them here, but if you get yourself a copy of *MORE Internet For Dummies* by John R. Levine and Margaret Levine Young (IDG Books, 1994) — no coffee table is complete without at least one copy — you can find these technical tidbits in Chapters 2 and 3.

Part II
Mail and Gossip

The 5th Wave   By Rich Tennant

"NO SIR, THIS ISN'T A DATING SERVICE. THEY INTRODUCE PEOPLE THROUGH A COMPUTER SO THEY CAN TALK TO EACH OTHER IN PERSON. WE INTRODUCE PEOPLE IN PERSON SO THEY CAN TALK TO EACH OTHER THROUGH A COMPUTER."

In this part...

Rumors, gossip, jokes, recipes, bad jokes, tourist travel tips, and really bad jokes (as if there aren't enough in here already): these are only a few of the things you can read and write about with electronic mail and news. Read on to find out how.

Chapter 7

Basics of Electronic Mail

● ●

● ●

*E*lectronic mail is without a doubt the most widely used Internet service. Every system on the net(other than specialized network support hosts and the like) supports some sort of mail service, meaning that no matter what kind of computer you're using, if it's on the Internet, you can send and receive mail.

Mail, much more than any other Internet service, is connected to many non-Internet systems, which means that you can exchange mail with many people not on the Internet in addition to all the people who are on it (see Chapter 8 for details).

Mailboxes Here, Mailboxes There

Before you do much mailing, you have to figure out your electronic-mail address so that you can tell it to people who want to get in touch with you. And you have to figure out some of their addresses so that you can write to them. (We suppose that if you have no friends or plan to send only anonymous hate mail, you can skip this section.)

Internet mail addresses have two parts, separated by @ (the *at* sign). The part before the @ is the *mailbox,* which is (roughly speaking) your personal name, and the part after is the *domain,* usually the name of the computer you use. Sometimes the domain used is the group that contains all the local computers. If you're with the Nuke the Whales Foundation, for example, your computer might be called `shamu.ntw.org`, but the mail domain might be just `ntw.org`. This lets the local mail system take care of getting your mail to the correct computer within the group, which is particularly handy if people switch computers a lot — it avoids your having to tell the rest of the world every time you move from one cubicle to another.

What's My Address?

The mailbox is usually your *username* (the name you use to log in to your computer, assuming that you're using a computer that needs a login), so your address may be king@ntw.org. Domain names are traditionally represented in uppercase (as in NTW.ORG), and mailbox names in lowercase or mixed case (as in *king*). But case never matters in domains and rarely matters in mailbox names. To make it easy on your eyes, therefore, most of the domain and mailbox names in this book are given in lowercase. If you're sending a message to another user in your domain (same machine or group of machines), you can leave out the domain part altogether when you type the address.

If you're using a machine such as a PC or a Mac that doesn't handle multiple users, you still have a mailbox name, but the way you set that name varies from system to system. In some cases, you set it when you start up the computer; in other cases, you log in when you start the mail program. If your incoming mail is stored on a mail server (see the sidebar "Are PCs real computers, mailwise?"), you had better use the same mailbox name on your PC as you have on the server if you ever want to get any answers to your outgoing mail.

A practical problem arises in figuring out e-mail addresses, because the way usernames are assigned is not consistent. Some usernames include first names, last names, initials, first name and last initial, first initial and last name, or anything else, including completely *made-up* names. Over the years, for example, John has had such usernames as john, john1, jrl, jlevine, jlevine3 (must have been at least three jlevines there), and even q0246.

Back when far fewer e-mail users were around and most users of any particular system knew each other directly, it wasn't all that hard to figure out who had what username. These days, it's becoming much more of a problem, so many organizations are creating consistent mailbox names for all users, most often by using the user's first and last names with a dot between them. In such a scheme, your mailbox name may be something like elvis.presley@ntw.org, even though your username is something else. (If your name isn't Elvis Presley, adjust this example suitably. On the other hand, if your name *is* Elvis Presley, please contact us immediately. We know some people who are looking for you.)

TIP

Mailing to the outside world

One of the best things about Internet mail is that it is surprisingly well connected to all sorts of other mail systems. In most cases, the connection is seamless enough that you send mail to off-net users in exactly the same way in which you send it to users directly on the net. In other cases, you have to type the address by using strange punctuation (such as ! and * and %), but in every other way you send and receive mail the same as always. See Chapters 8 and 9 for more information about addressing magic.

Are PCs real computers, mailwise?

Usually, no, unfortunately. Internet mail is passed around by using something called SMTP, for Simple Mail Transfer Protocol (presumably named by some programmers with a sense of humor, because it's only simple compared to, say, refinancing the national debt). SMTP was designed assuming that all the machines on the net are prepared to receive mail pretty much all the time. When one host has a piece of mail to deliver, it immediately contacts the destination host by using SMTP and delivers the message. (One of the nice things about Internet mail is that a message is normally delivered within a minute or two after you send it.)

This means that most systems always have an SMTP daemon (a program, usually named `smail` or `sendmail`, that lurks in the background, waiting for work to do) hanging around, waiting for the virtual phone to ring with incoming mail. If the destination machine doesn't respond, the sender's machine puts the message in a safe place and tries again every few hours, hoping that the destination machine will be working again soon. If the message can't be delivered after three days or so, the sending machine gives up.

This model of mail handling is a definite non-starter in the DOS world. DOS, not being a real operating system (we're not being snide here — it's just a fact), runs only one program at a time. So when someone wants to send you some mail, chances are that your machine is running Virtual Valerie or some other business-productivity-type application rather than a mail program. The chances of your mail program and a sending mail program getting together for SMTP, therefore, are roughly zero.

This problem can be finessed in one of three ways:

✔ If you have a workstation or a multiuser system nearby, you can let it handle all your mail and log in to it as necessary by using telnet (see Chapter 14).

✔ On a network with numerous PCs, many organizations run a PC-networked mail system, such as cc:Mail or Microsoft Mail, which keeps all the mailboxes on a mail-server PC. They then use an extra-cost gateway feature to pass stuff between the PC mail system and Internet SMTP mail. In that case, you send and receive messages in the usual way with your PC mail system, using some strange punctuation to tell it to pass messages to the Internet. You have to ask a local mail expert for advice because no two gateways are ever set up the same. Bad news: Network mail gateways are tricky to set up, and we've seen cases in which it took the better part of a year to get them working.

✔ For PC users whose machines are connected directly to the Internet, it's possible to have your mail stored on a UNIX workstation (or, in principle, on any other machine that can handle mail daemons, although in practice they're all UNIX boxes). When you want to check your mail, you run a program that uses POP2 or POP3 (which stand for Post Office Protocol, second and third attempts, respectively, to get it right) to retrieve your new mail from the machine that's been holding it. Then you use a local PC mail reader on the newly arrived mail.

Other than the extra step to pick up your mail, POP mail readers act pretty much like any other mail readers do. For outgoing mail, some POP mail readers pass it back to the mail host to have it sent from there; others use SMTP directly. Again, ask

(continued)

a local expert whether you're set up for POP. Depending on the mail program on your PC, using POP can be a pain in the neck because sometimes you have to use arcane commands to retrieve your new mail from the POP server. Unless you have a PC mail program that automates all this (most Windows mail programs do) or you have a text editor on your PC that you just adore (for writing new messages), it's usually just as easy and much less hassle to use the first technique: Log in to the mail host and read your mail there. Later in this chapter, we discuss Eudora, the most popular POP mail reader.

Having several names for the same mailbox is no problem, so the new, longer, consistent usernames are invariably created in addition to, rather than instead of, the traditional short nicknames.

If you don't know what your e-mail address is, a good approach is to send yourself a message, using your login name as the mailbox name. Then examine the return address on the message. Or you can send a message to Internet For Dummies Mail Central at internet@dummies.com, and a friendly robot will send back a message with your address. (While you're at it, tell us if you like this book, since we authors see that mail, too.) See Chapter 9 for more suggestions on finding e-mail addresses.

Mailers, Mailers, Everywhere

So now you know what your address is, or else you've decided that you don't care. Either way, it's time for some hand-to-hand combat with your e-mail system.

At least a dozen different *mailers,* e-mail reading and writing programs that people use on the Internet, are available for UNIX workstations alone, and many more exist for other kinds of computers attached directly and indirectly to the net. The examples here are representative mailers chosen by the highly scientific method of seeing what's already installed on our local computer.

- **Berkeley mail:** Called mail (or sometimes Mail or mailx), the basic mailer that comes with most UNIX systems. Like most people, we call it "Berkeley mail" because it was written (if that's the right word for such a pile of hacks) at the University of California at Berkeley.

- **xmail:** A graphical front end for Berkeley mail that runs on the *X Windows system.* (Readers familiar with the *Wizard of Oz* can think of xmail as the fire-breathing wizard that Dorothy and friends found in the Emerald City, and Berkeley mail as the man behind the curtain.)

✔ **elm:** A rather nice mail program with a full-screen terminal interface. Like much of the best Internet software, `elm` was written and is actively maintained entirely by volunteers. The original author of `elm` worked for Hewlett-Packard, and HP workstations all come with `elm` as the standard mail program.

✔ **Eudora:** A popular mailer that runs under Microsoft Windows. There's also a version of Eudora for Macs, which works nearly the same way.

Ahoy, there!

Sending mail is easy. You run your mail program and type the address you want to send mail to:

```
mail king@ntw.org
```

The traditional UNIX `mail` program operates under the traditional UNIX *no-news-is-good-news rule,* so at this point, unless you have some problem starting the mail program, it says nothing. Depending on how `mail` is configured (it has about 14 zillion options, most of them useless), it may ask you for a subject line. If it does, give it one, as in the following example (if it doesn't, you can give it one anyway, but we get to that later):

```
mail king@ntw.org
Subject: Hound dogs
```

Now you type your message. It can say anything you want, and it can be as long as you want. Here's a short example:

```
mail king@ntw.org
Subject: Hound dogs
When you said that I ain't nothing but a hound dog, did you
mean a greyhound, a basset hound, or some other kind of
hound? Signed,
A Curious Admirer
```

Now you're done. You can end your message in one of two ways (UNIX is always like this — you get used to it after a while). In most versions of `mail`, you can type a dot by itself on a line to say that you're finished. If it works, `mail` responds with EOT (for *end of text*). If a dot doesn't work, you can employ the usual Ctrl-D that UNIX always lets you use to mark the end of input. (*Note:* Be careful not to type Ctrl-D more than once or you're likely to log yourself out.) That's all you have to do. The message is delivered or, if not, you get back a cryptic response from the mail system explaining why it didn't deliver it.

By the way, about the `Subject:` line: If `mail` doesn't ask you for a subject and you want to add one, while you're typing your message, type a line with a ~ (tilde), the letter *s* (for Subject), and the subject itself, as in the following line:

```
~sHound dogs
```

This sort of thing is called a *tilde escape*. About two dozen of them exist, most of them not very useful.

If you are fortunate enough to use `elm`, it is considerably easier to send a message. You begin in nearly the same way, except that you run `elm` rather than `mail`.

```
elm king@ntw.org
```

A screen pops up and waits for you to enter a subject:

```
Send only mode [ELM 2.3 PL11] To: king@ntw.com
Subject:
```

After you put in the subject, `elm` may ask for `Copies to:`, which for the moment you can ignore (press Enter to skip it). Then `elm` automatically runs the standard local text editor, which, with any luck, you already know how to use. If not, see *UNIX For Dummies,* by John Levine and Margaret Levine Young (published by IDG Books Worldwide, 1993).

Type the message by using any old editor features you want. After you're finished and have saved the file (a temporary file, created by `elm`, for your message), `elm` comes back with a little menu:

```
And now: s
    Choose e)dit message, !)shell, h)eaders, c)opy file,
        s)end, or f)orget.
```

The `elm` program suggests that you press s to send the message. Resist, for the moment, the urge to try out all those swell options, and press s to send it. The `elm` program responds with a cheery `Mail sent!` message and you're all set.

If you're using `xmail`, life is considerably more complicated. First you have to start `xmail`, either by typing **xmail** to the UNIX shell or by some other allegedly user-friendly way set up by your local system administrator. After it starts, `xmail` shows up in a window like the one in Figure 7-1.

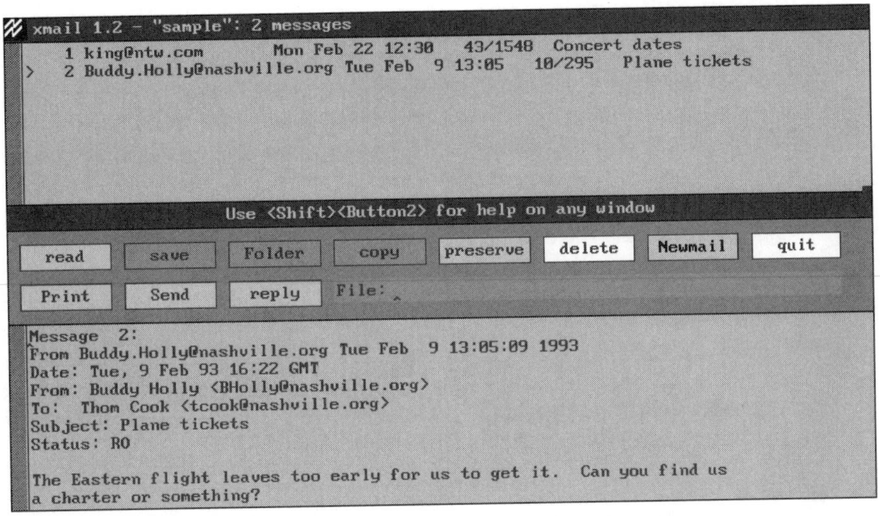

```
 xmail 1.2 - "sample": 2 messages
    1 king@ntw.com          Mon Feb 22 12:30   43/1548  Concert dates
>   2 Buddy.Holly@nashville.org Tue Feb  9 13:05  10/295   Plane tickets




             Use <Shift><Button2> for help on any window

  [ read ]  [ save ]  [ Folder ]  [ copy ]  [ preserve ] [ delete ] [ Newmail ]  [ quit ]

  [ Print ] [ Send ]  [ reply ]  File:

Message  2:
From Buddy.Holly@nashville.org Tue Feb  9 13:05:09 1993
Date: Tue, 9 Feb 93 16:22 GMT
From: Buddy Holly <BHolly@nashville.org>
To:  Thom Cook <tcook@nashville.org>
Subject: Plane tickets
Status: RO

The Eastern flight leaves too early for us to get it.  Can you find us
a charter or something?
```

Figure 7-1:
xmail starts
up.

If you look carefully at Figure 7-1, you notice that one of the dozen buttons in the middle of the window is labeled Send. When you click the Send button, xmail pops up a new window running a text editor (probably *vi,* the usual UNIX text editor).

"Hey, wait!" you may be saying. "What about the Subject line? Who the heck am I sending this to?" For some reason, xmail does everything backward: First you type the message and then you address it (whoever wrote xmail probably puts on socks after shoes, too). Play along with the gag. Write your message, save the file (it makes a temporary file for your message), and leave the editor.

After you leave the editor, xmail pops up yet another window that looks like the one in Figure 7-2.

Type the e-mail address of the person to whom you want to send the letter and then press Enter to get to the second line. Type the subject. Then click Deliver, and xmail sends the message. You may surmise from this example that xmail was designed more to make life easy for the man behind the curtain than to make it useful for mere users. Yes, but it's too late to do much about it now.

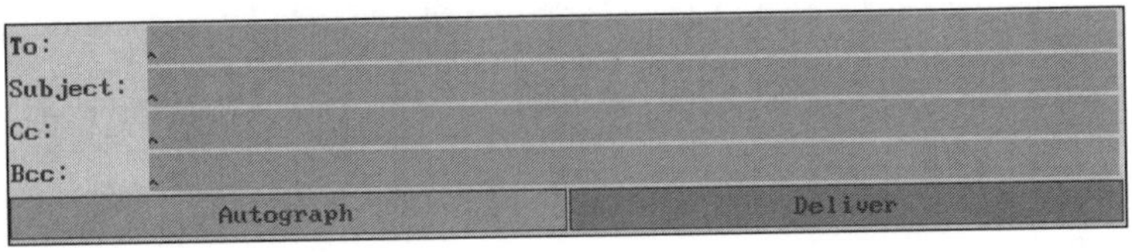

Figure 7-2:
xmail asks
for the
subject and
the address.

```
To:
Subject:
Cc:
Bcc:
      [    Autograph    ]        [    Deliver    ]
```

Eudora makes it easy

If your computer is a Windows PC, and if you're lucky, you may have a copy of Eudora, which is a nice Windows mail program. Eudora is popular for two reasons: It's easy to use, and it's really cheap. (You can try out a shareware version for free, and an enhanced commercial version costs only about $65. The examples here are made by using the commercial version, but the shareware looks nearly the same.) We assume here that your local mail guru has already set up Eudora for you. If not, you can find out the grisly details, along with lots more details about day-to-day use of Eudora, in Chapter 10 of *MORE Internet For Dummies.*

You start Eudora by clicking her Program Manager icon, which looks like an envelope. You should get an introductory "splash" window that goes away after a few seconds and then a screen like Figure 7-3.

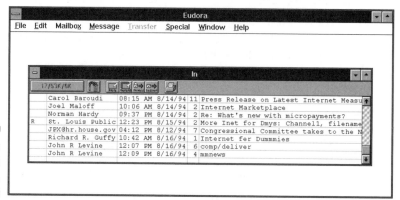

Figure 7-3:
Eudora says
hello.

Exactly what's in the window varies depending on what you were looking at the last time you ran Eudora.

To send a message, you choose Message➪New message from the menu (or if you're lazy and can remember shortcut keys, it's Control-N). Eudora pops up a new message window, like the one in Figure 7-4.

You type the recipient's address, press Tab to skip to the Subject field (it already knows who you are — you don't have to tell it that), and type a subject. Then press Tab a few more times to skip the Cc: and Bcc: fields (or type the addresses of people who should get carbon copies and blind carbon copies of the message). Then press Tab to move to the large area and type your message. When you're finished, it should look something like Figure 7-5.

Figure 7-4:
Eudora is
ready to
enter a new
message.

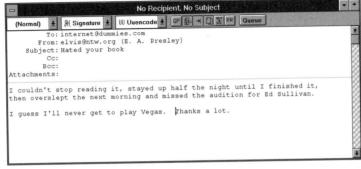

Figure 7-5:
Ready to
send!

To send the message, you click the button in the upper right-hand corner of the window, which, depending on how Eudora is set up, is marked Send or Queue. If it's marked Send, as soon as you click it, Eudora tries to send the message, putting up a little status window that contains incomprehensible status messages. If, on the other hand, it's marked Queue, your message is stashed in your outbox for sending later.

The usual reason to have a Queue button is that your computer isn't connected to the net all the time because you have a dial-up SLIP or PPP connection. In that case, to send the message, first you have to dial up and get your computer connected (usually by running a program called Custom or WinSock). After the connection is set, you switch back to Eudora and from the menu choose File⇨ Send Queued Messages (Ctrl-T for the lazy) to transmit the messages.

Unless you have a very fast permanent net connection, if you're sending several messages, it's much quicker to write and queue all of them and then use Send Queued Messages to send them all at one time.

What if I have some other kind of computer?

Part of the charm of the Internet is that hundreds of different kinds of incompatible computers are attached to it, all working slightly differently. Sending e-mail always involves more or less the same steps, but the details are never the same. If you're on a PC, depending on which of the dozens of different PC mail programs you're using, you may have to run a separate program after the mail program to upload outgoing messages to a *mail hub.*

If you're using a non-Internet mail system with a gateway, you may have to use some strange syntax to tell it that you're using Internet mail. On Digital VMS systems, for example, you usually have to use a mail address like this one:

```
IN%"king@ntw.org"
```

(That's *usually,* not always, because several different Internet software packages are available for VMS, and several different ways to set up the mail system exist. See Chapter 9 for a list of mail-addressing schemes.)

As mentioned, if you're running a PC network that doesn't use the Internet's native TCP/IP networking (see Chapter 6 for more about TCP/IP), zillions of ways are available to send Internet mail. Again, you have to ask a local expert for more info about those other zillions.

My mailer is better than yours

Particularly on UNIX systems, dozens of different mail programs are available, with such names as `pine`, `MH`, `mush`, and `zmail`. Each of them has different advantages and disadvantages. Some, such as `pine`, are easier for new users to use. Others, such as `MH`, are more flexible for heavy-duty users. (Serious e-mail users can easily get more than 100 messages per day — John gets about 95, counting all the mailing lists he's on.)

Something *every* e-mail program has is people who will tell you why it is the best mailer in the entire universe and that you would be a fool to use anything else. Be polite to these people because they can get violent if they're provoked. For plain day-to-day use, there isn't that much difference among mail programs. Use the mail program everyone else uses, because that makes it easier to pick up on local mail tricks and to find someone who can help you when you get stuck.

Mail Call!

If you start sending e-mail (and in most cases even if you don't), you'll start receiving it. The arrival of e-mail, which is always exciting, even when you get 50 messages a day, is often heralded by a hint from your computer. If you use a system with multiple windows on the screen (like a Mac or a Windows-like graphical environment), the flag on the mailer icon may flip up, looking something like Figure 7-6.

Figure 7-6:
Mail icons,
before and
after mail
arrives.

On some computers, arriving mail is announced by a sound from the computer's speaker, ranging from a quiet *boop* to (nerd alert here) trumpet flourishes and the like. Stick with the boop — your neighbors will thank you.

When you think that you may have e-mail, run your favorite mail program. You should see a list of new messages, sort of like the one shown by elm in Figure 7-7.

```
           Folder is 'chuckie' with 2 messages [ELM 2.3 PL11]

     1   Feb 22  Elvis Presley     (13)    Re: hound dogs
     2   Feb 9   Buddy Holly       (10)    Plane tickets




        |=pipe, !=shell, ?=help, <n>=set current to n, /=search pattern
   a)lias, C)opy, c)hange folder, d)elete, e)dit, f)orward, g)roup reply, m)ail,
     n)ext, o)ptions, p)rint, q)uit, r)eply, s)ave, t)ag, u)ndelete, or e(x)it

  Command: []
```

Figure 7-7:
elm lists
newly
arrived
messages.

TIP

If you have a totally antique mail program, it may immediately show you the first message. If this happens to you, demand something better. Budget limits are no excuse: Some of the nicest mail programs, such as elm and pine, are free for the taking.

Assuming that you have a *real* mail program, you usually read messages by moving the cursor to the message of interest (it starts by putting the cursor on the first new message, usually a good choice) and pressing Enter to view the message, as shown in Figure 7-8.

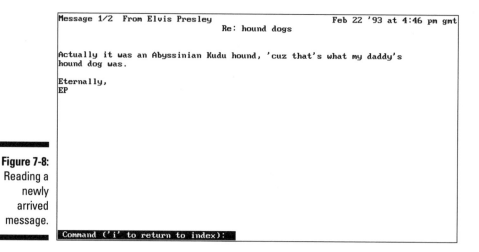

```
Message 1/2  From Elvis Presley                 Feb 22 '93 at 4:46 pm gmt
                         Re: hound dogs

Actually it was an Abyssinian Kudu hound, 'cuz that's what my daddy's
hound dog was.

Eternally,
EP
```

Figure 7-8:
Reading a
newly
arrived
message.

```
Command ('i' to return to index):
```

If you're using a line-oriented program such as Berkeley mail, it shows the messages by assigning a number to each one. Type the number of the message you want to see. In xmail, click the line with the message you want and then click the Read button. If you're using some other mail program, you have to do something similar (consult a local expert).

After you've seen the message, you can do a bunch of different things with it (much the same as with paper mail). Here are your usual choices:

- ✔ Discard it
- ✔ Reply to it
- ✔ Forward it to other people
- ✔ File it

Unlike paper mail, you can do any or all of these things to any message. The details vary (sorry to waffle, but if we put in the details of every option to every mail program, this book would be as long as a big city phone book — and about as readable). In general, you press r to reply, f to forward, s to save, and so on. If you don't tell your mailer what to do to a message, the message either stays in your mailbox for later perusal or sometimes gets saved to a file called mbox.

If your mailer automatically saves messages in mbox, be sure to go through your mbox every week or so or it will become enormous and unmanageable. See Chapter 8 for more hints about filing and forwarding messages.

Eudora Delivers

Reading mail with Eudora is simplicity itself. The hardest part is getting the mail into your mailbox. If you have a full-time net connection, Eudora probably is set up to retrieve your mail automatically, in which case you only have to start Eudora, and she'll get your mail. (In addition, if you leave Eudora running, even hidden at the bottom of your screen as an icon, she'll automatically check for new mail every once in a while.)

If you don't have a full-time net connection, follow these steps to get your mail:

1. **Make your net connection.**

2. **Start up Eudora.**

3. **If she doesn't retrieve mail automatically, choose File⇨Check Mail (or press Control-M) to retrieve your mail.**

The mail will appear in your inbox, a window Eudora labels In, one line per message. To see a message, click the mouse on its line. To stop looking at a message, double-click on the box in the upper left-hand corner of the message window (the standard way to get rid of a window.)

Buttons at the top of the In window let you dispose of your mail. First click (once) on the message you want, which should highlight it. Then click the trashcan button to discard the message, the printer icon to print it, and so on.

A Few Words from the Great Ladies of Etiquette

Sadly, the Great Ladies of Etiquette such as Emily Post and Amy Vanderbilt died before the invention of e-mail. But here is what they might have suggested about what to say and, more important, what *not* to say in electronic mail.

E-mail is a funny hybrid, something between a phone call (or voice mail) and a letter. On one hand, it's quick and usually informal; on the other hand, it's written rather than spoken, so you don't see a person's facial expressions or hear tone of voice.

Flame off!

Pointless and excessive outrage in electronic mail is so common that it has a name of its own: *flaming*. Don't flame. It makes you look like a jerk.

When you get a message so offensive that you just *have* to reply, stick it back in your electronic inbox for a while and wait until after lunch. Then, don't flame back. The sender probably didn't realize how the message would look. In about 20 years of using electronic mail, we can testify that we have never, never, regretted *not* sending an angry message. (But we *have* regretted sending a few. Ouch.)

When you're sending mail, keep in mind that someone reading it will have no idea of what you *intended* to say — just what you *did* say. Subtle sarcasm and irony are almost impossible to use in e-mail and usually come across as annoying or dumb instead. (If you are an extremely superb writer, you can disregard this advice, but don't say that you weren't warned.)

E-mail always seems ruder than it's supposed to

This means:

✔ When you send a message, watch your tone of voice.

✔ If someone sends you an incredibly obnoxious and offensive message, as likely as not it is a mistake or a joke gone awry. In particular, be on the lookout for failed sarcasm.

Sometimes it helps to put in a :-) (called a *smiley*), which means "this is a joke." (Try leaning way over to the left, if you don't see why it's a smile.) In some communities, notably CompuServe, <g> or <grin> serves the same purpose. Here's a typical example:

```
People who don't believe that we are all part of a warm,
caring community who love and support each other are no
better than rabid dogs and should be hunted down and shot. :-)
```

Smileys sometimes help, but if a joke needs a smiley, maybe it wasn't worth making. It may sound as though all your e-mail is supposed to be humorless. It's not that bad, but until you have the hang of it, limit the humor. You'll be glad you did.

How private is e-mail?

Relatively, but not totally. Any recipient of your mail might forward it to other people. Some mail addresses are really mailing lists that redistribute messages to many other people. In one famous case, a mistaken mail address sent a message to tens of thousands of readers. It began, "Darling, at last we have a way to send messages that is completely private."

The usual rule of thumb is not to send anything you wouldn't want to see posted next to the water cooler or perhaps scribbled next to a pay phone. The latest e-mail systems are starting to include encryption features that make the privacy situation somewhat better so that anyone who doesn't know the keyword used to scramble a message can't decode it. The most-common tools for encrypted mail are known as PEM (Privacy Enhanced Mail) and PGP (Pretty Good Privacy.) PGP is one of the most widely used encryption programs, both in the U.S. and abroad. PGP is good enough to deter all but the most determined and sophisticated snoop. (The National Security Agency doubtless has no trouble cracking it, but if the NSA wants to read your mail, you have more complicated problems than we can help you solve.) PGP is available free on the net; your system administrator should be able to download and install it within an hour or two. Ask locally whether any e-mail encryption is available and, if so, what set of recipients can arrange to read it.

BTW, what does IMHO mean? RTFM!

E-mail users are often lazy typists, and many abbreviations are common. Here are some of the most widely used:

Abbreviation	What It Means
BTW	By The Way
IMHO	In My Humble Opinion
RSN	Real Soon Now (vaporware)
RTFM	Read The . . . Manual — you could and should have looked it up yourself
TIA	Thanks In Advance
TLA	Three-Letter Acronym

Another possibility to keep in the back of your mind is that it is technically not hard to forge e-mail return addresses, so if you get a totally off-the-wall message from someone that seems out of character for that person, somebody else may have forged it as a prank. (No, we won't tell you how to forge e-mail. How dumb do you think we are?)

Hey, Mr. Postmaster

Every Internet host that can send or receive mail has a special mail address called postmaster that is guaranteed to get a message to the person responsible for that host. If you send mail to someone and get back strange failure messages, you might try sending a message to the postmaster. If king@ntw.org returns an error from ntw.org, for example, you might try a polite question to postmaster@ntw.org. The postmaster is usually an overworked volunteer system administrator, so it is considered poor form to ask a postmaster for favors much greater than *does so-and-so have a mailbox on this system?*

Chapter 8

More Mail Tricks

*O*kay, now you know how to send and receive mail. Now it's time for some tips and tricks to make you into a real mail aficionado.

Mail As Hot and Cold Potatoes

After you get a piece of e-mail, you can do roughly three things with it:

✔ Throw it away (even before you read it if you don't like the subject)

✔ Save it for posterity

✔ Pass it along to someone else

Throwing away mail is easy enough that you probably figured out how to do it already: Just delete it in the mail program. If you are using a decent mail program that shows you a screen of the subject lines, you can often throw away the really boring stuff without even reading it, just like with paper junk mail. In Eudora, for example, in the list of incoming messages you click once on the message of interest (or in this case, lack of interest) and then click the trashcan icon. Poof, it's gone.

Hot potatoes

You can forward e-mail along to someone else. Forwarding is one of the nicest things about electronic mail, and at the same time it's one of the worst things. It's good because you can easily pass messages along to people who need to know about them. It's bad because you (not you personally but, um, people around you — that's it) can just as easily send out floods of messages to recipients who would just as soon not hear yet another press release from the local Ministry of Truth. So you have to think a little about whether you will enhance someone's quality of life by forwarding a message to him or her. (If you don't care about the quality of life, pick some other criterion.)

Truth in forwarding

Two ways are available (computers never leave well enough alone) to forward stuff: remailing and forwarding. *Remailing* is the electronic version of scribbling another address on the outside of an envelope and dropping it back in the mailbox. Unlike paper mail, you can read e-mail without having to tear open the envelope (but these analogies are never perfect). Remailing makes sense when the letter is really for someone else. Remailing is sometimes also called *bouncing* because the R key is already used to Reply to messages, so it's B for Bounce.

What's usually called *forwarding* a message involves wrapping the message in a new message of your own, sort of like sticking Post-It notes all over a copy of it and mailing the copy and Post-Its to someone else. Usually, when you tell your mailer to forward a message, it copies the original contents into the new, forwarded message and precedes each line with > (the greater-than character). Replying to a message can work in much the same way, with the original message quoted the same way except that you're writing back to the person who wrote the message in the first place, as in the following reply:

```
>Is there a lot of demand for fruit pizza?
>
In answer to your question, I checked with our
research department and found that the favorite pizza
toppings in the 18-34 age group are pepperoni, sausage,
ham, pineapple, olives, peppers, mushrooms, hamburger,
and broccoli. I specifically asked about prunes and
they said that there was no statistically significant
response about them.
```

You then get to edit the message. Get rid of uninteresting parts. All the glop in the message header is included automatically in the forwarded message, and almost none of it is comprehensible, much less interesting, so get rid of it.

The tricky part is editing down the actual text. If the message is short, a screenful or so, you probably should leave it alone. If it's really long and only part of it is relevant, you should cut it down to the interesting part as a courtesy to the reader. We can tell you from experience that people pay much more attention to a concise, one-line e-mail message than they do to 12 pages of quoted stuff followed by a two-line question.

Sometimes it makes sense to edit down material even more, particularly to emphasize one specific part. Of course, when you do so, be sure not to edit to the point where you put words in the original author's mouth or garble the sense of the message, as in the following reply:

```
>In answer to your question, I checked with our
>research department and found that the favorite pizza
>toppings ... and
>they said that there was no statistically significant
>response about them.
```

That's an excellent way to make new enemies. Sometimes it makes sense to paraphrase a little — put the paraphrased part in square brackets, like this:

```
>[When asked about prunes on pizza, research]
>said that there was no statistically significant
>response about them.
```

People disagree about whether paraphrasing to shorten quotes is a good idea. On one hand, if you do it well, it saves everyone time. On the other hand, if you do it badly and someone takes offense, you're in for a week of accusations and apologies that will wipe out whatever time you may have saved. The decision is up to you.

Cold potatoes

Saving e-mail for later reference is like putting potatoes in the fridge for later (don't knock it if you haven't tried it — day-old boiled potatoes are yummy with enough butter or sour cream). Lots of your e-mail is worth saving, just like lots of your paper mail. (Lots of it *isn't,* but we already covered that.)

You can save e-mail in a few different ways:

- Save it in mailboxes full of messages
- Save it in regular files
- Print it and put it in a file cabinet with paper mail

The easiest method usually is to stick messages in a mailbox (a mailbox is usually no more than a file full of messages with some sort of separator between them). Most mail programs by default have a bad habit of saving all your incoming messages in a file named something like mbox, except for the ones you delete. This plan might have made sense back in the Paleozoic era, when on a really busy day you might have gotten five messages. Now it makes about as much sense as handling your paper mail by stuffing it all in your desk drawer. If you let your mailer save messages in this manner, your mbox file will grow like the giant blob in that old sci-fi movie until it devours all storage in sight. This is generally not considered Effective Disk Space Management, so don't let it happen to you.

To avoid death by blob, file or discard things yourself. First you have to make sure that your mailer doesn't stash messages in mbox without telling you. Disabling the automatic-filing feature is usually possible by twiddling a configuration parameter somewhere. Consult your local e-mail guru. If you're really desperate, you might try (gasp!) reading the manual, although too many manuals these days merely assert that the program is user-friendly and therefore intuitively obvious. Ho, ho. Find a guru. (Take along a few chocolate chip cookies.)

Two general approaches are used in mail filing: by sender and by topic. Whether you use one or the other or both is mostly a matter of taste. Often, mail programs help you file stuff by the sender's name, so if your friend Fred has the username fred@something.or.other, with a keystroke or two your mailer automatically files messages from Fred in a mailbox called fred. Of course, if some crazed system administrator has given him the username z92lh8t@something.or.other, the automatic naming can leave something to be desired, so make up names of your own.

For filing by topic, it's entirely up to you to come up with the mailbox names. The hardest part is coming up with memorable names. If you're not careful, you end up with four mailboxes with slightly different names, each with a quarter of the messages on a particular topic. Try to come up with names that are really obvious, and don't abbreviate. If the topic is accounting, call the mailbox accounting, because if you abbreviate, you'll never remember whether it's called acctng, acct, acntng, or any of a dozen other short abbreviations.

UNIX systems enable you to assign several names to a single file by using *links*. This capability offers a solution to the problem of slightly different names. If you can't remember which of four names to use for a project's mailbox, make one mailbox and link it to all four names. That way, you get the same mailbox no matter which name you use.

A related issue is where mailboxes live. Most mail programs have a favorite directory for mailboxes, usually called something creative like Mail. That's usually as good a place as any to put your mailboxes. Sometimes, though, it makes more sense to put the mailbox for messages about a project in the same directory as other files for that project. Again, with UNIX you can use links so that the mailbox is in both the Mail directory and the project directory.

Chain letters: Arrrrrggghhh!

One of the most obnoxious things you can do with e-mail is to pass around chain letters. Because all mail programs have forwarding commands, with only a few keystrokes you can take a chain letter and send it along to hundreds of other people. Don't do it. Chain letters are cute for about two seconds and then they're just annoying.

A few chain letters just keep coming around and around, despite our best efforts to stamp them out. Learn to recognize them now and avoid embarrassment later. Here are some of the hangers-on:

Dying boy wants greeting cards: (Sometimes it's business cards.) Not any more, he doesn't. Several years ago, an English boy named Craig Shergold was hospitalized with what was thought to be an inoperable brain tumor. Craig wanted to set the world record for most greeting cards. Word got out, and Craig received millions and millions of cards and eventually got into the *Guinness Book of World Records.* When it turned out that maybe the tumor wasn't inoperable, U.S. TV billionaire John Kluge paid for Craig to fly to the United States for an operation, which was successful. So, Craig is OK now and definitely doesn't want any more cards. (You can read all about this story on page 24 of the July 29, 1990, edition of the *New York Times.*) Guinness is so sick and tired of the whole business that it closed the category — no more records for the most cards will be accepted. If you want to help dying children, give the two dollars a card and stamp would have cost to a children's welfare organization, such as UNICEF.

The modem tax rumor: In 1987, the Federal Communications Commission (FCC) briefly floated a proposal for a technical change to the rules governing the way on-line services, such as CompuServe and GEnie, are billed for their phone connections. Implementing the proposal would have had the effect of raising the prices these services charge. Customers of on-line services made their opposition clear immediately and

loudly, members of Congress made concerned inquiries, and the proposal was dropped — permanently. Unfortunately, undated alarmist notices about the proposal have circulated around bulletin boards ever since. If you see yet another modem tax scare, demand the FCC's current docket number because the FCC — as a government bureaucracy — can't blow its nose without making announcements, accepting comments, and so forth. So no docket means no action, which means that it's the same old rumor you should ignore.

Make big bucks with a chain letter: Usually these letters have the subject MAKE.MONEY.FAST, are signed by "Dave Rhodes," contain lots of testimonials from people who are now rolling in dough, and tell you to send $5 or so to the name at the top of the list, put your name at the bottom, and send the message to a zillion other suckers. Some even say "this isn't a chain letter" (you're supposedly helping to compile a mailing list or something, your 100-percent-guaranteed tipoff that it is a chain letter). Don't even think about it. These chain letters are extremely illegal, and besides, they don't even work. (Why send any money? Why not just add your name and send it on?) Think of them as gullibility viruses. Just ignore them, or perhaps send a polite note to the sender's postmaster to encourage him to tell users not to send any more chain letters.

The "two fifty" cookie recipe: According to this one, someone was eating chocolate chip cookies somewhere (Mrs. Fields and Neiman-Marcus are frequently cited) and asked whether she (it was always a she) could have the recipe. "Sure," came the answer, "that'll be two-fifty, charged to your credit card." "OK." When the credit card statement came, it turned out to be two hundred and fifty dollars, not two dollars and fifty cents. So in retribution, the message concludes with the putative Mrs. Fields and/or Neiman-Marcus

(continued)

(continued)

recipe, sent to you for free. The story is pure hooey: Mrs. Fields doesn't give out her recipes, for money or otherwise; neither does Neiman's. The recipe, which varies somewhat from one version to the next, makes perfectly OK cookies, but we don't think that it's any better than the one on the back of the bag of chips. This same story, by the way, circulated hand-to-hand in the 1940s and 1950s, except that the recipe was for a red-velvet cake served at the restaurant at one of the big New York department stores. It wasn't true then either.

Filing in files

If you're lucky, mailboxes are editable files. On UNIX systems, they're usually plain text files in which each message is preceded by a line like this one:

```
From john1 Wed Apr 21 18:39:18 1993
```

If this seems like a pretty lame separator, that's because it is. This format was dreamed up in about two minutes by somebody who wrote an early mail program, and we've been stuck with it ever since.

An alternative format separates messages with lines containing four Ctrl-A characters, which look strange on the screen but are easy to handle in an editor, where they usually look like ^A^A^A^A, or smiley faces like this:

☺☺☺☺☺

On other systems, though, mailboxes are filled with impenetrable binary junk that makes them impossible to edit. In that case, if you want to use the contents of a message in another file, it may make sense to copy messages into plain text files, one per file, so that you can edit them.

Paper?

Well, sure. If most of your files on a topic are on pieces of paper in a folder in a file cabinet and you have a few mail messages, you might as well print the messages and put them in the folder so that all the stuff is in the same place.

Yes, this is unbelievably retro, but it works. In the Land of the Future, you scan everything into your computers and it all is stored in Object-Oriented Hypertextual Multimedia Databases (add more buzzwords to taste). In the Land of the Present, however, we all have big, old, paper files that aren't going away anytime soon, so we may as well make the best of them.

Just the fax, ma'am

One question that comes up frequently is whether there is an e-mail-to-fax gateway on the net. Quite a few of them exist, but few are open for public use, because no provision exists for charging back the cost of the phone calls. An alternative is to use a commercial service such as MCI Mail or AT&T Mail, both of which have gateways to the net, in which you mail a message to your account on one of those systems and then forward it on to a fax address.

If you want to send a large number of faxes, for $100 or so you (or more likely a local techie who is more interested in getting the software right) can get a fax modem, plug it in to your computer, and send the faxes yourself. With most e-mail systems, setting things up so that e-mail messages are passed to the fax modem is reasonably straightforward (as much as configuring e-mail software is ever straightforward). On Windows machines, the fax is invariably set up as a fake printer, so you fax a message by "printing" it to the fax.

Incoming faxes are more of a problem because although it is really easy to turn a text message into a fax, it is not at all easy to turn a fax back into text. (For example, what if it contains pictures or handwriting?) A frequent compromise is to put faxes in files you can look at with an image-display program and to e-mail you a message telling you that there's a fax file to look at.

As of mid-1994, a volunteer Internet fax-relay network known as TPC (for The Phone Company) had formed on the Internet, which offers free outgoing faxes in many U.S. cities and a few foreign ones (based on where the volunteers with the outgoing fax gateways can call for free.) The best way to find out about it is probably by way of the Usenet group `comp.dcom.fax` (see Chapters 11 and 12).

For the intrepid, here's how you send a TPC fax:

1. Begin with the full international phone number, including country code. (For numbers in North America, the country code is 1.) So the number might be 19175552468.

2. Then reverse the number to get 86425557191.

3. Splice `remote-printer@` on the front, put dots between each digit, and add `.tpc.org` to the end, which produces:

   `remote-printer@8.6.4.2.5.5.5.7.1.9.1.tpc.org`

If you're still with us, e-mail a message containing the word `help` to `tpc-faq@town.hall.org` for some hints on detailed fax instructions and how to get a list of places where faxes can be delivered this way.

Hey, Mr. Robot

Not every mail address has an actual person behind it. Some are mailing lists (which we talk about in the next chapter), and some are *robots*. Mail robots have become popular as a way to query databases and retrieve files because it's much easier to set up a connection that handles electronic mail than it is to set up one that handles the more standard file transfer. You send a message to the robot (usually referred to as a *mail server*), it takes some action based on the contents of your message, and it sends back a response. If you send a message to `Clinton-Info@Campaign92.Org`, for example, you get back a response telling you how to sign up to get speeches, press releases, and so on. (Yes, the campaign is over, but the press releases continue.)

Sound! Pictures! Action!

Most e-mail contains plain old typewriter-style text. It's perfectly readable, but let's face it — that's *boring*. And if there's one thing computer geeks can't stand, it's boredom. So as soon as their computers could handle anything better, they promptly set about improving e-mail to handle all sorts of other stuff. The result is called *MIME*. (If you care, which you don't, it stands for *Multipurpose Internet Mail Extensions*. Whoopee.)

MIME is a convention for including stuff other than plain text in e-mail messages. There is a long list of the kinds of stuff, ranging from slightly formatted text using characters (such as `*emphasis*` for *emphasis*) up through color pictures, full-motion video, and high-fidelity sound. The MIME group had enough sense to realize that not everyone has a computer that can handle all the fancy high-end stuff, so a single MIME message can contain alternative forms of the same thing, such as beautifully formatted, typeset text for people with fancy video screens and plain text for people on simple terminals. MIME also handles nested messages, so a single MIME message might contain a document and a couple of illustrations that go with it.

MIME is supposed to be a *four-wheel-drive mail system,* meaning that MIME messages can be delivered over all sorts of hostile and unhelpful mail links. They do this by disguising the MIME contents as plain old text. (At least it looks to the computer like text. To us, it looks more like `QW&IIdfhfFX97/$@`.) You can recognize a MIME message by looking for special mail headers that look something like this:

```
MIME-version: 1.0
Content-type: TEXT/PLAIN; CHARSET=US-ASCII
Content-transfer-encoding: 7BIT
```

The first line says that the message is using version 1.0 of the MIME standard (the only version defined to date). The second line says that this particular message contains plain old text. The third line says that the text is represented in the message as — get this — text. (Computers are so dim that even this isn't obvious to them.) Different kinds of messages use different Content-type headers. At this point, they all use the same Content-transfer-encoding.

> ✔ If you are using a mail program that is *MIME-compliant,* as the jargon goes, you know that you have a MIME message because as you're reading your mail, all of a sudden a window pops up with a picture or formatted text, or perhaps your computer starts singing the message to you (and you thought that singing telegrams were a thing of the past).

✔ If your mail program doesn't know about MIME and you get a MIME-ized message, it shows up as a large message in your mailbox. If it contains text, about half the kinds of tarted-up text are readable as is, give or take some ugly punctuation. The sound and pictures, on the other hand, are totally hopeless because they are just binary digitized images and not any sort of text approximation. Consult your local e-mail guru for help.

On UNIX systems, the most common MIME-compliant mail program is pine, a simplified and theoretically more user-friendly version of the widely used elm mailer. (Pine stands for Pine Is Nearly Elm.) On PCs and Macs, Eudora understands MIME messages, as do most of the mail programs provided with commercial Internet software packages.

Your Own Personal Mail Manager

After you begin sending e-mail, you probably will find that you are receiving quite a bit of it, particularly if you put yourself on some mailing lists (see Chapter 10). Your incoming mail shortly becomes a trickle, then a stream, then a torrent, and pretty soon you can't walk past your keyboard without getting soaking wet (metaphorically speaking).

Fortunately, most mail systems provide ways for you to manage the flow and avoid ruining your clothes (enough of this metaphor already). If most of your messages come from mailing lists, you should check to see whether the lists are available as *Usenet* news instead (see Chapter 11). Usenet newsreading programs generally enable you to look through the messages and find the ones of interest much quicker than your mail program does.

Even for mailing lists that don't have a Usenet equivalent, if you're using a reasonably capable system (such as a UNIX workstation) and have a cooperative system manager, it turns out to be easy to arrange the mail to make particularly chatty mailing lists look like Usenet news.

Finally, there is mail-sorting software. Depending on the enthusiasm of your system administrator and whether you can round up a volunteer willing to give you 20 minutes or so of programming help, you may have a mail-sorting program available that can automate much of the more mundane mail handling. If you get a large number of messages from a boring mailing list, for example, you can have it stuff them all in a separate mailbox. If your computer has a speaker, you can arrange for various boops and beeps to alert you to different kinds of mail, based on who sent it or what the topic is.

The most common UNIX mail-sorting programs are called delivermail and procmail. Both are available for free, although it takes a couple of hours for a system administrator to compile and install one of them. (They're in the comp.sources.unix archive at ftp.uu.net — see Chapter 18.) After one of them is installed, each user can have a *delivery script,* which is a command file interpreted by the usual UNIX shell, the command language.

Note: Someone who is familiar with shell scripts can easily write you a delivery script that looks for sender names and subject-line keywords and dispatches mail appropriately. (It helps to have chocolate chip cookies on hand to encourage your shell programmer to help.)

On Macs and PCs, Eudora users can create "filters" that can automatically check incoming messages against a list of senders and subjects and file them in appropriate mailboxes. Other Windows mail programs have similar filtering features.

All this automatic sorting nonsense may seem like overkill, and if you get only five or ten messages a day, it is. But after the mail really gets flowing, you find that dealing with your mail is taking much more of your time than it used to. So keep those automated tools in mind — if not for now, then for later.

Hail to the Chief

The White House, long a technological backwater, has finally crept into the computer age. (Legend has it that when President Eisenhower retired to Gettysburg in 1961, he picked up the phone, heard a dial tone, and had no idea what to do, because in the preceding 20 years when he had been a general, a college president, and U.S. President, he had never used a dial phone.) You can now send e-mail to the President and Vice President of the United States. Their addresses are

president@whitehouse.gov

vice.president@whitehouse.gov

At the moment, e-mail messages are printed and handled like paper mail, although they plan to fix that as soon as they can. (Don't hold your breath, though, waiting for Bill and Al to read them personally. The mail is still handled by the staff.) Your message should include your return address (paper mail — because they mail you a response) and should be reasonably formal, like normal correspondence. Feel free to use this sample letter as a model:

Gentle Reader

123 Mockingbird Lane

Anytown, USA 96943

Dear Mr. President:

I have just finished reading *The Internet For Dummies.* It is the most important book ever written. Every American, including Socks, must have a copy right away. I beg you to buy and distribute them immediately, as a matter of the greatest national urgency. Raise my taxes if you need to — it's worth it.

Sincerely,

G. Reader

Chapter 9

Tracking Down
Electronic-Mail Addresses

● ●

In This Chapter

▶ How to find an address

▶ On-line directories

▶ Lots and lots of mail systems

● ●

Where in Cyberspace Is Everyone?

As you've probably figured out, one teensy detail is keeping you from sending e-mail to all your friends: You don't know their addresses. In this chapter, you learn lots of different ways to look for addresses. But we save you the trouble of reading the rest of the chapter by starting out with the easiest, most reliable way to find out people's e-mail addresses:

Call them on the phone and ask them.

Pretty low-tech, huh? For some reason, this seems to be absolutely the last thing people want to do (see the sidebar "Top ten reasons not to call someone to get an e-mail address"). But try it first. If you know or can find out the phone number, it's much easier than any of the other methods.

They won't mind if you give them the finger

One of the most useful commands, if you generally know where someone receives mail, is finger. On most UNIX systems, you can use finger to find out who is logged in right now and to ask about particular users. If you run finger without asking for any particular user, you get a list of who's logged in now, something like the following:

Login Office	Name	TTY	Idle	When
root	0000-Admin(0000)	co	12:	Wed 16:04
john1	John R. Levine	vt	1d	Wed 16:03
john1	John R. Levine	p0		Wed 16:10
john1	John R. Levine	p1	1	Wed 16:10
john1	John R. Levine	p2	13:	Wed 16:10
john1	John R. Levine	p3	8:04	Wed 16:49
john1	John R. Levine	p4		Sat 19:45

This is a pretty typical response for a workstation. If the user is running a windowing system and has a bunch of windows open on the screen, each window shows up as a separate *pseudoterminal*. This doesn't mean that the user has six terminals with six keyboards arranged like a pipe organ; it's just a messy screen. The Idle column shows, for each terminal (or window), how long it's been since somebody typed something — a useful number if you're trying to see whether anyone is actually there. It's normally displayed in hours and minutes (or days if there's a *d*).

You can also finger a particular person. For example, because John's username is john1, if you type this line:

```
finger john1
```

TIP

Whaddaya mean, you don't know your own address?

It happens frequently — usually it's because a friend is using a proprietary e-mail system that has a gateway to the outside world that provides instructions for how to send messages to the outside but no hint on how outsiders send stuff in. Fortunately, the solution is usually easy: Tell your friend to send you a message. All messages have return addresses, and all but the absolute cruddiest of mail gateways put on a usable return address. Don't be surprised if the address has a great deal of strange punctuation. After a few gateways, you always seem to end up with things like this:

```
"blurch::John.C.Calhoun"%farp@slimemail.com
```
But usually if you type the strange address back in, it works, so don't worry about it.

You can find out your own address this way by sending a message to our ever-vigilant mail robot at internet@dummies.com, which will send you back a note telling you what the return address in your message was. (The human authors see those messages as well, so feel free to add a few words telling us whether you like the book.)

TIP

Top ten reasons not to call someone to get an e-mail address

✔ You want to surprise long-lost friend.

✔ You want to surprise long-lost *ex*-friend who owes you a large amount of money and thinks that he's given you the slip.

✔ You or your friend don't speak English. (Actually happens because many Internauts are outside the U.S.)

✔ You or your friend don't speak at all. (Actually happens—networks offer a uniquely friendly place for most people with handicaps because nobody knows or cares about the handicaps.)

✔ It's 3 a.m. and you need to send a message right now or you'll never get to sleep.

✔ You don't know the phone number and, because of an unfortunate childhood experience, you have a deathly fear of calling directory assistance.

✔ The phone takes only quarters; nobody around can break your $100 bill.

✔ The company installed a new phone system, nobody has figured out how to use it, and no matter what you dial, you always end up with Dial-a-Prayer.

✔ You inadvertently spilled entire can of soda into phone; can't wait for it to dry out to make the call.

✔ You called yesterday, didn't write down the answer, and forgot it. Oops.

you get back something like the following:

```
Login name: johnl                     In real life: John R.
            Levine
Directory: /usr/johnl                 Shell: /bin/sh
On since Jun 30 16:03:13 on vt01           1 day 9 hours Idle
            Time
Project: Working on "The Internet For Dummies"
Plan:
Write many books, become famous.
```

The exact format of the response varies a great deal from one system to another because fiddling with the finger program is a bad habit of many UNIX system hackers. (In this case, you would get six copies of the response, one for each window, but we thought that we would save the paper.)

Finger also, with some limitations, can match approximate names. If you type this line:

```
finger john
```

it finds all the people whose real names (according to the system password file) are *John something* or *something John.*

Fingering far-off friends for fun

The shrewd reader has probably noticed that so far we have discussed fingering only people on one's own machine, which isn't very interesting. What makes finger useful is that it can finger other machines equally well. If you type this line:

```
finger @ntw.org
```

it shows you who's logged in at ntw.org, assuming that it allows incoming finger requests (most but not all sites do). You can also ask about a particular person. If you type this line, for example:

```
finger elvis@ntw.org
```

you get back the same response as though a local user had typed finger elvis. If you know a user's name, you can usually use finger to figure out his or her e-mail address, which is generally the same as the username. If you finger chester@glorp.org, for example, and get back

```
User    Full name                What- Idle TTY -Console Location-
chet    Chester A. Arthur        csh   7:17 rb   ncd16 (X display 0)
```

you can be pretty sure that the mail address is chet@glorp.org.

Project that plan! (Or is it plan that project?)

On UNIX systems, the response to the finger command comes back with a *project* and a *plan.* You, too, can have a project and a plan so that you look like a well-informed, seasoned network user (appearances are everything).

Your project is a file called *.project* (yes, it begins with a dot), and your plan is a file called *.plan* (it begins with a dot too). You can put in them anything you want. The finger command shows only the first line of the project but all of the plan. Try not to go overboard. Ten lines or so is all people are willing to see, and even that's stretching it if it's not really, *really* clever.

The industrial-strength finger

Some places, universities in particular, have attached their finger programs to organizational directories. If you finger bu.edu (Boston University), for example, you get the following response:

```
[bu.edu]
   Boston University Electronic Directory (finger access)
This directory contains listings for Students, Faculty, Staff
and University Departments.
At present, most information about students is not accessible
off-campus or via finger on bu.edu. The primary directory
interface is ph; if this is not available, finger accepts
<user>@bu.edu where <user> can be a login name or FirstName
LastName (note dash '-' not space). Also note that <user> can
include standard Unix shell patterns.
...
```

So you can try fingering Jane-Smith@bu.edu and the like to find the address. Other universities with similar directories include MIT and Yale. It's worth a try — the worst that can happen is that it will say not found.

TIP

Hey, Ms. Postmaster

Sometimes you have a pretty good idea what machine someone uses, but you don't know the name. In that case, you can try writing to the postmaster. Every *domain*, the part of the address after @ (the at sign), that can receive Internet mail has the e-mail address postmaster, which contacts someone responsible for that machine. So if you're pretty sure that your friend uses moby.ntw.org, you might try asking (politely, of course) postmaster@moby.ntw.org what the address is. (We assume that, for some reason, you can't just call your friend and ask what the e-mail address is.)

Most postmasters are overworked system administrators who don't mind an occasional polite question, but you shouldn't expect any big favors.

Also keep in mind that the larger the mail domain, the less likely it is that the postmaster knows all the users personally. Don't write to Postmaster@ibm.com to try to find someone's e-mail address at IBM. (Fortunately for people who want to find correspondents in the Blue Zone, IBM has a *whois server* — see the next section, "Who zat?")

Postmaster is also the appropriate place to write when you're having trouble with mail to or from a site. If your messages to someone are coming back with a cryptic error message which suggests that the mail system is fouled up or if you're receiving a flood of mechanically generated junk mail from a deranged automatic mail server (see Chapter 10), the postmaster at the relevant site is the one to write to.

Who zat?

Quite a long time ago (at least, a long time ago in *network* terms — 15 or 20 years), some of the network managers began keeping directories of network people. The command that lets you look up people in these directories is called `whois`. Some systems have a `whois` command, so in principle you can type this line:

```
whois Smith
```

and it should contact the `whois` database and tell you about all the people named Smith. In practice, however, it isn't quite that simple. For one thing, around the end of 1992, the main system that keeps the Internet `whois` database moved, and many `whois` commands still haven't yet been updated to reflect that move. The old standard server most `whois` programs contact now holds only the names of people who work for the Department of Defense. Fortunately, you can tell the `whois` program to use a particular server, as in

```
whois -h whois.internic.net Smith
```

because the civilian Internet service is now at `whois.internic.net`. The `-h` stands for *host,* as in the host where the server is. But keep in mind that it still lists only network managers and administrative contacts. Here at Internet For Dummies Central, for example, `whois` will find John because he's the network manager (see the discussion of duct tape in Chapter 2), but you won't find Carol, who, instead of being a network manager, has a life.

Okay, how do I find people at IBM?

We thought that you would never ask. IBM has a mail server that lets you look up people's names. Send a message to `nic@vnet.ibm.com` that contains a line like this:

```
whois Watson, T
```

It lists any users with e-mail addresses whose names match. Although nearly all IBM employees have internal e-mail addresses, only a fraction can receive mail from the outside, and you can see only those addresses. (Makes sense — no point in telling you about mail addresses you can't use.)

Many other companies have a straightforward addressing system that gives everyone at the company an alias such as `Firstname.Lastname`. This works at AT&T, so mailing to this address:

```
Theodore.Vail@att.com
```

finds someone pretty reliably. This also works at Sun Microsystems (`sun.com`). It's always worth a try because the worst that can happen is that you get your message back as undeliverable. If several people have the same name, you usually get a mechanical response telling you how to figure out which of them you want and what the correct address is.

For systems that don't have the `whois` command, you can usually use telnet (see Chapter 14) instead. You can telnet to `whois.internic.net`; then at the prompt, type `whois whoever`. For European net people, try typing `whois.ripe.net`. A large list of `whois` servers (lots of organizations run their own `whois` service for their own employees) is in a file you can FTP (see Chapter 16) from `sipb.mit.edu`, filename `/pub/whois/whois-servers.list`.

Compatible Mail System — a Contradiction?

A zillion different networks are spliced into the Internet in one way or another. With many of them, you can barely tell that it's a different network. Many individual UNIX systems, for example, pass mail around by using *UUCP* (which stands for *UNIX to UNIX CoPy*), an ancient but sturdy and very cheap dial-up scheme. Most of them have arranged to register standard Internet addresses, so you can send mail to them in the same way you send mail to any other Internet mailbox.

But many proprietary mail systems are out there, and many of them are in fact connected to the Internet. Most of the connections seem to have been assembled with spit and baling wire, however, so you have to type something strange to get the mail through. In the section "A Parade of Mail Systems," later in this chapter, you should find the necessary strange stuff you need for this task.

X.400: We're from the government, and we're here to help you

After the Internet had been around for several years and e-mail had been flowing for far longer than that, the international organization in charge of standards for telephones and stuff like that, known then as the *CCITT* (a French acronym for the International Telephone and Telegraph Consultative Committee), decided that it too was going to get into the e-mail business.

You might think that the obvious thing to do would be to adopt the existing Internet standards because they had been shown to be reliable and robust. (Silly you — that just goes to show that *you'll* never get far as an international telecommunications standards developer.) The committee decided to come up with *X.400,* something all new, all singing, all dancing, and much, much more complex — as befits the grandeur of the international telecommunications establishment. In all fairness, X.400 does handle a few things that Internet mail (known as *RFC822*, after the document that describes it) doesn't, or at least didn't until recently. But X.400 is so complicated that it has taken nearly ten years from the publication of the first version for it to become at all common. And only the most wildly enthusiastic bureaucrats think that X.400 and its ilk will ever replace its Internet equivalents.

Incidentally, due to rumors that nonbureaucrats had begun to figure out who the CCITT was, it was reconstituted as the Telecommunications Branch of the International Telecommunications Union, now known as ITU-T. It's still the same well-paid international bureaucrats in Geneva, Switzerland, who have important meetings, often over an excellent (but rather expensive) lunch eaten at a restaurant overlooking beautiful *Lac Leman* and washed down with excellent (but rather expensive) Swiss regional wine, paid for by the taxpayers of the 100 countries that constitute the ITU (which is in turn a branch of the United Nations). For a more detailed discussion of what life at the ITU is like, see the first few chapters of Carl Malamud's *Exploring the Internet, a Technical Travelogue,* (Prentice-Hall, 1993), which, after you wade through the network geek parts, is screamingly funny. (True fact: Until recently, the headquarters of the ITU, which has 900 employees charged with coordinating the world's telecommunications and is by treaty entitled to free phone calls anywhere in the world, had only one fax machine.) But we digress.

An X.400 address isn't just a name and a domain: It's a bunch of attributes. The official specification goes on for dozens, if not hundreds, of pages, but we spare you the detail (which would have been fascinating if we had had the space, you can be sure) and report on the bare minimum. The attributes that are usually of interest and the codes used to represent them are the following:

- **Surname (S):** The recipient's last name

- **Given name (G):** The recipient's first name

- **Initials (I):** First or middle initial (or initials)

- **Generational qualifier (GQ or Q):** Jr., III, and so on (these folks think of everything)

- **Administration Domain Name (ADMD or A):** More or less the name of the mail system

- **Private Domain Name (PRMD or P):** More or less the name of a private system gatewayed into a public ADMD

- **Organization (O):** The organization with which the recipient is affiliated, which may or may not have anything to do with the ADMD or PRMD

- **Country (C):** A two-letter country code (see Appendix)

- **Domain Defined Attribute (DD or DDA):** Any magic code that identifies the recipient, such as username or account number

You encode these attributes in an address, using / (a slash) to separate them and writing each attribute as the code, an equal sign, and the value. Is that clear? No? (Can't imagine why.)

Here's a concrete example: Suppose that your friend uses Sprint's Sprintmail service (formerly known as Telemail, the ADMD), which has an X.400 connection to the Internet. Your friend's name is Samuel Tilden, he's in the United States, and he's with Tammany Hall. His attributes would be

- ✔ **G:** Samuel
- ✔ **S:** Tilden
- ✔ **O:** TammanyHall
- ✔ **C:** US

Because the Internet domain for the gateway is `sprint.com`, the address would be

```
/G=Samuel/S=Tilden/O=TammanyHall/C=US/ADMD=TELEMAIL/
          @sprint.com
```

We're not making up this syntax. Sorry. Notice that a slash appears at the beginning of the address and just before the @. The order of the slash-separated chunks doesn't matter.

Exactly which attributes you need for a particular address varies all over the place. Some domains connect to only a single country and ADMD, so you don't use those attributes with those domains. Others (such as Sprintmail) connect to many, so you need both. It's a mess. You have to find out for each X.400 system which attributes it needs. In theory, redundant attributes shouldn't hurt, but in practice, who knows?

One minor simplification applies to the hopefully common case in which the only attribute needed is the recipient's actual name. If the user's name is Rutherford B. Hayes, the full attribute form is

```
/G=Rutherford/I=B/S=Hayes/
```

But instead you can write

```
Rutherford.B.Hayes
```

Pretty advanced, eh? You can leave out the given name or the initial if you want. You can hope that most X.400 addresses can be written this way, but you are probably doomed to disappointment.

In most cases, the easiest way to figure out someone's X.400 address is to have your recipient send you a message and see what the From: line says. Failing that, you have to experiment.

X.500: We're from the government, and we're back

An official *white pages* directory-service model to look up people's e-mail addresses called *X.500* is brought to us by the same people who brought us X.400. Not surprisingly, considering who defined it, X.500 organizes its data like a shelf full of phone books (or in a large X.500 system, like a library of shelves organized by country). For any particular person, you have to tell X.500 which book or books to look in.

(Another true fact: If you're in one country, let's call it country A, and you want the phone number of someone in country B, the official ITU-T directory-assistance procedure is to connect you to someone in country A in a room full of old phone books from all over the world, in which they attempt to find the appropriate country B phone book and look up the person. If they can't find the number — because their country B phone books are all 15 years old and your friend moved 12 years ago, for example — tough. The scheme used in the U.S. in which they connect you to an actual directory operator in country B who is likely to have current phone numbers is in complete violation of standards. We feel that a moment of breathless admiration is appropriate for people who can invent standards like that.)

Note: It looks like X.500 will actually be used all over the place for two reasons. One reason is that it is somewhat more usable than X.400, and the other reason is that no other competing candidates exist. (We'll give you one guess about which is the more important reason.)

Currently, most X.500 services are *interactive,* which means that you log in to them and type your request. Generally, you enter the parts you know, such as the names of the person and the organization, and it shows you the account names that match. All the interactive systems have some sort of help, so if you're stuck, try pressing ? or typing **help**.

The most common X.500 service is called fred (which stands for FRont End to Directories). You can try it out by telnetting (see Chapter 14) to wp.psi.com or wp1.psi.com and logging in as fred. If you just type someone's name, fred tries to look it up in the local directory of people who work at PSI, the Internet network provider that offers the demonstration fred service. Most likely, the person you are looking for isn't at PSI, so you have to tell fred where to look.

The easiest thing to do, if you think that your friend is at an organization which begins with the letter *F,* for example, is to type

```
whois John Smith -org f*
```

Fred then goes through each of the matching organizations and asks you whether you want to look in their phone book. Press Y or N, depending. In theory, you should be able to type this line:

```
whois John Smith -org * -geo @c=US
```

to have it look in all the directories for companies in the United States. But in practice, the fred program is still sort of buggy and tends to die when you make complex queries.

Know what?

One more address-finding system worth trying is *knowbot.* You telnet (see Chapter 14) to it by typing this line:

```
telnet info.cnri.reston.va.us 185
```

(The *185* means that you want to log in to the knowbot server rather than the usual login prompt.) It then displays a prompt. Just type the person's name and wait, sometimes for as long as several minutes, as it looks through a bunch of directories and tells you what it finds. Knowbot has access to some directories not otherwise easily accessible, including the one for MCI Mail, so it's worth checking. In our experience, though, it sometimes misses things — John has an MCI Mail account, for example, but for some reason knowbot can't find him there.

A Parade of Mail Systems

Here is a short (well, *pretty* short) list of major mail and on-line systems that are connected to the Internet and how to send mail to people on that system.

America Online

An AOL user's mail address is the "screen name," usually the user's full name. To send mail to a user named Aaron Burr, type

```
aaronburr@aol.com
```

Note: Some AOL users have chosen mail names unrelated to their actual names; for them, you have to pick up the phone and call them. AOL makes it extremely easy to change your screen name, and a single user can have several screen names, so AOL addresses change frequently.

Applelink

Applelink users typically use their last name as their usernames:

```
reinhold@applelink.apple.com
```

AT&T Mail

AT&T Mail users have arbitrary usernames. To send mail to a user whose username is *blivet,* type

```
blivet@attmail.com
```

Note: AT&T Mail provides gateways to some companies' internal mail systems. In such cases, you may have an address like this:

```
argle!bargle!blivet@foocorp.attmail.com
```

We can report from bitter experience that these gateways don't work well. In one case, we've been trying for the better part of a year to get the gateway to transfer mail from the Internet with no success. (No matter what we send, even a two-line plain-text message, the gateway turns it into a message containing a mysterious embedded file that nobody can read.)

BITNET

BITNET is a network of mostly IBM mainframes. Each system name is eight characters long or less. System names often contain the letters *VM,* the name of the operating system used on most BITNET sites. Usernames are arbitrary, but they are usually also eight characters or less. Many BITNET sites also have Internet mail domain names, so you can send mail to them in the regular Internet way.

If the mailer you use is well configured, it probably has a BITNET support setup to handle BITNET systems not directly on the Internet. So you can send mail to *JSMITH* at *XYZVM3,* for example, by typing

```
jsmith@xyzvm3.bitnet
```

Failing that, you have to address mail directly to a BITNET gateway. Here are addresses using two gateways that tolerate outsiders' mail:

```
jsmith%xyzvm3.bitnet@mitvma.mit.edu
jsmith%xyzvm3.bitnet@cunyvm.cuny.edu
```

These two gateways are provided by MIT and the City University of New York (CUNY), respectively, as a courtesy to the net community.

BIX

BIX is a commercial system formerly run by *Byte* magazine and now run by Delphi. Usernames are arbitrary short strings. To mail to user *xxxxx*, type

```
xxxxx@bix.com
```

CompuServe

CompuServe is a large on-line service. (Is there anyone who doesn't know that?) For ancient, historical reasons, CompuServe usernames are pairs of *octal* (base eight) numbers, usually beginning with the digit 7 for users in the U.S. and 10 for users overseas. If a user's number is 712345,6701, the address is

```
712345.6701@compuserve.com
```

Note: The address uses a *period,* not a *comma,* because Internet addresses cannot contain commas.

Delphi

Delphi is an on-line service from the same people who run BIX, although the services are separate (Rupert Murdoch, the media baron, recently bought both of them.) Delphi usernames are arbitrary strings, most often the first initial and last name of the user. To send to user *support,* type

```
support@delphi.com
```

Digital's Easynet

Users on the Digital Equipment Corporation internal Easynet network have internal addresses of the form HOST::NAME, which correspond to:

```
name@host.enet.dec.com
```

Some users still use the old All-In-1 mail system, with addresses such as Ken Olsen @PDQ. These correspond to:

```
Ken.Olsen@pdq.mts.dec.com
```

Easylink

Easylink is a mostly mail service formerly run by Western Union and now run by AT&T. Users have seven-digit numbers beginning with 62. To mail to user 6231416, type

```
6231416@eln.attmail.com
```

FIDONET

FIDONET is a very large, worldwide BBS network. On FIDONET, people are identified by their names, and each individual BBS (called a *node*) has a three- or four-part number in the form 1:2/3 or 1:2/3.4. To send a message to Grover Cleveland at node 1:2/3.4, type

```
grover.cleveland@p4.f3.n2.z1.fidonet.org
```

If a node has a three-part name, such as 1:2/3, type

```
grover.cleveland@f3.n2.z1.fidonet.org
```

GEnie

GEnie is an on-line service run by General Electric. It's the consumer end of GE's commercial on-line service, which dates back into the 1960s. Each user has a username, which is an arbitrary and totally unmemorable string, and a mail name, which is usually related to the user's name. You have to know a user's mail name, something like J.SMITH7:

```
J.SMITH7@genie.geis.com
```

MCI Mail

MCI Mail is a large, commercial e-mail system. Each user has a seven-digit user number guaranteed to be unique and a username that may or may not be unique. You can send to the number, username, or the person's actual name, using underscores rather than spaces:

```
1234567@mcimail.com
jsmith@mcimail.com
john_smith@mcimail.com
```

If you send to a username or an actual name and the name turns out not to be unique, MCI Mail thoughtfully sends you a response listing the possible matches so that you can send your message again to the unique user number. MCI user numbers are sometimes written with a hyphen, like a phone number, but you don't have to use the hyphen in your address.

Prodigy

Prodigy is a large on-line system run by IBM and Sears. (We hear that they can have upward of 10,000 simultaneous users.) It has a hard-to-use mail gateway (for Prodigy users. It's a snap from the Internet side). Keep in mind that users pay for incoming mail, and the gateway can't handle very long messages. Users have arbitrary usernames like KS8GN3. Send mail to

```
KS8GN3@prodigy.com
```

Sprintmail (Telemail)

The Sprintmail e-mail system is provided by Sprintnet. Sprintmail used to be called Telemail because Sprintnet used to be called Telenet. (It was a techno-logical spinoff of the original ARPANET work that led to the Internet.) Sprintmail is the major X.400 mail system in the United States. As we mentioned in the earlier section that disparages X.400, to send a message to a user named Samuel Tilden who is with Tammany Hall in the United States, you type:

```
/G=Samuel/S=Tilden/O=TammanyHall/C=US/ADMD=TELEMAIL/
            @sprint.com
```

Many corporate and government e-mail systems are attached to Sprintmail. Each has a distinct organization (O=) name and sometimes a private mail domain (PRMD=) name also that have to be entered in the address.

UUCP

UUCP is an old and cruddy mail system still used by many UNIX systems because (how did you guess?) it's free. UUCP addresses consist of a system name and a username, which are both short, arbitrary strings. The system here at Internet For Dummies Central, for example, for historical reasons has a UUCP address — iecc — in addition to its normal Internet address, so you could address mail to iecc!idummies. (The ! is pronounced "bang," by the way, and this is called a *bang path address*.) Multihop UUCP addresses also exist: world!iecc!idummies says to send the message first to the machine called world, which can send it to iecc, where the address is dummies. (Think of it as e-mail's whisper down the lane.) Most often, UUCP addresses are written relative to an Internet host that also talks UUCP, so you could address mail to this address:

```
world!iecc!idummies@uunet.uu.net
```

(although it gets here faster if you send it to internet@dummies.com, because that avoids the UUCP nonsense). This address means to send the message to uunet.uu.net by using regular Internet mail, then by UUCP to world, and another UUCP hop to iecc, and there to the mailbox called idummies. If you think that this is ugly and confusing, you're not alone.

UUNET Communications is a large, nonprofit outfit that, among other things, brings e-mail to the UUCP-speaking masses, so it's the Internet system most often seen with UUCP addresses. Most of UUNET's customers also have regular Internet addresses that internally are turned into the ugly UUCP addresses. If you know the Internet address rather than the UUCP address, use it.

Chapter 10
Using Mailing Lists

In This Chapter

▶ Mailing lists

▶ Getting more or less junk mail

▶ A few interesting mailing lists

▶ Mail servers

Are You Sure This Isn't Junk Mail?

Now that you know all about how to send and receive mail, only one thing stands between you and a rich, fulfilling, mail-blessed life: You don't know many people with whom you can exchange mail. Fortunately, you can get yourself on lots of mailing lists, which ensures that you arrive every morning to a mailbox with 400 new messages. (Well, maybe you should start out with one or two lists.)

The point of a mailing list is quite simple. The list itself has a mail address, and anything (more or less) that someone sends to that address is sent to all the people on the list, who often respond to the messages. The result is a running conversation. Different lists have different styles. Some are fairly formal, hewing closely to the official topic of the list. Others tend to go flying off into outer space, topicwise.

Usenet news is another way to have running e-mail-like conversations, and the distinction between the two is blurry. (Some topics are available both as mailing lists and on Usenet, so people with and without access to news can participate.) Chapter 11 discusses Usenet.

Getting on and off Mailing Lists

The way you get on or off a mailing list is simple: You send a mail message. Two general schools of mailing-list management exist: the *manual* and the *automatic*. Manual management is the more traditional way: Your message is read by a human being who updates the files to put people on or take them off the list. The advantage to manual management is that you get personal service; the disadvantage is that the list maintainer may not get around to servicing you for quite a while if more pressing business (such as her real job) intervenes.

These days it's more common to have lists maintained automatically, which saves human attention for times when things are fouled up. The most widely used automatic mailing managers are a family of programs known as LISTSERV and Majordomo, which get their own sections later in this chapter.

For the manual lists, there is a widely observed convention regarding list and maintainer addresses. Suppose that you want to join a list for fans of James Buchanan (the 15th President of the United States, the only one who never married, in case you slept through that part of history class), and the list's name is buchanan-lovers@blivet.com. The manager's address is almost certainly buchanan-lovers-request@blivet.com. In other words, just add -request to the list's address to get the manager's address. Because the list is maintained by hand, your request to be added or dropped doesn't have to take any particular form, so long as it's polite. Please add me to the buchanan-lovers list does quite well. When you decide that you have had all the Buchanan you can stand, another message saying Please remove me from the buchanan-lovers list does equally well.

Messages to -request addresses are read by human beings who sometimes eat, sleep, and work regular jobs as well as maintain mailing lists. This means that they don't necessarily read your request the moment it arrives. It can take a day or so to be added to or removed from a list, and after you ask to be removed, you usually get a few more messages before they remove you. Be patient. Don't send cranky notes — they just cheese off the list maintainer.

LISTSERV, the studly computer's mail manager

The BITNET network (see Chapter 9) was originally set up so that the only thing it could do was ship files and messages from one system to another. As a result, BITNET users quickly developed lots and lots of mailing lists because no other convenient way — such as Usenet news — was available to stay in touch.

Maintaining all those mailing lists was (and still is) a great deal of work, so in order to manage the mailing lists, the BITNET crowd came up with a program called LISTSERV, which runs on great big IBM mainframe computers. Originally, only users on machines directly connected to BITNET could use LISTSERV, but anyone with an Internet address can use current versions. Indeed, LISTSERV has grown to the point where it is an all-singing, all-dancing mailing-list program with about 15 zillion features and options, almost none of which you care about.

LISTSERV is a little klunky to use, but it has the great advantage of being able to handle with ease enormous mailing lists containing thousands of members, something that makes the regular Internet mail programs choke.

You put yourself on and off a LISTSERV mailing list by sending mail to LISTSERV@some.machine.or.other, where some.machine.or.other is the name of the particular machine where the mailing list lives. Some lists live on several machines (see the section "Stupid LISTSERV tricks," later in this chapter). Because they're computer programs, LISTSERV list managers are pretty simple-minded, so you have to speak to them clearly and distinctly.

Suppose that your name is Roger Sherman you want to join a list called SNUFLE-L (LISTSERV mailing lists usually end with -L), which lives at ntw.org. To join, send a message to LISTSERV@ntw.org that contains this line:

```
SUB SNUFLE-L Roger Sherman
```

You don't have to add a subject line or anything else to this message. SUB is short for *subscribe*, SNUFLE-L is the name of the list, and anything after that is supposed to be your real name. (You can put whatever you want there, but keep in mind that it will show up in the return address of anything you send to the list.) Shortly afterward, you should get two messages back:

- ✔ A chatty, machine-generated welcoming message along with a description of some commands you can use to fiddle with your mailing-list membership.

- ✔ An incredibly boring message, telling you that the IBM mainframe ran a program to handle your request and reporting the exact number of milliseconds of computer time and number of disk operations the request took. Whoopee. (It is sobering to think that somewhere there are people who find these messages interesting.)

To send a message to this list, mail to the list name at the same machine — in this case, SNUFLE-L@ntw.org. Be sure to provide a descriptive Subject: for the multitudes who will benefit from your pearls of wisdom. Within a matter of minutes, people all over the world will be reading your message.

To get off a list, write to LISTSERV@some.machine.or.other, sending

```
SIGNOFF SNUFLE-L
```

or whatever the list's name is. You don't have to give your name again, because after you're off the list, LISTSERV has no more interest in you and completely forgets that you ever existed.

Some lists are harder to get on and off than others are. Usually you ask to get on a list and you're on the list. In some cases, however, the list isn't open to all comers, and the human list owner screens requests to join the list. In other cases, after you ask to subscribe, LISTSERV sends you a message to make sure that it got your address right, and you have to respond with OK or something. (These messages tend to say pretty clearly what you're expected to do.)

To contact the actual human being who runs a particular list, the mail address is OWNER- followed by the list name (for example, OWNER-SNUFLE-L). The owner can do all sorts of things to lists that mere mortals can't do. In particular, the owner can fix screwed-up names on the list or add a name that for some reason the automatic method doesn't handle. You have to appeal for manual intervention if your mail system doesn't put your correct network mail address on the From: line of your messages, as sometimes happens when your local mail system isn't set up quite right.

Stupid LISTSERV tricks

Here are some stupid LISTSERV tricks. For each of them, you send a message to LISTSERV@some.machine.or.other to talk to the LISTSERV program itself. You can send several commands in the same message if you want to do several tricks at one time.

- **Temporarily stopping mail:** Sometimes you're going to be away for a while and you don't want to get a lot of mailing-list mail in the meantime. But because you're coming back, you don't want to take yourself off all the lists, either. To *temporarily* stop mail from the SNUFLE-L mailing list, send

```
SET SNUFLE-L NOMAIL
```

and it will stop sending you messages. To turn the mail back on, send

```
SET SNUFLE-L MAIL
```

- **Getting messages as a digest:** If you're getting a large number of messages from a list and would rather get them all at one time as a daily digest, send

```
SET SNUFLE-L DIGEST
```

Not all lists can be digested (again, think of burritos), but the indigestible ones will let you know and won't take offense.

- **Finding out who's on a list:** To find out who subscribes to a list, send

```
REVIEW SNUFLE-L
```

Some lists can be reviewed only by people on the list, and others not at all. Some lists are enormous, listing thousands of subscribers.

- **Getting or not getting your own mail:** When you send mail to a LISTSERV list of which you're a member, it usually sends you a copy of your own message to confirm that it got there okay. Some people find this needlessly redundant. To avoid getting copies of your own messages, send

```
SET SNUFLE-L NOACK
```

To resume getting copies of your own messages, send

```
SET SNUFLE-L ACK
```

- Most LISTSERV servers have a library of files, usually documents contributed by the mailing-list members. To find out what's available, send:

```
INDEX
```

✔ To have it e-mail you a particular file, send:

```
GET fname
```

where *fname* is the name of a file from the INDEX command. On IBM systems, files have two-part names separated by a space (for example: GET SNUFLE-L MEMO).

✔ **Finding out what lists are available:** To find out what LISTSERV mailing lists are available on a particular host, send

```
LIST
```

Note: Keep in mind that just because a list exists doesn't necessarily mean that you can subscribe to it. But it doesn't hurt to try.

✔ **Getting LISTSERV to do other things:** Lots of other commands lurk in LISTSERV, most of which apply only to people on IBM mainframes. If you are such a person, or if you're just nosy, send a message containing

```
HELP
```

and you'll receive a helpful response listing other commands.

An excellent choice, sir

The third widely used mailing-list manager is Brent Chapman's Majordomo. It started out as a LISTSERV wannabe for workstations but has evolved into a system that works quite well. Majordomo commands are almost but not quite the same as their LISTSERV equivalents.

The mailing address for Majordomo commands, as you might expect, is majordomo@some.machine.or.other. Majordomo lists tend to have long and expressive names. One of our favorites is called explosive-cargo, a very funny weekly column written by a guy in Boston who in real life is a computer technical writer. To subscribe, since the list is maintained on host world.std.com, **send this to** Majordomo@world.std.com:

```
subscribe explosive-cargo
```

Unlike with LISTSERV, you *don't* put your real name in the subscribe command.

To unsubscribe:

```
unsubscribe explosive-cargo
```

Stupid Majordomo tricks

Not to be outdone by LISTSERV, Majordomo has its own set of not particularly useful commands. As with LISTSERV, you can send as many of these in a single message as you want.

- ✔ To find out which lists at a Majordomo system you are subscribed to:

    ```
    which
    ```

- ✔ To find all the lists managed by a Majordomo system:

    ```
    lists
    ```

- ✔ Majordomo also can keep files related to its lists. To find the names of the files for a particular list:

    ```
    index name-of-list
    ```

- ✔ To tell Majordomo to e-mail you one of the files:

    ```
    get name-of-list name-of-file
    ```

- ✔ To find out the rest of the goofy things Majordomo can do:

    ```
    help
    ```

- ✔ If you need to contact the human manager of a Majordomo system, send a polite message to owner-majordomo@*hostname*. Remember that humans eat, sleep, and have real jobs, so it may take a day or two to get an answer.

Sending messages to mailing lists

Okay, you're signed up on a mailing list. Now what? First, as we said a few pages back, wait a week or so and see what sort of messages arrive from the list — that way, you can get an idea of what you should or should not send to it. When you think that you've seen enough to avoid embarrassing yourself, try sending something in. That's easy — you mail a message to the mailing list. The list's address is the same as the name of the list: buchanan-lovers@blivet.com or snufle-l@ntw.org or whatever. Keep in mind that hundreds or thousands of people will be reading your pearls of wisdom, so try at least to spell things correctly (you may have thought this was obvious, but you would be sadly mistaken.) On popular lists, you may begin to get responses within a few minutes of sending a message.

Some lists encourage new subscribers to send in a message introducing themselves and saying briefly what their interests are. Others don't. So don't send anything until you have something to say.

Some mailing lists have funny rules about who is allowed to send messages, meaning that just because you're on the list doesn't automatically mean that any messages you send will appear on the list. Some lists are *moderated,* meaning that any message you send in gets sent to a human *moderator,* who decides what goes to the list and what doesn't. This may sound sort of fascist, but in practice the arrangement makes a list about 50 times more interesting than it would be otherwise, because a good moderator can filter out the boring and irrelevant messages, keeping the list on track. Indeed, the people who complain the loudest about moderator censorship are usually the ones whose messages most deserve to be censored.

Another rule that sometimes causes trouble is that many lists for some reason allow messages to be sent only from people whose addresses appear on the list. This becomes a pain if your mailing address changes. Suppose that you get a well-organized new mail administrator, and your official e-mail address changes from jj@shamu.pol.ntw.org to John.Jay@ntw.org, although your old address still works. You may find that some lists begin *bouncing* your messages (sending them back to you rather than to the list) because they don't understand that John.Jay@ntw.org, the name under which you now send messages, is the same as jj@shamu.pol.ntw.org, the name under which you originally subscribed to the list. Worse, LISTSERV doesn't let you take yourself off the list for the same reason. To resolve this mess, you have to write to the human list owners of any lists in which this problem arises and ask them to fix the problem by hand.

Replying to Mailing-List Messages

Lots of times you receive an interesting message from a list and want to respond to it. But when you send your answer, does it go *just* to the person who sent the original message, or does it go to the *entire list?* It depends, mostly on how the list owner set up the software that handles the list. About half the list owners set it up so that replies automatically go just to the person who sent the original message, on the theory that your response is likely to be of interest only to the original author. The other half set it up so that replies go to the entire list, on the theory that the list is like a running public discussion. In messages coming from the list, the mailing-list software automatically sets the Reply-To: header to the address where replies should be sent.

Fortunately, you're in charge. When you start to create a reply, your mail program should show you the address it's replying to. If you don't like the address it's using, change it. If you're using UNIX's hoary mail program, type **~h** to change the headers, including the To: address. If you're using some other mail program, a menu option should allow you to fix the headers, or in Windows you only have to click in the To: field and correct the address.

While you're fixing the recipient's address, you may also want to fix the `Subject:` line. After a few rounds of replies to replies to replies, the topic of discussion often wanders away from the original topic, and it is nice to change the subject to better describe what is really under discussion.

Some Interesting Lists

A great many lists reside on the Internet — so many, in fact, that entire *books* have been written that just enumerate all the *lists*. So, to get you started, here are a bunch of lists that we find interesting, along with short descriptions of what they are. Each is accompanied by at least one of the following codes, describing what kind of list it is:

- ✔ **Internet:** Internet-type list. To get on or off or to contact the human who maintains the list, write to `whatever-request@sitename`.

- ✔ **LISTSERV:** BITNET LISTSERV-type list. To get on or off, send a stylized "subscribe" or "unsubscribe" message to `LISTSERV@sitename`. To contact the relevant human, send mail to `owner-whatever@sitename`.

- ✔ **Majordomo:** A Majordomo list. To get on or off, send a "subscribe" or "unsubscribe" message to `Majordomo@sitename`.

- ✔ **Moderated:** Moderated list. Messages are filtered by the human list owner (moderator).

- ✔ **News:** List is also available as Usenet News, which is usually the best way to receive it Nearly all BITNET lists are also available as a special kind of newsgroup, so this marks only lists available as regular news. (See Chapter 11.)

- ✔ **Digest:** Messages normally arrive as a digest rather than one at a time.

Telecom Digest
telecom-request@eecs.nwu.edu
Internet, Moderated, News, Digest

Discussions of telephones ranging from the technical to the totally silly, like what the official telephone song should be. This is a heavily moderated, high-volume list with the only full-time moderator on the net.

Risks Digest
risks-request@csl.sri.com
Internet, Moderated, News, Digest

Forum on risks to the public in computers systems. Discusses the risks of modern technology, particularly computer technology. Great war stories.

Weather Talk
LISTSERV@vmd.cso.uiuc.edu
LISTSERV (list names below), Moderated

Weather discussions. Fairly technical. If you join WX-TALK, that's the discussion list. There are also several announcement-only lists that send out National Weather Service forecasts and reports. WX-NATNL is the nationwide forecasts delivered twice daily, which is probably more weather than you want in your mailbox unless you have some way to sort it out and discard it automatically after a day or two. Other Weather Service bulletins are:

- **WX-SWO:** For severe weather warnings in nearly incomprehensible weather shorthand
- **WX-WATCH:** For tornado and thunderstorm watches, also in shorthand
- **WX-WSTAT:** For other weather watches, in shorthand
- **WX-TROPL:** For daily tropical storm and hurricane outlooks
- **WX-PCPN:** For heavy rain and snow reports
- **WX-SUM:** For the national weather summary
- **WX-STLT:** For satellite observations
- **WX-LSR:** For local storm reports
- **WX-MISC:** For other weather bureau reports

Subscribe to them all and your mailbox will fill so fast that your head will swim. If you just want to check the weather now and then, see Chapter 15.

Privacy Forum Digest
privacy-request@vortex.com
Internet, Moderated

A running discussion of privacy in the computer age. Lots of creepy reports about people and organizations you would never expect were snooping on you (ambulance drivers, for example).

Tourism Discussions
LISTSERV@trearn.bitnet
LISTSERV (list name TRAVEL-L)

The TRAVEL-L list covers travel and tourism, airlines, guidebooks, places to stay — you name it. Participants come from all over the world (the system host is in France), so you get lots of tips you would never get locally.

Frequent Flyers
frequent-flyer-request@ames.arc.nasa.gov
Internet

`Frequent-flyer` is for and about frequent air travelers. It has lots of tips and war stories. Neophytes are welcome to join and listen in, but this isn't the right place to ask "How do I buy a plane ticket from New York to Chicago?"

Info-IBMPC Digest
info-ibmpc-request@brl.mil
Internet, Moderated, Digest

Moderately technical discussions of using, programming, and maintaining IBM PCs and clones. If you have access to Usenet, the Usenet equivalents are better.

Computer Professionals for Social Responsibility
LISTSERV@gwuvm.bitnet
LISTSERV (list name CPSR)

CPSR is an organization of computer people interested in the social effects of computing. This list mostly contains reports about CPSR activities.

Offroad Enthusiasts
offroad-request@ai.gtri.gatech.edu
Internet

The `offroad` list is partly about off-road driving, and mostly about four-wheel-drive vehicles. Full of fun-lovers.

White House Press Releases
clinton-info@campaign92.org
Moderated

Press releases and transcripts of press conferences direct from the White House. (A lot goes on at a press conference that they don't bother to report in the paper.) Subscribing is a little different from other lists: Send a message to `Clinton-Info@campaign92.org` containing the word *help,* and it sends back a subscription form for you to edit and return. This service was set up during the 1992 presidential campaign, hence the mailing address, but it proved so popular that it continued after the inauguration.

Compilers and Language Processors
compil-l@american.edu
Moderated, News, LISTSERV (list name COMPIL-L)

A totally technoid list about programs that translate one computer language into another. John moderates it, so of course he thinks that it's totally fascinating. (Your mileage may vary.)

Commercializing and Privatizing the Internet
majordomo@mcs.net
Majordomo (list name com-priv)

A running discussion of topics relating to the Internet's evolution from a government-sponsored research network into a privately operated, largely commercial network. Argumentative.

The HOTT (Hot Off The Tree) List
listserv@ucsd.edu
Moderated, LISTSERV (list name HOTT-LIST)

HOTT is a popular list (something like 100,000 subscribers) that is scheduled to come out every five weeks with summaries of interesting computer-related news from an enormous set of news services and publications. As of mid-1994, there had been only one issue, but the editors promise that by the time you read this, they'll be back on schedule.

Note: UCSD uses a mutant version of LISTSERV which requires that you do *not* include your name following SUBSCRIBE HOTT-LIST.

Finding Other Mailing Lists

SRI in Los Angeles keeps the *list of lists,* a long listing of Internet mailing lists. To get a copy by e-mail (Danger: It's really big, about 30,000 lines of text — so big that many mail systems can't handle it), send a message to mail-server@nisc.sri.com containing this line:

```
send netinfo/interest-groups
```

If you have access to FTP (see Chapter 16), you can more easily FTP it from ftp.nisc.sri.com, where it is called netinfo/interest-groups and a compressed version is called netinfo/interest-groups.Z. You can also buy it neatly printed and indexed as a book called *Internet: Mailing Lists,* edited by Edward T. L. Hardie and Vivian Neou (PTR Prentice Hall, 1993), although the book seems kind of pricey compared to getting the material on-line.

The Usenet group news.lists also has an extensive monthly list of mailing lists. If you get Usenet news, you can probably find this list there (see Chapter 11). Or you can get it by mail by sending this cryptic message to mail-server@rtfm.mit.edu:

```
send USENET/news.lists/P_A_M_L,_P_1_12
send USENET/news.lists/P_A_M_L,_P_2_12
```

(That last weird part stands for Publicly Accessible Mailing Lists, Part 1 of 12, and so forth. If you like what you see, you can get the rest of the parts the same way.) FTP users can FTP the list from rtfm.mit.edu, where it's in the directory pub/USENET/news.lists under the same names, or read it in Usenet where it's posted monthly to the newsgroup news.lists. The lists are growing fast, so by the time you read this, there may be more than 12 parts.

Chapter 11

Using Network News

● ●

In This Chapter

▶ What and why is net news?

▶ How to navigate around net news

● ●

All the News That Fits and More

Mailing lists are an okay way to send messages to a small number of people, but they're a lousy way to send messages to a large number of people. For one thing, just maintaining a big list with thousands of people is a great deal of work for a list manager, even if you automate most of it with something like LISTSERV, which we discussed in Chapter 10. For another thing, just shipping the contents of messages to thousands and thousands of addresses puts a huge load on the system that sends them out.

Usenet (also referred to by the name of the system that manages and transports its messages, *net news*) solves that problem and creates a whole host of others. Usenet is a very large, distributed *BBS (bulletin board system)*. The principle is simple: Every Usenet site ships a copy of all *articles* (news-speak for *messages*) it has received to all its neighbors several times a day. (To avoid wasted effort, each article contains a list of sites it's already been sent to.) News articles slosh around to nearly every directly connected Usenet site within a day or two of being sent. If your machine is directly on the Internet rather than connected over the phone, most news arrives within a few hours.

We assume that your local news system is set up and running (if not, persuade your system administrator to set it up), so a pile of news presumably is already waiting for you to read. Three Important News Skills:

✔ How to read the news that interests you

✔ How not to read the news that doesn't interest you, because far more news is sent every day than any single human could ever read

✔ How to post articles of your own (definitely optional)

Being a Newsgroupie

Every day more than 30,000 articles appear at a typical, well-connected news machine. To make it possible to sort through this mass of stuff, all items are assigned to *newsgroups,* which are topic headings. In all, several thousand newsgroups exist, ranging from the staid and technical to the totally goofy. Most news users pick a small number of groups to read and ignore the rest.

You can easily *subscribe* and *unsubscribe* to any group received by your machine — unlike getting on and off mailing lists, newsgroups just require an update to a local file. Many people begin reading a group by looking at a few articles and then stop reading it if it looks boring. Depending on how much time you plan to spend reading news, you may add groups when you're less busy and then drop all but the ones directly related to work when the crunch hits.

The newsgroup thicket

If you're eager to begin using news, you can skip this section and come back to it later when you want to refine your newsreading skills.

Newsgroups have multipart names separated by dots, as in `comp.dcom.fax` (a group devoted to fax machines and fax modems). The plan is that newsgroups are arranged into *hierarchies.* The first part of the name describes the general kind of newsgroup. When a bunch of newsgroups are related, their names are related too. So, for example, all the newsgroups having to do with data communication are filed as `comp.dcom.something`. Here are the top-level names of the *official* Usenet hierarchies distributed to nearly every news site:

- ✔ **comp:** Topics relating to computers (lots of fairly meaty discussions)
- ✔ **sci:** Topics relating to one of the sciences (also fairly meaty)
- ✔ **rec:** Recreational (sports, hobbies, the arts, and other fun endeavors)
- ✔ **soc:** Social newsgroups (both social interests and plain socializing)
- ✔ **news:** Topics having to do with net news itself (a few groups with introductory material and announcements should be read by everyone — otherwise, not very interesting unless you're a news *weenie*)
- ✔ **misc:** Miscellaneous topics that don't fit anywhere else (the ultimate miscellaneous newsgroup is called `misc.misc`)
- ✔ **talk:** Long arguments, frequently political (widely considered to be totally uninteresting except to the participants)

Note: Lots of less widely distributed — or less widely sanctioned — sets of newsgroups are mentioned in the next chapter.

Where did Usenet come from?

Usenet came from North Carolina originally. In 1980, two students came up with the first version to run on a couple of UNIX machines. Their original version, now known as *A*news, seemed pretty cool because it could transfer as many as a dozen articles a day from one machine to another by using a networking scheme called UUCP (UNIX-to-UNIX Copy), which is a clunky but reliable dial-up communications program that comes with all UNIX systems. Within a few years, Usenet had spread to several other universities and several software companies in a completely rewritten version called *B* news, then transferring as many as a thousand messages a day. Usenet was established enough to be featured in an article in the October 1983 issue of *Byte* magazine, which boasted that more than 500 news sites were in existence. (John can't resist pointing out that his site was called `ima` — you can find it near the upper right corner of the network map on page 224 of the issue.)

Throughout the ensuing decade, Usenet has spread like a disease. Now more than 30,000 sites send out news, and probably at least that many more sites just read it. Most of the original dial-up links have been replaced by permanently connected Internet network links using a communi-cation scheme called *NNTP,* for *Net News Transfer Protocol.* (And you thought that all acronyms were obscure.) A great deal of news is still sent over the telephone by way of UUCP, but an increasing amount of it is sent by way of exotic means, including satellite (using a spare channel that belongs to a national beeper company), CD-ROM, and even magnetic tapes (the tapes are sent to such countries as Malaysia, where long modem phone calls are impractical, and also to such places as the FBI, where internal computer users are prohibited from connecting to outside networks).

The volume of news has increased from a few hundred articles per day in 1983 to upward of 50,000 articles (more than 100MB of text) per day now. And Usenet is still growing.

Many sites still use B news, even though its own authors officially pronounced it dead more than five years ago. Current news systems include *C news,* which is a faster, more maintainable, complete rewrite of B news, and INN, a new version designed to work well in Internet networked environments. Fortunately, they all function pretty much the same way, so for the most part you don't have to worry about which version you're using.

Regional groups

All the mainstream groups, in theory at least, are of interest to people regardless of where they live. But many topics are quite specific to a particular place. Suppose that you live near Boston and you want recommendations of restaurants where you can take small children and not be snarled at (this topic came up recently). Although some `rec` newsgroups discuss food, most readers are likely to be nowhere near Boston, and you're likely to get more snappy comments than useful tips (for example, someone in Texas may note that if you don't mind driving to Dallas for dinner, you can find one there).

Fortunately, local and regional groups exist for local and regional discussions. An ne hierarchy for topics of interest to New England includes such groups as ne.food, which is just the place to ask about kiddie restaurants. State and regional hierarchies exist for most places that have enough Usenet sites to make it worthwhile: ny for New York, ba for the San Francisco Bay Area, and so on.

Universities and other organizations big enough to have a great deal of net news users often have hierarchies of their own, such as mit for MIT. Many companies have their own local sets of newsgroups for announcements and discussions about company matters. At a software company where one of us used to work, for example, every time someone logged in a change to one of our programs, the description of the change was sent out as a local news item so that everyone else could keep up with what was changing. Naturally, local company groups are sent around only within the company. Ask around to find out what organization or regional newsgroups your system gets, because it's basically up to your system manager to decide what to get.

Hand-to-Hand Combat with News

Okay, you're probably dying to try out news for yourself. (If you're not, you may as well skip ahead to Chapter 13.) Net news is designed so that anyone who wants to can write a new newsreading program, so many people have done so. Here we look mostly at two UNIX news programs called trn and its predecessor rn, which are the most widely used.

If you're using a PC to dial in to your Internet provider, remember that even though you're not running UNIX, your provider probably is, so this discussion of newsreading applies to you.

All newsreading programs do pretty much the same thing (they let you read news — what did you expect?), so most of them work in more or less the same way, give or take differences in the appearance of the screen and a few command letters. All news programs are written to be more or less full screen, although (as you will see) some of them take advantage of the screen better than others. They're all designed to enable you to flip though news as quickly as possible (because there's so much of it), so they all use single-letter commands, which are a pain to remember, of course, until you get used to them.

In nearly all newsreading programs, you don't have to press Enter after single-letter commands. Some commands, however, require that you type a line of text after the letter, such as a filename or a newsgroup name. In that case, you *do* press Enter to tell the program that you're finished with the line of text.

You start the newsreading program by typing **trn** (or if that doesn't work, **rn**). You should soon see something like this:

```
% trn
Trying to set up a .newsrc file
running newsetup...
Creating .newsrc in /usr/johnl to be used by news programs.
Done. If you have never used the news system before, you may
find the articles in news.announce.newusers to be helpful.
There is also a manual entry for rn. To get rid of newsgroups
you aren't interested in, use the 'u' command.
Type h for help at any time while running rn.
Unread news in general                              14 articles
(Revising soft pointers—be patient.)
Unread news in ne.food                              47 articles
Unread news in ne.forsale                         1177 articles
Unread news in ne.general                          268 articles
Unread news in ne.housing                          248 articles
etc.
********  14 unread articles in general—read now? [+ynq]
```

If the program complains that it cannot find either trn or rn, you have to ask for help to find out what the local news reader of choice is. Microsoft Windows users often have a program called Trumpet, which we discuss later and which uses a typical Windows screen interface to handle news. Even if you aren't using trn or rn, it's probably worth your while to look through the rest of this chapter because what you do with news is the same even if the exact keys you type are different.

Assuming that you manage to start trn or rn, it tells you that it sees that you've never used news before, so it's creating a file called .newsrc (yes, it starts with a dot, and you don't really want to know why), which it uses to keep track of which articles you've already seen. Then, in a fit of wild optimism, it guesses that you want to subscribe to every single newsgroup available on your system. Naturally, the list of newsgroups it shows depends on what's available on your system.

First things first: When you're tired of reading news, you leave it by pressing q (for quit). Depending on where you are, you may need to press it two or three times, but you can always q your way out.

Assuming that you're not ready to give up yet, trn or rn now goes through all the newsgroups. For each group, you basically have three choices: You can look at its articles now, you can choose to not look now but maybe come back later, or you can unsubscribe so that you never see that newsgroup again unless you specifically resubscribe. Press y to say yes (you want to read the newsgroup), n to skip it for now, or u to unsubscribe and never see the group again. (Of course, there's also q to quit trn or rn.)

If you press y, trn displays the first screen of the first unread article in the newsgroup general, which is the group for articles that are theoretically of interest to users of your machine only. (In practice, general tends to fill up with junk.)

While you're looking at an article, you again have a bunch of choices. If the article is more than one screenful, pressing the spacebar advances to the next screen, much like the familiar more and pg commands. If you're done looking at the article, press n to go on to the next article or q to leave the newsgroup and go on to the next newsgroup. If you find an article to be totally uninteresting, you can skip both the rest of that article and any other articles in the newsgroup that have the same boring title by pressing k (for kill). You can arrange to have articles with known boring titles killed every time you enter a newsgroup (see the sidebar "Arrgh! It's a kill file," later in this chapter).

After you get the hang of it, you mostly press the spacebar to go to the next article or newsgroup, n to skip to the next article or newsgroup, and k to skip a group of articles. Until you prune down to something reasonable in the set of newsgroups you're subscribed to, you'll probably also be pressing u frequently to get rid of the large majority of groups you don't want to read.

Where do newsgroups come from? Where do they go?

Here are two things you need to know that are related to getting rid of newsgroups. The first is that new newsgroups appear several times a week because Usenet is still growing like crazy. Every time you run rn or trn, you have the opportunity to subscribe to any new newsgroups that have appeared. The trn or rn program asks a question like this:

```
Checking active list for new newsgroups...
Newsgroup alt.comp.hardware.homebuilt not in .newsrc-sub-
            scribe? [ynYN]
```

You can answer y if you do or n if you do not want to subscribe. If you press y, it asks you where in the list of newsgroups you want to see this one appear.

```
Put newsgroup where? [$^L]
```

The most likely answers to this question are $ (to put it at the end) or + followed by the name of an existing group (to put it after that group).

Eventually, you may also regret having unsubscribed to a newsgroup, in which case you want to turn it back on. If so, press g followed by the name of the group you want to see. If you have never subscribed to the group, rn or trn may ask you where in the list you want to put it and offer you the same choices ($ or +). You can also use g to go directly to a particular newsgroup.

Ignoring articles faster with trn

If you're using trn rather than rn, you have a better way to choose which articles you want to see and which ones you don't. The important difference between trn and rn is that trn supports *threads* (that's what the *t* stands for), which are groups of related articles. You can select or ignore a thread at a time rather than an article at a time.

Arrgh! It's a kill file

In most newsgroups, a bunch of running discussions go on, and some of those discussions are much more interesting than others. You can arrange to permanently ignore the uninteresting ones by using a *kill file*. When you're reading along and you encounter a hopelessly uninteresting article, press K (capital K, for *KILL!*) to kill all current articles with the same title and also to put the title into the kill file for the current newsgroup. In the future, whenever you enter that newsgroup, rn or trn checks for any new articles with titles in the kill file and automatically kills them so that you never see any of them. Using kill files can save a great deal of time and lets you concentrate on discussions that are actually interesting.

You can edit kill files to remove entries for discussions that have died down or to add other kinds of article-killing commands. If you press Ctrl-K while you're reading a newsgroup, it starts the text editor (usually vi or emacs on UNIX machines) on the group's kill file. Kill files look like this:

```
THRU 4765
/boring topic/j
```

```
/was George Harrison in another
   band before Wings?/j
```

The first line notes how many articles have been scanned for killable topics (to save time by not rescanning the entire group each time). Subsequent lines are topics you don't want to read. You remove a topic by deleting its line in the kill file. After you're finished, save the file, leave the editor, and you're back where you were reading news.

Sometimes you may also find that *certain people* write articles you never want to read. You can arrange to kill all the articles they write! Press Ctrl-K to edit the newsgroup's kill file and at the end add a line like this:

```
/Aaron Burr/h:j
```

Between the slashes, type the author's name as it appears in the `From:` line at the beginning of his articles. You don't have to type the entire contents of the `From:` line, just enough of it to uniquely identify the guy. At the end of the line, after the second slash, place the magic incantation `h:j`. Then save the kill file, exit the editor, and you're set. *Sayonara,* pal.

If you press spacebar or + to enter a newsgroup, you see a table of contents screen like the following, which shows the titles of the unread messages.

```
general                           14 articles
a 0000-uucp(0000)   3  New mail paths
b 0000-Admin(0000) 10  backup
c Chet Arthur        1  System down to clean hamster cages

Select threads — All [Z>] —
```

Again, this newsgroup is called general, the group that exists on every machine for local messages that don't belong anywhere else. There are 14 unread articles. To make it easier to choose what to read, trn groups together related articles based mostly on the titles. In this case, three articles are called New mail paths, ten are called backup, and one is about hamsters. The letters in the left column are key letters you press to choose articles to read. For example, you press c to see the article about the hamsters.

After you're finished picking interesting-looking articles, you have a few choices. You can press the spacebar to go on to the next page of the table of contents, if any, and begin reading selected articles if you've seen all the titles. Or you can press D (uppercase) to read the selected articles and kill any unselected articles on the screen (d is for delete). Or you can press Z (uppercase) to read any selected articles and *not* kill the unselected ones.

Honest, It's a Work of Art

Usenet allows exactly one kind of message: plain old text. (A few versions of news handle MIME messages, which we mentioned in Chapter 8, and there are versions for Japanese and Russian characters, but this chapter is confusing enough without worrying about them.) A few widely used conventions exist, though, for sneaking through other kinds of files.

Binary files

Some newsgroups consist partly or entirely of encoded binary files, most often executable programs for IBM PCs, Macs, or other personal computers, or GIF or JPEG bitmap files (see Chapter 17 for details on file formats) of, um, artistic images. (If you must know, the newsgroup with the largest amount of traffic, measured in megabytes per day, is called alt.binaries.pictures.erotica, and it contains exactly what it sounds like. It's an equal-opportunity group — it

has about the same number of pictures of unclad men as of unclad women.)
The usual way to pass around binary files of whatever type is called *uuencode*.
You can recognize uuencoded messages because they start with a `begin` line
followed by lines of what looks like garbage, as in the following:

```
begin plugh.gif 644
M390GNM4L-REP3PT45G0OI-O5[I5-6M3OME,MRMK76OPI5LPTMETLMKPY
MEOT39I4905BO5YOPV3OIXKRTL5KWLJROJTOU,
6P5;3;MRUO5OI4J5OI4
```

You unscramble this with a program called uudecode. Fortunately, rn and trn
have a built-in decoder you can invoke by pressing e (for extract). For *really* big
files, it's customary to split the uuencoded file among several articles. Extract
is smart enough to handle this if you press e for each article in sequence.

Groups of files

Sometimes an article contains a group of files. These are packed up as *shell
archive* or *shar* files, which are UNIX shell (command language) scripts that,
when executed, re-create the desired files. Shar files usually start something like
this:

```
-cut here-
        # This is a shar file created on 4 Jul 1826 ...
```

You can also extract shar files with the trn or rn e command, just like
uuencoded messages. (It figures out which kind of message it is.)

Be aware that shar files are a horrendous *trojan horse* loophole (a way for a bad
guy to run his program but make it act as though you had done it) because a
shar file can contain any command you can type from the terminal. In the worst
case, it can delete all your files, send obscene e-mail with your signature, and so
on. In the past, prank shar files haven't been much of a problem, but it's worth
it to be a little skeptical. For the acutely apprehensive, shar-sanitizing programs
are available (your system administrator should have one handy that comes
with C news) that can scan a shar article, looking for suspicious commands.

Just a few notes for our files

Now and then an article is so interesting that you want to save it for posterity.
You save it with the s (for save) command. To save an article, press s followed
by the name of the file in which you want to save it. If the file doesn't already
exist, rn or trn asks you whether it should format the file as a plain file or a

mailbox (a special kind of file that usually contains mail messages). Usually, you should save it as a mailbox. If you save several articles into the same mailbox file, you can later use mail programs to review and change the contents of the mailbox. Saved files (or mailboxes) are put in your `News` directory, unless you give a different directory to the s command.

You can also save an article and pass it to a program. To do so, press | (vertical bar) rather than s and follow it with the command you want to execute. This choice is most often useful for printing a message by making the command `lpr` or `lp` or whatever your local print command is. UNIX pipelines, which pass the results of one program as input to the next are also permitted, as in

```
|pr -h "An important message" | lpr
```

A trn and rn cheat sheet

By this point, you've probably lost track of all the keys that control trn and rn. Here's a summary of the keys described in this chapter, along with a few others you might want to try. The rn program can be in two different *states: newsgroup state* (see Table 11-1), in which you pick which group to read, and *article state* (see Table 11-2), in which you're in a particular group and are looking at articles. The trn program adds a third state, the *table of contents state* (see Table 11-3), in which you're looking at a list of titles of unread articles in a group.

Table 11-1	Newsgroup State
Key	*Meaning*
Spacebar	Enter the next group that has unread news
y	Same as spacebar
n	Skip this group
u	Unsubscribe from this group so that you won't see it anymore
g	Go to a group, and type the group name after the g; if you're unsubscribed to the group, it resubscribes you
q	Quit, leave news
p	Go to the previous group with unread news
h	Show extremely concise help
^L	Redraw screen

Don't say we didn't warn you

You may occasionally find an article that is just plain gibberish, neither uuencoded nor a shar file (see the section, "Honest, It's a Work of Art," earlier in this chapter). Such articles use the infamous *rot13 cipher*. Rot13 is a simple-minded scheme that replaces each letter of the alphabet with the letter that is 13 places ahead of or behind it. For example, A turns into N and vice versa, B turns into O, and so on. This isn't a very secure code (we believe that it was cracked about 2,000 years ago by the Carthaginians), but it's not supposed to be.

The point of rot13 is to warn you that a message contains rude words or something else gross and offensive, so you shouldn't read it if you think that you may be offended. If you want to read it anyway, press X (uppercase) to get rn or trn to unscramble it.

Don't expect much sympathy if you complain about an offensive rot13 message. After all, you didn't have to read it.

Table 11-2	Article State
Key	**Meaning**
Spacebar	Read the next page of the current article, or the next unread article
n	Skip to the next article
k	Kill this article and any others with the same title
K	Same as k; also enters the title in the kill file so that the title is rekilled each time you enter the group
q	Leave this group
c	Catch up and pretend that you've read all articles in this group
u	Unsubscribe
spdq	Save article to file pdq
llpr	Feed (I) article to command lpr (easiest way to print an article)
/xyz	Find the next article whose title contains xyz
=	Show titles of unread articles
^L	Redraw screen
^R	Restart current article (redraws first page)
X	Unscramble rot13 message (not for the squeamish)
e	Extract uudecoded or shar file

(continued)

Table 11-2 *(continued)*

Key	Meaning
edir	Extract into directory dir
h	Show extremely concise help
q	Leave this group

Table 11-3 **Table of Contents State**

Key	Meaning
Spacebar	Read the next page of the table of contents, or start reading selected articles if there's no more TOC
d	Begin reading selected articles, and mark unselected articles as read
z	Read selected articles
/xyz	Select articles whose titles contain xyz
c-g	Select articles c through g in the current TOC
h	Show extremely concise help
q	Leave this group

Most letters and digits are used to mark articles to select.

The quick-reference manual entry for trn is 25 pages long, so it has many more commands. But you should be able to get along with just these.

What's in a Number?

Every Usenet message has a *message ID,* which is supposed to be different from the message ID of any other message ever, from the beginning to the end of time. (These people thought big.) A typical message ID looks like this:

```
<1994Jul9.055259.15278@chico.iecc.com>
```

The part after the @ is the name of the site where the article originated, and the part before the @ is some garbage made up to be unique and usually includes the date, time, phase of moon, and so on.

Messages also have numbers, which are assigned in order at each newsgroup as articles arrive. So the first message in comp.fooble is number 1, the second is number 2, and so on.

An important difference distinguishes the IDs and the numbers: The IDs are the same everywhere, but the numbers apply to only *your local system*. So don't refer to articles' message numbers when you write a response because people at other sites won't be able to tell which articles you mean.

If you use the rn or trn f or F commands to write a follow-up article, they automatically stick in a line that begins with `References:`, which has the message ID of the original article, along with any articles it in turn referenced. Trn uses the references to gather articles into related threads.

So You Want To Be Famous?

Sooner or later, unless you are an extraordinarily reticent person, you will want to send out some messages of your own so that people all over the world can at last find out just how clever you are. (This can be a mixed blessing, of course.) In this section, we look first at how you respond to an existing message and then take the plunge, writing an all-new message from scratch.

That's a Roger, Roger

The easiest and usually most appropriate way to respond to an article is to send e-mail to its author in case you want to ask a question or offer a comment. You can send e-mail by pressing r or R. In either case, rn or trn pops you into a text editor, where you can compose your message. The file you're given to edit contains header lines for the e-mail message, notably `Subject:` and `To:`, which you can edit if you want. The difference between r and R is that the uppercase R command also puts a copy of the text of the article into the message so that you can quote parts of it. Edit out irrelevant parts of the quoted article, keeping in mind that the author already knows what he or she said.

I'll follow you anywhere

If you have a comment on an article that is of general interest, you can post it as a Usenet article by using the f or F (follow-up) keys. The program asks you whether you're sure that you want to send a Usenet follow-up. If you respond that you are sure, you are popped into the editor, where you can compose your message. Uppercase F includes a copy of the original message, which you should again edit down to the minimum.

Give me a sign

Whenever you post an article, if a file called *.signature* exists in your home directory, the news system appends the file's contents to your article. Your .signature file should contain your name, e-mail address, and anything else you feel is relevant — so long as it all fits in no more than three lines. Some people have huge, fancy, 20-line signatures that are never as clever as they think they are. Keep it to three lines. **Note:** Many news systems enforce the three-line limit by including only the first three lines of the file, no matter how long it is.

You don't have to copy your .signature file into messages you send because the news-sending program adds it automatically. If you *do* include it yourself, your message will have two copies of your signature, which looks tacky and marks you as a rank amateur. You wouldn't want that to happen.

Many news systems reject messages that contain more quoted text than new material to discourage lazy typists who quote an entire 100-line message to add a two-line comment. Some people are under the peculiar impression that if an article is rejected with too much quoted text, they should add garbage lines at the end to pad out the unquoted part. *Don't ever do that.* It instantly marks you as a pompous ass. Edit down the text — your readers will thank you.

After you leave the editor, it again asks whether you want to send the article, edit it again, or abort. Press the appropriate key (s, e, or a).

When you send your follow-up, in most cases the article is posted either immediately or in a few minutes (the next time a background posting program runs). Some groups are moderated, which means your message is mailed to the group's moderator, who posts it if it meets the group's guidelines. Moderators are all volunteers, and all have work to do other than run their moderated groups, so it may take a while for your message to appear. Most moderators handle messages every day or two, but the slowest ones can take as long as two weeks. Remember: Patience is a virtue. As a newsgroup moderator (he runs one called `comp.compilers`, which discusses techniques of translating one computer language to another), one of the authors of this book can assure you that writing cranky letters to a moderator — in which you complain that it's taking too long to process your pearls of wisdom — is utterly counterproductive.

First Past the Post

The final topic we discuss in this chapter is how to send an all-new news article. You send your article with the *Pnews* command. You can either run Pnews directly from the UNIX command line or you can press period and then F when trn asks you something like `1 unread article in rec.food.restaurants — read now? [+ynq]`. When you run Pnews, it asks you a few questions. The first, if you ran it directly rather than from inside trn, is the name of the newsgroup or newsgroups. (You can post a single article to several groups at a time if it's appropriate.) Type the name of the group or groups (separate them with commas). It asks for the subject of the message and then for the distribution (see the following section, "Distributions Are Your Friends") with a suggested default. Then it asks once more whether you're absolutely, positively certain that you want to post an article, and if you say yes, it puts you into the text editor. From then on, it's just like you're sending a follow-up article (discussed earlier in this chapter).

Distributions Are Your Friends

Even though Usenet is a worldwide network, many times you're posting an article that doesn't really need to go to the whole world. For example, if you're posting something to `misc.forsale.computers` to advertise an old disk drive you want to sell, and you're in the United States, there's no point in sending the article outside the country. Usenet distributions enable you to limit where an article is sent. A line like the following in your article header limits its distribution to the United States:

```
Distribution: usa
```

If you're sending a new article using Pnews, you're asked which distribution to use. If you're sending a follow-up, the news system guesses that you want to use the same distribution the original article did. In either case, you can edit the `Distribution:` line in the message yourself as necessary.

A long list of possible distributions exists. Some commonly used distributions are shown in this list:

- ✔ **world:** Everywhere (default)
- ✔ **na:** North America
- ✔ **usa:** United States
- ✔ **can:** Canada
- ✔ **uk:** United Kingdom
- ✔ **ne:** New England
- ✔ **ba:** Bay Area (California)

TIP

Dying boy makes mailing list about modem tax

Back in Chapter 8, a sidebar lists well-known topics about which you should never, *never,* write to any mailing list. The same warning applies to Usenet news. For review, the top three topics to not write about are the following:

✔ Dying boy wants cards to set Guinness world record

✔ FCC will pass modem tax and impoverish us all

✔ Make big bucks with a chain letter

See Chapter 8 for details on why nobody wants to hear about any of these things.

All the regional hierarchy names, such as ne, ny, uk, ba, and so on, are also used as distributions. (People occasionally use worldwide hierarchy names such as comp and rec as distributions by

mistake — that doesn't do anything useful.)

Unless you're sure that people on the other side of the world will be as fascinated by what you say as people next door, you should use the smallest appropriate distribution for any articles you post, both originals and follow-ups.

In practice, distributions are pretty leaky, and articles often get sent to places the distribution says that they shouldn't go, due to peculiarities in the way news is passed from one system to the next. But it's a courtesy to faraway readers to at least *try* to avoid sending articles to places where the articles are not interesting. Keep in mind that international phone links are expensive, so if you avoid sending an article to countries where people aren't interested, you can save people some money.

Ta-Daa!

One area in which Windows newsreading differs from UNIX newsreading is that Windows machines never store the news locally. (You can keep copies of interesting articles locally, but the bulk of the news lives elsewhere.) If your PC has a fast permanent network connection such as an Ethernet, this doesn't have much effect, but if you have a dial-up SLIP or PPP link, the network discussions between your PC and the host where the news is can take a while when you move from one newsgroup to another.

The most popular Windows news program is called Trumpet, a shareware program written by Peter Tattam, at the University of Tasmania, Australia. Getting Trumpet installed is a pain, so we'll assume that someone has set it up for you already. If not, grab some cookies and ask a guru to do so. If you are stuck in a guru-free environment, see Chapter 11 of *MORE Internet For Dummies,* by John R. Levine and Margaret Levine Young (IDG Books, 1994).

Reading news with Trumpet

When you start up Trumpet, you should see a screen something like the one in Figure 11-1. The top part lists all the newsgroups you can read. There are many more newsgroups than fit in that window, so you can use the scrollbar to see the rest of them. When you find one you like, double-click it. This tells Trumpet to get from the news server all the subject lines of unread news articles in that group. (If it's a large group and you have a slow connection, this process can take a few minutes.) Trumpet shows the list of articles in the bottom half of the window, as shown in Figure 11-2.

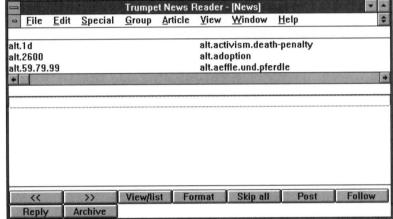

Figure 11-1:
A blast of
Trumpet.

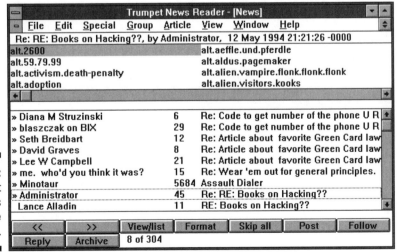

Figure 11-2:
Trumpet
proclaims
the article
subjects.

Reading an article is easy. Just double-click its line in the list of subjects. After you have an article on the screen, there are many things you can do:

- ✔ Click the << or >> buttons to see the preceding or next article. If you're looking at the last article in the group, it goes on to the next group.
- ✔ Click View/List to switch back to the list of article titles.
- ✔ Click Skip all to skip to the next group.
- ✔ Click on Reply or Follow to e-mail the author or post a follow-up.
- ✔ Click on Archive to save an archival copy of the message in a mail folder. (Trumpet also acts as a mail program.)

Other Trumpet tricks

Trumpet is a complex enough program to deserve a chapter of its own. (Indeed, it has one in *MORE Internet For Dummies.*)

Fortunately (and amazingly for a shareware program), it comes with a rather good help file. If you don't have a copy of *MORE Internet For Dummies* yet, choose Help⇨Procedures from the Trumpet menu for some short but understandable descriptions of the other things you can do with Trumpet.

Chapter 12

A Sampler of
Network News Resources

In This Chapter
▶ Favorite groups
▶ Standard and not-so-standard hierarchies
▶ Lots of news groups

So What Is There to Read Already?

Now that you have learned all about how to read and write Usenet news in Chapter 11, the only little detail remaining is to figure out what there is to read. This chapter lists some of the more interesting groups that exist as of mid-1994. Remember that new groups appear practically every day, old groups occasionally go away, and system managers can reject any groups they want to for lack of interest or other reasons. First we present some popular groups to get you acquainted with the mainstream hierarchies. Then you learn about hierarchies that are a tad more obscure. And finally, Tables 12-1 through 12-6 list numerous groups in the various hierarchies that you may want to explore.

Groups

Here are a few groups you may want to start with:

news.announce.newusers

Every new user should at least skim this group, which contains introductory material for new news users. One of the messages is pretty funny, but you have to read them to find out which one.

news.answers

This contains all the periodic (weekly and monthly, mostly) postings to all the groups on the net. Many of these have evolved into pithy and well-written introductions to their subjects. When you want to learn something fast about something that might have been discussed on the net, start here.

rec.humor.funny

This highly competitive, moderated group contains jokes, most of which are pretty funny. Compare to `rec.humor`, which contains articles that the authors think are funny but that usually aren't.

comp.risks

The *Risks Digest* (same digest that was discussed in Chapter 10 as a mailing list) has lots of swell war stories of computer screw-ups.

comp.compilers

John thinks it's interesting, but then he's the moderator.

alt.sex

Everybody reads it, but nobody admits to doing so. We certainly don't.

On Computers, about Computers

Traditionally, the largest set of newsgroups has been the computer-related ones under the hierarchy `comp` (many of which are listed in Table 12-1). It's not surprising: If you listen in on ham radio conversations, you realize that they're mostly about ham radio. So you may expect that when people used computers to create Usenet, they mostly talked about computers.

The `comp` groups can tend toward the esoteric and the technoid, but they're also a treasure trove when your computer acts up and you need advice from people who have seen it all before.

Many groups offer usable computer programs. The ones under `comp.binaries` are the places to look for free programs for PCs, Macs, and other systems.

Table 12-1	Groups in the Comp Hierarchy
Name	**Discussion**
comp.ai	Artificial-intelligence
comp.ai.nat-lang	Natural language processing by computers
comp.ai.neural-nets	All aspects of neural networks
comp.ai.philosophy	Philosophical aspects of artificial intelligence
comp.ai.shells	Artificial intelligence applied to shells
comp.answers	Repository for periodic Usenet articles (moderated)
comp.apps.spreadsheets	Spreadsheets on various platforms
comp.arch	Computer architecture
comp.arch.storage	Storage system issues, both hardware and software
comp.archives	Descriptions of public-access archives (moderated)
comp.archives.admin	Issues relating to computer archive administration
comp.bbs.misc	All aspects of computer bulletin board systems
comp.bbs.waffle	The Waffle BBS and Usenet system on all platforms
comp.benchmarks	Benchmarking techniques and results
comp.binaries.apple2	Binary-only postings for the Apple II computer
comp.binaries.atari.st	Binary-only postings for the Atari ST (moderated)
comp.binaries.ibm.pc	Binary-only postings for IBM PC and MS-DOS (moderated)
comp.binaries.ibm.pc.d	IBM PC binary postings
comp.binaries.ibm.pc.wanted	Requests for IBM PC and compatible programs
comp.binaries.mac	Encoded Macintosh programs in binary (moderated)
comp.binaries.ms-windows	Binary programs for Microsoft Windows (moderated)
comp.binaries.os2	Binaries for use under the OS/2 ABI (moderated)

(continued)

Table 12-1 *(continued)*

Name	Discussion
comp.cog-eng	Cognitive engineering
comp.compilers	Compiler construction, theory, and so on (moderated)
comp.compression	Data-compression algorithms and theory
comp.databases	Database- and data-management issues and theory
comp.dcom.fax	Fax hardware, software, and protocols
comp.dcom.lans.ethernet	Ethernet/IEEE 802.3 protocols
comp.dcom.modems	Data communications hardware and software
comp.dcom.servers	Choosing and operating data communications servers
comp.dcom.telecom	Telecommunications digest (moderated)
comp.doc	Archived public-domain documentation (moderated)
comp.doc.techreports	Lists of technical reports (moderated)
comp.dsp	Digital-signal processing using computers
comp.edu	Computer-science education
comp.emacs	EMACS editors of different flavors
comp.fonts	Type fonts — design, conversion, use, and so on
comp.graphics	Computer graphics, art, animation, image processing
comp.human-factors	Issues related to human-computer interaction (HCI)
comp.infosystems	Any discussion about information systems
comp.infosystems.gis	All aspects of geographic information systems
comp.infosystems.gopher	The Gopher information service
comp.infosystems.wais	The Z39.50-based WAIS full-text search system
comp.infosystems.www	The World Wide Web information system
comp.internet.library	Electronic libraries (moderated)

Name	Discussion
comp.lang.c	C
comp.lang.c++	The object-oriented C++ language
comp.lang.fortran	FORTRAN
comp.lang.lisp	LISP
comp.misc	General topics about computers not covered elsewhere
comp.multimedia	Interactive multimedia technologies of all kinds
comp.newprod	Announcements of new products of interest (moderated)
comp.object	Object-oriented programming and languages
comp.os.ms-windows.advocacy	Speculation and debate about Microsoft Windows
comp.os.ms-windows.announce	Announcements relating to Windows (moderated)
comp.os.ms-windows.apps	Applications in the Windows environment
comp.os.ms-windows.misc	Windows issues
comp.os.ms-windows.programmer.misc	Programming Microsoft Windows
comp.os.ms-windows.programmer.tools	Development tools in Windows
comp.os.ms-windows.setup	Installing and configuring Microsoft Windows
comp.os.msdos.apps	Applications that run under MS-DOS
comp.parallel	Massively parallel hardware and software (moderated)
comp.patents	Patents of computer technology (moderated)
comp.periphs	Peripheral devices
comp.programming	Programming issues that transcend languages and OSs
comp.risks	Risks to the public from computers and users (moderated)

(continued)

Table 12-1 *(continued)*

Name	Discussion
comp.robotics	All aspects of robots and their applications
comp.security.misc	Security issues of computers and networks
comp.simulation	Simulation methods, problems, uses (moderated)
comp.society	The impact of technology on society (moderated)
comp.society.cu-digest	The Computer Underground Digest (moderated)
comp.society.development	Computer technology in developing countries
comp.society.folklore	Computer folklore and culture, past and present (moderated)
comp.society.futures	Events in technology affecting future computing
comp.society.privacy	Effects of technology on privacy (moderated)
comp.sources.misc	Posting of software (moderated)
comp.speech	Research and applications in speech science and technology
comp.text	Text-processing issues and methods
comp.unix.questions	UNIX neophytes group
comp.unix.shell	Using and programming the UNIX shell
comp.unix.wizards	Questions for only true UNIX wizards
comp.virus	Computer viruses and security (moderated)

None of the Above

Despite all the careful (well, sort of careful) arrangement of Usenet into meaningful hierarchies, some topics just didn't fit anywhere else; these topics ended up in misc, the miscellaneous hierarchy (see Table 12-2). Topics range from the totally staid to the hopelessly argumentative. The ultimate miscellaneous group is misc.misc, for discussions that don't fit *anywhere*.

Table 12-2	Groups in the Misc Hierarchy
Name	**Discussion**
misc.answers	Repository for periodic Usenet articles (moderated)
misc.books.technical	Books about technical topics
misc.consumers	Consumer interests, product reviews, and so on
misc.consumers.house	Owning and maintaining a house
misc.education	The educational system
misc.entrepreneurs	Operating a business
misc.fitness	Physical fitness, exercise, and so on
misc.forsale	Short, tasteful postings about items for sale
misc.int-property	Intellectual property rights
misc.invest	Investments and the handling of money
misc.jobs.contract	Contract employment
misc.jobs.misc	Employment, workplaces, careers
misc.jobs.offered	Announcements of positions available
misc.jobs.offered.entry	Job listings only for entry-level positions
misc.jobs.resumes	Postings of résumés and *situation wanted* articles
misc.kids	Children and their behavior and activities
misc.kids.computer	The use of computers by children
misc.legal	Legalities and the ethics of law
misc.legal.computing	The legal climate of the computing world
misc.misc	Various discussions that don't fit in any other group

Fun and Games

Even computer weenies like to have fun. (Stop laughing, it's true.) Usenet has lots of recreational groups (in the rec hierarchy; see Table 12-3) for hobbies ranging from the strenuous, such as watching fish in an aquarium, to the totally relaxing — mountain climbing, for example. There are certainly a few here that you'll like.

Table 12-3	Groups in the Rec Hierarchy
Name	**Discussion**
rec.answers	Repository for periodic Usenet articles (moderated)
rec.antiques	Antiques and vintage items
rec.aquaria	Keeping fish and aquaria as a hobby
rec.arts.books	Books of all genres and the publishing industry
rec.arts.movies	Movies and movie making
rec.arts.movies.reviews	Reviews of movies (moderated)
rec.arts.poems	For the posting of poems
rec.arts.prose	Short works of prose fiction and follow-up discussion
rec.arts.sf.announce	Major announcements of the SF world (moderated)
rec.arts.startrek.current	New "Star Trek" shows, movies, and books
rec.arts.startrek.info	Information about the universe of "Star Trek" (moderated)
rec.arts.startrek.misc	General discussions of "Star Trek"
rec.arts.theatre	All aspects of stage work and theatre
rec.arts.tv	The boob tube, its history, and past and current shows
rec.audio	High-fidelity audio
rec.autos	Automobiles, automotive products, and laws
rec.autos.tech	Technical aspects of automobiles
rec.backcountry	Activities in the great outdoors
rec.birds	Bird-watching
rec.boats	Boating
rec.climbing	Climbing techniques, competition announcements, and so on
rec.crafts.brewing	The art of making beers and meads
rec.crafts.misc	Handiwork arts not covered elsewhere
rec.crafts.textiles	Sewing, weaving, knitting, and other fiber arts
rec.food.cooking	Food, cooking, cookbooks, and recipes
rec.food.recipes	Recipes for interesting food and drink (moderated)
rec.food.restaurants	Dining out
rec.games.chess	Chess and computer chess
rec.games.design	Game design and related issues

Name	Discussion
rec.gardens	Gardening methods and results
rec.humor	Jokes and the like — may be somewhat offensive
rec.humor.d	The content of rec.humor articles
rec.humor.funny	Jokes that are funny (in the moderator's opinion)
rec.nude	Naturist and nudist activities
rec.railroad	For fans of real trains
rec.roller-coaster	Roller coasters and other amusement park rides
rec.running	Running for enjoyment, sport, exercise, and so on
rec.scouting	Scouting youth organizations worldwide
rec.scuba	Scuba diving
rec.skiing	Snow skiing
rec.sport.football.college	U.S.-style college football
rec.sport.football.misc	American-style football
rec.travel	Traveling all over the world
rec.travel.air	Airline travel around the world

Ask Dr. Science

A lot of Usenetters are in university or industrial research labs, so you encounter a number of scientists in the sci hierarchy (both professional and amateur). You also find many computer-science types, although (despite its name) this area isn't really a science. In this hierarchy, you find pretty much any kind of pure or applied science you can think of, from archaeology to zoology and everything in between. Table 12-4 shows you a choice few.

Table 12-4	Groups in the Sci Hierarchy
Name	**Discussion**
sci.aeronautics	The science of aeronautics and related technology (moderated)
sci.aeronautics.airliners	Airliner technology (moderated)
sci.answers	Repository for periodic Usenet articles (moderated)
sci.archaeology	The study of antiquities of the world
sci.astro	Astronomy discussions and information

(continued)

Table 12-4 *(continued)*

Name	Discussion
sci.classics	The study of classical history, languages, art, and more
sci.crypt	Different methods of data encryption and decryption
sci.math	Mathematics and its pursuits
sci.med	Medicine and its related products and regulations
sci.military	Science and the military (moderated)
sci.misc	Short-lived discussions on subjects in the sciences
sci.skeptic	Skeptics discuss pseudoscience
sci.space	Space, space programs, space-related research

C'mon By and Stay a While

Usenet is a sociable place, so naturally there's a great deal of socializing going on in the soc hierarchy. About half the soc groups are in soc.culture, where they discuss particular countries or ethnicities, and the other half are devoted to other sociable topics (see Table 12-5). You find religious groups ranging all the way from fundamentalist Christianity to paganism to Buddhism.

Table 12-5	Groups in the Soc Hierarchy
Name	Discussion
soc.answers	Repository for periodic Usenet articles (moderated)
soc.college	College, college activities, campus life, and so on
soc.couples	For couples (compare with soc.singles)
soc.culture.british	Issues about Britain and those of British descent
soc.culture.canada	Canada and its people
soc.culture.tamil	Tamil language, history, and culture
soc.history	Things historical
soc.men	Issues related to men and their problems and relationships
soc.misc	Socially-oriented topics not in other groups
soc.religion.unitarian-univ	A hangout for Unitarians, Universalists, and their noncreedal friends
soc.singles	For single people, their activities, and so on
soc.women	Issues related to women, their problems, and relationships

Blah Blah Blah

A few topics provoke running arguments that never, *never* get resolved. Usenet puts these in the `talk` hierarchy, mostly to warn you to stay away (see Table 12-6). Most find these groups to be argumentative and repetitious and populated mostly by students. However, *you* may not mind this or you may feel differently — so take a look at any that seem interesting to you.

Table 12-6	Groups in the Talk Hierarchy
Name	*Discussion*
talk.abortion	All sorts of discussions and arguments about abortion
talk.answers	Repository for periodic Usenet articles (moderated)
talk.bizarre	The unusual, bizarre, curious, and often stupid
talk.religion.newage	Esoteric and minority religions and philosophies
talk.rumors	For the posting of rumors

More Hierarchies

Besides the standard hierarchies, there are a bunch of others.

alt

This name designates so-called *alternative* groups. Setting up a group in a regular hierarchy is relatively difficult, requiring a formal charter and an on-line vote by its prospective readers and nonreaders. On the other hand, any fool can (and often does) set up an `alt` group. Often, after an `alt` has been around awhile, its proponents go through the procedure to create a corresponding mainstream group, and the `alt` group goes away. The quintessential stupid `alt` group is called `alt.barney.die.die.die`. See Table 12-7.

bionet

This bunch of groups is of interest to *biologists,* with the latest news on fruit flies and the like. If you're not a biologist, don't bother.

bit

These BITNET mailing lists (see Chapter 10) are passed around as Usenet news.

biz

Designates *business* groups that are more commercial than the generally noncommercial traffic in the mainstream groups.

clari

ClariNet (see the sidebar "Listen to the ClariNet," later in this chapter).

gnu

The *GNU project* develops freely available software, including, eventually, a complete reimplementation of UNIX. (Stands for Gnu's Not UNIX.)

hepnet

HEPnet (High Energy Physics). Like bionet, you know if you're interested.

IEEE

IEEE, the professional organization for electrical and electronics engineers.

k12

The K-12 net is for elementary and high school students and teachers. Students and teachers are welcome on all of the other groups, of course, but these groups contain topics of particular interest.

relcom

These are Russian-language groups. Unintelligible unless you have a newsreader that handles Cyrillic characters. You have to read Russian too.

vmsnet

Discussing the VMS system that runs on some Digital (DEC) computers.

Of all these hierarchies, only `alt` has many groups that are of general interest. A few of them can be found in Table 12-7. The character of `alt` groups varies wildly. Some, like `alt.dcom.telecom`, are just as staid as any `comp` group. Others, like `alt.buddha.short.fat.guy`, verge on the indescribable.

Table 12-7	Groups in the Alt Hierarchy
Name	*Discussion*
alt.activism	Activities for activists
alt.angst	Anxiety in the modern world
alt.answers	As if anyone on alt has the answers (moderated)
alt.appalachian	Appalachian region awareness, events, and culture
alt.backrubs	Lower...to the right...aaaah!
alt.bbs	Computer BBS systems and software
alt.binaries.pictures.erotica	Gigabytes of erotic copyright violations

Name	Discussion
alt.binaries.pictures.erotica.d	Erotic copyright violations
alt.binaries.pictures.fine-art.d	The fine-art binaries (moderated)
alt.binaries.pictures.utilities	Posting of pictures-related utilities
alt.books.isaac-asimov	For fans of the late sci-fi/science author Isaac Asimov
alt.buddha.short.fat.guy	Religion and not religion, both, neither
alt.cobol	Relationship between programming and stone axes
alt.culture.electric-midget	What's that behind those shrubs?
alt.dcom.telecom	Telecommunications technology
alt.dreams	What do they mean?
alt.drugs	Recreational pharmaceuticals and related flames
alt.evil	Tales from the dark side
alt.flame	Alternative, literate, pithy, succinct screaming
alt.folklore.college	Collegiate humor
alt.folklore.computers	Stories, anecdotes about computers (some true!)
alt.folklore.urban	Urban legends, à la Jan Harold Brunvand
alt.hackers	Descriptions of projects under development (self-moderated)
alt.online-service	Large, commercial on-line services and the Internet
alt.paranormal	Phenomena that are not scientifically explicable
alt.parents-teens	Parent-teenager relationships
alt.party	Parties, celebration, and general debauchery
alt.pave.the.earth	Futuristic visions of global asphalt sheet & cars
alt.save.the.earth	Environmentalist causes
alt.sex	Postings of a prurient nature
alt.supermodels	Famous and beautiful models
alt.surfing	Riding the ocean waves
alt.tv.mash	Nothing like a good comedy about war and dying
alt.tv.mst3k	Hey, you robots! Down in front!
alt.tv.prisoner	"The Prisoner" television series from years ago

Listen to the ClariNet

It had to happen someday — Usenet meets real life. A guy named Brad (same guy who created `rec.humor.funny`, Usenet's most widely read group) had a simple goal for his computer: He wanted to get his weekly Dave Barry column in his electronic mail. How hard could that be, considering that newspaper features are all distributed by satellite, anyway? Pretty hard, it turned out, mostly because of the legal issues of who owns what on the satellite.

Brad kept at it, though, and ended up with the right to distribute by network not just Dave Barry but also the entire UPI newswire and many other features too. That was *far* too much data to send out as e-mail, so Brad did the obvious thing and decided to use Usenet software instead. The result is a group of about 250 newsgroups known as ClariNet. Each group contains a particular category of news (actual newspaper-type news, not just net news), such as `clari.news.economy` for stories about the economy.

If your system has a direct (not just dial-up) Internet connection, you can get ClariNet news about as fast as the news comes off the ticker. It costs money, of course, but for a site with dozens or hundreds of users, the price per user is low — on the order of a few dollars per user per month. For information, e-mail to `info@clarinet.com`.

Brad also did get his e-mail Dave Barry, for about two years until the syndicate that distributed him decided that there was more copyright piracy of Dave's articles than they cared for. You can still get other syndicated columns, including Mike Royko, Miss Manners, and Joe Bob Briggs, for less than $10 per year (less than the cost of a Sunday paper each week). If your system gets ClariNet news, they may already be filed under `clari.feature.*`.

Chapter 13

While-You-Wait Conversation:
Talk and Chat

Talking the Talk

Sometimes e-mail just isn't fast enough. If you want to get in touch with some-one right now, what's the best way to establish contact? Pick up the phone, of course. But sometimes that's not practical (see the sidebar "Why use talk if you have a telephone?"). When calling isn't practical, the next best thing is the Internet *talk* command. To talk to some other user somewhere, type

```
talk username@hostname
```

If the other person is on the same machine as you are, you can leave out the @hostname part (although leaving it in never hurts). If you're using a fancy windowed system, such as Microsoft Windows or Motif, you probably double-click the talk icon in a program menu and then type the victim's — er, recipient's — name in a box. The talk command clears your screen and draws a dotted line across the middle. (The top half of the screen is where you type, and the bottom half is where the other person's typing appears, so even if you both type at the same time, the messages don't get scrambled.) The program then says something like [Checking for invitation on caller's ma-chine].

That means talk is checking to see whether the other person has already asked to talk to *you*. Most likely that's not the case, and if not, talk displays something like this on their screen (you don't see this):

```
Message from Talk_Daemon@whitehouse.com at 10:08 ...
talk: connection requested by elvis@ntw.org.
talk: respond with:  talk elvis@ntw.org
```

The recipient (if someone else were trying to talk to you, you'd be the recipient) should then type a corresponding talk command, and then the connection is established.

Now the two of you can talk back and forth:

```
How about some lunch?
_____

Sure, call me at 6-3765 and we'll figure out where to meet.
```

When you're finished, either party can exit talk by typing the local system's *interrupt character,* usually Ctrl-C or Delete. On windowed systems, you disconnect by clicking a menu item. If there's no answer, talk keeps sending the message until you press Ctrl-C or Delete.

Finding your victim

If your intended recipient (or *talkee,* making you the *talker*) is using a workstation with a windowing system, talk picks, more or less at random, one of the windows on the screen and sends that window the invitation to talk. As likely as not, your friend isn't looking at that window at that moment. The window may not even be visible on the screen. Try fingering (see Chapter 9) the machine to see which window is active, as shown in the following example:

```
finger @tammany.org
[suit.tammany.org]
Login     Name                TTY Idle     When        Where
tweed     Boss Tweed          co 1:35      Wed 02:37
tweed     Boss Tweed          p0   4d      Wed 02:37    :0.0
tweed     Boss Tweed          p1           Wed 02:37    :0.0
tweed     Boss Tweed          p2 1:35      Wed 02:38    :0.0
```

In this case, the user has several windows on the screen. (The glop in the Where column means that it's a window; the colon is the giveaway, so all but the first here are windows.) Only one of them is active at the moment. You can tell that p1, in the TTY column, the name of the *pseudoterminal* the window uses, is the active window because all the other windows have entries in the Idle column showing that the window has been idle for more than an hour or, in one case, four days. You can include a terminal name in the talk command, after the name of the talkee, **talk tweed@suit.tammany.org ttyp1**.

Note: You have to type **ttyp1**, not just **p1**. (You don't really want to know why, just prefix **tty** to whatever finger shows as the terminal name.) Now talk sends its invitation to ttyp1, where your friend presumably will see it.

Why use talk if you have a telephone?

A darned good question. Most of the time, if you can call someone on the phone, it's much more effective to call them than to use `talk`. (Using `talk` has been likened to communicating with someone on the moon.) Here are a few examples of times when it is sensible to use `talk` rather than the phone:

✔ The other person isn't answering the phone or isn't logged in from her usual office, so you use `talk` to encourage her to call you from wherever she is.

✔ The other person isn't near a phone. (Unlikely — how many networked computers don't have a phone nearby?)

✔ The other person is on another continent, and phone calls are difficult or very expensive. (We hear that people at the Amundsen-Scott Base at the South Pole use the Internet as their primary means of communication.)

✔ One or both of you don't speak English very well, so it's easier to type than to speak.

✔ The other person can't hear at all. (Quite a few deaf people are on the Internet, and you never know who they are unless they decide to tell you.)

✔ You don't know the other person's phone number, so use `talk` to find out the number to call.

Talk with care

Unlike e-mail, `talk` sends everything you type directly to the recipient as soon as you type it. You can backspace over errors, but the recipient *sees you do it.* This means that if your fingers slip, and type something really rude, even if you backspace over it you're *in deep sneakers.* For example, don't do this:

```
Can you come by for a meeting?
```

```
stick it←←←←←←←←Sure, Boss, no problem.
```

Serious Time Wasting

The `talk` command enables you to talk to only one person at a time. Chat programs let you talk to *dozens* of people at a time, who can be located all over the world. Most of the people you chat with are students who appear to have nothing better to do.

The most widely used chat program is called *Internet Relay Chat,* or *IRC.* Some systems (particularly UNIX workstations and Windows PCs) may have an IRC client program, in which case you merely type the command `irc` or click the IRC icon to get on it. (You can ask your system manager to install IRC, but don't expect much sympathy unless your manager is also a chat addict.)

In the absence of a local chat client, you can *telnet* (see Chapter 14) to a *public IRC server* and chat from there. IRC servers come and go all the time because they are widely (and not without justification) viewed as useless resource hogs. The best way to find current IRC telnet servers is to look at the Usenet newsgroup `alt.irc` (see Chapters 11 and 12).

After you're connected to IRC, you have to choose a nickname to identify yourself for the duration of your chat (your username does nicely). Then you have to decide which *channel* (discussion topic) you want to join. Type

```
/list
```

to see the names of all the channels available on your IRC and the number of people on them. (Many channels have only a single person, presumably lonely souls.) To join one called #penpals, for example, type

```
/join #penpals
```

and wait a minute for IRC to find the others on your channel and announce their nicknames on your screen. Then begin typing. Contributions are prefaced with the appropriate nickname. It tends to be pretty vapid:

```
<Gier> Why do people start doing quickies today.
<DrScott> re Buster!
<Gier> Do a quick one and you're dead Buster!
<DrScott> Gier: well, just for fun :))
<Gier> I ain't gonna say anything...
<Gier> til I'm sure...
<DrScott> Gier.... ;)
> That could take a while.
```

When you lose interest, **/QUIT** to exit.

There are lots of other commands. Type **/HELP** to find out what they are.

In principle, IRC could be used for on-line help desks and stuff. In practice, though, it isn't. It's just gossip. Oh well. Occasionally, when we're feeling bored (or looking for an excuse to avoid working), we turn on an IRC channel called #dummies. If you're on IRC when we do, feel free to drop by and say hi.

Part III
Instant Gratification

The 5th Wave   By Rich Tennant

@RICHTENNANT

"I THINK WHAT WE LIKE MOST ABOUT IT IS ITS TRANSPARENCY IN THE SYSTEM."

In this part...

So far we've been looking at staid, slow-moving ways to communicate with other people and other computers. But face it, mail is *still* mail. How exciting is walking down to the mailbox? In this part, you start using the Internet for while-you-wait communication. If you're into instant gratification (and who isn't these days?), read on.

Chapter 14

The Next Best Thing To Being There

● ●

In This Chapter

▶ Being there

▶ A few words from IBM

▶ Host-hopping with remote login

● ●

How You Can Be in Two Places at a Time

By far the most widely used interactive Internet services are the various forms of remote login. What these services do is simple: You log in to a remote *host* (computer) as if your *terminal* (workstation, PC, whatever) were attached directly to that host. Because all hosts on the Internet are officially equal, you can log in to a host on the other side of the world as easily as you can log in to one down the hall, with the only difference being that the connection to the distant host may be a little slower.

Although *telnet,* the most commonly used remote login program, is in principle simplicity itself, because computers are involved, simplicity isn't what it used to be. To run telnet, you type the `telnet` command followed by the name of the host you want to use. If everything goes well, you are then connected to that host.

In the following example, John telnets to his home computer and logs in as himself. (No, you can't have his password. Sorry.)

```
% telnet iecc.com
Trying 140.186.81.1 ... Connected to iecc.com.
Escape character is '^]'.

System V UNIX (iecc)
login: john1
Password:

Terminal type (default VT100):
...
```

Notice a couple of points here:

- Some versions of telnet report the numeric addresses of the hosts they contact. If your version does this, take note of that number in case of later trouble with the network connection.

- The thing that's absolutely essential to note is the *escape character,* which is your secret key to unhooking yourself from the remote host if it becomes recalcitrant and stops doing anything useful.

- The escape character in our example, the most common one on UNIX systems, is ^], which means that you hold down the Ctrl key and press] (the right bracket character on your keyboard).

- If you use a program on the remote system that needs to use that escape character for its own purposes, you can choose another escape character. See the section "Whipping telnet into line," later in this chapter.

After you're logged in, you can work pretty much as though you were indeed directly logged into the remote host. The main difference is that characters take a little longer to appear on-screen — as long as a full second or more. In most cases, you can keep typing even when what you typed hasn't yet appeared; the remote host eventually catches up.

Terminal Type Madness

If you use a full-screen program, such as the UNIX text editors emacs and vi or the mail programs elm and pine, you have to set your *terminal type.* This problem shouldn't exist in the first place. But it does, so you have to deal with it.

The problem is that about a dozen different conventions exist for screen controls such as *clear screen, move to position (x,y),* and so on. The program you're using on the remote host has to use the same convention your terminal does (if you're using a terminal) or that your local terminal program does (if you're on a PC or a workstation).

If the conventions are not the same, you get garbage (funky-looking characters) on-screen when you try to use a full-screen program. In most cases, the remote system asks you what terminal type to use. The trick is knowing the right answer:

- If you're using a PC, the best answer is usually ANSI because most PC terminal programs use ANSI terminal conventions. *ANSI* stands for the *American National Standards Institute.* One of its several thousand standards defines a set of terminal control conventions that MS-DOS PCs — which otherwise wouldn't know an ANSI standard if they tripped over one — invariably use.

✔ If you're using an X Window-based system, such as Motif or Open Look, the answer is more likely to be VT-100, a popular terminal from the 1970s that became a de facto standard.

✔ In places in which a great deal of IBM equipment is used, the terminal type may be 3101, an early IBM terminal that was also quite popular.

The ANSI and VT-100 conventions are not much different from each other, so if you use one and your screen is only somewhat screwed up, try the other.

More than you want to know about terminal types

Back in the good old days — like around 1968 — only one kind of terminal was ever used: a genuine Teletype brand teletype. Teletype machines, direct descendants of the news teletypes (familiar from old movie footage of newspaper production), were simple beasts. That is, they were simple conceptually — physically, they had an incredible number of moving parts. The only things these machines did other than type text was return the carriage and ring the bell.

Then people realized that you could combine a keyboard with a slightly modified television screen and build a video terminal. Dozens of manufacturers appeared, most now long forgotten, and they all noticed that you could do a great deal more with a screen than you could with an old teletype. For example, you could clear the screen, draw text in specific places, shift text up and down — all sorts of handy stuff. So each manufacturer assigned otherwise unused character codes as control characters to handle these special functions. Naturally, no two terminals used the same assignment.

Meanwhile, on a small planet far, far away — oops, sorry, wrong book. Meanwhile, in Berkeley, California, in the late 1970s, what is now known as Berkeley UNIX was taking shape. People at Berkeley had amassed large and completely miscellaneous collections of incompatible terminals. Which terminals would Berkeley UNIX support? Here's a hint: Terminals had to be bought from outside and cost real money, whereas software

was written by students and was free. Naturally, they supported every single terminal type on the campus, using a large database of hundreds of terminal types with the particular control sequences needed for each terminal.

By the early 1980s, it was apparent that the dominant terminal in the non-IBM market was the DEC VT-100. Many clone terminals began to appear that understood exactly the same control sequences as VT-100s, so they would work in all the places that VT-100s did. ANSI, the organization in charge of technical standards in the United States, adopted as an official standard control sequences almost identical to the VT-100 sequences.

So now you can assume that every terminal is a VT-100, right? Well, no. For one thing, many of those old terminals refuse to die. For another, terminal manufacturers progressed far beyond the VT-100, adding such features as color and graphics that the VT-100 didn't have. So most terminals made today are more or less ANSI-compatible, but with their own grotty warts. The world is stuck with multiple terminal types for the foreseeable future. But at this point, if you don't know what kind of terminal you have, either VT-100 or ANSI is your best guess.

For another failed attempt at terminal standardization, see the sidebar called "Disregard this discussion about network virtual terminals," later in this chapter.

Depending on how well-implemented your local version of telnet is, it may automatically tell the remote system which kind of terminal you're using. So with luck, you don't actually have to set your terminal type, or perhaps you just have to reply **y** when it says something like Terminal type VT100 OK?

Help! I've Telnetted and I Can't Get Out!

The normal way to leave telnet is to log out from the remote host. When you log out, the remote host closes its end of the telnet connection, which tells your local telnet program that it's finished. Easy enough — normally. Sometimes, though, the other end gets stuck and pays no attention to what you type. Or it doesn't get permanently stuck, but the host responds so slowly that you have no interest in waiting for it anymore. (This sometimes happens when network congestion occurs between you and the other host.)

Some versions of host software, which we won't name for looking-gift-horses-in-the-mouth-type reasons, get hopelessly slowed down by congestion, much more than the congestion itself causes. So you have to know how to escape from telnet. Here's where the magic escape character comes in handy:

- First, you have to get telnet's attention by pressing the escape character. (If nothing happens after a few seconds, try pressing Enter as well.) Telnet should come back with a prompt telling you that it's there.

- Then type **quit** to tell it that you're done. You should see something like the following:

```
^]
telnet> quit
Connection closed.
```

You can give telnet a dozen other commands (press **?** to see them), but none of them is anywhere near as useful as quit.

Terminals Served Here

One specialized host increasingly found on the Internet is a terminal server. The *terminal server* is basically a little computer with a bunch of modems or hard-wired terminal ports, and all it does with its life is telnet to other hosts. This makes sense if you have a large number of regular terminals around the office or many people who dial in over the phone, because it enables many terminals to get on the net at low cost. (Terminal servers are so carefully tuned to their task that even though a typical one has the computing power of a 1985 PC, it can handle upward of 30 modem connections at 14,000 bps *each.*)

Using a terminal server is similar to logging in to a single-minded computer (indeed, that's just what it is). You dial in and usually have to enter a site password that keeps 12-year-old hackers from calling in at random. (Or hackers of any age, for that matter.) Then you type the name of the host you want to connect to, and you're telnetted in. Here's a session on a typical Cisco terminal server:

```
User Access Verification Password: *****
TS>iecc.com
Translating "IECC.COM"...domain server (155.178.247.101) [OK]
Trying IECC.COM (140.186.81.1)... Open

System V UNIX (iecc)
login:

. . . regular telnet session deleted here ...

[Connection to IECC.COM closed by foreign host]
TS>
```

Terminal servers have escape characters just like regular telnet programs do, although they tend to be harder to guess. The usual escape for Cisco servers, the most popular brand, is two characters, Ctrl-^ (which you usually enter as Ctrl-Shift-6), followed by a lowercase *x*. Other brands of terminal servers have different escape sequences; inquire locally to find out which ones to use.

Most terminal servers also have a small set of commands that you can use to customize your terminal session. Press ? rather than a host name and see what it says.

PCs Can't Leave Well Enough Alone

If you use a Macintosh, a PC under Microsoft Windows, or some other windowing system, you start telnet somewhat differently from how you do it on a UNIX system. You start the telnet program from an icon, and a window pops up with menu choices at the top. One of the choices is usually Connect (or something like it). Click that choice, to get a Connect window. Figure 14-1 shows a typical window you get from the Connect menu item. Then type the name of the host you want, or maybe select it from a list, click OK, and away you go.

Connect To

Host Name: chico.iecc.com

Port: 23

Emulate: VT100

Description list:

OK   Cancel   Help

Figure 14-1:
Connecting
by way of a
Windows
telnet
program.

Disregard this discussion about network virtual terminals

Back in 1983 when telnet was defined, the folks working on it were acutely aware of the various kinds of terminals in use. Their solution to the incompatible terminal explosion was to define a network virtual terminal (NVT). The plan was that the telnet client (the program you run) would turn the local control glop into standard NVT codes; the telnet server (the program at the other end that makes your network connection act like a terminal on that host) would turn NVT codes into whatever the local convention was. So long as each system was configured correctly for the terminals physically attached to it, NVTs would take care of everything.

This didn't work. What happened? The problem was that telnet came along slightly too early, and the kinds of terminals they were worried about were line-at-a-time printing terminals, particularly some IBM terminals known by four-digit numbers such as 2741 and 1050. The 2741 was a slightly beefed-up Selectric typewriter with a computer interface, but it wasn't beefed up quite enough to handle the wear and tear of being run at full speed by a computer rather than at 30 words per minute by a typist. One of the authors of this book used for several years a terminal room that contained about a dozen 2741s and cannot remember all of them ever being in working order at the same time.

NVTs magnificently solve incompatibilities among 2741s, Teletypes, Flexowriters, and many other utterly obsolete printing terminals. Unfortunately, video terminals were just coming into fashion, and NVTs didn't address them. So Internet users are stuck with multiple terminal types on all the hosts.

(That's not quite true. Major manufacturers such as Digital Equipment Corporation, or DEC, tend to support only their own terminals, so if you telnet into a DEC VMS system with anything other than a DEC terminal or clone thereof, you lose. Fortunately, the ubiquitous VT-100 was made by DEC.)

Figure 14-2 shows the same session as shown earlier in this chapter, but this time from a Windows machine using the `telnet` program from the widely used Chameleon TCP/IP package from NetManage. A windowing system has no escape character because you do all the escape-type stuff from the program's menu. To disconnect from a recalcitrant host, for example, click a menu item called Disconnect (or something similar).

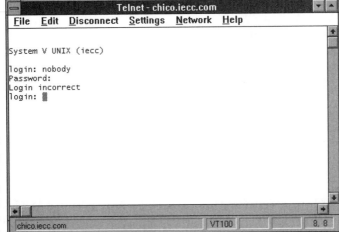

Figure 14-2:
A connected
Windows
telnet
session.

Whipping Telnet into Line

You can tell telnet to change its behavior in a few ways. The two most notable are to turn on and off *local echo* and *line mode*. Local echo means that the characters you type are sent to your screen by the local host (the one running telnet) rather than the one you have telnetted to. If your remote host echoes slowly or doesn't echo at all (some IBM hosts are like that), you can try to turn on local echo. Usually, pressing Ctrl-E turns local echo on and off.

Nearly all hosts on the Internet want to process the characters you type one at a time, as soon as you type them. A few ancient ones prefer a line at a time. You usually can recognize them because they don't handle any backspacing over errors. To work around that problem, type the telnet escape character (Ctrl-]) and then:

```
telnet> mode line
```

This line tells your local host to save up the characters and send them along a line at a time, handling the backspaces before passing them on. The number of hosts using line mode is small and shrinking. If you think that you have found a host that needs it, ask around to see whether you have overlooked something.

If the host sends text a screen at a time and uses acronyms such as VM or MVS (the two most common IBM operating systems), you probably have run into an IBM host and should use *tn3270* instead. See the section "We're from IBM and We Know What's Good for You," later in this chapter.

Any Port in a Storm

When you telnet into a remote host, you have to select not just the host but also a *port* on the host. The port is a small number that identifies what service you want. The usual port for telnet is (for obscure historical reasons) the number 23, which is taken to mean that you want to log in to the host. You choose another port by putting the port name after the host name as follows:

```
telnet ntw.org 13
```

Port 13 is the *daytime* port. It tells you that host's idea of the time of day and then disconnects. This exercise is not terribly useful, although occasionally you may need to see what time zone another host is in.

Some hosts are set up so that the regular telnet to port 23 gets a login prompt for regular users of the system, whereas telnet to some other port gets you into a special, publicly usable subsystem. Some of these systems are mentioned in Chapter 15.

We're from IBM and We Know What's Good for You

All the terminals discussed earlier that are handled by telnet are basically souped-up teletypes, with data passed character by character between the terminal and the host. This kind of terminal interaction can be called *teletype-ish.*

IBM developed an entirely different model for its 3270-series display terminals. The principle is that the computer's in charge. The model works more like filling in paper forms. The computer draws what it wants on the screen, marks which parts of the screen the user can type in, and then unlocks the keyboard so that users can fill in whichever blanks they want. When the user presses Enter, the terminal locks the keyboard, transmits the changed parts of the screen to the computer, and awaits additional instructions from headquarters.

To be fair, this is a perfectly reasonable way to build terminals intended for dedicated data-entry and retrieval applications. The terminal on the desks at your bank, electric company, and such are probably 3270s — or more likely these days, cheap PCs *emulating* (pretending to be) 3270s. The 3270 terminal protocol squeezes a great deal more on to a phone line than teletype-ish, so it's common to have all the 3270s in an office sharing the same single phone line, with reasonable performance.

The Internet is a big place, and plenty of IBM mainframes run applications on the net. Some of them are quite useful. Most of the large library catalogs, for example, speak 3270-ish. Usually, if you telnet to a system that wants a 3270, it converts from the teletype-ish that telnet speaks to 3270-ish so that you can use it anyway. But some 3270 systems speak only 3270-ish, and if you telnet to them, they connect and disconnect without saying anything in between.

A variant of telnet that speaks 3270-ish is called *tn3270*. If you find that a system keeps disconnecting or if you see full-screen pictures like the one shown in Figure 14-3, try typing the command **tn3270** instead. (Large amounts of UPPER-CASE LETTERS and references to the IBM operating systems VM or MVS are also tipoffs that you're talking to a 3270.) Even if a 3270 system allows regular telnet, you get a snappier response if you use tn3270 instead.

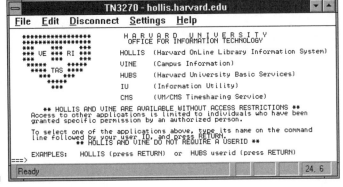

Figure 14-3: Using tn3270 to log into the Harvard University Catalog.

Remote Login: The Next Best Thing to Being There

Most UNIX systems also include a different, somewhat incompatible telnetlike program called *rlogin*. (Most PC network packages that support telnet have rlogin as well.) We use rlogin in the following example:

```
rlogin pumpkin.ntw.org
Last login: Fri Jan  8 14:30:28 from squash
SunOS Release 4.1.2 (PUMPKIN) #3: Fri Oct 16 00:20:44 EDT
         1992
Please confirm (or change) your terminal type.
TERM = (vt100)
```

Hey! It didn't ask you to log in. What happened? That's the main advantage of rlogin over telnet. When you find yourself logging in to the same machines over and over again, you easily can arrange it so that after you log in to one of them, you can rlogin to any of them. The rlogin program automatically passes your username and terminal type to the remote system so that you don't have to retype them yourself. By and large, if the hosts you use support rlogin, it's more convenient to use than telnet. But not every host supports rlogin, so sometimes you have to use telnet. If you try to rlogin to a system that doesn't accept it, you see a message like the following, which means that you should try telnet instead:

```
% Connection refused by remote host
```

Parting Is Such Sweet Sorrow

The rlogin program has a completely different set of escape characters from telnet. (Honestly, are you surprised?) All rlogin escapes begin with ~ (the tilde) at the beginning of a line. The most important escape sequence you can type is exit, which is ~. (a tilde followed by a period or dot). So to get out of a stuck rlogin, your key to escape is to press Enter (to make sure that you're at the beginning of a line) and then type ~. (that's tilde followed by a period followed by another Enter).

Be My Guest

In some cases, a group of hosts share the same complete set of users, so that anyone logged in to one of them can log in to any of the others. In this case, a system file lists all the hosts whose users are equivalent to this one. It's called /etc/hosts.equiv on UNIX systems and something similar on other machines. If machine Able has a hosts.equiv file that contains the name of host Baker, anyone on Baker can rlogin to Able without giving a password.

Some groups of workstations, particularly Suns, use something called *NIS* (Network Information System), which provides a groupwide database of usernames and the like. If you're using NIS, the system consults an NIS `hosts.equiv` database in addition to its regular file. To see it, type `ypcat hosts.equiv`. (Don't ask us why the command is called `ypcat`; you don't want to know. But if you insist, see "The Yellow Plague" in Chapter 4.)

Be My Host

In another situation, you have accounts on several hosts, but they're not all under the same management. You can arrange your own `rlogin` setup. On each of your accounts, create a file called `.rhosts` (that's a dot in front of the *r*) that lists all the other hosts on which you have accounts. For systems in which you have a different username, put your username on that system *after* the host name, separated by a space. Then, when you use rlogin, the system you're logging in to checks your `.rhosts`, sees that it's you, and you're all set. If you're using rlogin to log in to a host where you have a different name, specify it like this (assuming that your username at `ntw.org` is `king`):

```
rlogin ntw.org -l king
```

If you're bewildered by now, here's an example that may help. Suppose that you have accounts on three machines called `Able`, `Baker`, and `Clarissa`. On `Able` and `Baker`, your username is `sam`, and on `Clarissa` it's `tilden`. You want to be able to `rlogin` from any of them to any of the others. Your `.rhosts` file on `Able` could contain the following:

```
Baker
Clarissa tilden
```

Your `.rhosts` on `Baker` could contain this:

```
Able
Clarissa tilden
```

Your `.rhosts` on `Clarissa` could contain

```
Able sam
Baker sam
```

But here's an easier way. It doesn't hurt to include the username, even if it's the same, and it also doesn't hurt to include a line for the local system. So all three `.rhosts` files can be the same:

```
Able sam
Baker sam
Clarissa tilden
```

If rlogin doesn't recognize you, it asks for your name and password just like telnet does. Who would ever have expected something that sensible?

How to Hardly Be There at All

The rlogin program has a junior version called *rsh* (for *remote shell*). It executes a single command on a remote system:

```
rsh Able ls -R
```

If you have a different username on that system, you give it the same way as for rlogin:

```
rsh Clarissa -1 tilden ls -R
```

You can't run full-screen programs using rsh, although you can run programs that read their input a line at a time. (We won't bore you with the obscure technical reasons for this.) This means that you can use clunky line-at-a-time mail programs such as mail or mailx, but not nice ones such as elm or pine. A simple work-around is available, however: Use rlogin instead.

Finally, rsh never asks for a username or password. If it can't recognize you using `hosts.equiv` or `.rhosts`, it just fails.

In practice, we find rsh most useful for listing directories on remote systems. For anything more complicated, rlogin or telnet is easier.

Chapter 15

Some Interesting
Computers to Log In to

. . . .

In This Chapter

▶ Telnetting around the world

▶ More useful information than any sane person would want

. . . .

Come On By, Anytime

The Internet is a remarkably friendly place. Many systems let you telnet in with little or no prearrangement. Most just let you telnet in without restriction. Others require that you register the first time you log in but still don't ask you to pay anything. They just want to have some idea who their users are.

This list doesn't include any of the many places where you can telnet to Gopher, Archie, WAIS, or WWW servers — those servers are covered in Chapters 19 through 22.

Libraries

Nearly every large library in the country (indeed, in the developed world) now has a computerized catalog, and most of those catalogs are on the Internet. Most of the on-line catalogs also have other research info that is certainly more interesting than the catalogs themselves. This section lists some of the more prominent library systems and how to access them.

Library of Congress
Address: locis.loc.gov, Access code: Telnet or TN3270

The Library of Congress is the largest library in the world, and it certainly has the biggest catalog system, called LOCIS. (It's your tax dollars at work, or maybe at play.) In addition to the regular card catalog, in which you can look up pretty much any book ever published in the United States, the Library of Congress has an

Your secret decoder ring

In the list of services in this chapter, the codes have the following meanings:

Codes	Meaning
Telnet	Connect by way of regular telnet.
Port 123	Specify a port number after the host name in your telnet command (see Chapter 14 for details).
TN3270	Connect by way of tn3270, a version of telnet that acts like an IBM data-entry terminal. Most tn3270 systems listed in this chapter also allow regular telnet for people without tn3270. For systems that have both, TN3270 is faster, and its screens usually look better.
Register	Registration required. The first time you log in, you have to say who you are and get an account. No money required, though.
Account	Account required. You have to sign up and arrange to pay money. (Not many of these are listed.)

extensive and useful congressional legislation system you can use to look up bills. You can find out what bills have been introduced; what has happened to them (getting a bill through Congress is somewhat more complicated than getting someone canonized as a saint); who sponsored them; and what they say (in summary).

Figure 15-1 shows the summary of a bill that was, in 1993, passed by the House of Representatives and waiting for committee action in the Senate. You also can check for bills by the name of their sponsor, if you're wondering what your local representative or senator has been up to.

Figure 15-1:
LOCIS showing the summary of a bill in Congress.

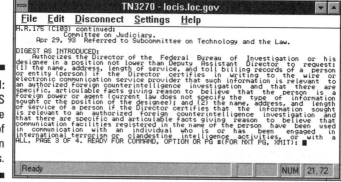

Note: LOCIS is available only during the hours when the Library is open, generally from 9 a.m. to 9 p.m. weekdays (Eastern time), with shorter hours on weekends. Other times, it disconnects immediately.

Dartmouth College Library
Address: library.dartmouth.edu, Access code: Telnet

In addition to the card catalog, this service includes the full text of William Shakespeare's plays and sonnets and the works of other great authors. To search the plays, type **select file s plays**; for sonnets, type **select file s sonnets**. For example, Figure 15-2 shows a search string found in *Hamlet,* which was written by our literary colleague, Shakespeare.

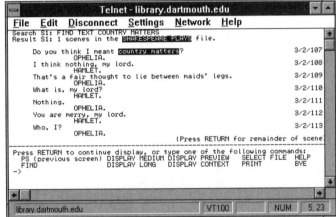

Figure 15-2:
A
memorable
scene in
Hamlet.

Harvard Library
Address: hollis.harvard.edu, Access code: Telnet or TN3270

Harvard has another huge library, and the service also provides campus info.

Yale Library
Address: orbis.yale.edu, Access code: TN3270

This is yet another large library (and the only one in which you can find a copy of John's thesis, "A Data Base System for Small Interactive Computers," which may not matter to you, but he thinks it's interesting).

Victoria University of Wellington
Address: library.vuw.ac.nz, Access code: Telnet

This library catalog is in New Zealand. After you connect, press Enter a few times until it asks you to log in, and then type **OPAC**.

Other Libraries

A service called *hytelnet* is a database of and gateway to many other libraries. If you log in to any one of them, it helps you find catalog information for dozens or hundreds of libraries. Current hytelnet servers include the following:

- access.usask.ca (login: `hytelnet`)
- info.ccit.arizona.edu (login: `hytelnet`)
- laguna.epcc.edu (login: `library`)
- info.anu.edu.au (login: `library` — *Note:* located in Australia)
- nctuccca.edu.tw (login: `hytelnet` — *Note:* located in Taiwan)

Large lists of on-line libraries also are available by FTP (see Chapter 18 for more information). For most purposes, we find that the Library of Congress is the most useful for finding names of books, unless you're planning to physically visit one of the other libraries.

Miscellaneous Databases

On-line information on an astounding range of topics is only a few keystrokes away, as you can see in the following sections.

Agriculture and nutrition databases

PENpages
Address: psupen.psu.edu, Access code: Telnet
Log in as your two-letter state abbreviation. This database provides a wide range of agricultural info. It's handy if you are (or like to think of yourself as) a farmer.

Clemson Forestry and Agriculture Network
Address: eureka.clemson.edu, Access code: Telnet
Log in as `PUBLIC`. This database offers plenty of forestry facts.

Geography databases

Geographic Server
Address: martini.eecs.umich.edu, Access code: Telnet, Port 3000
This database contains the name, location, and other facts of every place in the United States. If you have ever wondered where Surf City, U.S.A. really is, then

this database is for you. (It's in New Jersey, by the way. It doesn't tell you, however, to not miss the Surf City Fire Breakfast, held on the fourth Sunday in August from 8 a.m. to 12, but it looks like we just did.)

Earthquake info
Address: geophys.washington.edu, Access code: Telnet
Log in as quake, and use the password quake. Did you know that the United States has earthquakes almost every day? And you thought you were paranoid!

GLIS
Address: glis.cr.usgs.gov, Access code: Telnet, Register
This is the government's *Global Land Use Info System (GLIS)*. An enormous amount of map data is available, and GLIS enables you to locate and order it. Whip out a computerized map of your town, state, or planet.

Ham radio databases

Ham radio call signs on-line, indexed by call, name, and address. If you're a ham or want to find hams in your area, this is for you.

Ham call signs
Address: ns.risc.net, Access code: Telnet
Log in as hamradio.

Ham call signs
Address: callsign.cs.buffalo.edu, Access code: Telnet, Port 2000
Ham call signs
Address: pc.usl.edu, Access code: Telnet, Port 2000

History databases

History buffs can find lots of good stuff around the net.

University of Kansas
Address: ukanaix.cc.ukans.edu, Access code: Telnet
Log in as history for databases on history or as ex-ussr for databases on Russia and its neighbors. They list documents, bibliographies, and other info.

Other history resources are available by Gopher (see Chapter 20) and FTP (Chapter 16.) Also see the Usenet group soc.history for announcements of any newly available resources.

Outer-space databases

Care to roam the far reaches of the universe (or talk to people who do)? Then the outer space databases are for you.

NASA
Address: nssdc.gsfc.nasa.gov, Access code: Telnet, Register
Log in as `nodis`. This is NASA's *National Space Science Data Center*. This database contains many facts for the outer-space crowd.

Spacelink
Address: spacelink.msfc.nasa.gov, Access code: Telnet, Register
This database contains NASA news, including the shuttle launch schedule.

European Space Agency
Address: esrin.esa.it, Access code: Telnet
This database tells you what's new in the European part of outer space.

FIFE
Address: pldsg3.gsfc.nasa.gov, Access: Telnet
Login as `FIFEUSER`. This has lots of databases of satellite science data.

Aviation database

Interested in the wild, blue yonder? Here is someplace you can roam.

DUATS
Address: duats.gtefsd.com, Access code: Telnet, Register
This database provides pilot info, briefings, and flight plans. If you're a real certified pilot, log in to `duat.gtefsd.com` instead. Log in by using your last name as the login name.

Book databases

Looking for books, tapes, and CDs? Here are a few starting points.

CARL
Address: pac.carl.org, Access code: Telnet, Account
This database of book reviews, magazines, and articles includes fax article delivery. For many of the services, you need a library card (or at least the number of a library card) from a participating library in Colorado or Wyoming, such as the Denver Public Library.

Consumer Access Services
Address: columbia.ilc.com, Access code: Telnet, Register
Books, CDs, and videotapes are listed here. If you register, you can order these goodies by using a credit card. Log in as CAS.

Wordsworth Books
Address: wordsworth.com, Access code: Telnet
Wordsworth is a large, general-interest discount bookstore in Cambridge, Massachusetts, with, among other things, an excellent selection of *Dummies* books. Your authors happen to live within walking distance and drop by to autograph copies of their books from time to time. Log in as wordsworth to search the catalog or as order to order or ask a question.

Gateway Systems

The following act as gateways to other systems, like hytelnet does for libraries.

World Window Gateway at Washington University
Address: library.wustl.edu, Access code: Telnet
This gateway to hundreds of other services around the net is the best place to begin browsing. When you find an interesting service, make a note of its name (and port and login, if necessary) so that you can telnet in directly next time.

MERIT Network
Address: hermes.merit.edu, Access code: Telnet, Account
MERIT is the regional network that serves Michigan, and it also runs some national network facilities. MERIT offers access to some commercial services, at a modest hourly rate. The publicly available service is a gateway to Sprintnet, a commercial packet network from which you can reach many commercial services not otherwise connected to the Internet. You can sign up for a paid (but inexpensive) service that lets you dial out to local Detroit numbers, which for some services ends up being several dollars per hour less expensive than Sprintnet.

Commercial Services

Several commercial on-line services are available too. These have local dial-in numbers as well as telnet access, but if you already have an Internet connection through school or work, telnet can be faster and cheaper than dialing in.

DELPHI Internet
Address: delphi.com, Access code: Telnet, Account

Log in as `joindelphi` and use the password `info` to find out about Delphi terms and services, or use password `dummies` to sign up for an account. You get five free hours before they charge you.

The World
Address: world.std.com, Access code: Telnet, Account

A large on-line provider in suburban Boston with a complete suite of Internet services. Log in as `new` for both information and to sign up.

Netcom
Address: netcom.com, Access code: Telnet, Account

One of the largest national Internet providers. Log in as `guest` to look around.

CR Labs
Address: crl.com, Access code: Telnet, Account

Another large, national Internet provider. Log in as `guest` to look around.

CompuServe
Address: compuserve.com, Access code: Telnet, Account

If you don't already know who CompuServe is, we don't have room to explain it. Log in as `CIS` to get to the CompuServe prompt.

PC Travel
Address: pctravel.com, Access code: Telnet, Register

PC Travel lets you look at airline schedules on-line, make reservations, and order tickets. It is (as far as we know) the only no-charge on-line reservation system.

QUOTE.COM
Address: quote.com, Access code: Telnet, Register

This service offers daily on-line stock quotes and other stock market information delivered by e-mail or other means. Some services are free, some cost money.

Fun and Sheer Goofiness

Here are a few services you can access if you're just plain bored.

Thought for the day
Address: astro.temple.edu, Access code: Telnet, Port: 12345

Every time you telnet to this service, you get a pithy saying. Here's one:

```
telnet astro.temple.edu 12345
Trying ASTRO.OCIS.TEMPLE.EDU (129.32.1.100, 12345)... Open
Nihilism should commence with oneself.
```

Internet Relay Chat
Address: various, Access code: Telnet

You can telnet to various systems to join the running on-line IRC (Internet Relay Chat) discussion (see Chapter 13 for more details). In each case, log in as `irc`. Here are a few servers that currently work, but be warned that they come and go frequently. Try to use one on your continent.

- ✔ sci.dixie.edu (Port 6677)

- ✔ exuokmax.ecn.uoknor.edu (Port 6677)

- ✔ caen.fr.eu.undernet.org (Port 6677) France

- ✔ obelix.wu-wien.ac.at (Port 6996) Austria

- ✔ irc.tuzvo.sk (Port 6668) Slovakia

- ✔ irc.nsysu.edu.tw (Login: `irc`) Taiwan

Consult the Usenet group `alt.irc` for more recent information.

Scrabble
Address: next7.cas.muohio.edu, Access code: Telnet, Port 8888
seabass.st.usm.edu, Access code: Telnet, Port 7777

Play the game Scrabble against the computer or other people.

Network Go
Address: hellspark.wharton.upenn.edu
Access code: Telnet, Register, Port 6969

Play the Oriental strategy game of Go against other people.

Sports Info
Address: culine.colorado.edu, Access code: Telnet, Port (see below)

Telnet to port 859 for NBA schedules, 860 for NHL, 861 for Major League Baseball, or 862 for the NFL.

Chess server
Address: rafael.metiu.ucsb.edu or telnet ics.uoknor.edu, Access code: Telnet, Register, Port 5000

Telnet to either of these two systems to find fellow chess lovers for a game, gossip, or advice. The server takes care of the mechanics of tracking moves in a game and helping match up players of similar ratings.

The Tübingen Game Server
Address: herx1.tat.physik.uni-tuebingen.de, Access code: Telnet

Everything from Tetris to multiuser Colossal Cave. Log in as `games`.

Chapter 16

May We Have a Copy for Our Files?

In This Chapter

▶ Getting files from all over the net

▶ Stashing files all over the net

▶ Doing the same thing another way, for the easily bored

You See It, You Can Almost Touch It, but Where Is It Anyway?

Being on the Internet feels at times like being in a hall of mirrors. It's easy to lose track of where you are and how you got there, especially if you're using Gopher or the World Wide Web. (See Chapter 22 for the exciting details.) Often it doesn't really matter where you are as long as you're having a good time and finding what you're looking for. When it's time to go home, however, and you want to take some souvenirs with you, such as bringing home some of those nifty games to play on your own computer, it begins to matter where you are. You have to know where stuff is if you want to make a copy of it. It's that simple. Except that nothing's that simple.

How Can You Be in Two Places at Once When You're Not Anywhere at All?

We have to make an important distinction here between two kinds of Internet users: those directly connected to the Internet, including SLIP and PPP users, and those who use a modem and communications software (not SLIP or PPP) to connect to the net. For folks in the first category, getting things home is relatively easy: You can use FTP to copy files directly to your computer, as we're about to discuss. If you use a modem to dial in from your PC or Mac, you first have to get stuff to your Internet service provider and then get it to your very own machine — not so easy.

In the next section, we talk about copying files from system to system. Remember that if you're not directly connected to the net, you have do this, and you're only half the way home. After it's on your provider's computer, you still have to download it to your computer. We talk about that subject later in this chapter.

What's on File?

File transfer means to copy files from one system to another. You can copy files from other systems to your system and from your system to others. In this section, when we say "your system," we mean your system if you are directly connected to the net, and we mean your Internet provider's system if you're not directly connected. So when we say, "If your system has blah, blah, blah," we mean, "If your Internet provider's system has blah, blah, blah."

The Internet features two different and (how did you know that we were going to say this?) incompatible file-copying programs: FTP and RCP. This chapter spends more time discussing FTP because it's more widely available and somewhat more flexible.

If your system doesn't have FTP or RCP, all is not necessarily lost. See Chapter 17 to find out how to FTP, slowly, by e-mail.

How hard can it be to copy a file from one place to another?

Basically, it's pretty simple to copy a file from one place to another (but don't forget — computers are involved). Here's how it works: Log in to the other computer for FTP and tell it what you want to copy and where you want it copied to.

Here's an example in which one of the authors of this book FTPs to his computer and retrieves a file called README.

```
% ftp iecc.com
Connected to iecc.com.
220 iecc FTP server (Version 4.1 8/1/91) ready.
Name (iecc.com:johnl): johnl
331 Password required for johnl.
Password:
230 User johnl logged in.
```

```
ftp> get README
150 Opening ASCII mode data connection for README (12686
            bytes).
226 Transfer complete.
local: README remote: README
12979 bytes received in 28 seconds (0.44 Kbytes/s)
ftp> quit
221 Goodbye.
```

Look at the preceding example step by step. First he runs FTP, telling it the name of the host (computer) he wants to talk to. After the host answers (the line starting with 220), it asks for a username because you have to log in the same way you do for a telnet login. Invariably, it also asks for the password, so type that. (Usually, the password doesn't appear when you type it, just like when you log in by way of telnet.) Then he gets the file README, which provokes a flurry of messages. Finally, he tells FTP to quit.

That's basically how FTP works, but of course you need to know about 400 other odds and ends to use FTP effectively.

When is a file not a file?

When it's a text file. The FTP definition specifies six different kinds of files, of which only two types are useful: ASCII and binary. An ASCII file is a text file. A binary file is anything else. FTP has two modes, ASCII and binary (also called image mode), to transfer the two kinds of files. When you transfer an ASCII file between different kinds of computers that store files differently, ASCII mode automatically adjusts the file during the transfer so that the file is a valid text file when it is stored on the receiving end. A binary file is left alone and transferred verbatim.

Why is it called FTP?

We could say that FTP is short for *file-transfer program* and you probably would believe us, but that would be wrong. It really stands for *file-transfer protocol.* Way back in 1971, the Internet Powers That Be decided on a *protocol,* a set of conventions for copying files from one place to another on the net. Then many people wrote programs that implemented the protocol and called them all FTP. Is this clear? Never mind.

By the way, RCP stands for *remote copy.* Nothing fancy there.

You tell FTP which mode to use with the binary and ASCII commands:

```
ftp> binary
200 Type set to I.
ftp> ascii
200 Type set to A.
```

In the preceding example, the I is for binary or image mode (after 20 years, the Internet protocol czars still can't make up their minds what to call it), and the A is for ASCII mode. Like most FTP commands, `binary` and `ascii` can be abbreviated by lazy typists to the first three letters — so `bin` and `asc` will suffice.

How to foul up your files in FTP

The most common error made by inexperienced Internet users (and by experienced users, for that matter) is transferring a file in the wrong mode. If you transfer a text file in binary mode from a UNIX system to an MS-DOS or Macintosh system, the file looks something like this (on a DOS machine):

```
This file
          should have been
                           copied in
                                     ASCII mode.
```

On a Mac, the entire file looks like it's on one line. When you look at the file with a text editor on a UNIX system, you see strange ^M symbols at the end of each line. You don't necessarily have to retransfer the file. Many networking packages come with programs that do expost facto conversion from one format to the other.

If, on the other hand, you copy something that isn't a text file in ASCII mode, it gets scrambled. Compressed files don't decompress; executable files don't execute (or they crash or hang the machine); images look unimaginably bad. When a file is corrupted, the first thing you should suspect is the wrong mode in FTP.

If you are FTP-ing files between two computers of the same type, such as from one UNIX system to another, you can and should do all your transfers in binary mode. Whether you're transferring a text file or a nontext file, it doesn't require any conversion, so binary mode does the right thing.

Patience is a virtue

The Internet is pretty fast, but not infinitely so. When you are copying stuff between two computers on the same local network, information can move at about 200,000 characters per second. When the two machines are separated by a great deal of intervening Internet, the speed drops—often to 1,000 characters per second or less. So if you're copying a file that's 500,000 characters long (the size of your typical inspirational GIF image; see Chapter 17), it takes only a few seconds over a local network, but it can take several minutes over a long-haul connection.

It's often comforting to get a directory listing before issuing a get or put command so that you can have an idea of how long the copy will take.

The Directory Thicket

Every machine you can contact for FTP stores its files in many different directories, which means that to find what you want you have to learn the rudiments of directory navigation. Fortunately, you wander around directories in FTP pretty much the same way as you do on your own system. The command you use to list the files in the current directory is dir, and to change to another directory you use the command cd, as in the following example:

```
ftp> dir
200 PORT command successful.
150 Opening ASCII mode data connection for /bin/ls.
total 23
drwxrwxr-x  19 root      archive       512 Jun 24 12:09 doc
drwxrwxr-x   5 root      archive       512 May 18 08:14 edu
drwxr-xr-x  31 root      wheel         512 Jul 12 10:37 sys-
                                                        tems
drwxr-xr-x   3 root      archive       512 Jun 25  1992
                                                        vendorware
    ... lots of other stuff ...
226 Transfer complete.
1341 bytes received in 0.77 seconds (1.7 Kbytes/s)
ftp> cd edu
250 CWD command successful.
ftp> dir
200 PORT command successful.
150 Opening ASCII mode data connection for /bin/ls.
total 3
```

```
 -rw-rw-r—    1 root       archive       87019 Dec 13  1990 R
  -rw-rw-r—   1 root       archive       41062 Dec 13  1990 RS
  -rw-rw-r—   1 root       archive      554833 Dec 13  1990 Rings
drwxr-xr-x    2 root       archive         512 May 18 09:31 admin-
                                                            istrative
drwxr-xr-x    3 root       archive         512 May 11 06:44 ee
drwxrwxr-x    8 root       234             512 Jun 28 06:00 math
226 Transfer complete.
200 bytes received in 63 seconds (0.0031 Kbytes/s)
ftp> quit
221 Goodbye.
```

In a standard UNIX directory listing, the first letter on the line tells you whether something is a file or a directory. *d* means that it's a directory — anything else is a file. In the directory edu in the preceding example, the first three entries are files, and the last three are other directories. Generally, you FTP to a host, get a directory listing, change to another directory, get a listing there, and so on until you find the files you want; then you use the get command to retrieve them.

You often find that the directory in which you start the FTP program is not the one in which you want to store the files you retrieve. In that case, use the lcd command to change the directory on the local machine.

To review: cd changes directories on the other host; lcd changes directories on your own machine. (You might expect cd to change directories correspondingingly on both machines, but it doesn't.)

The File-Retrieval Roundup

Sometimes on your machine you have to give a file a name that is different from the name it has on a remote machine. (This is particularly true on DOS machines, where many UNIX names are just plain invalid.) Also, if you want to get a bunch of files, it can be pretty tedious to type all the get commands. Fortunately, FTP has work-around solutions for both those problems. Suppose that you have found a directory with a bunch of files in it, as in the following:

```
ftp> cd r
250 CWD command successful.
ftp> dir
200 PORT command successful.
150 Opening ASCII mode data connection for /bin/ls.
```

```
-rw-rw-r—    1 root      archive      5248 Nov  1  1989 rose
-rw-rw-r—    1 root      archive     47935 Nov  1  1989 rose2
-rw-r—r—     1 jlc       archive    159749 Aug 16  1992 rtrinity
-rw-r—r—     1 jlc       archive     71552 Feb 10  1993 ruby
-rw-r—r—     1 jlc       archive    220160 Feb 10  1993 ruby2
-rw-r—r—     1 jlc       archive      6400 Jul 14  1992 ruger_pistol
-rw-rw-r—    1 ftp       archive    133959 Nov 30  1992 rugfur01
-rw-r—r—     1 jlc       archive     18257 Jul 14  1992 rush
-rw-r—r—     1 jlc       archive    205738 Sep  3  1992 rush01
-rw-r—r—     1 jlc       archive    202871 Sep  3  1992 rush02
-rw-r—r—     1 jlc       archive     51184 Jul 14  1992 ruth
226 Transfer complete.
9656 bytes received in 3.9 seconds (2.4 Kbytes/s)
```

In this example, you want to get the file rose2 but you want to name it
rose2.gif because it contains a GIF-format image (see Chapter 17). First
make sure that you're in binary mode and then retrieve the file with the get
command. This time, however, you give two names to get — the name of the
file on the remote host and the local name — so that it renames the file as
the file arrives:

```
ftp> bin
200 Type set to I.
ftp> get rose2 rose2.gif
200 PORT command successful.
150 Opening BINARY mode data connection for rose2 (47935
         bytes).
226 Transfer complete.
local: rose2.gif remote: rose2
47935 bytes received in 39 seconds (1.2 Kbytes/s)
```

Next suppose that you want to get a bunch of the files that begin with ru. In
that case, you use the mget (which stands for *multiple get*) command to
retrieve them. The names you type after mget can be either plain filenames
or wildcard patterns that match a bunch of filenames. For each matching
name, FTP asks whether you want to retrieve that file, as in the following:

```
ftp> mget ru*
mget ruby? n
mget ruby2? n
mget ruger_pistol? n
```

```
mget rugfur01? n
mget rush? y
200 PORT command successful.
150 Opening BINARY mode data connection for rush (18257
          bytes).
226 Transfer complete.
local: rush remote: rush
18257 bytes received in 16 seconds (1.1 Kbytes/s)
mget rush01? y
200 PORT command successful.
150 Opening BINARY mode data connection for rush01 (205738
          bytes).
local: rush01 remote: rush01
205738 bytes received in 200.7 seconds (1.2 Kbytes/s)
mget rush02?
```

Note: If you find that `mget` matches more files than you expected, you can stop it with the usual interrupt character for your system — typically Ctrl-C or Delete:

```
^C
Continue with mget? n
ftp> quit
221 Goodbye.
```

You can even interrupt in the middle of a transfer if a file takes longer to transfer than you want to wait.

This game of 20 questions is okay for three or four files, but it can get darned tedious if you want to copy a bunch of them. Fortunately, you also can do an express `mget`, which doesn't ask any questions and enables you to find exactly the files you want, as in the following:

```
ftp> dir 92-1*
200 PORT command successful.
150 Opening ASCII mode data connection for 92-1*.
-rw-rw-r—  1 johnl    staff      123728 Jul  1 20:30 92-10.gz
-rw-rw-r—  1 johnl    staff      113523 Jul  1 20:30 92-11.gz
-rw-rw-r—  1 johnl    staff      106290 Jul  1 20:30 92-12.gz
226 Transfer complete.
remote: 92-1*
192 bytes received in 0.12 seconds (1.5 Kbytes/s)
```

Suppose that you want all those 92-1 files and don't feel like hammering on the y key to tell FTP to get all the files. Use the prompt command, which tells FTP to not ask any questions in mget but to just do it:

```
ftp> prompt
Interactive mode off.
ftp> mget 92-1*
200 PORT command successful.
150 Opening BINARY mode data connection for 92-10.gz (123728
          bytes).
226 Transfer complete.
local: 92-10.gz remote: 92-10.gz 123728 bytes received in 2.8
          seconds (43 Kbytes/s)
200 PORT command successful.
150 Opening BINARY mode data connection for 92-11.gz (113523
          bytes).
226 Transfer complete.
local: 92-11.gz remote: 92-11.gz 113523 bytes received in 3.3
          seconds (34 Kbytes/s)
200 PORT command successful.
150 Opening BINARY mode data connection for 92-12.gz (106290
          bytes).
226 Transfer complete.
local: 92-12.gz remote: 92-12.gz 106290 bytes received in 2.2
          seconds (47 Kbytes/s)
ftp> quit
221 Goodbye.
```

About, Face

Okay, now you know how to retrieve files from other computers. How about copying the other way? It's just about the same procedure, except that you use put rather than get. The following example shows how to copy a local file called rnr to a remote file called rnr.new:

```
ftp> put rnr rnr.new
200 PORT command successful.
150 Opening ASCII mode data connection for rnr.new.
226 Transfer complete.
local: rnr remote: rnr.new
168 bytes sent in 0.014 seconds (12 Kbytes/s)
```

(As with `get`, if you want to use the same name when you make the copy, leave out the second name.)

The mput command works just like the mget command does, only in the other direction. If you have a bunch of files whose names begin with uu and you want to copy most of them, issue the mput command, as in the following:

```
ftp> mput uu*
mput uupick? y
200 PORT command successful.
150 Opening ASCII mode data connection for uupick.
226 Transfer complete.
local: uupick remote: uupick
156 bytes sent in 0.023 seconds (6.6 Kbytes/s)
mput uupoll? y
200 PORT command successful.
150 Opening ASCII mode data connection for uupoll.
226 Transfer complete.
local: uupoll remote: uupoll
200 bytes sent in 0.013 seconds (15 Kbytes/s)
mput uurn? n
```

(As with `mget`, you can use `prompt` to tell it to go ahead and not to ask any questions.)

Most systems have protections on their files and directories that limit where you can copy files. Generally, you can use FTP to put a file anywhere that you could create a file if you were logged in directly by using the same login name. If you're using anonymous FTP (see the section "No Names, Please," later in this chapter), you generally cannot `put` any files at all.

A bunch of other file-manipulation commands are sometimes useful, as in the following example of the delete command:

```
delete somefile
```

This command deletes the file on the remote computer, assuming that the file permissions enable you to do so. The mdelete command deletes multiple files and works like `mget` and `mput`. The mkdir command makes a new directory on the remote system (again assuming that you have permissions to do so), as in the following:

```
mkdir newdir
```

After you create a directory, you still have to use `cd` to change to that directory before you use `put` or `mput` to store files in it.

If you plan to do much file deleting, directory creation, and the like, it's usually much quicker to log in to the other system by using telnet to do your work and using the usual local commands.

What's with All These Three-Digit Numbers?

You may notice that whenever you give a command to FTP, the response from the remote host begins with a three-digit number. (Or you may not notice — in which case — never mind.)

The three-digit number is there so that the FTP program, which doesn't know any English, can figure out what's going on. Each digit means something to the program.

Here's what the first digit means:

- ✔ 1 means that it has begun to process your request but hasn't finished it.
- ✔ 2 means that it finished.
- ✔ 3 means that it needs more input from you, such as when it needs a password after you enter your username.
- ✔ 4 means that it didn't work but may if you try again.
- ✔ 5 means "You lose."

The second digit is a message *subtype,* namely, a digit that distinguishes this message from other similar ones.

The third digit distinguishes messages that would otherwise have the same number (something that in the computer world would be unspeakably awful).

If a message goes on for multiple lines, all the lines except the last one have a dash rather than a space after the number.

Note: Most FTP users have no idea what the numbers mean, by the way, so now that you're one of the few who does know, you're an expert.

No Names, Please

So far, you have seen how to FTP to systems on which you already have an account. What about the other 99.9 percent of the hosts on the net, where nobody's ever heard of you? You're in luck. On thousands of systems, you can log in with the username anonymous. For the password, enter your e-mail address. (This is strictly on the honor system — if you lie about who you are, they still let you log in.) When you log in for *anonymous FTP*, most hosts restrict your access to only certain directories that are allowed to anonymous users. But you can hardly complain because anonymous FTP is provided free out of sheer generosity. Here's a typical example of what you see when you log in to a large, anonymous FTP host:

```
ftp wuarchive.wustl.edu
Connected to wuarchive.wustl.edu.
220 wuarchive.wustl.edu FTP server (Version wu-2.1b(1) Fri
        Jun 25 14:40:33 CDT 1993) ready.
Name (wuarchive.wustl.edu:johnl): anonymous
331 Guest login ok, send your complete e-mail address as
        password.
Password: (typed our  e-mail address here)
230-  If your FTP client crashes or hangs shortly after login
        please try
230-  using a dash (-) as the first character of your pass-
        word.  This will
230-  turn off the informational messages that may be confus-
        ing your FTP
230-  client.
230-
230-  This system may be used 24 hours a day, 7 days a week.
        The local
230-  time is Thu Aug 13 12:15:10 1994.
230-
230-  You are user number 204 out of a possible total of 250.
230-
230-  All transfers to and from wuarchive are logged.  If you
        don't like
230-  this then disconnect now!
230-
230-  Wuarchive is currently a DEC Alpha AXP 3000, Model 400.
        Thanks to
230-  Digital Equipment Corporation for their generous sup-
        port of wuarchive.
230-
```

```
230-Please read the file README
230-  it was last modified on Mon May 17 15:02:13 1993 - 87
          days ago
230-Please read the file README.NFS
230-  it was last modified on Tue Jun 29 12:12:27 1993 - 44
          days ago
230 Guest login ok, access restrictions apply.
ftp> dir
200 PORT command successful.
150 Opening ASCII mode data connection for /bin/ls.
total 23
-rw-r—r—  1 root      wheel         782 Aug  9 10:45 .Links
-rw-r—r—  1 root      archive         0 Nov 28  1990 .notar
-rw-r—r—  1 root      archive      2928 May 17 14:02 README
... tons of other stuff, this is a very large archive ...
```

After you're logged in, you use the same commands to move around and retrieve files as you always do.

A few anonymous FTP tips

Some hosts limit the number of anonymous users or the times of day that anonymous FTP is allowed. Please respect these limits because no law says that the owner of the system can't turn off anonymous access.

Don't store files in the other computer unless the owner invites you to do so. Usually a directory called INCOMING or something similar is available where you can put stuff.

Some hosts allow anonymous FTP only from hosts that have names. That is, if you try to FTP anonymously from a host that has a number but no name, these hosts don't let you in. This is most often a problem with personal computers that, because they generally offer no services that are useful to other people, don't always have names assigned.

PCs don't leave well enough alone

If you are running under Microsoft Windows or some other windowing environment, you may find that the version of FTP you're using has been *user-friendlyized*. Figure 16-1 shows a list of remote files and directories you can click with a mouse. Under the covers, in fact, these FTP programs are doing the same things you would do with a regular FTP program. You tell it to change directories, copy files, and perform other operations by clicking with the mouse, but what you can do is just the same as it always was.

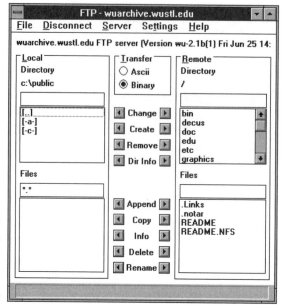

Figure 16-1:
A Windows
FTP
program.

The full-screen FTP programs can take awhile to start up because before you can start pointing and clicking, they have to ask the remote host for a list of file and directory names to fill in the selection lists on the screen, and because retrieving the list of files, particularly by way of a relatively slow SLIP or PPP connection, can be slow.

An FTP Cheat Sheet

Table 16-1 gives a short list of useful FTP commands, including a few not otherwise mentioned:

Table 16-1	Useful FTP Commands
Command	*Description*
get old new	Copies remote file old to local file new; can omit new if same name as old
put old new	Copies local file old to remote file new; can omit new if same name as old

(continued)

Table 16-1 *(continued)*

Command	Description
del *xxx*	Deletes file *xxx* on remote system
cd newdir	Changes to directory newdir on the remote machine
cdup	Changes to next higher directory
lcd newdir	Changes to directory newdir on the local machine
asc	Transfers files in ASCII mode (use for text files)
bin	Transfers files in binary or image mode (all other files)
quit	Leaves FTP
dir pat	Lists files whose names match pattern pat; if no pat, lists all files
mget pat	Gets files whose names match pattern pat
mput pat	Puts files whose names match pattern pat
mdel pat	Deletes remote files whose names match pattern pat
prompt	Turn name prompting on or off in mget and mput

A Few Words from Berkeley

Berkeley UNIX systems and systems written by programmers who (for some reason) *like* Berkeley UNIX, have another file-copying command called *RCP*. The idea of RCP is that it works just like the standard file-copying command cp except that RCP works on remote files you own or have access to. The RCP command uses the same username rules as do rlogin and rsh, so before you can use RCP, the remote computer must be set up so that you can use rlogin and rsh as well (see Chapter 14 for details).

To refer to files on another host, put the host name followed by a : (colon) before the filenames. To copy a file named mydata, for example, from the host named pumpkin to the local machine and call it pumpkindata, enter the following command:

```
rcp pumpkin:mydata pumpkindata
```

To copy it the other way, use this command:

```
rcp pumpkindata pumpkin:mydata
```

If your username on the other system is different from your username on your *own* system, put the username and an at-sign (@) before the host name, as follows:

```
rcp steph@pumpkin:mydata pumpkindata
```

If you want to copy files that belong to another user on the other system, the username goes after a tilde (~) and is separated by a slash from the filename. For example, to copy a file called `trfile` belonging to user `tracy`:

```
rcp pumpkin:~tracy/trfile tracyfile
```

When you want to copy an entire directory at a time, you can use the `-r` flag (`-r` is short for *recursive,* which is computerese for "go into the directory and do the same thing it's already doing") to tell it to copy the entire contents of a directory, as in the following:

```
rcp -r pumpkin:projectdir .
```

The preceding line says to copy the directory `projectdir` on host `pumpkin` into the current directory (that's what the period or dot is, the nickname for the current directory) on the local machine.

You can combine all this notation into an illegible festival of punctuation, as follows:

```
rcp -r steph@pumpkin:~tracy/projectdir tracy-project
```

The preceding line means to go to host `pumpkin`, where your username is `steph`, and get from user `tracy` a directory called `projectdir`. Copy `projectdir` and its contents to a directory on this machine called `tracy-project`. Whew!

In the finest UNIX tradition, RCP is extremely taciturn and says nothing unless something goes wrong. Copying many files over a network can take awhile, like a couple of minutes, so you may have to be more patient than usual while waiting for RCP to do its work.

If you copy stuff to another host and want to see whether it worked, try using rsh to run an ls command afterward to list the directory and see what files are actually there:

```
rcp -r projectdir pumpkin:squashproject
rsh pumpkin ls -l squashproject
```

RCP is pretty reliable. If it doesn't complain, the copy almost certainly worked — but it never hurts to make sure.

Meanwhile, Back at the Ranch

"All this FTP and RCP stuff is fine and dandy and works just great for getting stuff from one UNIX machine to another, but how about all us other folks out here who just plan to dial in to the net — what about us, huh, huh?" You should ask this question because, just like we warned you, it ain't over yet.

Down and dirty

To get stuff to your very own PC or Macintosh, you have to *download* it. In order for this to work, you need to have matching software on your PC or Mac and on your Internet service provider. Most service providers have a range of stuff to choose from, and the software that came with your modem probably has something to do the trick. Commonly available software includes Kermit, xmodem, ymodem, zmodem, and MacTerminal. Because downloading varies from provider to provider, you may actually have to call your service to get the scoop on how to download from its system.

Generally speaking, though, you have to go through these basic steps.

1. **Prepare your computer to receive data.**

   This step may not be anything other than ensuring that its file-transfer settings are appropriate to the software you'll be using from your Internet service provider.

2. **Tell the Internet service provider's computer to send stuff.**

3. **Wait.**

   For PCs, a good hunch is that zmodem is around on the provider's side. One way you can check is to type this command:

   ```
   man sz
   ```

   If zmodem is present, the directions for how to use it are displayed.

   For Macs, check your provider's MacTerminal availability by typing

   ```
   man macput
   ```

   If MacTerminal is present, the directions for how to use it are displayed.

What goes down goes up

If you want to share something of yours with other users on the net, you have to upload it. *Uploading,* as you probably guessed, is just the reverse of downloading. Uploading, just like downloading, varies from system to system, but here's the basic plot. It works on The World, our local Unix shell provider, and something similar will work on whatever system you're on.

1. **Prepare your computer to send data.**

   This step may not be anything other than ensuring that its file-transfer settings are appropriate to the software you'll be using from your Internet service provider.

2. **Tell the Internet service provider's computer to prepare to receive stuff.**

3. **Tell your computer to send the data.**

4. **Wait.**

For PCs, a good hunch is that zmodem is around on the provider's side. One way you can check is to type this command:

```
man rz
```

If zmodem is present, the directions for how to use it are displayed.

For Macs, check your provider's MacTerminal availability by typing

```
man macget
```

If MacTerminal is present, the directions for how to use it are displayed.

For helpful hints about rooting around on UNIX machines to find useful stuff, see *UNIX For Dummies,* by John R. Levine and Margaret Levine Young (IDG Books Worldwide). For more information about uploading and downloading, see *Modems For Dummies,* by Tina Rathbone (IDG Books Worldwide).

Chapter 17

Now That I've Got It, What Do I Do with It?

Now that you know how to use FTP and RCP and how to download, you probably have already retrieved zillions of files (well, maybe three or four). But when you look at them with your text editor, you may notice that they're garbage. In this chapter, we consider the various kinds of files on the net, how to tell what they are, and what to do with them.

How Many Kinds of Files Are There?

Hundreds, at least. Fortunately, they fall into some general categories.

Text files

Text files contain readable text (what did you expect?). Sometimes the text is actually human-readable text (such as the manuscript for this book, which we typed into text files the first time we wrote it). Sometimes the text is source code to computer programs in languages such as *C* or *Pascal*. And occasionally the text is data for programs. PostScript printer data is a particular kind of text file discussed later in this chapter.

Executable files

Executable files are actual programs you can run on a computer. Executable programs are particularly common in archives of stuff for PCs and Macs. Some executable programs are also available on the net for other kinds of computers, such as various workstations. Any single executable file runs on only a particular kind of computer: A Mac executable is useless on a Windows machine, and vice versa.

Archives and compressed files

Often a particular package requires a bunch of related files. To make it easier to send the package around, the files can be glommed together into a single file known as an *archive*. (Yes, the term "archive" also refers to a host from which you can FTP stuff. Sorry. So sue us. In this chapter, at least, archive means *a multifile file*.) After you retrieve an archive, you use an *unarchiving program* to extract the original files.

Some files are also *compressed,* which means that they're encoded in a special way that takes up less space but that can be decoded only by the corresponding *uncompressor*. Most files you retrieve by anonymous FTP are compressed because compressed files use less disk space and take less time to transfer over the net. In the PC world, archiving and compression usually happen together by using utilities such as PKZIP. In the Mac world, the StuffIt program is very popular. In the workstation world, however, the two procedures are usually done separately — the programs tar or cpio do the archiving, and the programs compress, pack, or gzip do the compressing.

Data files

Some files are not text, executable, archived, or compressed. For lack of a better term, we refer to these as *data files*. Programs often arrive with some data files for use by the program. Microsoft Windows programs usually come with a data file that contains the help text.

Macintosh files usually come in two or three chunks, one of which is the data file. You can't really see the chunks on your very own Macintosh from the user's point of reference, but you will see them if you try to upload them to a UNIX machine. In the Macintosh world, the three files are all pieces of one file and are referred to as *forks* — the data fork, the resource fork, and the optional information fork. When you upload what you think is one file from the Macintosh, it often appears as three separate files with the extensions .data, .resc, and .info appended to the filename.

The most common kinds of data files you find on the net are pictures, most often digitized photographs in *GIF* or *JPEG* format. An increasing number of digitized movies are also being made available in *GL* and *MPEG* formats.

You also occasionally find formatted word-processor files to be used with such programs as WordPerfect and Microsoft Word. If you encounter one of these files and don't have access to the matching word-processor program, you can usually load them into a text editor, where you will see the text in the file intermingled with nonprinting junk representing formatting information. In a pinch, you can edit out the junk to recover the text. Before you resort to that, however, try loading them with whatever word processor you have. A great deal of word-processing software can recognize a competitor's format and make a valiant effort to convert it to something usable by you so that you aren't tempted to buy the other product.

The most commonly used text-processing programs on the net remain the elderly but serviceable TeX and troff. Both of them take as their inputs plain text files with formatting commands in text form, something like this:

```
\begin{quote}
Your mother wears army boots.
\end{quote}
```

If you want to know more about TeX, see the Usenet newsgroup `comp.text.tex`. Free versions of TeX are available for most computers, described in a monthly posting on the newsgroup.

Troff is commonly distributed with UNIX systems; see `comp.text.troff`. Most ordinary human beings find troff something worth avoiding. For one thing, it's not *wysiwyg,* common desk-top publishing jargon for "*what you see is what you get.*" This means that it's really difficult to figure out what something will look like after it has gone through the program that interprets all the little codes you stick in. Some people, however (we won't mention any names, but his initials are JRL), get a strange satisfaction from using it, and the first version of this book was written using troff, which JRL then filtered into something more usable by our regarded publishers. What can you say?

Just Plain Text

There isn't much to say about text files — you know them when you see them. As mentioned in Chapter 16, the way text is stored varies from one system to another, so you should FTP text files in ASCII mode to convert them automatically to your local format.

If you encounter a text file that starts out something like the following, you have a PostScript document:

```
%!PS-Adobe-2.0
%%Title: Some Random Document
%%CreationDate: Thu Jul 5 1990
/pl transform 0.1 sub round 0.1 add exch
  0.1 sub round 0.1 add exch itransform bind def
```

A PostScript document is actually a program in the PostScript computer language that describes a document. Unless you are a world-class PostScript weenie, the only sensible thing to do with this type of document is to run the program and see the document. And the normal way to do that is to send it to a PostScript printer. PostScript interpreter programs, such as GNU Ghostscript (see Chapter 18), are also available that can turn PostScript into other screen and printer formats for users without PostScript printers.

Any Last Requests Before We Execute You?

The most commonly found executable programs are for DOS and Windows. These files have filenames like FOOG.EXE, FOOG.COM, or (sometimes for Windows) FOOG.DLL. You run them the same way you run any other DOS or Windows program.

Some chance always exists that any new PC or Mac program may be infected with a computer virus. (Because of the different ways in which the systems work, it's much less likely for workstation executables to carry viruses.) Stuff from such well-run repositories as SIMTEL-20 and wuarchive (see Chapter 18 for details) is unlikely to be infected; but if you run a random program from a random place, you deserve whatever you get.

Executable programs for workstations don't have easily recognizable filenames, although any file whose filename contains a dot is unlikely to be an executable. Even though nearly every kind of workstation runs UNIX, the executables are not interchangeable. Code for a SPARC, for example, doesn't work on an IBM RS/6000, or vice versa. Several different versions of UNIX run on 386 PCs, with different executable formats. Generally, newer versions of PC UNIX run executables from older versions, but not vice versa.

Packing It in

If you retrieve many files from the net, you have to learn how to uncompress stuff. The four main compression schemes are compress, gzip, ZIP, and StuffIt.

Compression classic

Back in 1975, a guy named Terry Welch published a paper on a swell new compression scheme he had just invented. A couple of UNIX programmers implemented it as the program compress, and it quickly became the standard compression program. Better compressors are available now, but compress is still the standard.

You can easily recognize a compressed program because its name ends with .Z. You recover the original file with uncompress (which is actually the same program as compress running in a different mode), as shown in this example:

```
uncompress blurfle.Z
```

This line gets rid of blurfle.Z and replaces it with the original blurfle. Sometimes uncompress is unavailable, in which case you can do the equivalent by using compress:

```
compress -d blurfle.Z
```

On PCs, compressed files often have names ending with Z, such as BLURFLE.TAZ. A UNIX-compatible version of compress is available in the SIMTEL archive in the directory /msdos/compress as COMP430D.ZIP. (You have to unzip that; see the section "ZIPping it up," later in this chapter.)

Frequently, UNIX files are archived and compressed and have names such as blurfle.tar.Z. In that case, you first uncompress to get blurfle.tar and then unarchive. If you want to see what's in a compressed file without uncompressing the entire thing, you can use zcat, which sends an uncompressed copy of its input to the screen. Any file big enough to be worth compressing is longer than one screenful, so you should run it through a paging program, such as more:

```
zcat blurfle.Z | more
```

It's patently obvious

Something that the people who wrote compress didn't realize is that Welch not only published the scheme that compress uses but also patented it. (Two guys at IBM named Miller and Wegman independently invented the same scheme at the same time and also got a patent on it — something that's not supposed to happen because only the first person to invent something is allowed to patent it. Yet the patents are definitely there.) UNISYS, which employs Welch, has said from time to time that it might someday start to collect royalties on compress, although to date it has never done so.

So the Free Software Foundation, which runs the GNU free software project, wrote gzip, which uses 100-percent nonpatented algorithms. Files that are gzip-ed end with `gz` and are uncompressed with the command gunzip:

```
gunzip blurfle.gz
```

It turns out that although compress's compression is patented, nobody bothered to patent the *de*compression technique, so gunzip can also decompress .Z files from compress as well as from some other earlier and less widely used schemes. It can even uncompress a ZIP archive as long as only one file is in it. If you have a mystery compressed file, try feeding it to gunzip and see what happens. There is also gcat, which, like zcat, sends its output to the screen. So a good way to peek inside a mystery file is to enter this command:

```
gcat mysteryfile | more
```

UNIX versions of gzip and gunzip are available in the GNU files at `ftp.uu.net` and elsewhere, and a DOS version is in the SIMTEL repository (see Chapter 18) as GZIP123.ZIP in `/msdos/compress`.

ZIPing it up

The most widely used compression and archiving program for DOS is the shareware program PKZIP. Zipped files all end with .ZIP and can be uncompressed and unarchived with PKUNZIP, available at SIMTEL as well as at virtually every BBS in the world. There's also WinZip (also shareware), which handles the same files but is easier to use from Windows.

Compatible UNIX zip and unzip programs called zip and unzip (the authors are creative programmers but not creative namers) are available at `ftp.uu.net` and elsewhere. For situations in which the shareware nature of PKUNZIP is a problem, a DOS version of UNIX unzip is available, although it's only about half as fast as PKUNZIP.

Just StuffIt!

The favorite Macintosh compression and archiving program is a shareware program, by Raymond Lau, known as StuffIt. StuffIt comes in many flavors, including a commercially available version called StuffIt Deluxe. StuffIt files of all varieties generally end in .SIT.

For decompression, you can use the freeware programs UnStuffIt, StuffIt Expander, or Extractor.

Other archivers

Dozens of other compressing archivers are out there with names like HARC, ZOO, and ARC. Unarchivers for all of them are in the SIMTEL repository.

In the Archives

Two different UNIX archive programs are tar and cpio. They were written at about the same time by people at two different branches of Bell Laboratories in different parts of New Jersey. They both do about the same thing; they're just different.

An important difference between UNIX-type archives and ZIP files is that UNIX archives usually contain subdirectories; ZIP files almost never do. You should always look at a UNIX archive's *table of contents* (the list of files it contains) before extracting the files so that you'll know where the files will end up.

The tar pit

The name *tar* stands for *Tape ARchive*. Although tar was originally designed to put archives of files on old reel-to-reel tapes, it will write to any medium. Files archived by tar usually have filenames ending with .tar. To see what's inside a tar archive, enter the following command:

```
tar tvf blurfle.tar
```

The *tvf* stands for *Table of contents Verbosely from File. Verbosely* in this case means tar actually tells you what it finds by echoing the files to your screen. If you don't use the v, tar gets the table of contents, but you'll never know.

To extract the individual files, use this command:

```
tar xvf blurfle.tar
```

Copy here, copy there

The name cpio stands for *CoPy In and Out*. The program was also intended to copy archives of files to and from old reel-to-reel tapes. (It was a pressing issue back then because, at the time, the disks on UNIX systems failed about once a week — tape was the only hope for getting your work back.) Files archived by cpio usually have filenames ending with .cpio. To see what's in a cpio archive, type the following line:

```
cpio -itcv <blurfle.cpio
```

Notice the < (left bracket) before the name of the input file. (If you wonder why it's necessary, see *UNIX For Dummies*. The answer is pretty technoid.) The -itcv means *Input, Table of contents, Character headers* (as opposed to obsolete *octal* headers), *Verbosely*. To extract the files, enter this line:

```
cpio -icdv <blurfle.cpio
```

The letters here stand for *Input, Character headers, Verbosely,* and *create Directories as needed.*

PAX vobiscum

Modern versions of UNIX, versions since around 1988, have a swell, new program called pax for *Portable Archive eXchange*. It speaks both tar and cpio, so it should be able to unpack *any* UNIX archive. If your system has pax, you'll find it easier to use than either tar or cpio. To see what's inside an archive, enter this command (the v is for *verbose* listing):

```
pax -v <tar-or-cpio-file
```

And to extract its contents, enter this line:

```
pax -rv <tar-or-cpio-file
```

(That's Read, Verbose output).

For the Artistically Inclined

A large and growing fraction of all the stuff the Internet is made of is increasingly high-quality digitized pictures. About 99.44 percent of the pictures are purely for fun, games, and worse. But we're sure you're in the 0.56 percent who need them for work, so here's a roundup of picture formats.

I could GIF a . . .

The most widely used format on the Internet is CompuServe's *GIF* (Graphics Interchange Format). The GIF format is well-matched to the capabilities of the typical PC computer screen — no more than 256 different colors in a picture and usually 640×480, 1024×768, or some other familiar PC screen resolution. Two versions of GIF exist: *GIF87* and *GIF89*. The differences are small enough that nearly every program that can read GIF can read either version equally well. GIF is very well standardized, so you never have problems with files written by one program being unreadable by another.

Dozens of commercial and shareware programs on PCs and Macs can read and write GIF files. On UNIX, under the X Window system, are quite a few free and shareware programs, probably the most widely used of which are ImageMagick and XV. You can find them in the Usenet `comp.sources.x` archives, such as the one at wuarchive in `/usenet/comp.sources.x`. (These are all in source form, so you have to be able to compile C programs to install them. Grab some chocolate chip cookies and sweet-talk a local nerd into doing it for you.)

The eyes have it

A few years back, a bunch of digital-photography experts got together and decided that it was time to have an official standard format for digitized photographs and that none of the existing formats was good enough. So they formed the *Joint Photographic Experts Group (JPEG),* and after extended negotiation, JPEG format was born. JPEG is specifically designed to store digitized, full-color or black-and-white photographs, not computer-generated cartoons or anything else. As a result, JPEG does a fantastic job of storing photos and a lousy job of storing anything else.

A JPEG version of a photo is about one-fourth the size of the corresponding GIF file. (JPEG files can actually be *any* size because the format allows a trade-off between size versus quality when the file is created.) The main disadvantage of JPEG is that it's considerably slower to decode than GIF is, but the files are so much smaller that it's worth it. Most programs that can display GIF files now also handle JPEG. JPEG files usually have filenames ending in .peg or .jpg.

The claim has occasionally been made that JPEG pictures don't look anywhere near as good as GIF pictures do. What is true is that if you take a full-color picture and make a 256-color GIF file and then translate that GIF file into a JPEG file, it won't look very good. For the finest in photographic quality, however, demand full-color JPEGs.

A trip to the movies

As networks get faster and disks get bigger, people are starting to store entire digitized movies (still rather *short* ones at this point). The standard movie format is called *Moving Photographic Experts Group (MPEG).* MPEG was designed by a committee down the hall from the JPEG committee and — practically unprecedented in the history of standards efforts — was designed by using the earlier JPEG work.

MPEG viewers are found in the same places as JPEG viewers are. You need a reasonably fast workstation or a top-of-the-line power-user PC to display MPEG movies in anything like real time.

Let a hundred formats blossom

Many other graphics file formats are in use, although GIF and JPEG are by far the most popular on the Internet. Other formats include the following:

- **PCX:** A DOS format used by many paint programs — also okay for low-resolution photos.

- **TIFF:** A complicated format with hundreds of options — so many that a TIFF file written by one program often can't be read by another.

- **TARGA** (called TGA on PCs): The most common format for scanned, full-color photos; in Internet archives, TARGA is now supplanted by the much more compact JPEG.

- **PICT:** A format common on Macintoshes.

A few words from the vice squad

We bet that you're wondering whether any on-line archives contain, er, *exotic* photography but you're too embarrassed to ask. Well, we'll tell you — they don't. Nothing in any public FTP archive is any raunchier than fashion photos from *Redbook* or *Sports Illustrated*.

That's for two reasons. One is political. The companies and universities that fund most of the sites on the Internet are not interested in being accused of being pornographers or in filling up their expensive disks with pictures that have nothing to do with any legitimate work. (At one university archive, when the *Playboy* pictures went away, they were replaced by a note that said that if you could explain why you needed them for your academic research, they would put them back.)

The other reason is practical. From time to time someone makes his (almost always *his,* by the way) private collection of R-rated pictures available for anonymous FTP. Within five minutes, a thousand sweaty-palmed undergraduates try to FTP in, and that corner of the Internet grinds to a halt. After another five minutes, out of sheer self-preservation, the pictures go away.

If someone you know is in desperate need of such works of art (not you, of course, but, er, someone down the hall needs it for sociology research), you might direct him to the Usenet group `alt.binaries.pictures.erotica`.

WAAHHH! I Can't FTP!

Oh, no! You only have an e-mail connection to the Internet, so you can't FTP any of this swell stuff! Life isn't worth living!

Wait. There's hope even yet. Several kind-hearted Internet hosts provide FTP-by-mail service. You e-mail a request to them, and a helpful robot retrieves the file and mails it to you. It's not as nice as direct FTP, but it's better than nothing. Only a few FTP-by-mail servers exist, so treat them as a precious resource. In particular, observe the following:

- ✔ Be moderate in what you request. When it mails you a nontext file (remember that compressed or archived files are nontext for FTP purposes, even if what they contain is text), it has to use a textlike encoding that makes the mailed messages 35 percent bigger than the file itself. So if you retrieve a 100K file, you get 135K of mail, which is a great deal of mail. If you use a commercial system in which you pay for incoming mail, you probably will find FTP by mail to be prohibitively expensive. (In that case, try a service such as AT&T Mail or MCI Mail that doesn't charge for incoming mail or a public Internet provider that provides direct FTP access.)

- ✔ Be patient. Nearly all FTP-by-mail systems ration their service. This means that if many people are using them (which is always true), there may be a delay of several days until they can get to your request. If you send in a request and don't hear back right away, *don't send it again.*

- ✔ Before you use a general-purpose FTP-by-mail server, check to see whether the system from which you want to retrieve stuff has a server of its own that can send you files from just that system. If it does, use it, because that is much quicker than one of the general servers.

The most widely available FTP-by-mail server is known as BITFTP. It was originally intended for users of BITNET, an older, mostly-IBM network, which has great mail facilities but no FTP. In the United States, a BITFTP server is at Princeton University at `bitftp@pucc.princeton.edu`. European users should try `bitftp@vm.gmd.de` in Germany.

Here's a list of other FTP by mail servers. To minimize expensive international network traffic, please try to use one in your own country.

- ✔ ftpmail@decwrl.dec.com (California, USA)

- ✔ ftpmail@sunsite.unc.edu (North Carolina, USA)

- ✔ ftpmail@cs.uow.edu.au (Australia)

- ✔ ftpmail@lth.se (Sweden)

✔ ftpmail@ftp.uni-stuttgart.de (Germany)

✔ ftpmail@grasp.insa-lyon.fr (France)

✔ ftpmail@ieunet.ie (Ireland)

✔ bitftp@plearn.edu.pl (Poland)

✔ mail ftpmail@doc.ic.ac.uk (Britain)

Before you send any requests to an FTP-by-mail server, send a one-line message containing the word *help.* You should do this for two reasons: to see whether the help message contains anything interesting and to verify that you and the server can send messages to each other. Don't try to retrieve any files until you get the help message.

The message you send to a BITFTP server is more or less the sequence of commands you would issue in an interactive FTP session. For example, to retrieve a text file with the index of FYI notes from INTERNIC (*INTER*net *Net*work *I*nformation *Center*), send this message to BITFTP:

```
FTP ftp.internic.net
USER anonymous
cd fyi
get fyi-index.txt
quit
```

You can enter multiple cds and get commands if necessary, but keep in mind that you don't want to overwhelm your mailbox with huge numbers of incoming messages full of files.

How am I supposed to know what files to ask for?

An excellent question. We're glad you asked. You can get a directory listing and then ask for a file in a later request, like this:

```
FTP ftp.internic.net
USER anonymous
cd fyi
dir
quit
```

Many systems have a complete directory listing available as a file in the top-level directory. The file is usually called something like `ls-1R` or `ls-1R.Z`. (The odd name comes from the name of the UNIX command used to create it.) If such a file exists, try getting it instead of doing a zillion dir commands. If no ls-1R is available but the file *README* is, get that, because it often tells you where the directory listing is hidden.

If u cn rd ths u mst b a cmptr

So far, we've considered retrieving text files by mail. But what about the 95 percent of available files that aren't text? For those files, there's a subterfuge called uuencode. (We mentioned this subject in Chapter 11 because it's the same way binary files are sent as Usenet news.) The uuencode program disguises binary files as text, something like this:

```
begin plugh.exe 644
M390GNM4L-REP3PT45GOOI-O5[I5-6M3OME,MRMK76OPI5LPTMETLMKPY
MEOT39I4905B05YOPV3OIXKRTL5KWLJROJTOU,6P5;3;MRUO5OI4J5OI4
...

end
```

Unless you are fortunate enough to have a mail program like Eudora that automatically decodes uuencoded messages, you have to feed the message through the program `uudecode` (or, for Windows users, WinCode) to get back the original file. If a file is really big, its uuencoded version is sent as multiple mail messages, in which case you have to save all the messages in the correct order to a file and then uudecode that file.

To retrieve a binary file, you give a uuencode *keyword* on the FTP line to tell it to uuencode what it retrieves and, as always, a binary command to tell it to FTP the file in binary mode. For example, to retrieve the compressed directory listing from */INFO* on `wuarchive.wustl.edu`, send this to BITFTP:

```
FTP wuarchhive.wustl.edu uuencode
USER anonymous
binary
cd info
get ls-1R.Z
quit
```

After you have uudecoded this file, you uncompress it (just like a file you FTP-ed directly) to get the file listing.

If you don't have a copy of uudecode but you have access to a C compiler (or someone who knows how to use a C compiler), the first file you retrieve should be a uudecoder. At `wuarchive.wustl.edu` in the directory `/info/ftp-by-mail` is a file called uuconvert.c, a superior version of uudecode that can decode large uuencoded files that have been sent as multiple mail messages.

Macintosh files are often encoded with a different uuencode-like scheme called BinHex (see Chapter 5 for details).

Chapter 18
FTP's Greatest Hits

· ·

· ·

There's Gigabytes Out There

Hundreds of gigabytes of stuff are available for FTP, if you know where to find them. (Remember that FTP stands for file-transfer protocol. It's the way you can get files from one place to another on the net, discussed in Chapter 16.) This chapter suggests some places to look. But first, a few words about strategy.

Ms. Manners says . . .

Please recall that all *anonymous FTP* servers (hosts that allow you to log in for FTP without having an account there) exist solely because someone feels generous. They can go away if the provider feels taken advantage of. So:

✔ Pay attention to restrictions on access times noted in the welcome message. Remember that servers are in time zones all over the world. So if the server says use only between 6 p.m. and 8 a.m., but it's in Germany and you're in Seattle, you can use it between 9 a.m. and 11 p.m. your time.

✔ Do not upload material unless you're invited to. (And don't upload material inappropriate to a particular archive — we would hope that this would be obvious, but experience suggests otherwise.)

Mirror, mirror, on the net

Many archives are *mirrored,* which means that the contents of an archive are mechanically copied from the home server to other servers. Usually the mirroring systems are larger and faster than the home server, so it's easier to get material from the mirror than from the home system. Mirrors are usually updated daily, so everything on the home system is also at the mirrors.

When you have a choice of mirrors, use the one closest to you. You want the one that's closest in terms of the number of network links between you and it. But because the number of hops is practically impossible to figure out, use the mirror that's physically closest. In particular, use one in your own country if possible, because international links are relatively slow and congested.

A Few Words about Navigation

All the FTP servers discussed in this chapter require you to log in using the username anonymous. For the password, use your e-mail address. When we say "log in," remember that we're talking about using the FTP command that requires you to log in when it reaches the machine you have specified. FTP actually gets you to the remote site through a specific entrance. Many FTP servers (machines that support FTP) don't allow you to log in through telnet, for example, or any method other than anonymous FTP.

Many servers have a small file called README, which you should retrieve the first time you use the server. That file usually contains a description of the material available and the rules for using the server.

If you log in to an FTP server and don't see any interesting files, look for a directory called pub (for public). For reasons lost in the mists of history, it's a tradition on UNIX systems to put all the good stuff there.

The FTP Hit Parade

The rest of this chapter lists some available FTP systems. Each section in the chapter includes the following information:

- ✔ Name and location of the system
- ✔ Particular rules for use
- ✔ Mail or other non-FTP access, if any
- ✔ What's there

UUNET

UUNET Communications, Virginia
Accepts FTP only from hosts with registered names.
All material also available for uucp (dial-up system available on UNIX and DOS systems) via 1-900-GOT-SRCS, 50 cents per minute

UUNET is probably the largest archive available on the net. It has masses of software (mostly for UNIX in source form), archives of material posted on Usenet, files and documents from many publishers and vendors, and mirrors of many other archives around the net.

WUARCHIVE

wuarchive.wustl.edu
Washington University, Missouri

This large program and file archive includes mirrors of many other programming archives, with megabytes of stuff for DOS, Windows, Macintosh, and other popular computer systems. WUARCHIVE also contains the largest collection of GIF and JPEG pictures (all suitable for family viewing, by the way) on the net.

RTFM

rtfm.mit.edu
Massachusetts Institute of Technology, Massachusetts
Mail server: mail-server@rtfm.mit.edu

RTFM is the definitive archive of all the *FAQs (frequently asked questions)* messages on Usenet. RTFM is therefore a treasure trove of information for everything from the state-of-the-art in data compression to how to apply for a mortgage to sources of patterns for Civil War uniforms. Look in the directories `pub/usenet-by-group` and `pub/usenet-by-hierarchy`.

RTFM also has an experimental Usenet address database, containing the e-mail address of every person who has posted a message to Usenet in the past several years. That database is in `pub/usenet-addresses`.

RTFM is one of the most popular FTP sites on the net, but it lets only 50 outside users on at a time. (It also lets in 50 people from within M.I.T., where it's located.) As a result, it can be difficult to connect to RTFM, particularly at popular times. So try it at off hours, like really early in the morning, or use the mail server.

INTERNIC

ftp.internic.net
Internet Network Information Center, California

This central repository for information about the Internet itself includes copies of all the standards and RFC documents that define the network. Also, INTERNIC has information about many other FTP archives available on the net.

NSFNET

nis.nsf.net
National Science Foundation c/o MERIT, Michigan

The NSFNET is (or at least used to be) the largest backbone network in the Internet. It has a great deal of boring administrative stuff and some interesting statistics on how big the net is and how fast it's growing. Look in `statistics/nsfnet`.

Desperately seeking software

archive.umich.edu or sumex-aim.stanford.edu
The software archives at the University of Michigan and Stanford University

If you're looking to expand your computer's skills, check out the software for the PC, Macintosh, Amiga, Apple II, Apollo — you name it.

oak.oakland.edu
The Oak Software Repository, Oakland University, Rochester, Michigan

Here's software for your UNIX machine and more for your PC. It includes a mirror of the enormous SIMTEL archive of PC software.

The list of lists

sri.com
SRI International, California
Mail server: mail-server@sri.com

Look in the directory `netinfo` for the file `interest-groups`, or the compressed version, `interest-groups.Z`. This is a relatively complete list of public mailing lists on various topics. From 1992 to 1994 it languished unchanged, but as of mid-1994, it appears as though it's being updated again.

Of Academic Interest

Many sites are full of stuff that is fascinating to the academic community.

Coombs Papers

Coombs.anu.edu.au
Australian National University

This data bank of social-science papers, offprints, bibliographies, directories, abstracts of theses, and other materials is in Australia, so the slant is different from what you get in the United States.

Behavioral brain sciences

princeton.edu in directory pub/harnad/BBS
Behavioral Brain Sciences Archive, Princeton University, New Jersey
This is the main meeting point for brain and cognitive scientists. It's also tied in to a conventional print journal for those seeking publication.

EJVC

byrd.mu.wvnet.edu in directory /pub/ejvc
Arachnet Electronic Journal of Virtual Culture, West Virginia

We wouldn't dream of telling you what Virtual Culture is. You have to look for yourself. For more info about this journal, e-mail a polite note asking for info to m034050@marshall.wvnet.

For a history database, check out /pub/history. Also at the same site is an archive on fractals, chaos, and more of that kind of stuff in /pub/estepp/fracha.

Kermit

watsun.cc.columbia.edu in directory kermit
Kermit Archive, Columbia University, New York

Kermit is a popular dial-up communications program that runs on practically every kind of computer known to humankind. You can find versions of it here for your computer. If you have some computers on the Internet and others not on the Internet with modems, you can Kermit them all together.

Numerical software

netlib.att.com
Bell Labs, New Jersey
Mail servers: netlib@netlib.att.com (New Jersey), netlib@nac.no (Norway), and netlib@draci.cs.uow.edu.au (Australia) — use the one closest to you

For upward of 30 years, scientists have been writing programs to do such things as solve sparse systems of linear equations. If you know what that means and are interested in doing some of it yourself, don't even consider writing any software of your own until you check in `netlib`.

Compilers

iecc.com
I.E.C.C., Massachusetts
Mail server: compilers-server@iecc.com

Complete archives of the `comp.compilers` Usenet group, in addition to various documents, bibliographies, and programs of interest to compiler writers, are available from this service. It also contains documents for the *Journal of C Language Translation*. Incidentally, unlike most archives, which are sponsored by large organizations, this one is maintained and funded by a single individual who thinks that having an Internet node in his house is fun.

NIH

ftp.cu.nih.gov
National Institutes of Health, Maryland

This system contains many NIH documents and interesting reports from the General Accounting Office in the directory GAO-REPORTS, such as this:

```
Although GAO notes much good news in the enforcement of
federal milk bid-rigging laws, more work needs to be done.
On the plus side, the Justice Department continues to
aggressively investigate milk bid-rigging cases and has taken
legal action against a number of violators. . . .
```

It's the Law

Finally you can take the law into your own hands. Well, at least into your computer. Don't rely on bigoted media reports. Check out the unedited goings-on on-line.

Supreme Court rulings

ftp.cwru.edu

For text files of the Supreme Court rulings, look in /hermes. Decisions are available in both plain ASCII and WordPerfect format, which can be read by most other word processors. Each file is stored both uncompressed and gzipped (see "It's patently obvious" in Chapter 17). The filenames are based on the docket number, so you have to do some guessing to find what you want.

Note to users of "user friendly" FTP programs: Some of the directories are enormous, so if you use an FTP program that retrieves a list of the files to display in a window, getting the list of files can take a couple of minutes.

Here's a typical shorter decision:

WEDNESDAY, MAY 11, 1994
CERTIORARI DENIED

93-9087   WHITMORE, JONAS H. V. GAINES, MIKE, ET AL, (A-937)

The application for stay of execution of
sentence of death presented to Justice Blackmun
and by him referred to the Court is denied.
The petition for a writ of certiorari is denied.
    Justice Blackmun dissenting:
        Adhering to my view that the death penalty
cannot be imposed fairly within the constraints of
our Constitution, see my dissent in *Callins v.
Collins*, 510 U.S. _, _ (1994), I would grant
the application for stay of execution and the
petition for a writ of certiorari and would remand
with instructions to enjoin petitioner's execution.

Congressional mail

ftp.senate.gov
Mail server: congress@hr.house.gov
The United States Senate

Provided by the Office of the U.S. Senate Sergeant at Arms and the Senate Committee on Rules and Administration, this server contains general information files about the Senate plus files from each state senatorial office.

Law libraries

sulaw.law.su.oz.au
The Sydney University Law School, Sydney, Australia

If you're into doing your own legal research, log in as `lawlib` and look into `/pub/law`.

Fun and Frolic

There's plenty of fun on the net. Here are some of our favorite fun spots.

Hamming it up

oak.oakland.edu
The Oak Software Repository, Oakland University, Rochester, Michigan
Mail server info@arrl.org

Amateur radio talk on the Internet might seem redundant to most people, but if it's your thing, check out `pub/hamradio`.

Shop 'til you drop

ftp.netcom.com
Netcom On-line Communications Services

When the malls close everywhere else, you can still drop in on the Internet Mall. You may even find that the selection is better. Look at `/pub/Guides`.

For music lovers

ftp.uwp.edu
The University of Wisconsin at Kenosha, Wisconsin,

You can find lyrics, chords, tablature, and music pictures in `/pub/music`.

Attention, sports fans

etext.archive.umich.edu
A volunteer-staffed archive at the University of Michigan

Check out the baseball archives in `pub/Sports/Baseball`.

News

ftp.voa.gov
The Voice of America

"Every week tens of millions of listeners around the world tune their radios to the Voice of America. They know that they can rely on VOA . . . ." It also has CNN Headlines and European news and weather. You can find overview information, schedules, and programs. If your computer has a sound card and a fast network connection, you can download copies of their audio programs as well. Note that, by law, VOA materials are not intended for domestic U.S. listeners, but anyone can retrieve material from the server.

TV (and movie) guide

quartz.rutgers.edu
Rutgers University

If you want to have on your screen what's on the screen, look at `/pub/tv+movies`.

Travel tips

ftp.cc.umanitoba.ca
The University of Manitoba, Winnipeg, Canada

Draw from a world of experience and check out travelogues, guides, and answers to frequently asked questions, gleaned from the Usenet group `rec.travel`. They're in the directory `rec-travel`.

Yummy finds

You'll never want for a new dish if you look for recipes on the net!

FTP to	And see
gatekeeper.dec.com	pub/recipes
mthvax.cs.miami.edu	pub/recipes
ftp.neosoft.com	pub/rec.food/recipes
cs.ubc.ca	pub/local/RECIPES

One of the authors points with pride to his key-lime pie recipe at gatekeeper, but he wants you to know that contrary to what the recipe says, you can in fact get bottled key-lime juice. (See Chapter 21 for more on this.)

FTP by e-mail

Lots of FTP servers are ready to service your e-mailed FTP request. See "WAAHHH! I can't FTP" in Chapter 17.

Go ask Archie

This chapter gives you only a handful of the FTP sites available on the net. *Far* too many exist to list them all here, and new sites appear daily.

Fortunately, you have an ally to help you find the FTP material you need: Archie. See Chapter 19 to learn all about Archie, the on-line FTP locator.

Part IV
Finding Stuff on the Net

The 5th Wave   By Rich Tennant

"I think this answers our question—no, it's not a good idea to try to download the entire Internet at one time."

In this part...

As we've already said too many times, the Internet is
really big. It's so big that finding all the swell stuff
that's available for the taking is itself a daunting task.
(Imagine a very large library that has no card catalog, in
which each shelf is arranged independently by the person
who brought in the books on that shelf.) In these chapters,
you learn about four new tools to help you navigate around
and find the goodies: Archie, Gopher, WAIS, and the World
Wide Web.

Chapter 19
Ask Archie

I Know I Saw a Note about It Here Somewhere . . .

Somewhere on the Internet is probably everything you really want and a great deal more you might want if you knew it existed. "But how do I *find* it?" you ask. Good question.

If it's software you're looking for, ask Archie.

If you know the name of what you're looking for — or kind of know the name, enough that you can come up with a reasonable guess — Archie goes running around the world, checking database after database, looking for files that match your description.

Archie servers exist all over the world, but you should pick one close to home to help minimize traffic on the net. Different Archie servers get different amounts of use, so you may have to try a few before you find one with a reasonable response time. If everything you try seems painfully slow, try early in the morning or late at night, or try sending your Archie request by e-mail (see the section "E-mail Archie," at the end of this chapter).

Table 19-1 lists several Archie servers you can try. If you try one and it doesn't let you on because it's too full, chances are it provides you with another list of Archie servers you can try. Eventually you'll get on.

Table 19-1	Archie Servers
Server Name	*Location*
archie.rutgers.edu	New Jersey
archie.sura.net	Maryland
archie.unl.edu	Nebraska
archie.ans.net	New York
ds.internic.net	U.S.A. (run by AT&T)
archie.mcgill.ca	Canada
archie.au	Australia
archie.th-darmstadt.de	Europe (Germany)
archie.funet.fi	Europe (Finland)
archie.luth.se	Europe (Sweden)
archie.univie.ac.at	Europe (Austria)
archie.doc.ic.ac.uk	UK and Europe
archie.cs.huji.ac.il	Israel
archie.ad.jp	Japan
archie.kuis.kyoto-u.ac.jp	Japan
archie.sogang.ac.kr	Korea
archie.nz	New Zealand
archie.ncu.edu.tw	Taiwan

You can access Archie servers in several ways:

- ✔ If you have *Archie client software (*archie or xarchie), you can run directly from your machine (see the sections "Straight Archie" and "Xarchie" later in this chapter).

- ✔ You can telnet to an Archie server (see the following section, "Telnet Archie").

- ✔ You can e-mail your request to an Archie server (see the section "E-mail Archie").

Telnet Archie

Unless you have Archie client software available to you locally (try using the archie command or, on a machine with X Windows or one of its variants such as Motif, xarchie), you probably want to telnet to an Archie server. Before you do, however, if you can, you probably want to start a *log file* (a file in which all the text displayed in your window is captured), because Archie's output may come fast and furiously, gushing filenames, host names, and Internet addresses that you really don't want to have to copy down by hand if you can avoid it. If you're running on a machine with X Windows or one of its variants such as Motif, hold down Ctrl, press the left mouse button, and choose Log to File from the Main Options window. If you're not running X, it's worth asking around to see whether there is some locally available program that can capture the text on the screen to a file. Windows users have wsarchie, which we consider later.

For now, pick a server, use telnet, and log in as archie, as in the following:

```
% telnet archie.ans.net
Trying...
Connected to forum.ans.net.
Escape character is '^]'.Archie
AIX telnet (forum.ans.net) IBM AIX Version 3 for RISC System/
       6000
(C) Copyrights by IBM and by others 1982, 1991.
login: archie
```

Archie returns with an Archie prompt:

```
archie>
```

Tell Archie how to behave: The set and show commands

Every Archie server is set up with features you can tune to suit your needs. You may have to change them to make Archie do what you want. Not all Archie servers are alike, and you have to pay attention to how things are set up on the server you land on.

To see how the server you're on is set up, use the show command:

```
archie> show
#  'autologout' (type numeric) has the value '15'.
#  'mailto' (type string) is not set.
#  'maxhits' (type numeric) has the value '100'.
#  'pager' (type boolean) is not set.
#  'search' (type string) has the value 'sub'.
#  'sortby' (type string) has the value 'none'.
#  'status' (type boolean) is set.
#  'term' (type string) has the value 'dumb 24 80'.
```

You can also use show to see specific values one at a time (try typing **show term**, **show search**, and so on). Although all these values are explained next, the variables you need to pay careful attention to are *search* and *maxhits*. We also suggest setting the *pager*, which tells Archie to stop after every screenful of text and wait for you to press the spacebar, to avoid the extremely irritating situation in which you wait 15 minutes for an Archie search and then the output flies off the screen before you can read it.

Searching is such sweet sorrow, or something

Normally, Archie searches for a name that contains the string you type, disregarding uppercase and lowercase. So if you search for *pine,* it matches *PINE, Pineapple,* and *spineless,* among other things. If you use Archie much, you find that you want more control over the searching process, so you probably want to use one of the other search methods for matching what you type. How much you know about the name of the file you're looking for should determine the search method you use.

To set the search method, use the set command:

```
archie> set search sub
```

The search methods Archie supports are called *sub, subcase, exact,* and *regex.* The next sections discuss how they work.

The sub method

This method searches to match the substring anywhere in the filename. This search is case insensitive, meaning that case doesn't matter. If you have an idea of a character string that's likely to be contained in the filename, choose sub.

The subcase method

This method searches to match the substring exactly as given anywhere in the filename. This search is case sensitive. Use this method only if you are sure of the case of the characters in the filename.

The exact method

This method searches for the exact filename you enter. This search is the fastest, and you should use it if you know exactly what file you're looking for.

The regex method

Use UNIX *regular expressions* to define the pattern for Archie's search. This is a particular kind of substring search, and Archie tries to match the expression to a string anywhere in the file's name. In regular expressions, certain characters take on special meaning, and regular expressions can get absurdly complicated, if you want them to be.

- ✔ If you know that the string begins the filename, start your string with the ^ (caret) to tie the string to the first position of the filename.
- ✔ If you know that the file ends with a particular string, end your string with the $ (dollar sign) to tie the string to the end of the filename.
- ✔ The . (period) is used to specify any single character.
- ✔ The * (asterisk) means zero or more occurrences of the preceding regular expression.
- ✔ Use [and] (square brackets) to list a set of characters to match, or a range of characters to match. Combined with ^ (caret) in the first position, square brackets list a set of characters to exclude or a range not to include.
- ✔ You can specify more than one range in the same search. If you need to use a special character as part of your string, put a \ (backslash) in front of it.

For example, to find any files containing the string *birdie* and ending with *txt,* type

```
prog ^birdie.*txt$
```

To find filenames containing numeric digits, type

```
prog [0-9]
```

To exclude filenames containing lowercase letters, type

```
prog [^a-z]
```

How long do you want to look?

The *maxhits* variable determines how many matches Archie tries to find. On many servers, the default for this number is 1,000 — but for most searches that's ridiculous. If you know the name of the file you want, how many copies do you want to choose from? Ten or 20 should give you sufficient choice. But if you don't reset *maxhits,* Archie continues traveling around the net, looking for as many as 1,000 matches.

Remember too that Archie's output is going to your screen and maybe to your log file — so think about how much data you can handle. After you decide just how much you want to know, set maxhits equal to that number (suppose that it's 100):

```
archie> set maxhits 100
```

Table 19-2 lists more set settings.

Table 19-2	Other Nifty Features to Set from Set
Variable	**What It Does**
autologout	Sets how long Archie waits around for you to do something before kicking you off.
mailto	Sets the e-mail address used by the mail command.
pager	Sends Archie's output through the pager program *less,* which stops after each screenful of output and waits for you to press the spacebar. Using the command *set pager* switches the pager from off to on or from on to off, so do a *show* before you change the pager setting so that you don't do the opposite of what you intend.
sortby	Sorts Archie's output in one of the following orders: by *hostname* in alphabetical order or reversed (*rhostname*); by most recently modified (*time*) or oldest (*rtime*); by *size,* largest first, or by smallest first (*rsize*); by *filename* in lexical order, or reverse (*rfilename*); *unsorted* (usually the default). You type something like **set sortby time**.
status	Makes Archie show the progress of the search. Can be reassuring when Archie is very slow.
term	Sets the type of terminal you're using so that Archie can tailor your output (try *vt100* if you're not sure).

Find It!

Archie's basic command is the prog command, and it takes this form:

```
prog searchstring
```

And that's it. That command launches the whole search. The nature and scope of the search are determined by the variables you set or didn't set.

Here's an example. Suppose that you want to find out what kind of font software is around:

```
archie>  prog font

Host csuvax1.murdoch.edu.au    (134.115.4.1)
Last updated 00:23 31 Jul 1993

     Location: /pub/mups
        FILE        rw-r-r-       4107   Nov  16   1992     font.f
        FILE        rw-r-r-       9464   Nov  16   1992
             fontmups.lib

Host sifon.cc.mcgill.ca    (132.206.27.10)
Last updated 04:22 11 Aug 1993

     Location: /pub/packages/gnu
        FILE        rw-r-r-     628949   Mar   9 19:16     fontutils-
             0.6.tar.z

Host ftp.germany.eu.net    (192.76.144.75)
Last updated 05:24  7 May 1993

     Location: /pub/packages/gnu
        FILE        rw-r-r-     633005   Oct  28   1992     fontutils-
             0.6.tar.z
     Location: /pub/gnu
        FILE        rw-r-r-    1527018   Nov  13 16:11
             ghostscript-fonts-2.5.1.tar.z

Host ftp.uu.net    (192.48.96.9)
Last updated 08:17 31 Jul 1993

     Location: /systems/att7300/csvax
```

```
        FILE       rw-r—r—    1763981  Mar  5 23:30    groff-
              font.tar.z

Host reseq.regent.e-technik.tu-muenchen.de
            (129.187.230.225)
Last updated 06:26 10 Aug 1993

      Location: /informatik.public/comp/typesetting/tex/
            tex3.14/DVIware/laser-sett ers/umd-dvi/dev
        FILE       rw-r—r—         51  Sep 24  1991    fontdesc

Host nic.switch.ch    (130.59.1.40)
Last updated 04:48  7 Aug 1993

      Location: /software/unix/TeX/dviware/umddvi/misc
        FILE       rw-rw-r—       607  Oct  2  1990    fontdesc
```

As you quickly find out, a great deal of duplication is out there. If you're looking for variety, you can make a series of inquiries that eliminate the stuff you've already found and make subsequent queries more fruitful.

After you have found it, or some of it . . . what is it?

There sure is a lot of *stuff* out there. But what the heck is it? Sometimes Archie can help you to figure that out. We say *sometimes* because Archie's information is only as good as that provided by the folks who hung the stuff out there in the first place. But for those packages that have been supplied with a description, the *whatis* command might provide you with useful information. The whatis command is actually another kind of search — it searches a database of software descriptions provided by the individual archive managers looking for the string you provide rather than search directories for filenames. If you're looking for software of a specific nature, regardless of what it's called, you can use the whatis command to augment your search.

If we use whatis rather than prog in my search for font software, for example, we get the following:

```
archie> whatis font
afm2tfm          Translate from Adobe to TeX
fage support)
gftodvi          Converts from metafont to DVI format
gftopk           Converts from metafont to PK format
gftopxl          Converts from metafont to PXL format
her2vfont     Hershey fonts to 'vfont' rasterizer
hershey       Hershey Fonts
hershey.f77Hershey Fonts in Fortran 77
hershtools    Hershey font manipulation tools and data
hp2pk           HP font conversion tool
jetroff/bfont             Jetroff Basic Fonts
jis.pk           The JTeX .300pk fonts (Japanese language
             support)
k2ps               Print text files with Kanji (uses JTeX
             fonts) (Japanese language support)
mkfont         Convert ASCII font descriptions <-> device-
             independent troff (ditroff) format
ocra-metafont             METAFONT sources for the OCR-A
"Alphanumeric Character Sets for
Optical Recognition"
```

Note: The string *font* appears in some of these filenames, but only in the description of others.

You can't get there from here

Archie's great for *finding* stuff but no help at all in actually *retrieving* stuff for you. (Xarchie and wsarchie are a big help, so if you have one of them, you probably want to use it.) To actually get stuff off the net, you have to do what Archie did to find it in the first place: Use FTP (File Transfer Protocol) to copy it from the archive where it lives back to your computer. Because you're not likely to have an account on any of the systems Archie finds, you can use *anonymous FTP* (logging in as the generic user `anonymous`). After you have logged in for FTP, you use the cd command to move to the appropriate directory, and get or mget to retrieve the files (see Chapter 16 for details).

If you're on a quest for related software, after you have FTP'd to a host that has relevant stuff, you might want to look around in the directory containing the file you know about (use the FTP dir command to list the contents of a remote directory) and in any subdirectories near it.

Straight Archie

If you try to type the archie command directly and it returns a comment telling you how to use it, you're in luck. You can use the Archie client software directly without telnetting to an Archie server. One big advantage of using Archie from a command line is that you can easily redirect its output to a file, as in the following:

```
$ archie -ld font > fontfiles
```

(This line stores the result of the search in a file called `fontfiles`, which you can later peruse at your leisure using any text editor or file viewer.) Be aware, however, that the client software is limited and that you may want to telnet to an Archie server to take advantage of more of Archie's capabilities. For one, you can't set all the tuning variables described in the section "Telnet Archie," earlier in this chapter. Also, you cannot use the whatis command.

Using Archie directly means using a command line that may get complex. You can specify the kind of search and the Archie server you want to use and format the output to a limited extent. If you supply the search string and no modifiers, Archie defaults to an exact search with a maximum of 95 matches. For details on selecting a search method and other available options, see the section "Telnet Archie," earlier in this chapter.

Table 19-3 lists the modifiers you can supply.

Table 19-3	Search String Modifiers	
Archie Modifier	**Telnet Equivalent**	**Archie Meaning**
-c	subcase	Set search mode for a case-sensitive substring
-e	exact	Set search mode for an exact string match (default)
-r	regex	Set search mode for a regular expression search
-s	sub	Set search mode for a substring search
-l		List one match per line
-t	sortby	Sort Archie's output by date, newest first
-m#	maxhits	Set the maximum number of matches to return (default 95)
-h		Specify the Archie server to use
-L		List the known Archie servers and the current default

For example, to use the server `archie.ans.net` to do a regular expression search for no more than 50 files that contain digits in their names:

```
$ archie -r -m50 -h archie.ans.net "[0-9]"
```

(Note that the pattern [0-9] is enclosed in double quotes to avoid having it misinterpreted as the name of a file to match locally. In general, put your patterns in quotes if they contain anything other than letters and digits.)

Xarchie

If you're lucky enough to be running X Windows or a near relative of X Windows and xarchie is available to you, use it. It enables you to set most Archie settings from the main menu and the settings menu. Furthermore, after completing the search, xarchie enables you to scroll through the hosts and filenames and click the selections that interest you (see Figure 19-1).

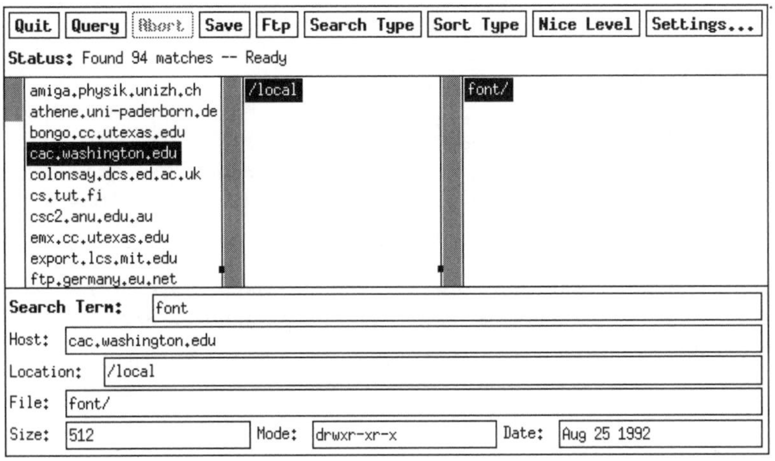

Figure 19-1:
Using
xarchie to
search for
files.

After you find something you want, you can choose Ftp from the main menu; xarchie turns itself into a junior version of the FTP program and retrieves the remote file for you and puts the file in your current directory or in the directory you specify from the Settings menu (see Figure 19-2).

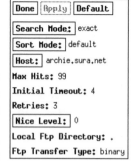

Done	Apply	Default

Search Mode: exact
Sort Mode: default
Host: archie.sura.net
Max Hits: 99
Initial Timeout: 4
Retries: 3
Nice Level: 0
Local Ftp Directory: .
Ftp Transfer Type: binary

Figure 19-2:
Xarchie's
option
menu.

Windows Archie

A couple of Archie clients are available on Windows, the nicest of which is
David Woakes' wsarchie.

You start it up by clicking its icon. Then fill in the search for string, pick a
server if you don't like the default one, and click Search. It contacts the server
and comes back with an optimistic estimate of how long you have to wait. (At
the bottom of Figure 19-3, Queue 2 means that we're second in line, and Time
18s means 18 seconds to wait. Ha!)

After the results come back, you can scroll through the lists of matching hosts,
directories, and files. If you find a file you like, double-click its name, and
wsarchie starts up an FTP program and automagically retrieves it for you.
Pretty cool.

One of the nicest things about running Archie under Windows is that you can
start your query, shrink wsarchie to an icon, and go do something else until the
answer comes back.

E-Mail Archie

If you're unable to telnet to an Archie server either because of the limitations of
your network connection or because you have been unsuccessful in logging in
to an Archie server, you can send your request to Archie by using e-mail. If
you're planning to launch a major search and don't want to wait for the response, using Archie from e-mail is a good way to go in any case.

Not all of telnet Archie's capabilities are available to you through e-mail, but
you can still carry out a substantial search. To send a request to Archie, send
mail to `archie@servername`, where *servername* is any of the Archie servers
mentioned at the beginning of this chapter.

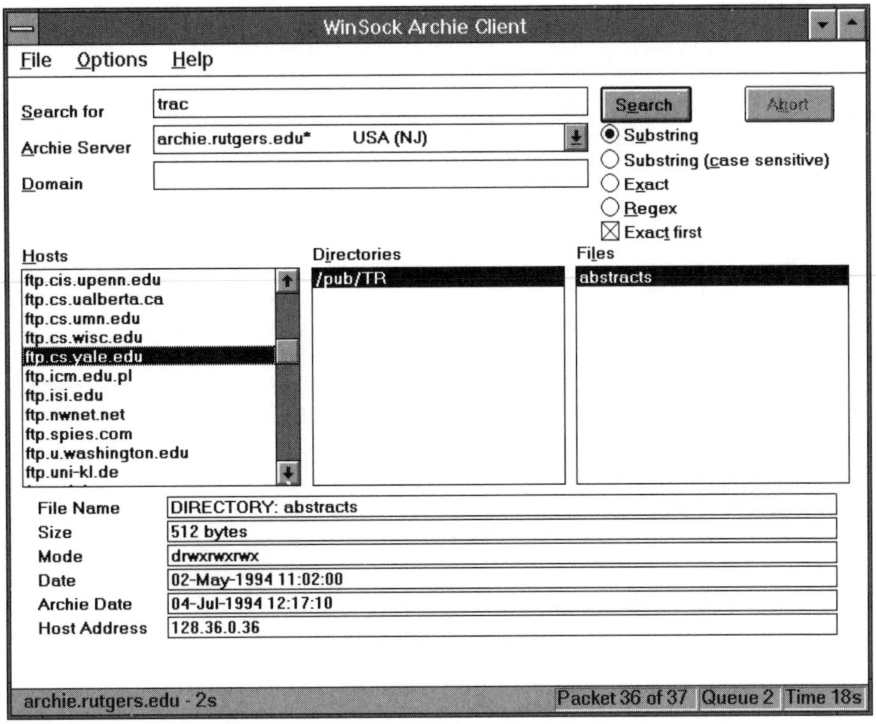

Figure 19-3:
wsarchie.

The body of the e-mail message you send contains the commands you want to issue to Archie. Enter as many commands as you like, each beginning in the first column of a line. Choose from the following available commands:

Command	What It Does
prog	Searches for matching names; assumes a regular expression search (regex)
whatis	Supplies the keyword for the software description database search
compress	Sends the reply in a compressed and encoded format
servers	Returns a list of Archie servers
path	Gives the e-mail address you want Archie to use to respond to your mail request if the automatically generated return address on your e-mail isn't correct
help	Returns the help text for e-mail Archie
quit	Ends the request to Archie

The most-common commands are prog and whatis, which take exactly the same form you use in telnet Archie. For example:

```
prog font.*txt
whatis font
```

Archie has become extremely popular, so popular that it's common for each server to be handling several dozen requests at a time, all the time, all day. That means that telnet or command-line Archie can be s-l-o-o-o-w-w, like 10 or 15 minutes to do a search. If it's going to be *that* slow, you may as well send in your request by e-mail and go do something else. As soon as Archie finishes your request, it drops its answer in your mailbox, where you can peruse it at your leisure. An added advantage of e-mail is that if the response turns out to be 400 lines long, it's much easier to deal with a 400-line e-mail message than with 400 lines of stuff flying off your screen.

Chapter 20

Gopher Baroque

. . . .

In This Chapter

▶ Looking for documents and files with Gopher

▶ Having considerably more fun with fancy Gopher programs

. . . .

Welcome to Gopherspace

As the Internet has grown, users have run into two related problems. One is that so much information is available that nobody can find it all. (Archie addresses this problem.) The other is that umpteen different ways exist to get to different resources (telnet, FTP, finger, Archie, and so on), and it's getting hard to remember what you say to which program in order to make it do its tricks.

Gopher solves these problems quite well by reducing nearly everything to menus. You start up Gopher, it shows you a menu. You pick an item, it shows you another menu. After a certain amount of wandering from menu to menu, you get to menus with actual, useful stuff. Some of the menu items are files that Gopher can display, mail to you, or (usually) copy to your computer. Some are telnet items that start a telnet session for you to a host that provides a particular kind of service. And some are search items that ask you to enter a *search string,* the name or partial name of what you're looking for, and then use the search string to decide what to get next — more menus, files, or whatever.

Another way to look at Gopher is like directories on your disk, in which some of the entries are files of various sorts, and other entries are other directories. Whether you think of it as menus or directories, Gopher gets much of its power from the fact that any item in any menu can reside on any host in Gopherspace. It's quite common to have a menu where every item refers to a different host. Gopher automatically takes care of finding whatever data you want, no matter where it is. You may use a dozen or more different Gopher servers in a single session, but you hardly know it.

This extremely simple model turns out to be very powerful, and Gopher is usually the fastest, easiest, and most fun way to wander around the net looking for and frequently finding the information you need.

The Good, the Bad, and the Ugly

All the services discussed to this point have had a bunch of different client programs that run on different systems (the client is the program you run on your computer, and the server is the one on the other end). Although they look different, anything you can do with one client you can do with another.

Gopher is different. You can do much more with a good client than with a bad one. In particular, Gopher is moving into the multimedia era with a vengeance, but the classic UNIX client (the original Gopher program you get at all the telnet sites) handles only text. For anything else, it goes into what one may call *cruel joke mode,* in which it tells you that it has a swell picture you would just love to look at but you can't. A good client, on the other hand, finds the picture, copying it to your computer, and popping it up in a window on your screen.

We look at two Gopher clients: the original, ugly, UNIX terminal Gopher and HGOPHER, a Windows client written in England by Martyn Hampson. (Both are free, so we know which one *we* would choose.)

Why did they name it Gopher?

They named it Gopher for two reasons: One is that the gopher is an industrious little animal, always busy, scurrying about on behalf of its family. The other is an obvious pun on "go fer" because Gopher *goes fer* your files.

The fact that the mascot of the University of Minnesota, where Gopher was written, is a gopher is, of course, *completely* irrelevant.

Gopher has been so successful that an improved version has appeared, called *Gopher+.* Fortunately, the main difference between the two is that Gopher+ can handle more and different kinds of information than plain Gopher can. Other than that, they're so similar that you can think of them as interchangeable, and plain Gopher and Gopher+ items can intermix in the same menu.

Where Do I Find a Gopher?

In your vegetable garden, of course, *yuk yuk* — oh, sorry, you mean the other one. The number of systems that have Gopher servers grows daily. But most of the servers talk only to Gopher clients, not to mere mortals using telnet. If you have a Gopher Client on your system, use it, because it's faster and more flexible than the telnet version. The exact name of the program varies. The most common Mac version is called Turbogopher. There are lots of Microsoft Windows versions, including Gopherbook, which makes Gopher menus look like pages in a book, WinGopher which makes each menu a separate subwindow, and so on. Ask around locally if you don't see any obvious Gophers available.

If you don't have your own client, telnetting to Gopher is much better than no Gopher at all. Fortunately, quite a few Gopher systems offer telnet access. Table 20-1 lists hosts offering telnet to Gopher. Because nearly all Gopher servers have references to each other (or at least to the master *every gopher in the world* list in Minnesota), you can get to any Gopher information from any Gopher system. So pick one close to you. **Note:** Unless otherwise instructed, if it asks you to log in, log in as gopher. If it asks for a password, just press Enter.

The first thing most of these systems do when they start up is to ask you what type of terminal you have. If you don't know, the correct guess is probably vt100 (an extremely obsolete terminal that, for sentimental reasons, most PC and Mac terminal programs emulate) or ansi. If you guess wrong, your screen becomes scrambled; press q and Enter to escape and try again.

Table 20-1	Gopher Servers	
Country	*Server Address*	*Special Instructions*
Australia	info.anu.edu.au	Log in as info
Austria	finfo.tu-graz.ac.at	Log in as info
Britain	info.brad.ac.uk	Log in as info
Chile	tolten.puc.cl	
Denmark	gopher.denet.dk	
Ecuador	ecnet.ec	
Germany	gopher.th-darmstadt.de	
Italy	siam.mi.cnr.it	
Japan	gan.ncc.go.jp	
Poland	gopher.torun.edu.pl	

(continued)

Table 20-1 *(continued)*

Country	Server Address	Special Instructions
Spain	gopher.uv.es	
Sweden	info.sunet.se	
U.S.A.	consultant.micro.umn.edu	
	sailor.lib.md.us	
	gopher.msu.edu	
	cat.ohiolink.edu	Log in as `ohiolink`
	wsuaix.csc.wsu.edu	Log in as `wsuinfo`
	scilibx.ucsc.edu	Log in as `infoslug`
	infopath.ucsd.edu	Log in as `infopath`
	sunsite.unc.edu	
	panda.uiowa.edu	
	gopher.virginia.edu	Log in as `gwis` (pronounced "gee whiz")
	ecosys.drdr.virginia.edu	
	gopher.ora.com	
	enews.com	Log in as `enews`

Taking Gopher for a Spin

Enough of this Theory of Pure Gopherology — let's take Gopher for a test drive. If you have a Gopher client on your system, type `gopher` (if you're not sure, try it). With any luck, you get a copyright screen, and when you press Enter, you get a screen like the following:

```
                Internet Gopher Information Client v1.1
                Root gopher server: gopher.micro.umn.edu  —
 > 1.   Information About Gopher/
   2.   Computer Information/
   3.   Discussion Groups/
   4.   Fun & Games/
   5.   Internet file server (ftp) sites/
   6.   Libraries/
   7.   News/
   8.   Other Gopher and Information Servers/
   9.   Phone Books/
   10.  Search Gopher Titles at the University of Minnesota <?>
   11.  Search lots of places at the University of Minnesota
            <?>
   12.  University of Minnesota Campus Information/
 Press ? for Help, q to Quit, u to go up a menu          Page: 1/
            1
```

If you don't have a local Gopher client, telnet to one of the systems listed in the section "Where Do I Find a Gopher?" earlier in this chapter. The items in the menu differ, but the general appearance of the screen is the same for local client Gopher and telnet Gopher. (If you're using Windows and HGOPHER, you see a screen like the one in Figure 20-1, which displays the same items, only more attractively.)

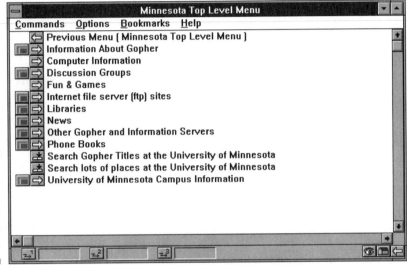

Figure 20-1:
A typical
top-level
menu
displayed by
HGOPHER.

This particular menu contains two kinds of items. The ones that end with / (slash) are other menus, and the ones with <?> are search items, which we consider later. In HGOPHER, the icon to the left of the line tells you what kind of item it is. A large arrow means another menu, and a little arrow pointing into a book is a search item. (The square icons to the left of some of the items mean that extra Gopher+ info exists for that item. Ignore for now.)

Although Minnesota is a swell place, gophers and all, let's look farther afield in our Gopher tour. So choose number eight, Other Gopher and Information Servers. That is, either move the cursor down to line 8 or go there directly by pressing 8 and then press Enter. When you press Enter, the next menu appears. (***Note:*** We're leaving out the top and bottom headers to save space.)

```
 ->    1.   All the Gopher Servers in the World/
       2.   Search titles in Gopherspace using veronica/
       3.   Africa/
       4.   Asia/
       5.   Europe/
       6.   International Organizations/
```

```
 7.   Middle East/
 8.   North America/
 9.   Pacific/
10.   South America/
11.   Terminal Based Information/
12.   WAIS Based Information/
```

Picking North America and then USA gives you a menu that lists all the states. The menu is too big to fit on a single screen, which it tells you by putting `Page: 1/3` at the bottom (meaning that this is page one of three). You move from page to page in the listing with + and – or to a particular item by typing its number. If you know the name of the item you want, you can search for it by typing / (slash), then part of the name, and then pressing Enter, at which point Gopher finds the next menu item that matches what you typed.

Eventually (in this example), we end up at the National Bureau of Economic Research because we're looking for a position paper it published. The menu looks like the following:

```
-->   1.   NBER Information.
      2.   About this Gopher.
      3.   Search for any NBER publication <?>
      4.   Penn-World Tables v. 5.5/
      5.   Phone books at other institutions/
      6.   NetEc (Universal) Economics Working Paper Server/
```

These indexes are a mess

If you use Gopher much, you quickly notice that there isn't a great deal of consistency from one menu to another. That's because Gopher is a totally decentralized system. That is, anyone who wants to can put up a Gopher server. It's pretty easy to do, requiring only that the system manager install a few programs and create some index files containing the text of the local menus. If one site wants to include in its Gopher menu a link to an item or menu somewhere else, it can just do so without requiring any cooperation from the manager of the item or menu linked to.

So the *good* news is that thousands of Gopher servers are on the net, put up by volunteers who want to make it easier to get to their data. The *bad* news is that almost none of these people has any experience in indexing and information retrieval (for that, you need a degree in library science), so the same item may appear on five different menus under five different names, and no two Gopher menus are quite the same.

It can take some experimenting and poking around, therefore, to figure out where people have hidden stuff. But it's invariably worth the effort.

Yoo-Hoo, Gopher

Now let's take advantage of a search item, indicated by <?>. When we choose it, Gopher pops up a box in which we type words to search for. In this case, we type the name of the author of the paper, and it shortly returns a menu of papers he has written:

```
Search for any NBER publication: Krugman  —
>       1.    |TI| Pricing to Market when the Exchange Rate
              Changes
        2.    |TI| Industrial Organization and International
              Trade
        3.    |TI| Is the Japan Problem Over?
        ...
```

Gopher search items are a very general feature. In this case, we searched through a local database, but the interpretation of any particular search key is entirely up to the Gopher server that does the search. People have written extremely clever servers that do all sorts of searching (see the section "Veronica, My Darling," later in this chapter).

Finally, Some Files

Now we have a menu of file items, which in this case contains citations of the papers we want. Choosing any of the items starts displaying its file on the screen, a page at a time. When the entire file has been displayed (or after you press Q to shut it up), Gopher says:

```
Press <RETURN> to continue, <m> to mail, <s> to save, or <p>
            to print:
```

If you decide that you liked that file, you can arrange to get a copy of it. If you press m, Gopher asks for your e-mail address and mails you a copy. If you press s, it asks for a filename and copies the file (invisibly, using FTP) to your computer. If you press p, it sends a copy to the printer. If you're telnetted in, the only option is m because the disk and the printer on the computer on which the gopher program is running may be thousands of miles away.

If you've dialed in from a PC running a terminal program such as Crosstalk or Procomm, you can usually download files by using a scheme such as Kermit or zmodem. At the end of a document, press Enter to get back to the menu and then D to download. Gopher pops up a box asking which download method to use. If your access to the Internet is by way of a PC, this is by far the easiest way to get copies of files because it combines FTP retrieval and downloading into one step. (For more info about downloading, see the section "Meanwhile, Back at the Ranch," in Chapter 16). Gopher can download any file in its menus, even if it's not text.

UNIX Gopher Cheat Sheet

Table 20-2 contains all the keys for the basic UNIX Gopher. Except as noted, each key takes effect immediately as you type it.

Move the cursor up and down to move up and down in the current menu. Moving the cursor to the left moves you back to the preceding menu. Moving the cursor to the right selects the current item.

Table 20-2	Basic UNIX Gopher Commands
Command	**What It Does**
Enter	Selects current item; same as cursor right
u	Moves up, goes back to preceding menu; same as cursor left
+	Moves to next menu page
−	Moves to preceding menu page
m	Goes to main menu
digits	Goes to particular menu item, terminates with Enter
/	Searches menu for string
n	Searches for next match
q	Quits, leaves Gopher
=	Describes current item
Bookmark commands	
a	Adds current item to list
A	Adds current menu to list

(continued)

Command	What It Does
v	Views bookmarks as a menu
d	Deletes current bookmark
File commands	
m	Mails current file to user
s	Saves current file (not for telnet)
p	Prints current file (not for telnet)
D	Downloads current file

Leaping Tall Systems in a Single Bound

Some menu items are flagged with <TEL>. These are telnet items. When you choose one of these, Gopher automatically runs telnet (see Chapter 14) to connect you with a system that provides a service. More often than not, you have to log in to the remote system — if so, it tells you the login name to use.

If your short-term memory isn't great, you may want to write down the login name the telnetted-to system requires, because it can take a while before it gets around to asking you for the login name.

To get back to Gopher, log out of the new system. If you can't figure out how to do that, press Ctrl-] and then at the telnet> prompt type **quit**. (*Note:* If you have telnetted to Gopher instead of running it directly, read the sidebar, "How many telnets would a telnet telnet if a telnet . . ." before trying this maneuver.)

Some telnet items actually invoke *tn3270,* a mutant version of telnet that works with IBM mainframes. The principle is the same, but figuring out the escape keys to use can be difficult (see Chapters 14 and 15).

When Gopher telnets to a system, it's not doing anything magical — if Gopher can telnet somewhere, so can you. If you find one of Gopher's on-line systems to be interesting, make a note of its host name, which is displayed just before connection. Next time, you can telnet there yourself without Gopher's help.

How many telnets would a telnet telnet if a telnet ....

Here's one of those problems that nobody had to worry about before computers existed. Suppose that you're working on your UNIX system and you telnet to a Gopher system. You use that Gopher to telnet to a *third* system, and your session on the third system is messed up, so you want to stop it. As Gopher never tires of pointing out, you can interrupt its telnet session by pressing Ctrl-].

But wait a minute. Ctrl-] also interrupts the telnet session from your computer to the Gopher system. If you press Ctrl-], which one does it interrupt? The first session (you to Gopher) or the second session (Gopher to third system)? Both? Neither?

The answer is that it interrupts the first session. But in that case, how do you interrupt the second session? For that, a trick is available: Change your interrupt character. Do this:

        Ctrl/]

        telnet> set escape ^X

Note: That last line ends with the two keys ^ (caret) and X. They tell the first telnet that henceforth you will press Ctrl-X to interrupt it. Now, if you press Ctrl-], you interrupt the second telnet session, which is what you wanted to do in the first place. If Gopher itself messes up, you can use Ctrl-X to get the local telnet's attention.

Incidentally, after you have telnet's attention, the command to tell it to quit is **quit**.

Attention Mac and Windows users: If you're using SLIP or PPP, you don't have to worry about this nonsense because your version of telnet has a sensible way to disconnect. If you type Ctrl-], that interrupts the second session, so you can type **quit** and get back to gopher. If you want to hang up on gopher, you use the menu item (usually called Disconnect) that your telnet provides, as usual.

Veronica, My Darling

Gopher quickly became a victim of its own success. So many Gopher servers are out there that finding the Gopher menu you want has become difficult. *Veronica* comes to the rescue. Like Archie, Veronica has a big database of available services. Veronica tracks all the Gopher menus that can be accessed directly or (often very) indirectly from the mother Gopher in Minnesota.

Using Veronica is easy — it's just another search item. You can find Veronica under "Other Gophers" or a similar name in most public Gophers.

For example, one time we wanted to find the on-line computerized *Jargon Dictionary* (which has been around in various forms since the late 1960s). I picked a Veronica Gopher item — there are usually several, one for each of the available Veronica servers — and for the search string we entered `jargon dictionary`. Veronica constructed for us a custom menu that contained only entries that matched our search string:

```
->   1.  The Jargon Dictionary File/
     2.  The Jargon Dictionary File/
     3.  The Jargon Dictionary File/
     4.  The Jargon Dictionary File/
     5.  The New Hacker's Dictionary (computer jargon) <?>
     6.  jargon: The New Hacker's Dictionary <?>
     7.  jargon: The New Hacker's Dictionary <?>
     8.  Fuzzy search in "The New Hackers Dictionary"
             (jargon.txt) <?>
     9.  The Jargon Dictionary <?>
    10.  Computer Jargon Dictionary <?>
```

Redundant items mean that a resource is available at more than one place. It usually doesn't matter which one you use.

Making Book

The final Gopher feature is *bookmarks*. As you move through Gopherspace, you often come to a menu that you want to revisit later. One way to do that is to carefully note the sequence of menus that led up to the one you like — but that's exactly the sort of thing that computers do better than people. Gopher bookmarks, then, note your favorite places in Gopherspace.

To remember the current item, press a (lowercase), for *add* a bookmark. To remember the entire current menu, press A (uppercase).

To use your bookmarks, press v (for *view*) and Gopher constructs a menu that contains all your bookmarks. You can use that menu like any other menu and move ahead from there. You can prune that menu if you want by pressing D to *delete* the current item.

Why did they name it Veronica?

According to its authors, the name Veronica is just a coincidence, unrelated to Archie, because it's an acronym for the true name, which is *Very Easy Rodent-Oriented Net-wide Index to Computerized Archives.*

But the next index searcher is called *Jughead,* which is supposed to stand for *Jonzy's Universal Gopher Hierarchy Excavation And Display.* How gullible do they think we are? And what about Betty? And Moose?

We find that we've come up with sets of bookmarks that are close to most of the items we regularly use. That lets us get to our regular Gopher haunts in only one or two keystrokes, starting from our bookmark menu.

If you're running the Gopher client directly, your bookmarks are saved in a file so that they're available each time you go Gophering. If you telnet in, the bookmarks are discarded (unfortunately) at the end of each session.

High-Class Gopher

Well, enough of that grotty old user interface. Let's try HGOPHER (see Figure 20-2).

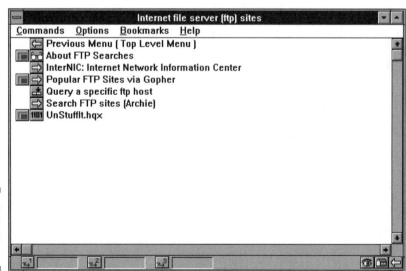

Figure 20-2:
Typical
HGOPHER
menu.

Figure 20-2 shows a typical HGOPHER screen. The column of icons describes the file types. The eyeglasses mean a text file, arrows are menus, and the little arrow pointing at the book is a search item. The 1101 is a binary file, and telnet items (none is shown here) appear as little terminals.

Because Microsoft Windows lets you have lots of windows active at a time, items that aren't menus show up in windows of their own. Text items appear in the standard Notepad editor, telnet items start a telnet window, and so on. When you click on a file, normally HGOPHER retrieves the file, runs a suitable program to display it, and then throws the file away. To save a file that HGOPHER retrieves, switch from *view* mode (click the little eye in the lower-right corner of the screen) to *copy to file* mode; for any incoming file, HGOPHER asks you for the name under which you want to store the incoming info.

If you've retrieved a file in view mode, you can keep a copy by telling the application that's viewing it to save the file under a *different* name from the one HGOPHER assigned. When the viewer exits, HGOPHER deletes the file it made, but if you made another copy, that copy stays on the disk.

HGOPHER understands Gopher+, so it knows considerably more about the formats of files than plain Gopher clients do. For example, Gopher+ can tag a file as being a picture stored in GIF or JPEG format (see Chapter 17) and can even say that a file is available in multiple formats, perhaps as a beautifully formatted PostScript file and also as plain text. The optional icon to the left of the file-type icon is the Gopher+ file type, which you can click on to see the types of the file.

Because HGOPHER keeps a list of viewer programs, if you have a shareware program that can display GIF files and you enter it in the viewer list, when you click on a Gopher+ file item that is a GIF file, the file is automatically copied to your machine and displayed with your GIF viewer. It's really cool.

But by far the coolest thing is that HGOPHER can do three things at a time. You can click three file items, and it copies all three at the same time into separate windows. You can continue to browse the Gopher menus while the transfers are happening — subject to a limit of three simultaneous transfers (moving from one menu to the next also requires a transfer) at any time.

You can therefore ask for a large item, such as a high-resolution picture, and keep Gophering along while the picture is being copied. This feature alone would make HGOPHER worth it, even if it *weren't* free.

There's considerably more to HGOPHER, but like most Windows applications, it's much easier to learn by using it than by reading about it. You can also find out more about HGOPHER in Chapter 12 of *MORE Internet For Dummies* (IDG Books, 1994).

TIP

It's a breath mint! No, it's a floor wax! No, it's both!

The astute reader (you, of course) may be wondering why Archie and Gopher both exist. They both let you look for files and retrieve them. Don't they really do the same thing?

Yes and no. Their original goals were quite different: Archie is an index to FTP files, and Gopher is a menuing system.

But they turn out to be quite complementary. In Chapter 19, you saw that at least five different ways are available to send a request to Archie (telnet, mail, and so on). The Gopherologists figured that a Gopher search item is as good a way

as any to send a request to Archie. They then went beyond that and arranged to intercept the response from Archie so that the directory names Archie returns turn into Gopher menus, and the files turn into items. This arrangement enables you to use Gopher to retrieve the files that Archie found. A marriage made in heaven, no?

To find one of these Gopher-to-Archie gateways, use Veronica to search for the keyword archie. We don't list any here because the list of gateways changes so often that any list printed here would be obsolete by the time you read it.

Chapter 21

We Have WAIS
of Finding Your Information

● ●

In This Chapter

▶ "There are more things in heaven and earth, Horatio, than are dreamt of in your philosophy . . ."

▶ Finding documents by keyword

▶ Some great recipes

● ●

*I*f you're keen on finding all there is to find about a given topic, it behooves you to learn to use WAIS, the software that knows its way around the databases of the world. *WAIS,* which stands for Wide Area Information Servers (pronounced "ways," incidentally), is a system designed for retrieving information from networks.

WAIS's original developers were information-retrieval and database gurus at Thinking Machines, Apple Computer, and Dow Jones (yes, the Dow Jones that publishes the *Wall Street Journal*). Although it was developed to provide access to proprietary databases, such as the ones that Dow Jones sells, most of the information accessible by way of WAIS at this point is available free. Thinking Machines even maintains a CM-5 Connection Machine supercomputer on the Internet for free WAIS access.

With WAIS, you enter a set of words that describe what you're looking for, and WAIS digs through whatever libraries you specify, looking for documents that match your request. Unlike Archie and Veronica, WAIS looks at the *contents* of documents rather than just at the titles. This requires much more work by the server (that's one reason that Thinking Machines is involved — its supercomputer does this kind of searching well), but it makes it much easier to find what you want because you're not dependent on someone's coming up with properly descriptive titles.

WAIS also uses *relevance feedback,* which means that after WAIS performs a search it returns a list of documents that seem to match your request. You can then look at some of those documents, and if WAIS didn't find quite what you want, you can identify a few of the documents that matched best (the most *relevant* ones) and tell WAIS to find stuff more like that.

The Bad News about Using WAIS

Unless you're thrilled at the thought of parallel parking an 18-wheeler in the city, you're probably not going to be really excited by the standard UNIX command-line interface for WAIS. The people who *like* WAIS say that the standard UNIX WAIS interface is clumsy, ugly, and nearly unusable. We can't tell you what the people who *dislike* WAIS think about that interface (at least not in a PG-rated book like this one).

Fortunately, window-based interface programs are available for most window systems (including X Windows and its variants, Microsoft Windows, and Macs) that make WAIS quite usable.

If you do have access to a window-based interface, by all means use it. Not only will you be happier, but you can also do more than is available through the command-line interface.

Why Z39.50 is good for you

In an anonymous building in Times Square in New York City, a little known organization called the *American National Standards Institute (ANSI)* labors away to make our lives easier. For example, an ANSI standard for lightbulbs ensures that no matter which brand of lightbulb you buy, it fits into your socket at home.

The scheme that WAIS uses to communicate between its clients and servers is based, amazingly enough, on an official ANSI standard called Z39.50. (All the standards have strange names like that. It means simply that it's the 50th standard approved by the 39th subgroup of the library science division.)

Z39.50 defines rules for one computer to use when passing an information-retrieval query to another computer and the rules for passing back the result. Systems all over the world use Z39.50 because most libraries insist on it.

Splicing WAIS on to most existing information-retrieval systems that already speak Z39.50-ese should be relatively simple, so you can expect many more WAIS sources in the future as existing library databases get WAIS-ized.

We should tell you that all the information accessible by WAIS is also available to Gopher and through WWW (World Wide Web). We tell you this now so that if you lose patience with the WAIS interface program — or if it loses you (not unheard of) — you know that you have other alternatives. Anyway, the sidebar "Go fer WAIS" tells you how to get started.

WAIS and Means

Unless you're fortunate enough to have a WAIS client program available to you locally (try the commands wais, swais, and xwais), you have to telnet to a machine that does. Telnet to quake.think.com, the home of WAIS, log in as wais, and be prepared to wait for a while as it starts up.

New WAIS of thinking

Although WAIS provides access to tons of stuff, it's not exactly user-friendly. You kinda have to learn how to talk to it. If you want to know more about the Internet, for example, you can't just say, "Tell me about the Internet." You have to take it step by step. No subject is too obscure. WAIS includes such databases as these:

- Astropersons
- Supreme Court
- Tantric News
- Livestock
- Quran (better known as the Koran, the Islamic holy book)

Go fer WAIS

Using WAIS through Gopher is simplicity itself. Find a WAIS menu in Gopherspace. (From the mother Gopher's main menu, choose Other Gopher and Information Sites and then WAIS Based Information.) From there, select a WAIS source (which appears as a search item) and type the words to search for. Gopher conducts a WAIS search and gives you a menu of the matching documents. You don't get to select multiple sources, and you can't use the relevance feedback features (described later in this chapter), but it's *much* easier than fighting with the standard horrible WAIS interface.

You also can get to WAIS from the World Wide Web (see Chapter 22 for details).

Where to look

Some WAIS servers begin by displaying a lengthy list of databases that WAIS is ready to search. The folks at Thinking Machines think that 25 screens of WAIS databases is not most people's idea of fun, so they jump over this part and start you at the directory of servers. What this means is that your *first* search is for which of the more than 500 servers you want WAIS to search:

```
SWAIS  Source          Selection             Sources:  1
  #    Server          Source                Cost
 001   quake.think.com]  directory-of-servers  Free
```

To start a search, you provide *keywords* telling WAIS what it is you're after. To specify words, press w. Enter your words at the keyword prompt and press Return. If you enter **Internet**, for example, WAIS turns up 40 listings in the Directory of Servers (the default source for the search):

```
S                           Search Results
               Items: 40
  #   Score  Source           Title
                   Lines
001: [1000] (directory-of-se) ANU-Internet-Voyager-Guide   79
002: [ 955] (directory-of-se) internet_services            24
003: [ 910] (directory-of-se) internet-mail               131
004: [ 864] (directory-of-se) Internet-user-glossary       29
005: [ 819] (directory-of-se) internic-internet-drafts     63
006: [ 819] (directory-of-se) ripe-internet-drafts         16
007: [ 773] (directory-of-se) comp.internet.library        14
008: [ 773] (directory-of-se) internet-intros              13
009: [ 773] (directory-of-se) internet-standards-merit     15
010: [ 773] (directory-of-se) internet_info                15
011: [ 728] (directory-of-se) internet-rfcs-europe         13
012: [ 728] (directory-of-se) internet-standards           64
013: [ 409] (directory-of-se) SURAnetGuide-All             23
014: [ 318] (directory-of-se) UCSC_directory_of_servers    55
015: [ 318] (directory-of-se) conf.announce                64
016: [ 318] (directory-of-se) dynamic-archie               65
017: [ 318] (directory-of-se) dynamic-netfind              69
018: [ 318] (directory-of-se) eros-data-center             94
```

You can enter many keywords, and WAIS tries to match them all. WAIS scores its search results on a scale of 0 to 1000, with 1000 assigned to the item that most closely meets your search criteria. (The numbers are relevant only within your search; the best match is always 1000, even if it didn't match all that well.) The search results are ordered, with the highest score appearing first.

What are all these things anyway?

WAIS just looked at its list of servers and came up with 40 different *databases* that have information that *might* be of interest to us. But how can we tell, and how do we actually get to that information?

Slogging through WAIS lists

As you look through the list of databases, select those that you think are likely to contain the information you're looking for. Press ↓ or j (lowercase) to move down the list. Press ↑ or k (lowercase) to move up the list.

Sources are listed alphabetically, and you can page down by pressing upper-case J or Ctrl-V or Ctrl-D. You can page back up by pressing uppercase K or Ctrl-U. The list of sources wraps around so that if you go past the bottom, you find yourself at the top of the list again (and if you go above the top, you find yourself at the bottom).

If you know the name of a source, you can search for it by name by pressing / (slash) followed by the name. You don't have to know the entire name; WAIS searches for whatever string you give it, starting with the first character of the entry. If you give it USE, it finds USENET, but if you give it NET, it doesn't. WAIS always begins at the top of the list, so you should try to use a string that's likely to be unique.

After you see the source in the list, you can position the cursor on it by pressing the number of the source. *Note:* Positioning the cursor on the source and actually selecting that source as one that WAIS is to use are *not* the same thing. That would be too simple.

To select a database, position your cursor on the line containing the database that interests you and press the spacebar or . (period). WAIS then displays a little blurb about this database. If you like what you see and want WAIS to look at it and tell you what's in it, press u, telling WAIS to *use* this database as a source for your next search. Patience, please, we're not finished yet.

Not again!

After you've looked through the list and picked out the databases you want to use as your sources, press s to return to the sources menu. Now you may think that you have told WAIS where to look during your next search, but you haven't exactly. What you really told WAIS is the list you want to possibly search, but really, of this list the ones you really want to search are — don't say that we didn't warn you.

Are we there yet?

To tell WAIS which of the databases you've just selected you actually like, you must *select* them. Again. From this screen. So position yourself next to each one you want to use (pressing its item number or the up- and down-arrow keys) and press the spacebar. You should see an asterisk appear next to it. If an asterisk is next to something you don't want to search (like maybe you don't want to search the directory of servers again), deselect it by navigating to it and pressing the spacebar.

What's wrong with this picture?

What's wrong is that you've finished all this work and you haven't started your search yet. Suppose that you've selected your databases — now what? You have to specify the keywords (the same way as before) and begin the search again. In keeping with the horribleness of this interface, to actually get to the information you want, you have to use anonymous FTP (see Chapter 16) to get to the site listed and copy the files, if found, to your computer (or Internet service provider, as the case may be). Yikes!

There are easier WAIS

You can use WAIS through Gopher (see Chapter 20) or World Wide Web (see Chapter 22). And, as you see later in this chapter, not all WAIS interfaces are this nasty.

Strictly optional

The WAIS server display format is determined by options, some of which may prove helpful to you. To see and set the options settings, press o (lowercase):

```
SWAIS                     Option Settings          Options: 6
   #     Option          Value
  001:   widetitles      on
  002:   sortsources     on
  003:   sourcedir       tmp/sources-user.13337/
  004:   commondir       /sources/
  005:   pagerpause      on
  006:   maxitems        40
```

The widetitles option provides you with the Internet name or address of the server. If you aren't interested in these, you can turn off its display. If sortsources is off, the sources are displayed in the order in which WAIS finds them rather than by relevance. The maxitems option determines how many matches WAIS finds before returning.

To actually change an option, select it as you select a source (by first positioning the cursor on the line of the correct option and pressing the spacebar or by referencing the option by number). To change a value from on to off or vice versa, press the spacebar. To change other values, press the spacebar and then enter the new value at the prompt.

Simpler Searches

WAIS does know about a number of things, and if you pick the right thing, you may be easily satisfied. Suppose that you want new recipes for cherry pie. If you select the sources recipes and usenet-cookbooks and the keywords cherry and pie, WAIS happily provides you with a great selection:

```
SWAIS                    Search Results                Items: 40
  #  Score                                               Source
              Title Lines
001: [1000] (cmns-moon.think)      CHERRYCHEESE-1(D)
            USENET Cookbook          60
002: [1000] (       recipes)               shafer@rig Re:
            BAKERY COLLECTION VEG App   445
003: [ 917] (cmns-moon.think)      BLKFOREST-PIE(D)
            USENET Cookbook          61
004: [ 760] (cmns-moon.think)      CHERRY-PILAF(M)
            USENET Cookbook          110
005: [ 732] (cmns-moon.think)      CHEESECAKE-4(D)
            USENET Cookbook          65
006: [ 693] (       recipes)               Sanjiv Sin Re:
            REQUEST Pumpkin Pie          302
007: [ 654] (       recipes)               shafer@rig Re:
            COLLECTION BAKERY Pumpkin    291
008: [ 519] (cmns-moon.think)      PUMPKIN-PIE-3(D)
            USENET Cookbook          87
009: [ 500] (cmns-moon.think)      GRAPE-PIE(D)
            USENET Cookbook          57
010:   [ 491] (cmns-moon.think)      STRAW-RHU-PIE(D)
            USENET Cookbook          73
011:   [ 482] (cmns-moon.think)      SWEEPTO-PIE(D)
```

```
              USENET Cookbook        48
012:   [ 482] (cmns-moon.think)        LEMON-PIE(D)
              USENET Cookbook        56
013:   [ 481] (          recipes)              arielle@ta Re:
              COLLECTION: Vinegar PIE                 155
014:   [ 473] (cmns-moon.think)        FRANGO-PIE(D)
              USENET Cookbook        64
015:   [ 462] (          recipes)              arielle@ta Re:
          Sweet Potato Pie
          180
016:   [ 462] (          recipes)              arielle@ta Re:
          Cheesecakes
          1105
017:   [ 454] (cmns-moon.think)        SPANAKOPITA-2(M)
              USENET Cookbook       108
018:   [ 454] (cmns-moon.think)        PUMPKIN-PIE-2(D)
              USENET Cookbook        51
```

BlkForest_Pie looks enticing, so we select item 3 and press the spacebar.
WAIS goes and gets it, presenting us with the following:

```
BLKFOREST-PIE(D)          USENET Cookbook          BLKFOREST-
          PIE(D)


BLACK FOREST PIE

     BLKFOREST-PIE - A rich chocolate/cherry pie

     I got this recipe from my mom, I don't know where she
          got it. It is very rich, so be careful!


INGREDIENTS (1 pie)
     1              pie crust, cooked
     3/4 cup        sugar
     1/3 cup        unsweetened cocoa
     2 Tbsp         flour
     1/4 cup        butter
     1/3 cup        milk
     2              eggs, beaten
     1 1/4 lb       cherry pie filling (one large can)
     8 oz           whipped cream
     1 oz            unsweetened chocolate, coarsely grated
```

```
PROCEDURE
   (1)   Prepare your favorite crust for a filled 1-crust pie.

   (2)   Preheat oven to 350 deg. F. In a medium saucepan,
         combine sugar, cocoa, and flour; add butter and
         milk. Cook until mixture begins to boil, stirring
         constantly. Remove from heat.

   (3)   Add small amount of hot mixture to eggs, mix well,
         then fold egg mixture into the chocolate mixture.

   (4)   Fold 1/3 of the pie filling into chocolate mixture;
         save the rest for the topping. Pour chocolate
         mixture into pie crust.

   (5)   Bake at 350 deg. F for 35-45 minutes or until center
         is set but still shiny. Cool, and chill one hour.

   (6)   Whip the cream. Combine 2 cups whipped cream and
         grated chocolate and spread over cooled pie. Top
         with remaining pie filling, and the remaining
         whipped cream. Chill at least half an hour before
         serving.

NOTES
   I use a pre-mixed whipped topping rather than real whipped
         cream when I make this pie.

RATING
   Difficulty: easy. Time: 30 minutes preparation, 3 hours
   cooking and cooling. Precision: measure the ingredients.
CONTRIBUTOR
   Darrell Walker
   Hewlett Packard, Cupertino, California, USA
   hplabs!hpesoc1!walker
```

To display the next screen, press the spacebar.

If you want WAIS to mail you the article, press m (lowercase). WAIS prompts you for your e-mail address.

After you're finished with the current selection, press q (lowercase). WAIS prompts you with Press any key to continue. When you do that, you are returned to the Search Results screen. Look through any of the goodies WAIS has brought you.

After you're finished, press s (lowercase) to return to the Sources Selection screen to begin another search or q (lowercase) to quit.

For searches of more obscure topics, begin with broad, general keywords. As WAIS finds articles, you can refine the search by choosing more-specific keywords.

Windows into WAIS

If you have serious research to do or if you expect to do it on an ongoing basis, investigate getting access to a decent WAIS client, such as xwais on UNIX or WinWais on Microsoft Windows. They provide extra functions that enable you to add sources or even set things up so that when new information becomes available, the client lets you know. Let's try a search with WinWais.

WinWais is a WAIS client that was written at the United States Geological Survey (your taxes at play — er, work). It has some special features that enable you to choose geographical coordinates by rotating and zooming in and out of a picture of the earth, but because most WAIS databases don't include any longitude or latitude to match, we stick to the basics.

When you start WinWais, you get a busy screen bristling with fields and buttons, as befits a complex application like WAIS. WinWais doesn't know about all the possible data sources, so before you do any searching, you have to begin by searching the Directory of Servers to find sources of interest and then add the sources it finds to the list that WinWais knows about.

First you have to select the source to use by clicking the Sources button, the large one in the upper-left corner under the File menu, as shown in Figure 21-1. At this point, there's only the Directory of Servers source, so click that to include it in the list to search. Then click Done.

Searching for recipes worked fairly well last time, so let's try it again. Type **food cooking recipes** into the top window and click Search to have WinWais look for sources on those topics. After a few seconds, it comes back with a list, shown in the bottom window in Figure 21-2.

Rather than score sources on a scale of 0 to 1000, WinWais scores them like movies, giving them from one to four stars. The first two sources seem promising.

To retrieve any found item, double-click it. After double-clicking the first item found, `recipes.src`. WinWais displays it in a window, as shown in Figure 21-3.

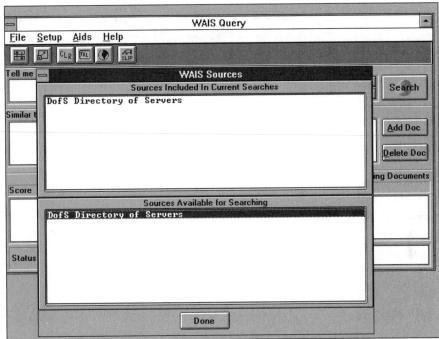

Figure 21-1:
Selecting
the source.

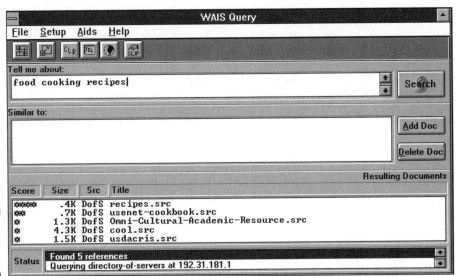

Figure 21-2:
Found some
sources.

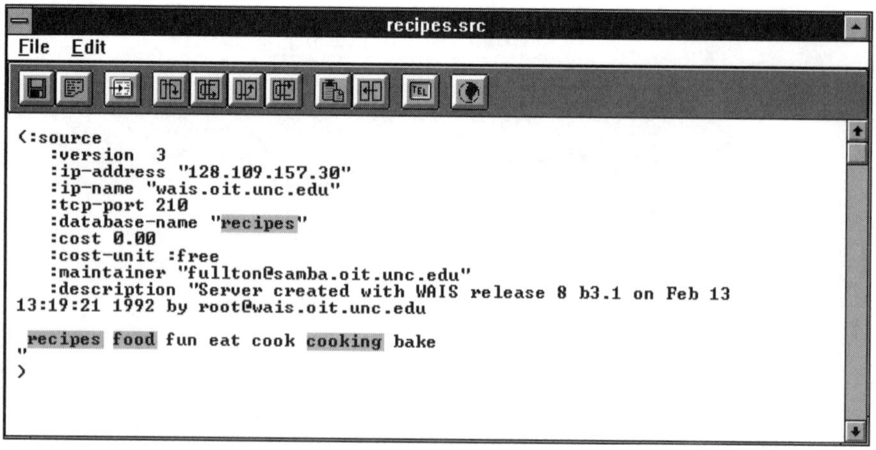

Figure 21-3:
A recipe
source.

The sources are in a special, rather ugly format that WAIS itself specifies. This looks like a plausible source, so we add it to our permanent list of sources by clicking the Save button (the one with the picture of the disk on it in the upper-left corner of Figure 21-3). If this were a regular document, this action would save it to a file. But because it's a WAIS source, the Save button pops up a window that enables you to edit the parameters of the source — something that is rarely a good idea. Click Add and then Done to add the source to WinWais's list. Then add the second source in the same way.

Search ho!

Now you're ready to do some searching. First you add the two sources you just found to the list of sources to search. (What you just did added them to the list of sources known to WinWais, but *not* to the list to search right now.) You add the sources again by clicking the Sources button and then clicking the two new sources that now appear in the lower window in the Sources screen. Click Done to get back to the main screen.

Performing the search is practically anticlimactic. Just type in the top window the words to search for (**florida pie**, in this case, to try to find a recipe for a pie John had on his last trip to Florida) and then click Search. WinWais queries each of the sources in turn and comes up with a ranked list of matches, as shown in Figure 21-4.

The first pie in the list is indeed an old Florida favorite, so double-click it to retrieve the recipe, as shown in Figure 21-5.

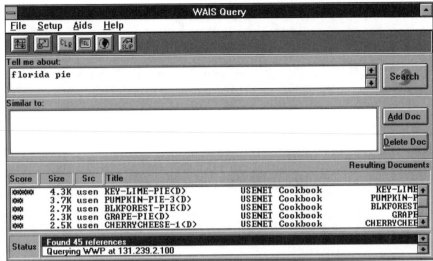

Figure 21-4:
WAIS found
some pies.

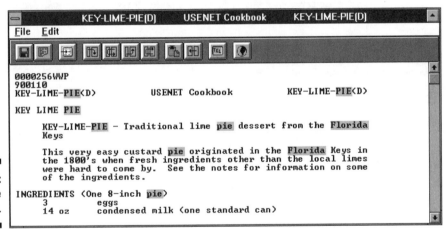

Figure 21-5:
Key Lime pie
— yum.

WinWais highlights the words in the screen that matched the query. You can save this recipe into a file by clicking the Save button (the one with the disk); print it by clicking the Print button (next to Save); and do some other document wrangling, which you can find out about easily enough from the help screen, so we don't belabor it here. After you're finished looking at the recipe (and saving it if you want to), return to the main screen by choosing File⇨Done from the menu.

Relevantly speaking

Having saved a copy of the Key Lime Pie recipe, scroll down through the list of documents to look for other interesting ones. A recipe for pumpkin cake looks interesting. Are other similar recipes available? That's where *relevance searching* comes in. Click once on the interesting recipe (clicking once selects it without going out to the server to retrieve the whole thing) and drag it into the middle window. That action adds it to the Similar To list of relevant documents. Click Search again, and WAIS then looks for more recipes like pumpkin cake, as shown in Figure 21-6.

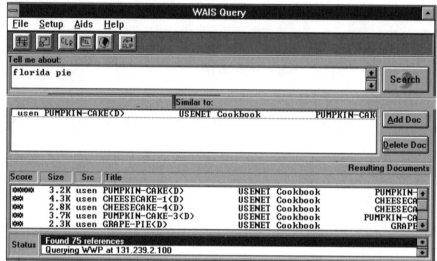

Figure 21-6:
Seeking
pumpkin
cakes.

As you might expect, the pumpkin cake recipe is the most relevant here, although some other possibilities look interesting.

WAISing into the Sunset

With a decent client program, WAIS is an extremely powerful way to search through databases. Several hundred free WAIS sources are available on the Internet, and many more proprietary ones are coming on-line. Dow Jones, for example, participated in the WAIS work to use for its on-line news service, which contains the text of many years of the *Wall Street Journal* and other magazines.

Chapter 22

It's More Than Super, It's Hyper: The World Wide Web and Mosaic

*I*f you're beginning to think there has to be an easier way, there is. One giant leap forward in making computers useful for ordinary mortals has been the attempt to improve the interaction between computers and ordinary mortals. The efforts that have been put forth toward making computers do what humans would do seem to be much more fruitful than the typical approach of making humans act like computers.

The *World Wide Web* — or *WWW* or the *Web* to its friends — is a major step forward in making the process of looking for information fast, powerful, and intuitive. WWW is based on a technology called *hypertext* (or now, more accurately, *hypermedia,* because it can handle graphics and sounds in addition to text). Hypertext was first described 20-odd years ago but only now is finding its way into widely used software.

Although the hypertext concepts have been around for a while, creating the technology to bring them to life has been a challenge. So even though hypertext may be the *coolest* way to retrieve data, it's not necessarily the *quickest.* Setting up information for hypertext retrieval is still cumbersome, and that's one more reason that information isn't already available in hypertext form.

Hypertext: a reminiscence

John writes:

The term and concept of *hypertext* were invented around 1969 by Ted Nelson, a famous computer visionary who has been thinking about the relationship between computers and literature for at least 25 years now — starting back when most people would have considered it stupid to think that such a relationship could *exist*. Twenty years ago he claimed that people would have computers in their pockets with leatherette cases and racing stripes. (We haven't seen any racing stripes yet, but otherwise he was dead on.)

Back in 1970, Ted Nelson told John that we would all have little computers with inexpensive screens on our desks with super-whizzo graphical hypertext systems. "Naah," John said. "For hypertext, you'll want a mainframe with gobs of memory and a high-resolution screen." They were both right, of course, because what we have on our desks in 1994 are little computers that are faster than 1970s mainframes and have more memory and better screens.

Various hypertext projects have come and gone over the years, including one at Brown University (of which Ted was a part) and one at the Stanford Research Institute (which was arguably the most influential project in computing history because it invented screen windows and mice).

Ted's own hypertext system, Project Xanadu, has been in the works for about 15 years, under a variety of financing and management setups, but with many of the same people slogging along and making it work. The project addresses many issues that other systems don't. In particular, Ted figured out how to pay authors for their work in a hypertext system, even when one document has pieces linked from others and the ensuing document consists almost entirely of a compendium of pieces of other documents. For a decade, we have been hearing every year that Xanadu, and now a smaller "Xanadu Light," will hit the streets the next year. This year we hope that they're right.

What's the Big Deal?

If you have ever done research in an area you know little about, you found yourself in a library, staring at the card catalog. You begin with one bit of information, such as a subject or a name. You look up one subject and begin reading the cards. All kinds of new ideas flash into your mind about ways you can continue your search with other subjects or other names. Even if you write down all the ideas, you inevitably have to pick one of them to follow and have to leave your current drawer and find the next. Here you begin again, and again your search may send you in an entirely different direction.

As you follow more and more leads, you may have to back up, look at choices you made earlier, and see what trying a different tack would bring. If you take careful notes, this process may be relatively easy, but chances are that you have to retrace many of your steps.

Hypertext organizes data to help this kind of information retrieval. It keeps one finger in one drawer and another finger in another drawer and so on to help you to go down one path and then go back and try a different one. And hypertext can have a hundred or more fingers in drawers all over the *planet*. (You might think of it as an extremely large but friendly alien centipede made of information.)

In traditional libraries (both the kinds with books and the kinds in computers), information is organized hierarchically yet somewhat arbitrarily, in the order it's found or in alphabetical order. These orders reflect nothing of the relationships among different pieces of information. In the world of hypertext, information is organized in relationship to other information. In fact, the relationships between different pieces of information are often much more valuable than the pieces themselves.

Hypertext also allows the same set of information to be arranged in multiple ways at the same time. In a conventional library, a book can be on only one shelf at a time, so a book on mental health, for example, is shelved under medicine or psychology, but it can't be in both places at a time. Hypertext is not so limited, and it's no problem to have links from both medical topics and psychological topics to the same document.

Suppose that you are interested in what influenced a particular historical person. You can begin by looking at the basic biographical information: where and when she was born, the names of her parents, her religion, and other basic stuff like that. Then you can expand on each fact by learning what else was happening at that time in her part of the world, what was happening in other parts of the world, and what influence her religion may have had on her. You draw a picture by pulling together all these aspects and understanding their connections — a picture that's hard to draw from just lists of names and dates.

A hypertext system creates the connections between pieces of information that enable you to easily find related information. As you draw the connections between the pieces of information, you can begin to envision the web created by the links between the pieces. What's so remarkable about WWW (the Web) is that it connects pieces of information from all around the world, on different machines, in different databases, all pretty much seamlessly (a feat you would be hard pressed to match with a card catalog).

My Spider Sense Is Tingling

Different WWW servers have implemented hypertext *browsing* programs differently. (They're called browsers rather than readers partly because you usually spend more time puttering about the links than reading any individual document and also because they all potentially give you the ability to add links and comments of your own.) If you understand what hypertext is about, you more easily understand how it works through any particular browser. Further-more, if you find that the browser you're using is particularly difficult, you can try another. Different browsing programs make different assumptions about their output and your machine, and a different one may be more suitable for you. It's like underwear — you like what you like, and nobody can persuade you any differently.

Very few Internet hosts have their own WWW browsers installed yet, so you begin by telnetting to a WWW server (see Chapter 14 for more details about telnet). Some public servers are shown in this list:

- info.cern.ch (Switzerland)

- www.njit.edu (New Jersey)

- hnsource.cc.ukans.edu (Kansas; log in as www)

- sunsite.unc.edu (North Carolina; log in as lynx)

- gopher.msu.edu (Mississippi; log in as web)

At least three different text-only browsing programs are available, with different public sites using different programs, so it's worth trying all three to see which one you prefer. The most popular is called Lynx, so that's the one we show here.

Using the University of Kansas machine, log in as www:

```
          Welcome to WWW at the University of Kansas

You are using a new WWW Product called Lynx.  For more
     information about obtaining and installing Lynx
     please choose About Lynx

     The current version of Lynx is 2.0.10.  If you are run-
          ning
     an earlier version PLEASE UPGRADE!

                    WWW sources
     For a description of WWW choose Web Overview
     About the WWW Information Sharing project
     WWW Information By Subject
     WWW Information By Type
```

```
                          Lynx sources
                University of Kansas CWIS
                History Net Archives


                         Gopher sources
        University of Minnesota Gopher Server (Home of Gopher)
        All the Gopher servers in the world
```

In this WWW system, the hypertext links are highlighted (bold). Use the arrow keys to navigate to the area that interests you and press Enter. In other systems, such as www.njit.edu, hypertext links are indicated by numbers enclosed in square brackets, and you choose by number the link that interests you:

```
NJIT WWW entry point[1]
gopher://chronicle.merit.edu/[2]
Overview of the Web[3]
NJIT Information Technology and World Wide Web Help[4]
```

The information the WWW systems have available is largely the same, because regardless of where you start, it's all linked together. We use the University of Kansas server in our example because from our machine it behaves the best. We want to see what topics are available, so we choose By Subject by positioning the cursor there and pressing Enter. Here's part of what it shows:

```
Mathematics    CIRM library (french).The International
               Journal of Analytical and Experimental Modal
               Analysis.
                         Complex systems


Meteorology    US weather, state by state.  Satellite Images.
                    Weather index. ANU weather services


Movies         Movie database browser.


Music                    MIDI interfacing,  Song lyrics
                         (apparently disabled for copyright
                         reasons), UK Independent Music.
```

We love the movies, so we move the cursor to Movie database browser and press Enter again.

```
[IMAGE]A Hypertext move the Movie

[IMAGE]

  Aug 25th.. Images Soon ?

   [IMAGE]

Select the type of search you want to perform:

      Movie people.....(multi Oscar winners) or

      Movie titles .....(multi Oscar winners)

Searches the rec.arts.movies movie database system, main-
tained by Col Needham et-al, using a mixture of Col Needham's
movie database package v2.6, and specially written scripts
and programs to search the databases.

Here is some information on list maintainers.
Local users can access the database from the command line.
            See the Movie
Database  directory in /well/lot.

If you have a comment or suggestion, it can be recorded here

   [IMAGE]

HERE is a pre-1986 movie information gopher server. (at
          Manchester UK)

rec.arts.movies.reviews can be found here
```

This is just a taste of the wonderful things WWW can do. It can not only connect you to all the databases it highlights but also even send Gopher on a search for you. The [IMAGE] blocks show where links to pictures are; telnet handles only text rather than pictures, so it can't show these links. (If you're fortunate enough to have a WWW browser on your own computer, it pops up a window with the appropriate picture if you select an [IMAGE] block. You'll see some real images later in this chapter with Mosaic.)

The Gopher server we have selected contains information about movies dated before 1986. It asks for a string to search. We type **Nicholson**, and it responds with this:

```
HERE:  Nicholson

 (FILE) THE BRIDGE ON THE RIVER KWAI
 (FILE) CHINATOWN
 (FILE) THE LAST DETAIL
 (FILE) ONE FLEW OVER THE CUCKOO'S NEST
 (FILE) EASY RIDER
 (FILE) THE SHINING
 (FILE) THE POSTMAN ALWAYS RINGS TWICE
 (FILE) FIVE EASY PIECES
 (FILE) TERMS OF ENDEARMENT
 (FILE) REDS
 (FILE) CARNAL KNOWLEDGE
 (FILE) THE LAST TYCOON
```

and pages more, with each movie title linked to more information about the movie. In other instances, WWW happily launches WAIS for you if the links happen to lead in that direction (see Chapter 21 for more information about WAIS).

Fame and Fortune

Another wonderful feature of WWW is that the network is ever-expanding, and *you* can add to it. While viewing the information from the Gopher server, WWW prompted us for our comments. WWW solicits comments at different levels so that you can really be involved in its growth. You can comment on the topic you're reading about, a new topic you want to discuss, WWW in general, this version of WWW, or whatever. You can enter your comments with your name or anonymously. WWW even lets you request a response from subsequent readers.

Another Way around the Web

The material WWW displays resides on many different servers all around the world; WWW automatically contacts servers as necessary when you move to materials they contain. In addition to providing a subject list as a starting point for *Web-walking*, WWW also provides access to many other network services, such as WAIS (see Chapter 21), telnet (Chapter 15), anonymous FTP (Chapter 16), Network News (Chapter 11), Gopher (Chapter 20), WHOIS, and X.500 (the last two are white-pages directory services mentioned in Chapter 9). The Web provides lists of all these kinds of servers (and indexes into these servers) so that you can literally go from machine to machine and look at all that's available. For example, here is part of the WAIS index provided by WWW:

```
WAIS INDEXES BY NET DOMAIN

Generated automatically at CERN from the TMC directory of serv-
        ers. See also: by index name, by Subject.

ariel.its.unimelb.EDU.AU    unimelb-research,
orion.lib.Virginia.EDU      bryn-mawr-classical-review,
wais.wu-wien.ac.at            cerro-1, earlym-1, rec.music.early,
archie.au                      aarnet-resource-guide,
                                archie.au-amiga-readmes,
                                archie.au-ls-lRt,
                                archie.au-mac-readmes,
                                archie.au-pc-readmes,
                                au-directory-of-servers,
services.canberra.edu.adir   sun-fixes,
wraith.cs.uow.edu.au          acronyms, netlib-index,
uniwa.uwa.oz.au                netinfo-biblio, netinfo-docs,
                                s-archive, sas-archive,
                                spss-archive, stats-
                                archive,
alfred.ccs.carleton.ca        amiga-slip, ocunix-faq,
qusuna.qucis.queensu.ca      software-eng,
```

After you choose a server, WWW connects you to it and allows you to search. Again, you can start up WAIS yourself, but WWW integrates it all into one big Web. WWW is a uniquely powerful way to look for and retrieve information, and we're sure that you'll be seeing more of it in the future. If you can only persuade your system manager to install one of the new services (such as Archie, Gopher, WAIS), WWW is definitely the way to go.

Battle of the titans: Gopher versus WAIS versus WWW

Okay, we've told you that you can use Gopher to search Archie and WAIS, you can use WWW to search Gopher, and you can use WWW to search WAIS. If you can use any of them to search anything, which one should you use and when? Confusion reigns! You need guidance.

You're in luck: *Guidance* is our middle name. (Actually, John's middle name is *Robert,* but he's been thinking about changing it.) Here are some rules of thumb.

✔ Use Archie if you're trying to locate software or files available for FTP.

✔ Use Gopher if you're looking for something for which you suspect someone has built a Gopher menu. (After Gophering around for a while, you learn what to suspect.)

✔ Use WAIS to search documents by content.

✔ Use WWW if you're not sure what you're looking for because it subsumes all the previous ones.

✔ Archie servers are all overloaded, so it's slow no matter how you use it. Use a local Archie client, telnet, or e-mail as the mood strikes you.

✔ If you have a local Gopher, WAIS, or WWW client (that is, a program on your own machine), use it instead of telnetting to some other system, because your client is faster and easier to use than telnet. Local Gopher clients can retrieve files directly to your disk, screen, and (if you have one) loudspeaker, whereas telnet versions have to e-mail them to you or download them by using Kermit or zmodem (PC telecommunications software).

✔ If at all possible, avoid the standard-text WAIS program (the one you get if you telnet to quake.think.com) because it's very difficult to use. Use a local, graphical WAIS, such as WinWais or xwais, if available; otherwise, use Gopher or WWW to get to WAIS. *Note:* Relevance feedback is available only with the local WAIS clients and not by way of telnet, Gopher, or WWW.

✔ If you're not sure which to use, start with WWW. If you find that what you want is provided by Gopher or WAIS, switch.

So What About Mosaic?

You have doubtless heard all about Mosaic, the "killer application of the Internet." So why haven't we discussed it yet? Well, it's somewhat overrated, but it's still pretty cool, so here it is.

Ms. Universe

One of the more useful innovations in the Web is what are known as *Universal Resource Locators,* always abbreviated as URLs. The point of a URL is to have a short and consistent way to name any resource that one might find on the net. Although URLs were originally intended for use only within WWW, they're so useful that you see them all over the place as a shorthand for FTP archives, Gopher menus, telnet servers, and of course WWW pages. Here's a typical URL:

http://sunsite.unc.edu/Dave/drfun.html

The http part says that this is a WWW page (if you care, it's HyperText Transfer Protocol), the name after the two slashes is the host name where the resource can be found, and the rest of the URL is the resource name on that host. Here's a typical URL for a gopher menu:

gopher://fcc.gov/

The part after the two slashes is still the host name. There's nothing after the last slash in this case, which means that it refers to the top-level menu at the FCC (the same FCC that regulates TV, radio, and telephone companies.) You can either give this URL directly to a WWW client or take it apart and use the host name to start a regular gopher client.

The last kind of popular URL is one for a file in an anonymous FTP archive:

ftp://iecc.com/pub/jclt/sell.txt

Here, iecc.com is the host name, and pub/jclt/sell.txt is the filename on that host. Again, WWW clients can use this URL directly, or if you don't have or don't feel like using a WWW client, you can use it yourself by starting your FTP program, connecting to iecc.com, going to the directory pub/jclt, and retrieving the file sell.txt.

NCSA Mosaic is the name for a set of WWW client programs that run on Windows, Macs, and UNIX (under X Windows.) The NCSA part stands for the National Center for Supercomputing Applications at the University of Illinois, which wrote the first versions of Mosaic. Since then, several commercial vendors have licensed NCSA's code (and in several cases hired away NCSA's programmers) to produce enhanced versions of their own. At least one commercial Mosaic is unrelated to NCSA's. So "Mosaic" is rapidly becoming a generic term for a graphical WWW client program.

Here we take a quick look at NCSA Mosaic for Windows, probably the most popular version of Mosaic in use. It's full of bugs, but NCSA gives it away for free. All the NCSA versions deliberately look about the same, so although the details of the locations of the buttons differ, the basic functions are the same.

When you start Mosaic, it automatically fetches an initial Web page to display, as shown in Figure 22-1. "Out of the box" (hot off the net), Mosaic fetches NCSA's home page. (With luck, someone will have configured it to start somewhere else, because with a million copies of Mosaic all starting up with the NCSA home page, starting up can be a wee bit slow as you wait your turn to fetch a copy of that page over the net.)

After you start it, using Mosaic is a snap. The links to other documents are underlined if they're text or heavily outlined, if they're pictures. (If you have a color screen or if this were a glossy coffee-table-type book, you would also be able to see that the links are blue.) As soon as you click on something, Mosaic runs out on the net to get whatever the link is linked to.

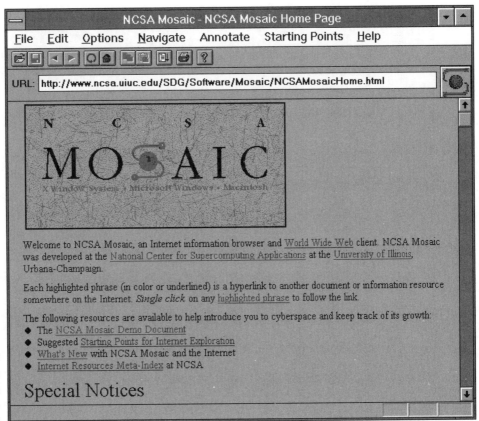

Figure 22-1:
Mosaic's
Home Page.

Mosaic comes with references to a number of interesting pages built-in. The Starting Points menu lists lots of interesting pages to start from; choose any of them from the menu, and Mosaic will fetch it for you.

The People's hypermedia

WWW and Mosaic are now established well enough that it is relatively easy for an individual (admittedly, an individual with some technical savvy and considerable patience) to create his or her own WWW page. So we have some pretty funky pages. Figure 22-2, for example, is the Doctor Fun page, with a new cartoon five days a week written by a guy who should have been fixing computers in Chicago.

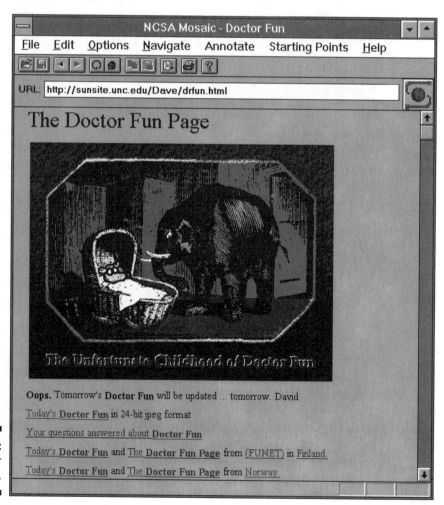

Figure 22-2:
The Doctor
Fun page.

Indexes galore

Since any WWW page can link to any other web page, we're starting to find a number of pages that exist solely to be indexes to collections of resources around the net. One of the best is Scott Yanoff's Special Internet Connections list, updated twice a month, part of which you can see in Figure 22-3. It rates a menu item of its own in Mosaic; you can see it by choosing Starting Points⇨Other Documents⇨Internet Services List.

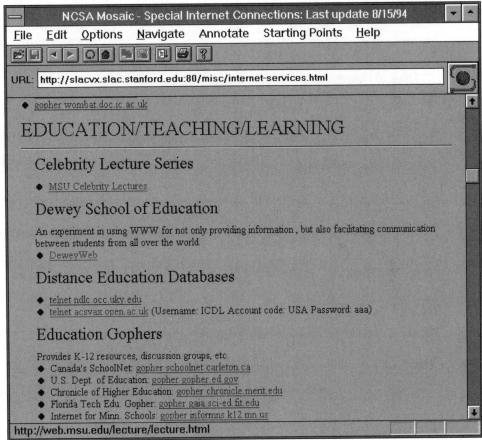

Figure 22-3:
Special
Internet
Connections.

Mosaic's dirty little secret

One major thing keeps NCSA Mosaic from being the perfect Internet program. It's slow. Really, really slow. Readers of a certain age may remember an old Bob and Ray radio skit about the STOA. That's the Slow...Talkers...Of...America. The head of the S...T...O...A (played by Bob) put long...pauses...between...his...words, so long that you wanted him to just hurry up and finish his sentences. Mosaic can feel like that.

There are two separate slowness problems. One is that fancy multimedia screens require a great deal of data, which means that they take a long time to transfer over any but the fastest networks. The other is that Mosaic itself is, to use a technical computer term, a pig. Even the authors of Mosaic say that you need a 486/33 with 8 megabytes of RAM to get reasonable performance, and we can report from experience that if you run Mosaic on a computer of that size, it still spends an awful lot of time swapping pieces of itself back and forth from the disk. Presumably, if you have a Pentium and 32M, it's fast.

You can do a few things to perk up Mosaic. The best way to deal with the network speed problem is to tell it not to fetch all the swell graphics in each page automatically. You do this by choosing Options⇨Display Inline Images from the menu. Henceforth, wherever a page has a graphics image, Mosaic puts a placeholder (a sort of blue, swirly doozit) where the picture is supposed to go. If you want to see what the picture looks like, you click the doozit with the *left* mouse button, at which point Mosaic goes and gets the picture. People usually find that they can live without about 90 percent of the graphics, and it makes pages much faster to load.

Mosaic automatically *caches* (saves internal copies of) as many of the pages and images that it fetches as it can, which means that if you later redisplay the same page, Mosaic can reuse the copy it already has rather than refetch it. Even if you have graphics turned off, if Mosaic sees that it already has an image in its cache, it displays it because it takes no extra time to do so.

As far as Mosaic's basic pigginess, there's not much you can do about that, short of buying a bigger and faster computer. You shut down as many of your other programs as you can (everything except the Program Manager and, if necessary, your TCP/IP system) and hope for the best. Some of Mosaic's competitors, notably Cello, from the Cornell Law School, work better in systems with limited memory. If you find Mosaic too slow for words, it's worth seeing whether you can get someone to install Cello for you. Mosaic's developers claim they're working on the piggy problems, so by the time you read this, Mosaic, we hope, will be svelte and speedy.

Part V
The Part of Tens

"I DON'T THINK OUR NEWEST NETWORK CONFIGURATION IS GOING TO WORK. ALL OF OUR TRANSMISSIONS FROM OHIO SEEM TO BE COMING IN OVER MY ELECTRIC PENCIL SHARPENER."

In this part...

Some things just don't fit anywhere else in the book, so they are grouped into lists. By the strangest coincidence, exactly *ten* facts happen to be in each list. (*Note to the literal-minded:* You may have to cut off and/or glue on some fingers to make your version of ten match up with ours. Perhaps it would be easier just to take our word for it.)

Chapter 23

Ten Common Problems and How to Avoid Them

• •

In This Chapter

▶ Opportunities for embarrassment and humiliation

▶ Easy ways not to be embarrassed and humiliated

• •

The Network's Dead!

Actually, it's probably not. Suppose that you try to use a service on some remote computer and you can't get to it. You know that you didn't change anything on *your* computer, so the network or the remote computer must be kaput, right? Not so fast.

Many moving parts (conceptually speaking) lie between your computer and a computer on the other side of the country (or world). The Internet is a bunch of interconnected networks, so your data probably moves along a dozen different networks between here and there. In theory then, a failure could come from any one of them. In practice, the networks in the middle are *high-speed, shared* networks with *multiple redundant paths, automatic rerouting, 24/7 monitoring,* and many other buzzword features that mean that they're not likely to break and that even if they *do* break, bells start ringing in less than a second, network connections are rerouted, and people fix things.

Consider this: In more than 20 years, the Internet has experienced only one major backbone failure, and that was because of a software glitch, not because of cable failures. On the other hand, if you accidentally kick your computer's network connection out of the wall, who's going to notice but you? So here's a list of things to check.

Is your computer working?

Does your computer act normally when you tell it to do nonnetwork things? Yes, we know that it's obvious, but it never hurts to check. (True story: "Hello, help desk? My computer won't boot up." "Is it plugged into the wall correctly?" "I can't tell; the power failed and all the lights are out.")

Is your computer connected to the net?

The next step is to see whether you have any connection to the outside world. If you do, the best command to use is *ping,* which sends packets to another host that is supposed to echo them back. The ping command depends only on the very lowest level of networking software. So if ping can't reach another computer, that strongly suggests either a network break or that the other computer is dead. For some reason, on UNIX systems the ping command is often hidden away, so you have to type something like /etc/ping or /usr/ ucb/ping to run it. (Make a note of the correct incantation.) When you run ping on a UNIX system, its output looks something like this:

```
% ping nearbyhost
PING nearbyhost: 56 data bytes
64 bytes from 127.186.80.3: icmp_seq=0. time=9. ms
64 bytes from 127.186.80.3: icmp_seq=1. time=9. ms
64 bytes from 127.186.80.3: icmp_seq=2. time=9. ms
64 bytes from 127.186.80.3: icmp_seq=3. time=9. ms
^C
—nearbyhost PING Statistics—
4 packets transmitted, 4 packets received, 0% packet loss
round-trip (ms)  min/avg/max = 9/9/9
```

The ping command usually runs until you interrupt it with Ctrl-C on UNIX or the equivalent mouse click in Windows. The times it reports are the approximate times it took for each message to reach the other computer and come back, measured in milliseconds (1/1,000 of a second, abbreviated as *ms*). For computers on the same Ethernet, the time should be in the vicinity of 10 ms. For computers on the other side of the world, it can be as much as 2,000 or 3,000 ms — two or three seconds. Now and then a ping can get lost in the network. If it happens only now and then, it's no problem. But if it happens frequently (more than 5 percent of the time), you have either severe network congestion or, more likely, a flaky network connection with one of the computers.

If you don't have ping, any other network command, like finger or telnet, will do. First, see whether you can contact a nearby computer — ideally one on the same physical network cable. (The closer another computer is, the more likely it's on the same cable.) Three results are possible:

- ✔ Your computer can't even find the other computer.
- ✔ Your computer can find the other computer, but the other computer doesn't answer.
- ✔ It works.

If it works, you know that your computer and local network are okay, so you can go on to the next step.

If your computer claims that no such computer as the one you're trying to contact exists, you may have lost contact with your *name server* — the computer whose job it is to translate host names to four-part numeric addresses. Assuming that you know the numeric address of your neighboring machine, try contacting it by using the numeric address, four numbers separated by periods. (If you don't know the other machine's number, try going to the machine and telling it to ping itself, which should report its address. Failing that, ask a local expert where the list of addresses can be found.)

If your computer can contact the neighbor by numeric address but not name, you have name server trouble. (See the section "What's in a Name?" later in this chapter.) Contact an expert, politely, and ask for help. If you can report that a numeric address works, but the corresponding name doesn't, you narrow down the possibilities considerably. If you want to do some more sleuthing, and you know which computer on your local network is the name server (usually the one that has the big disk, if you use remote files), try pinging it by name and number to see whether the route to that machine is broken.

If your computer tries to contact the other computer and can't, the most likely problem is that your computer has come unhooked from the network. Other than checking whether you've accidentally knocked out the network cable, you can't do much about this. You have to ask for help.

Note to users with computers on Token Rings: If your local network uses a Token Ring (the cable looks like phone wire and uses big, square connectors — see Chapter 3) and you unhook your computer by mistake, just plugging the connector back in isn't enough to get you back on the network. Your computer has to do a *network insertion,* a special processing step that reintroduces itself to its neighbors. The insertion requires at least restarting your computer's network software and may require a complete reboot. Check locally. And put that cable someplace where people are less likely to trip over it.

Is the other end okay?

If you can get in touch with a neighboring computer, that pretty much proves that your computer is okay. The next thing to think about is whether the computer at the other end is on. In particular, what are its scheduled hours?

Some services are available only part-time. The United States Library of Congress LOCIS system, for example, is available only during library hours. Or maybe they're doing some maintenance at the other end. In what time zone is the other computer? If you're in Los Angeles, it may be 5 p.m. there, but if the other computer is in France, it's 2 a.m. there — a prime time for hardware and software maintenance.

Also, some companies use low-cost, dial-up access to connect their local network to the Internet, which means that they're on the net only when someone at that company is using some outside network resource. Otherwise, they're off the net.

If you've determined that the other computer is indeed supposed to be available, maybe it's just broken. Try some other computers several network hops away from you. (The various network information centers such as `is.internic.net` are good candidates.) If you can get to them, the network is probably okay. If you know someone where the computer you're trying to use is located, call on the phone and ask whether there is a problem.

Maybe it's the network after all

If you can get in touch with a neighboring computer, that proves that your computer is okay. But if you can't contact any computers in the outside world, it sounds like a network problem. At this point, it's often informative to wander down the hall and peer into the closet where the network routing equipment lives to see whether perhaps someone is working on it. Remember: Local network failures are the most likely. It may also help to try pinging computers in the same department, on different floors, in different buildings, and so on, to get an idea of how far away you can contact someone, because that helps to pinpoint where the failing network-to-network connection may be.

What's in a Name?

Occasionally you'll be running perfectly normally, and a program you're using will give you a strange message like the one in Figure 23-1. What's going on?

Figure 23-1:
Mosaic
can't figure
out a name.

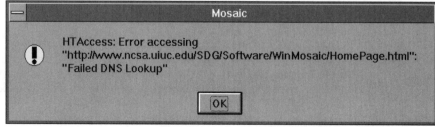

TIP

Things to know before your network breaks

It's much easier to diagnose network foul-ups if you gather a few important facts before it breaks. Here's a minimal set:

Your computer's host name_____

_____

Its numeric address_____

_____

Your name server_____

_____

Name server's numeric address_____

_____

A nearby computer_____

_____

Its numeric address_____

_____

A remote computer_____

_____

Its numeric address_____

_____

Your ping command_____

_____

The problem has to do with the way the Internet's Domain Naming System works. When you tell a program to contact a computer by name, first it has to find the corresponding numeric address for the name. To do that, it asks a local *name server,* a computer running a program, to do the translation. Because there are upward of three million named computers on the net, as you might imagine, no single name server knows all the names. So if you ask your local server for a name it doesn't know, it goes out by way of the net to find out about the name from other, better connected, servers. Now and then, translating a perfectly good name fails, most likely because one of the net messages got garbled and your program got impatient and gave up waiting before the name server could get back to it with the name.

The solution is quite simple: Just try it again. The local server will have gotten the translation details (the amounts of time here are measured in fractions of a second), and your computer will get its numeric address.

If you get `address not found` errors two or three times in a row, that suggests that either the local network or the name server is broken. See "The Network's Dead!" for some suggestions about what to do in that case.

What's My Address?

Before you begin sending out a great deal of e-mail and news articles, make sure that you know your electronic mailing address. Keep in mind that your address relative to the Internet as a whole may be different from your address within your company. For example, your in-company address may be

```
tom@calmari
```

but your address from the outside may be one of these:

```
tom@calmari.mktg.nebraska.plexxcal.com
Thomas.A.Hendricks@plexxcal.com
```

or even

```
tom%calmari@mktg-gateway.plexxcal.com
```

 One easy and nonembarrassing way to make sure that you have your address right is to send a message to an automated mail server (see Chapter 9). When the server sends you a response, look at the `To:` line in the response's message header to see what your address is. If you're at a loss for a mail server to use, send a message right here to The Internet For Dummies Central Headquarters, where the address is

```
internet@dummies.com
```

While you're at it, add a few words about whether you like this book, because messages go to both an automatic mail responder and to a mailbox where the authors can read your comments.

 Also, find out the numeric Internet address of your computer (a four-part number, something like 127.99.88.77). It can come in handy when someone needs to track down a network problem between your computer and the rest of the Internet world.

Real Network-Type Problems

If you attempt to contact another host and get a response like `no route to host` or `connection refused`, that usually means that a network problem has occurred. See the next chapter for details.

Making Enemies via E-Mail and News

The quickest way to make a bad name for yourself is to send obnoxious e-mail or news. See Chapters 8 and 11 for more, but here are things not to do:

✔ **Don't send junk mail.** Just because it's easy to send e-mail to 10,000 people doesn't mean that it's a good idea. You can expect to find your mailbox clogged, minutes later, with 10,000 irate responses.

✔ **Don't send advertisements.** Traditionally, Internet e-mail is used for noncommercial purposes. It's perfectly okay to talk about work-related topics, but don't send out unsolicited ads to drum up business. If you do, expect to receive buckets of hate mail and for your system manager to boot you off the system.

✔ **Don't send junk news either.** It's technically not difficult to send 10,000 copies of a message to every possible Usenet newsgroup, to make sure that everyone in the world who reads news will see it. That's known as *spamming* (after the Monty Python "I don't like Spam" skit) and is universally loathed. Expect 100,000 irate messages, followed shortly by having your account canceled.

✔ **Don't send any messages about dying boys, modem taxes, or chain letters.** Internet users have heard them all and don't want to hear them again. (See Chapter 8 for the sorry details.)

✔ **DON'T SEND MESSAGES IN ALL UPPERCASE LIKE THIS BECAUSE PEOPLE ASSUME THAT YOU'RE TOO DIM TO FIND AND TURN OFF THE CAPS LOCK KEY ON YOUR KEYBOARD.** Use upper- and lowercase, just like on a real typewriter. Some e-mail users evidently feel that neatness no longer counts, but they're wrong.

✔ **Don't forget: E-mail always comes across ruder or more obnoxious than you intend.** Over and over, people have discovered this important fact the hard way. E-mail is a funny medium, not really like the phone or paper mail. And it's unexpectedly easy to fly off the handle in response; so easy that the term for this is *flaming*. Don't flame. If you do, people assume that you're a flaming . . . um, well, you know what we mean.

Mailing List and Usenet News Etiquette

Discussed in greater length in Chapter 10, but here's a brief review:

✔ Know the difference between the address you use to get on or off a mailing list and the address you use to send messages to the list itself.

✔ Read a mailing list or newsgroup for at least a week before you try to send anything to it so that you understand what topics it covers and grasp the level of discussion. (For example, a Usenet group called comp.arch is about computer architecture. But every month or so some clueless newcomer who's never looked at the contents sends in a question about archiving programs. We're sure that you'll never make that kind of mistake now.)

- ✔ Most lists have an introductory message, and most newsgroups periodically post FAQ (frequently asked questions) messages that introduce the topic and answer the most common questions. Before you send in your question, make sure it's not already answered for you.

- ✔ When you're responding to a message, if you include a copy of the original message, trim it down to the minimum needed.

Don't Be a Pig

Because most Internet services are free (after you've paid for the network connection), the popular ones can become slow and overloaded. Don't be a pig. Use what you need, but don't FTP megabytes of junk just because you think that you might need it someday.

Help — I've Telnetted and I Can't Get Out

You can use telnet and rlogin to connect to services on other computers all over the world. Amazingly, some of the programs and systems you telnet to contain *bugs* (computerese for errors). Some even hang (freeze up completely) and become catatonic.

Right up there in the top ten embarrassing moments is the one in which your computer is working flawlessly but your console has gone dead because you're telnetted to something that's hung and you can't make telnet go away. There's always some way to escape, but you have to know what it is, preferably *before* you get stuck.

Note: On UNIX systems, you usually escape with Ctrl-]. Then when it says `telnet>`, you type `quit`. If you're logged in through a terminal server, the escape may be two or more letters, like Ctrl-^ followed by X. If you're using a machine with windows (a Mac, Microsoft Windows, or a UNIX system with the X Window system), a menu item (probably at the top of the telnet window) enables you to disconnect from the remote system.

The rlogin command is much like telnet, to the point that it has the same problem. For most versions of rlogin, you disconnect by pressing Enter, and then ~. (tilde followed by period), and then Enter again. Your version of telnet or rlogin may be different. Telnet usually tells you what the escape character is at start-up; rlogin is extremely taciturn, and you may have to consult an expert or — perish the thought — look it up in the manual.

A Not-So-CAPITAL Idea

Back in the Dark Ages of computing, nobody worried about upper- and lower-case. Keypunches and terminals had only capital letters so EVERYTHING WAS IN UPPERCASE, INCLUDING FILENAMES AND MAIL ADDRESSES. BUT IT SEEMED AN AWFUL LOT LIKE SHOUTING, SO AS SOON AS TERMINALS COULD HANDLE LOWERCASE, THEY switched to mixed case like normal people use — at least some of them did.

The problem is that some computers (notably those running UNIX) consider upper- and lowercase to be different, whereas others (running most other systems) consider it to be the same. For example, on a UNIX system, README, ReadMe, and readme are three different files, but on most other systems they're merely three different ways to type the name for the same file. What this means is that when you are retrieving files by FTP or RCP, make sure that you type the name in the same mixture of upper- and lowercase that appears in a directory listing. It can't hurt and it may well help.

Another place where this occasionally causes trouble is in e-mail addresses. According to the official standard for e-mail addressing, case doesn't matter in the *domain* part of the address (the part after the @). But the *local* part (the part before the @), can be handled any way the recipient mail system wants. In theory, this means that a really perverse system could interpret Fred@perverse.org and FRED@perverse.org to be different mail addresses, although we have never seen a mail system that does so. In a few cases, you have to type the local part of the address in the same case as the recipient system handles it; so if the recipient's address is fred, it doesn't accept Fred. (These systems are gradually being stamped out, but a few still exist.)

Fortunately, a reliable rule of thumb is that systems that care about upper- and lowercase addresses want the address in lowercase, so use fred to be sure.

If you have to use mixed UUCP (an old dial-up networking system we mention at the end of Chapter 9) and domain addresses like flipper!fred@ntw.org, be aware that the UUCP site name (flipper, in this case), is case sensitive. A few mixed-case UUCP host names used to exist, but they are — as far as we can tell — all gone. So use all lowercase to be sure.

Why FTP Mangled Your Files

Finally, here's a mistake that everyone makes sooner or later: You use FTP to retrieve a program or a compressed file (ZIP, .Z, or the like), and the file is messed up. The program hangs, the ZIP file doesn't unzip, or the compressed file uncompresses to trash. Is the disk broken? Is the network corrupt? Nope. It's just that you forgot to tell FTP to transfer the file in *binary* mode, so it copied it in *ASCII* mode under the misimpression that the file contained plain text. Just transfer it again, in binary mode this time. (Type the command **binary** or **image** to the FTP program before transferring the file.)

An easy way to check for this problem is to compare the size of the file on your computer to the one from which you retrieved it. In binary mode, the two copies should be exactly the same size. If the size differs by a few percent (one copy is 87,837 bytes, and the other is 88,202, for example), you've been bitten by the ASCII copy gremlin. Oops. Don't be embarrassed — even experts forget this one from time to time. Yes, that includes us.

Chapter 24

Ten Problems That Aren't Your Fault and How to Circumvent Them

In This Chapter

▶ Mysterious network failures

▶ Hostile hosts

▶ Dread version creep

When Networks Go Bad

Actually, networks almost never go bad, as we mentioned in the preceding chapter. But there are a few messages that *do* mean that the network isn't doing what you want.

"Connection refused"

This message means just what it sounds like. Your computer asked to talk to some other host, and the host said no. There are several possible reasons for this:

- ✔ You've tried to use a service that the host doesn't offer. Not every Internet host offers every service. It's up to a host's manager to decide what services are available and what services aren't.

- ✔ Some hosts don't offer any services at all. For example, if you try to finger, FTP, telnet, or nearly anything else to *xuxa.iecc.com,* you get Connection Refused. It's nothing personal — xuxa lives in John's attic, as I've mentioned, and she won't connect to us either, because she's a little old 286 PC that just routes data from one network to another. (She does respond to a *ping,* however, if you want to see that she exists.)

✔ The host may accept requests only from certain addresses. Frequently, for security reasons, a host accepts telnet and FTP only from other FTP hosts on the same network, which means that they're in the same organization.

✔ In a few cases, services are available only during certain hours. Many anonymous FTP servers are available only outside of office hours to avoid slowing them down while local users are trying to get work done.

"No route to host" or "Network unreachable"

Sometimes this message actually means that no network connection exists between where you are and where the other host is. This situation may occur if one of the network routers near you or near the other host fails. More likely explanations are

✔ The numeric address of the host doesn't exist, either because you typed an address incorrectly, a hard-coded address in a program changed, or some part of the database that translates host names to host numbers is out of sync. (That database is, like much of the rest of the Internet, largely maintained by volunteers who occasionally goof.)

✔ A *firewall* system between you and the other host decided that you're not authorized to communicate with systems beyond it; so as far as you're concerned, there really *is* no route from here to there. If the firewall is inside your organization, and you're trying to contact a host outside the organization, a special procedure to persuade the firewall that you're OK may be available. Failing that, unless you have pull with the people who run the firewall, you're probably out of luck.

Total silence

Sometimes you try to contact another host and get no response at all. This silence means that the host has a valid numeric address on an actual network somewhere, but the host itself doesn't exist, at least not at the moment. (Think of a street in a subdivision that has all the addresses assigned, but some of the lots are vacant.) Most often this means that the host is down, so try again later.

Sometimes total silence means that the host exists and is working just fine, but doesn't offer the service that you want. Or a firewall in front of the host has declined to pass on your request. Ideally, a host should send an explicit `refused` message when it receives a request for a service it doesn't offer, but sometimes it just ignores the request. Try *pinging* the same address (see Chapter 23). If that works, you're being ignored. If you think that the host is supposed to offer that service, you can send a polite message to its *postmaster,* asking whether the host is broken or the service has been moved somewhere else.

The FTP That Wouldn't

As we mentioned in Chapter 23, 90 percent of the time, if you copy a file with FTP, it works. When it doesn't work, 90 percent of the time it's because you copied a file in *ASCII* mode rather than *binary* mode. In a few instances, though, FTP can't do what you want it to do for some other reason.

One reason is that on some computers, notably Macintoshes, filenames can contain spaces. This is a problem for FTP programs on most other kinds of computers, which tend to screw up requests for names that have spaces in them, because in most cases the programs assume that spaces separate one name on the command line from another. (A careful reading of the FTP spec shows that FTP programs are supposed to be capable of handling this, but most FTP programs were written long before Macs appeared on the Net in significant numbers.) The usual symptom is that you try to retrieve a file called *read me,* and FTP complains that there's no file called *read.* The only good way around this is to change the name of the file you want to copy.

A bunch of seldom-used options are available in FTP (so seldom are they used that many FTP programs don't support them). Many of these options were put in place to support the peculiarities of the DEC-20, the most common machine on the ARPANET (the Internet's predecessor) in the early 1970s but nearly extinct now. This means that, occasionally, when you need to use one of these older computers from your newer one, your version of FTP may not be up to the task. The most likely scenario is that you try to retrieve MS-DOS programs from the FTP archive at SIMTEL-20 *(wsmr-simtel20.army.mil),* which may be the last remaining DEC-20 on the net. You need to give a *tenex* command to FTP to tell it to use a peculiar data transfer format that TOPS-20 uses. Some of the snazzy, windowed versions of FTP don't have a tenex button, so if you use one of these, you're out of luck. Fortunately, the SIMTEL-20 collection is mirrored at many other sites that, not being DEC-20s, don't *need* tenex mode (see Chapter 18). Indeed, by the time you read this, SIMTEL will probably have been scrapped because it's 20 years old.

It can have problems with some of the structured file types found on systems such as IBM VM and MVS and DEC's VMS. Usually, local conventions can be used either to tell FTP about the file types or to pack up the files in a way that enables you to transfer them by using regular FTP commands and then unpack them after they arrive. Ask a local expert.

Dread Version Creep

Finally, there is *version creep*. All facilities on the Internet have evolved over the years. The older ones, such as telnet, FTP, and finger, have become quite stable, whereas the newer ones, such as Gopher, WAIS, and WWW are still changing. Any successful facility is implemented dozens of different times on dozens of different kinds of computers. That's why, for example, you can use telnet to log into pretty much any kind of computer on the net. Even though their internal structures are quite different, they all provide compatible telnet servers.

With the more recent services, however, people add new features all the time. This means that if you're using Gopher, for example, you may occasionally get a strange message like the one shown in Figure 24-1. This message means that the remote Gopher has offered your system an item that your system doesn't know how to handle. The only solution for this is to get a more recent version of the program. As services become better understood and settle down, they change less often. For now, the more on the cutting edge something is, the more of a pain it is to keep up to date. (But really, are you surprised?)

Figure 24-1:
Version
creep
sneaks up
on Gopher.

Chapter 25

Ten Handy Shortcuts for Better Internet Use

In This Chapter

▶ Timesaving tricks

▶ Handy hints

▶ Snazzy shortcuts

Remote Commands for Lazy Typists

If you use the UNIX rsh command much to run commands on other computers, you soon grow sick and tired of typing such things as

```
rsh lester cat somefile
```

to tell it to run a command (in this case, on a computer called lester). A clever
shortcut (at least it seemed clever at the time) is available: If the name under
which rsh is invoked is something *other* than rsh, it assumes that *that's* the
name of the computer to use. So if you make a copy of rsh and call it lester,
you can just type

```
lester cat somefile
```

If everyone made dozens of copies of rsh with dozens of different names,
considerable space would be wasted. Fortunately, you can use UNIX *links* to
make a new name for rsh *without* making a new copy.

First make sure that you have a bin directory (see Chapter 14 of *UNIX For
Dummies* if you're not familiar with bin directories). Then type this line:

```
ln -s /usr/ucb/rsh bin/lester
```

Note: You probably don't use a host called `lester`, so substitute the name of a host you do use. The name you use can be a full Internet name if it's a faraway host, like `mobydick.ntw.org`, in which case the linking command is

```
ln -s /usr/ucb/rsh bin/mobydick.ntw.org
```

(On a few systems, the true name of rsh is something other than `/usr/ucb/rsh`, in which case you can use the command `whereis rsh` to find the name to use in the ln command.) You can make as many links to rsh as you want, one for each system you want to use.

After you make the links, type **rehash** to tell the *shell* (the UNIX program to which you type your commands) that you have added some new commands; then you can go ahead and use them.

If your office has many computers sharing the same set of accounts, a directory called `/usr/hosts` may exist, which has links for all the commonly used computers. If so, you can put it in your program search path by typing the following, if you use the *C shell:*

```
set path=($path /usr/hosts)
```

Or if you use the *Korn* or *Bourne shell,* type these lines:

```
PATH=$PATH:/usr/hosts
export PATH
```

Using `/usr/hosts` doesn't preclude making your own links in `bin` for names of systems you use that aren't in the local list.

Host Naming for Lazy Typists

You may have noticed that Internet host names, particularly those in large organizations, tend to be pretty long. A system may be named something like `thirdbase.yankees.bronx.nyc.ny.us`. Do you really have to type the entire name every time you want to refer to that host? The answer, as long as the name has something in common with yours, is *no.*

The authors of the Internet naming system assumed that the closer a host is to you, the more likely you are to need to refer to it and the less typing you should have to do. So in many cases, you can abbreviate the host name, and your system can still figure out what you mean.

The name system uses a *search path* — a list of partial names based on your host name — to figure out what you mean when you use an abbreviated name. If you're living at third base, for example, your search path includes

```
yankees.bronx.nyc.ny.us
bronx.nyc.ny.us
ny.us
```

You can enter just the first few parts of a host name. When the name system discovers that the name you've entered isn't a full host name, it guesses the host you want by trying the name you entered relative to the various names in the search path. To talk to leftfield.yankees.bronx.nyc.ny.us, for example you can abbreviate the name as leftfield, and the rest is filled in from the search path. The abbreviations leftfield.yankees and leftfield.yankees.bronx and leftfield.yankees.bronx.nyc work too because the name system can fill in the rest from the search path.

If you want to do a little scouting at homeplate.mets.queens.nyc.ny.us, the abbreviation homeplate.mets.queens is adequate because the rest of the name is in the search path.

In practice, this scheme enables you to abbreviate the host names of computers in your department to a single component and names elsewhere in your organization to the first two or three components.

In theory, each system's search path can be changed to include whatever the system manager wants, not just the trailing parts of the local computer's name — but nobody does that because it would be too confusing. It's rare to use anything other than a simple name (for hosts with all but the first name the same as yours) and full names (for everyone else), and there are some places where those are in fact the only names that work.

A Compendium of FTP Tricks

Navigating around FTP and transferring many files can be tedious, particularly if you already know which files you want and you just want to get to the darned things. This section gives you some hints to make FTP less tedious.

Automate that login

Most UNIX versions of FTP let you store a list of the usernames and passwords for your frequent FTP targets in a file called .netrc (yes, it begins with a dot). When you start FTP, it consults the file to see whether the system you're FTP-ing to is on the list. If so, FTP uses the name from the file. A typical .netrc:

```
machine shamu.ntw.org login elvis password sinatra
default login anonymous password elvis@ntw.org
```

If you FTP to shamu.ntw.org, FTP logs you in as elvis with the password sinatra. Anywhere else, FTP logs you in as anonymous with password elvis@ntw.org. (Use your own e-mail address, of course.) Some versions of FTP don't understand the default line, so with them you have to put in individual lines for each of the systems you log in to for anonymous FTP, like this:

```
machine ftp.uu.net login anonymous password elvis@ntw.org
machine ftp.internic.net login anonymous password
          elvis@ntw.org
```

On Windows and Mac systems, all but the cruddiest versions of FTP have a way to store a list of your favorite FTP sites along with login and password and other details such as what directories to use on the local and remote system. Figure 25-1 shows the Connect screen from John Junod's excellent and free WS_FTP with a typical FTP configuration.

How can I keep the blasted directory listing on the screen?

One of the charmingly annoying bad habits of UNIX FTP is that it sends its output to your screen as fast as it can. (The UNIX FTP program was written back in the era of slow typewriter terminals that actually *printed stuff on paper,* if you can imagine such a thing.) When you get a directory listing, the list tends to fly off the screen before you can read it. To avoid this problem, you can take advantage of a heretofore unmentioned feature of the FTP dir command. You can type two things after the dir command:

✔ The directory to list

✔ The local file into which you want to store the listing

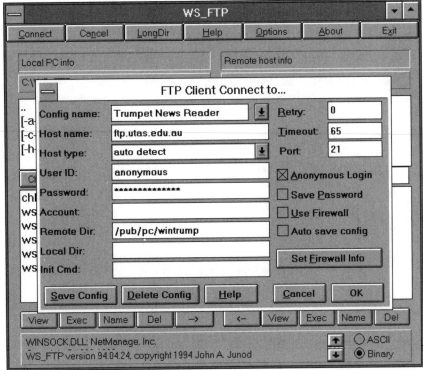

Figure 25-1:
WS_FTP
and its
configuration
screen.

If you want to get a listing of a remote directory called `virtval`, for example, you can type

```
ftp> dir virtval val-dir
```

This line puts the directory into the local file `val-dir`. That's still kind of a pain because you have to interrupt FTP to look at the file (although sometimes files with listings of popular FTP archives can be handy to keep around for reference).

Another even more obscure feature of dir is that if you give FTP a name that begins with | (a vertical bar) rather than a local filename, it treats the rest of the name as a command, as in the following example:

```
ftp> dir virtval |more
```

This command feeds the directory to the more command that displays info one page at a time.

How to look at a remote file without FTP-ing the whole thing first

You can use the same trick on get commands. If you want to look at the remote file README but don't want to store it locally, type this line:

```
ftp> get README |more
```

Compression is your friend

If you're transferring large files (meaning files that take longer to transfer than you want to wait), *compress* them first. For typical text or executable files, compression programs such as zip (or its compatible competitors WinZip or PKZIP), compress, or gzip squash down the files to about half their original size, which means that they take half the time to transfer. If you're using a slow link (slower than a megabit per second), telnetting in and doing the compression can take much less time than waiting for the usual transfer. If you are transferring many separate files, you also can save time by using tar, cpio, or one of the zip programs to combine them into a single archive file, because a significant amount of network overhead is involved when FTP moves from one file to the next.

Compressing applies at least as much when you're using RCP rather than FTP. Before you use RCP to copy a file, you can use rsh to compress or archive the file on the other machine. For example:

```
rsh lester zip tmpzip file1 file2 file3
... zip does its thing ...
rcp lester:tmpzip.zip tmpzip.zip
unzip tmpzip.zip
```

In this example, we first used rsh to run the zip command on remote host lester and created an archive called tmpzip.zip. Then we used RCP to copy that archive to our machine, and finally we unzipped it locally.

Hopping around in FTP land

The usual way to move from one directory to another in FTP is to issue a cd command, look at a directory listing, do another cd, and so on. But if you know exactly where you want to go, you can cd there in one swell foop, as follows:

```
cd pub/micro/pc/windows/games/new/prnotopa
```

Most systems — UNIX and DOS, at least — require a / (slash) between components in directory names (DOS takes a \ — backslash — also). On other
systems, you have to use whatever the local convention is.

Getting more than one directory at a time

Note: This particular trick assumes that you have an FTP program similar to
the standard UNIX one. If you have a spiffy, graphical, windowed FTP
program, it doesn't work. Sorry.

Suppose that you want to use FTP to copy several entire directories from one
machine to another. With a little planning, you can arrange to do all this in one
uninterrupted command that you can give at, say, 11:59 a.m. so that it does all
the work while you're at lunch. For example, assume that the files you want are
everything in the remote machine in the directories pc/tools, pc/editors,
and pc/games (you don't want to miss that last one).

Before you FTP, create the corresponding lowest-level directories on your
machine — in this case tools, editors, and games. Then FTP to the other
machine and issue the following commands after you log in:

```
binary
cd pc
prompt off
mget tools/* editors/* games/*
```

The first command, binary, sets binary transfer mode, which is essential if
you're transferring nontext files. The second command, cd pc, changes to the
pc directory on the host, the parent directory of the ones you want to copy.
The third command, prompt off, turns off the usual file-by-file prompting that
the mget command usually uses. (If you forget this step, mget asks you about
each file before it copies it, which totally defeats the point of doing it all in one
command.) The fourth command, mget . . ., asks to copy everything in the
directories tools, editors, and games.

The mget command copies files by using the exact same names on the local
machine as they have on the remote machine, which is why you need local
directories tools, editors, and games ready to receive the incoming files from
the corresponding remote directories.

As it copies each file, the mget command tells you what it just did, so you can
see that it's doing what you want. If many files are to be copied, it can take quite
a while, but mget does it all unattended.

People who use RCP to copy files should be pleased to learn that this same trick is available to them with considerably less work, as shown in the following command:

```
rcp -r ntw.org:pc/tools ntw.org:pc/editors tw.org:pc/games
       ntwstuff
```

This single line tells RCP to copy *recursively* (that's what the -r is for) the three remote directories into a local directory called ntwstuff. Recursive copying means that the directories *and* everything in them are copied. The RCP command even creates the local directories if they don't already exist. Lazy typists who use the UNIX C shell can abbreviate this to

```
rcp -r ntw.org:pc/tools,editors,games ntwstuff
```

If you're the victim of a user-friendly windowed FTP program, all is not necessarily lost. In WS_FTP, for example, you can highlight as many of the filenames in one of the directory windows as you want by using the standard Windows trick of holding down the Ctrl key as you click the names. Then when you click the "transfer" button, it copies all the highlighted files without more intervention. This shortcut doesn't let you do multiple directories at a time, but it can be much more convenient than clicking all the files in a large directory one at a time.

Hey, make up your mind

The astute reader (that's you) has noticed that we just said on the one hand that you should zip up or archive a bunch of files and then FTP the archive, and on the other hand that you can use FTP and mget or plain RCP to get them one at a time. Which method is better?

It depends. (The astute reader no doubt sees that we're waffling. Next time, we'll write a book for less-astute readers. It's easier.) If the computer you're getting the files from is connected to you by a fast link such as an Ethernet (see Chapter 3), the transfer is fast enough that compressing files isn't worth it. On the other hand, if the other computer is connected by a slow phone line, compression saves a great deal of time.

The question of whether to compress is usually moot if you're retrieving files using anonymous FTP, because you don't have the option of logging in and doing compression yourself. But a few anonymous FTP systems do compression automatically. If a file is called zorplotz, for example, and you try to get zorplotz.Z or zorplotz.zip, these particular FTP systems understand that you want a compressed version and compress the file for you. This also works the other way, in case their version is compressed and you don't have a copy of the requisite uncompressor program handy. This trick works in only a few places, but it doesn't hurt to try. The worst that can happen is that it tells you that no such file as zorplotz.Z exists.

Tricks for Windows Users

If you're using a windowing system such as Microsoft Windows, you can usually create Program Manager icons for your most commonly used commands and hosts. Suppose that you're using Windows and, for lack of a local Archie program, you telnet to a system with a telnet Archie server. You can create an icon that runs telnet and gives the name of the host to telnet to on the command line, which is passed to the program as it starts up, as shown in Figure 25-2.

Figure 25-2:
Creating a
specialized
icon in
Windows.

Program Item Properties		
Description:	Telnet archie	OK
Command Line:	telnet archie.sura.net	Cancel
Working Directory:	c:\junk	
Shortcut Key:	None	Browse...
	☐ Run Minimized	Change Icon...
		Help

The details of icon creation vary from one system to another, but it's usually pretty simple. Look at a similar icon (the regular telnet icon is a good choice if you want to make a specialized telnet), copy that, usually by holding down the Ctrl key while you click it and drag it somewhere else, and then open it and add some extra text on the command line.

If you're using X Windows, a main menu usually appears whenever you click the mouse outside any window. The entries in that menu come from a file called something like .twmrc or .mwmrc. Contact a local guru to find out how to add items to the menu. It's not difficult after someone shows you where to add them. On our system, the menu lines look like this:

```
"L of C" !"xterm -name Library -e telnet locis.loc.gov &"
```

The -name is the name to display at the top of the window, and the text after -e is the command to run.

Chapter 26

Ten Cool Things You Can Do on the Internet

In This Chapter

▶ Ten random fun things to do on the net

▶ Humor!

▶ Education!

▶ Plain time wasting!

The Internet is one of the world's best resources for Work Avoidance, the fundamental principle that says when you really, really have to get a report out this afternoon, *first* you must play a game of Tetris. So here are ten ways to use the Internet toward this noble goal.

Learn a New Joke

Everybody needs a new joke now and then, right? Usenet has long had a newsgroup called `rec.humor`, in which people post what they consider to be their funniest jokes. Tastes vary, and most of what's there isn't very funny. Indeed, much of what's there consists of complaints that a joke isn't funny, and then more complaints that the complaint isn't funny, and so on.

Fortunately, a civic-minded Usenetter named Brad Templeton stepped into this disgraceful situation and came up with the improved newsgroup `rec.humor.funny`, in which he selected jokes that he likes from those sent in. The competition is fierce, and probably 95 percent of the putative jokes never make it. Brad has retired to Executive Moderator, but Maddy, the new person who does the jokes, is also pretty good at it. Having carefully followed `rec.humor.funny` for several years (for research purposes only, of course), we can testify that most of the jokes are indeed pretty funny. So the next time you're reading news, give it a look. You'll be in good company: Readership statistics almost always report that `rec.humor.funny` is among the most widely read groups on the net.

If you like the jokes, you can buy printed *best of* compendia from previous years. See Brad's monthly posts regarding how to order.

Learn a Foreign Language

This subject at least isn't wasting time — it's self-improvement. Because the Internet spans the world, many languages other than English are spoken on it.

Round the world on Usenet

Usenet features several dozen `soc.culture` groups for different countries (considerably more groups than there is room in Chapter 12 to list them), most of which present discussions partly in the native language. So if you're interested in French, try `soc.culture.french`. For German, try `soc.culture.german` (you get the idea).

Also, Gopher lets you find Gophers all over the world. From the every-Gopher-in-the-world menu at the mother Gopher in Minnesota — which is usually an item on every *other* Gopher menu because it's so useful — you can find Gophers on every continent (well, not on Antarctica yet, but as we mentioned, Internet hosts are already there, so who knows?).

Everyone's second-favorite language

The computing community has always exhibited a quiet but persistent interest in Esperanto, an invented language from the late 1800s. Although nobody is a native speaker of Esperanto, it is designed to be simple, regular, and easy to learn so that it can be a common international language. (Nobody then could foresee that by the late 20th century, the common international language would be broken English, but such are the vagaries of history.)

Mac users can find a HyperCard stack that teaches the rudiments of Esperanto. Use either Archie or Gopher to look for `esperanto` to find a copy near you. Esperanto mailing lists, text editors, and discussion groups are also available. On Usenet, the group is `soc.culture.esperanto`.

Write a Letter to the President

Has the government done something lately that you approve of? (Hmm, thought not.) Something that you disapprove of? (More likely.) Don't just gripe about it — write a letter to the President and let him know how you feel. While you're at it, drop a note to the Vice President. Their addresses are

- ✔ president@whitehouse.gov
- ✔ vice.president@whitehouse.gov

Until the White House upgrades its networks, it prints the messages and handles them with the paper mail. So include your regular mailing address if you want a response. For more info and a sample letter, see the sidebar "Hail to the Chief," in Chapter 8.

Learn about the Law

Do you know all the laws that affect your work, home, and hobbies? Surely you know that ignorance of the law is no defense. Better get started now learning about it — you never know when you may need it.

Some experimental Gopher and WWW servers are loaded up with U.S. Supreme Court decisions, which are a good place to begin because (unlike most laws) they're written in something resembling English. Also found on these servers: patent and copyright law, the Uniform Commercial Code, and many other things. To find them, you can Gopher to fatty.law.cornell.edu or gopher.law.csuohio.edu. If you don't have Gopher locally, you can telnet to either and log in as gopher.

The Internet Town Hall has several interesting government databases available at http://town.hall.org/govt/govt.html. There's the full text of thousands of recent patents, with searching facilities, in addition to the SEC EDGAR database in which publicly held companies (which means pretty much any company you've ever heard of) disclose all sorts of interesting financial details as required by law. Until recently, the only way to get EDGAR data was through expensive proprietary services, but for Internauts it's now available for free. (Well, not exactly free since, as taxpayers, we've already paid for it, but you know what we mean.)

Study History

Is it true that the Articles of Confederation said that Canada could be admitted as a state? (If you paid attention in seventh-grade history, you remember that the Articles of Confederation effectively *were* the Constitution during the American Revolution.) Well, wonder no more about questions such as this — a wealth of historical documents and resources awaits you on the Internet.

Enough documents to put anyone to sleep

Quite a few archives of historical documents are on the net. They're all pretty new, and their coverage is spotty.

At `ra.msstate.edu` in `pub/docs/history` is a collection of historical documents ranging from the Articles of Confederation (yes, they said that about Canada) to Civil War papers and foreign documents. The archive at `jade.tufts.edu` in `pub/diplomacy` has a slightly different slant: It's not so much historical as it is diplomatic, with many treaties and related documents from this century.

Forward into the past

The University of Kansas has an interactive service for historians, about half of which is history and half of which is the history biz, featuring appointments, grants, and the like. To reach this service, telnet to `hnsource.cc.ukans.edu` and log in as `history`. What you log in to is actually a version of WWW (see Chapter 22), and it has connections all over the place, not just to historical stuff. It even has a connection to the mother Gopher, so you can get to nearly any Gopher resource in the world by using WWW commands.

Make New Friends

One of the most ancient (if not exactly honored) of human activities is gossip. The Internet, because it is largely populated by humans, is as gossipy a place as any. For small-scale gossip, use the talk command, which enables you to type back and forth to another person on the net. But for real, *serious* gossip, IRC (Internet Relay Chat) has no substitute. The global on-line gossip network enables people from all over the world to gossip 24 hours a day about nothing in particular. See Chapter 13 for details.

Make New Enemies

IRCs are generally pretty friendly. The same cannot be said of MUDs (Multi-User Dungeons), also known as MUSEs (Multi-User Shared Environments). You may have played an old text-mode game called Adventure or Dungeon or Colossal Cave, in which you type commands to travel around a huge multiroom cave, looking for treasure and trying to avoid getting killed. (You may recall responses like "I see no Spam here.")

A MUD is just what it sounds like. It's the same idea, only with many players all over the net (in other words, all over the world). You interact with other players in ways that range from the extremely hostile to the, uh, highly affectionate. Often, you can create your own rooms and carve out your own part of the cave. Many different MUDs with many different styles are played on the net.

Because MUDs come and go frequently, listing them here is pointless — the list would be instantly out-of-date. Consult the Usenet newsgroup `rec.games.mud.announce` and look for the weekly MUD listing posted every Friday. Send a polite message asking for a list of MUDs to `mudlist@glia.biostr.washington.edu`. Or you can FTP to `caisr2.caisr.cwru.edu` and look in `/pub/mud`.

Visit a Coke Machine

A long-standing tradition is that real hackers drink Coke. And an almost-as-long-standing tradition is that real hackers have an on-line Coke machine. Different Coke machines on the net are automated to a greater or lesser degree. Some just provide status reports so that you can tell whether you can have a cold one if you walk down the hall (or fly several thousand miles, depending on where you are relative to the Coke machine). Others have fancy accounting systems on which users can set up accounts. You can pop up a Coke machine panel on the workstation screen and click on your favorite flavor, and your account is debited as the machine drops a can for you. (A few years back in California, an on-line machine called the Prancing Pony had a double-or-nothing option, in which you had a 50-50 chance of either getting your soda free or at double the regular price.)

Here's the current list of Internet Coke machines. In each case, you can check the status with the `finger` command:

```
drink@csh.rit.edu
graph@drink.csh.rit.edu
coke@cmu.edu
```

```
bargraph@coke.elab.cs.cmu.edu
mnm@coke.elab.cs.cmu.edu          (candy machine, actually)
coke@cs.wisc.edu
coke@gu.uwa.edu.au    (Australian hackers drink Coke,too)
```

Use a Supercomputer

Ever wanted to use a multimillion-dollar supercomputer? No? How about being able to impress your geeky friends and coworkers? You can casually tell them that you have been using a state-of-the-art Thinking Machines CM-5 massively parallel supercomputer by way of a peer-to-peer client/server networked interface. (It doesn't matter whether you know what all those buzzwords mean, only that you can rattle them off without stumbling. You can practice in the shower, perhaps.)

Using the massively parallel blah blah blah is easy. Whenever you use WAIS (see Chapter 21) to search any of the databases at quake.think.com at Thinking Machines, you're using a CM-5. They attached it to the net partly as an experiment and partly as advertising — because many people thought that the machine was so exotic that you couldn't do anything useful with it. (The fact that the guy who designed it was already famous for building a tic-tac-toe machine out of Tinker Toys and fishing line — *and* for driving down the middle of the Charles River on sunny days in his 1960s AquaCar — didn't help.)

Read a Book

A book? Pretty retro, eh? A surprising amount of plain, old text can be found on the net, ranging from the works of Shakespeare to the works of Bill Gates. Some files are pretty big, such as a complete copy of *Moby Dick.*

The two main repositories are

- ✔ The Internet Wiretap at wiretap.spies.com (certainly one of the most ominously named machines on the net)
- ✔ The Online Book Initiative at obi.std.com (the std stands for Software Tool and Die)

You can get to them by either anonymous FTP or Gopher. If you go by FTP, at Wiretap the books are in the directories /Library and /Etext, and at OBI they're in /obi. If you go by Gopher, the menus are self-explanatory.

Given a choice, Gopher is easier to use and has better descriptions of what's what — for example, *Mark Twain: A Connecticut Yankee in King Arthur's Court* as opposed to /Library/Classic/yankee.mt (an actual example at Wiretap).

Think of all the money you can save if you use FTP or Gopher to get a copy of that book. You can print it on your laser printer, which will cost (let's see now, 272 pages at five cents per page, carry the three) around $13.60, whereas a bound copy at your local bookstore easily costs as much as five bucks. Hmmn. Maybe it's not that much cheaper if you print it. But it's a steal if you read it on your screen. Plus, if you do that, you will look like you're working. Just don't laugh too loud at the jokes.

Visit Internet for Dummies Central

We authors will do anything to avoid writing. Some of us (John in particular) even in desperation set up Internet Web and Gopher servers. To see what he's been up to lately and what's new in *Internet For Dummies* Land, Gopher and WWW users can drop by Internet For Dummies Central.

Gopher users can point their gopher programs at dummies.com.

WWW (Mosaic, Cello, Lynx) users can look at http://dummies.com/.

Lots More Cool Things

Scott Yanoff, at the University of Wisconsin, keeps a list of special Internet connections with far more cool stuff than this chapter has room for. To find out how to get a current copy, finger yanoff@csd4.csd.uwm.edu.

Part VI

Resource
Reference

The 5th Wave　　By Rich Tennant

"WELL, I NEVER THOUGHT I'D SEE THE DAY I COULD SAY I
TELNETTED TO A BRAZILIAN HOST, THEN USED THE WORLD
WIDE WEB TO GET A GOPHER MENU, ONLY TO FIND OUT I
HAVE TO ANONYMOUS FTP."

In this part...

Now that you're an Internet expert, only one tiny detail remains: How do you get on in the first place? These last three chapters list places that provide access, places that provide software you need to use that access, and finally, some points of departure for continuing on your Internet journey.

Chapter 27

Public Internet Service Providers

• •

In This Chapter

▶ Types of access

▶ A bunch of places that can provide you Internet access

▶ Some places that can provide free access

• •

What's in This List?

This chapter concentrates on places where individuals can get dial-up Internet access at prices that make sense for individuals. There are also vendors that can supply high-speed dedicated access for organizations; these are not listed here on the theory that it's probably not your job to get the entire company on the net.

If it *is* your job to attach your company's network to the Internet and you have a dial-up account somewhere, telnet to the INTERNIC Info Server at `is.internic.net`. Log in as `gopher` and from the first menu choose Getting Connected to the Internet. There you can find an up-to-date list of regional and national networks to contact. Connecting networks together is still a major technical challenge, so you will need lots of help from your local network weenies.

All the U.S. systems listed in this chapter provide at least interactive telnet and FTP in addition to e-mail and Usenet news, or they provide on-demand dial-up network connections (using SLIP or PPP) so that you can run any Internet program you want on your own computer. We have excluded systems that only provide access to e-mail because there are thousands of them, ranging from international providers such as MCI Mail and AT&T Easylink down to local hobbyist bulletin-board systems. Pretty much any BBS that exchanges mail with other BBSs can exchange mail with the Internet by way of FIDO (a dial-up network of PC BBSs) and other gateways.

In an effort to further global access, we have included sites around the world. They may not all meet the criteria we set for U.S. sites, but we thought that in many cases *any* access might be desirable. Some say that the Internet grew an astonishing 81 percent last year and that most of that growth was on foreign soil. We can't tell how real that number is, but we can show you that there's access almost everywhere you turn.

Two Kinds of Access

Two basic varieties of dial-up access are available: dialing in as a *terminal* or dialing in as a *network host.* In the first case, you dial in to a system by using either a regular terminal or, more likely, a computer running a terminal program such as Procomm or Crosstalk. You can use whatever network programs the system you've dialed in to provides. If you want to transfer files to or from your computer, use Kermit, zmodem, or something similar (see Chapter 3), just like you would upload or download files to or from a BBS.

If you dial in as a network host, your computer becomes an Internet host for the duration of your call and acts as any other Internet host (except, perhaps, a little smaller and slower, but nobody other than you needs to know that). The advantage of dialing in as a host is that you can run any network application on your computer you want. If you have a multitasking system such as Microsoft Windows or Macintosh System 7, you can even run several programs at a time, so you can telnet to one system while retrieving files by FTP in the background. As new services are introduced, you can use them as soon as you can get client software (most often by downloading the client from the net) rather than have to wait for your dial-up provider to install the software on its machine.

The disadvantage of dialing in as a host is that you need more software than a terminal emulator on your end, and it's considerably harder to set up. (You need to know about things like host numbers, subnet masks, and other network voodoo.) ***Note:*** If you're dialing in as a host, you should have a modem that runs at *at least* 9600 bps (bits per second). Slower modems work, but they make the network transactions so slow that only the extraordinarily patient find them usable.

It probably makes sense to try a dial-up terminal service first and then try trading up to being a host if you get really hooked. Two variants of host service are called SLIP and PPP. They both work, but, given a choice, PPP is a little faster and more reliable. (See Chapters 3 and 5 for more info.)

Signing Up

Most of the dial-in services allow you to sign up on-line. If a modem number is listed, you can dial in on that number. Log in using the password provided or follow the prompts after you connect.

Sign-up generally involves providing your name, address, and telephone number, along with billing information, such as a credit-card number. Often, access is granted immediately, or the service may call you on the phone to verify that you are who you said you are.

Where to find your provider

An important topic to consider in choosing your provider is the cost of the phone call, because calls to on-line systems tend to be long. Ideally, you want to find a provider who has a dial-in number that's a local call for you — either a direct number or by way of a network such as Tymnet or Sprintnet or CompuServe's network.

A few providers have 800 numbers, but their hourly rates have to be high enough to cover the cost of the 800 call. It's almost invariably cheaper to dial direct and pay for the call yourself rather than use an 800 access number (800 access is attractive to people who travel frequently or who don't have to pay their own phone bills).

Your secret decoder ring

This chapter includes a listing of national and regional providers, and within each listing entry are some code letters you need to know. The following table tells you what the code letters mean:

Code Letter	What It Means
D	Dial-in interactive service providing at least telnet, FTP, e-mail, and Usenet news
T	Dial-in telnet access to other systems
S	SLIP or PPP host access
F	System available for free (except perhaps for the cost of the phone call)

Code Letter	What It Means
R	Flat-rate plan available with no hourly charge (800 or network access usually costs extra)
8	Toll-free 800 access
N	Dial-up network access by way of Tymnet, Sprintnet, CompuServe, or other network
H	High-speed modem number (faster than 2400 bps)
M	Medium-speed modem number (1200 or 2400 bps)

National Providers

The national providers have 800 access, dial-in numbers in many cities, or provisions for access by way of a national network such as Tymnet or Sprintnet or CompuServe's network.

Cooperative Library Agency for Systems and Services: D8

Phone: 800-488-4559
E-mail: class@class.org

Note: Available only to libraries and similar organizations

CR Laboratories Dialup Internet Access: DS8R

Phone: 415-837-5300
Modem: 415-705-6060, other numbers in major cities
E-mail: support@crl.com

General Videotex DELPHI: DN

Phone: 800-544-4005
Modem: 800-365-4636 (for sign-up only)
            Log in as JOINDELPHI, password DUMMIES
E-mail: info@delphi.com

Note: Free five-hour test drive usually available when you sign up

HoloNet: DN

Phone: 510-704-0160
Modem: 510-704-1058
E-mail: info@holonet.net

Netcom Online Communication Services DS

Phone:	800-501-8649	
Modem:	206-547-5992	510-865-9004
	310-842-8835	619-234-0524
	408-241-9760	916-965-1371
	408-459-9851	404-303-9765
	415-328-9940	617-237-8600
	415-985-5650	703-255-5951
	503-626-6833	214-753-0045
	510-426-6610	714-708-3800
E-mail:	info@netcom.com	

Novalink: DN

Phone: 800-274-2814
Modem: 800-825-8852 for access, dial-ups in major U.S. cities
E-mail: info@novalink.com

The Portal System: DNR

Phone: 408-973-9111
Modem: 408-973-8091H, 408-725-0561M
               Log in as info
E-mail: cs@cup.portal.com, info@portal.com

PSI's Global Dialup Service: DTNR

Phone: 703-620-6651
E-mail: all-info@psi.com, gds-info@psi.com

UUNET Communications: SR

Phone: 800-4-UUNET-3, 703-204-8000
Modem: Major U.S. and Canadian cities
E-mail: info@uunet.uu.net

The WELL (Whole Earth 'Lectronic Link): DN

Phone: 415-332-4335
Modem: 415-332-6106
               Log in as newuser
E-mail: info@well.sf.ca.us

Northeast Providers

DMConnection: DSR

Phone: 508-568-1618
Modem: Dial-ups available in Boston and Hudson, Massachusetts
E-mail: info@dmc.com

The IDS World Network: DSR

Phone: 401-884-7856
Modem: 401-884-9002, 401-785-1067
E-mail: `sysadmin@ids.net`

MindVOX: DR

Phone: 212-989-2418
Modem: 212-989-4141
            Log in as `mindvox`, **password** `guest`
E-mail: `info@phantom.com`

MV Communications, Inc.: DS

Phone: 603-429-2223
Modem: 603-429-1735
E-mail: `mv-admin@mv.mv.com`

NEARnet: SR

Phone: 617-873-8730
Modem: Dial-ups available in Boston, Massachusetts and Nashua, New
            Hampshire
E-mail: `nearnet-join@nic.near.net`

NYSERnet: SR

Phone: 315-443-4120
Modem: Dial-ups available throughout New York state
E-mail: `luckett@nysernet.org`

PANIX Public Access UNIX: DR

Phone: 212-877-4854 Alexis Rosen
            212-691-1526 Jim Baumbach
Modem: 212-787-3100
            Log in as `newuser`
E-mail: `alexis@panix.com, jsb@panix.com`

The World: DSN

Phone: 617-739-0202
Modem: 617-739-9753
            Log in as `new`
E-mail: `office@world.std.com`

Middle Atlantic Providers

Clark Internet Services: DS8

Phone: 1-800-735-2258
Modem: Washington, D.C., Maryland, and Virginia
E-mail: info@clark.net

Digital Express Group — Online Communications Service: DS

Phone: 800-969-9090, 301-220-2020
Modem: 301-220-0462M   301-220-0258H
          410-766-1855M   410-768-8774H
          714-377-9784   908-937-9481
          215-836-4832
          Log in as new
E-mail: info@digex.net

Grebyn Corporation: DR

Phone: 703-281-2194
Modem: 703-281-7997
          Log in as apply
E-mail: info@grebyn.com

The John von Neumann Computer Network — Dialin' Tiger: DSR8

Phone: 800-35-TIGER, 609-258-2400
Modem: Dial-ups available in Princeton and Newark, New Jersey; Philadel-
          phia, Pennsylvania; Garden City, New York; Bridgeport, New
          Haven, and Storrs, Connecticut; Providence, Rhode Island
E-mail: info@jvnc.net

PREPnet: TSR

Phone: 412-268-7870
          Modem: Dial-ups available in Philadelphia, Pittsburgh, and
          Harrisburg, Pennsylvania
          E-mail: prepnet@cmu.edu

Telerama BBS: D

Phone: 412-481-3505
Modem: 412-481-5302
          Log in as new
E-mail: info@telerama.pgh.pa.us

Southern Providers

Interpath: DS

Phone: 800-849-6305
Modem: Sites in parts of North Carolina
E-mail: info@interpath.net

Texas Metronet: SDR

Phone: 214-401-2800
Modem: 214-705-2902H, 214-705-2917M
             Log in as info, password info
             or log in as signup, password signup
E-mail: srl@metronet.com, 73157.1323@compuserve.com

Vnet Internet Access: DR

Phone: 704-374-0779
Modem: Dial-ups available in major cities in North Carolina

NeoSoft's Sugar Land Unix: DR

Phone: 713-438-4964
Modem: 713-684-5900
E-mail: info@NeoSoft.com

Midwestern Providers

APK — Public Access UNI* Site: DR

Phone: 216-481-9428
Modem: 216-481-9436M, 216-481-9425H
E-mail: zbig@wariat.org

InterAccess: DSHR

Phone: 800-967-1580
Modem: 708-498-3960, 312-705-6633, 708-716-6633
             Log in as guest
E-mail: help@interaccess.com

GENESIS/MCSNet: DR

Phone: 312-248-8649
Modem: 312-248-0900H, 312-248-0970H, 312-248-6295 (Telebit)
E-mail: info@genesis.mcs.com

Merit Network, Inc. — MichNet Project: TSNR

Phone:	313-764-9430
Modem:	Michigan; Boston, Massachusetts; Washington, D.C.
E-mail:	info@merit.edu

MSen Inc.: DS

Phone:	313-998-4562
Modem:	313-998-1302
E-mail:	info@mail.msen.com

OARnet: D8

Phone:	614-292-8100
Modem:	Dial-ups avilable in major cities in Ohio
E-mail:	nic@oar.net

XNet Information Systems: DS

Phone:	708-983-6064
Modem:	Dial-ups avilable in major cities in Illinois
E-mail:	info@xnet.com

Mountain States Providers

Community News Service: D8

Phone:	719-579-9120
Modem:	719-520-1700
	Log in as new, password newuser
E-mail:	klaus@cscns.com

Colorado SuperNet, Inc.: DS8

Phone:	303-273-3471
Modem:	Dial-ups available throughout Colorado: Alamosa, Boulder/ Denver, Colorado Springs, Durango, Fort Collins, Frisco, Glenwood Springs/Aspen, Grand Junction, Greeley, Gunnison, Pueblo, Telluride
E-mail:	info@csn.org

Old Colorado City Communications: DR

Phone:	719-632-4848, 719-593-7575, 719-636-2040
Modem:	719-632-4111
	Log in as newuser
E-mail:	dave@oldcolo.com or thefox@oldcolo.com

Western Providers

a2i communications: DR

Phone:	408-293-8078
Modem:	408-293-9010H, 408-293-9020 (Telebit)
	Log in as guest
E-mail:	info@rahul.net

CTS Network Services: DRS

Phone:	619-637-3637
Modem:	619-637-3660
E-mail:	info@ctsnet.cts.com

Sublight SRW: DR

Modem:	408-866-0262
	Log in as guest
E-mail:	info@sunlight.com

RainDrop Laboratories: D

Modem:	503-293-1772M, 503-293-2059H
	Log in as apply
E-mail:	info@agora.rain.com

The Cyberspace Station: DR

Modem:	619-634-1376
	Log in as guest
E-mail:	help@cyber.net

DIAL n' CERF: DS8

Phone:	800-876-2373, 619-455-3900
Modem:	Dial-ups available in major cities in California
E-mail:	help@cerf.net

Eskimo North: DR

Phone:	206-367-7457
Modem:	206-367-3837M, 206-362-6731H, 206-742-1150 (Telebit)
E-mail:	nanook@eskimo.com

Halcyon: DR

Phone:	206-955-1050
Modem:	206-382-6245
	Log in as new
E-mail:	info@halcyon.com

Northwest Nexus Inc.: S

Phone:	206-455-3505
Modem:	Seattle area
E-mail:	info@nwnexus.wa.com

Canadian Providers

Communications Accessibles Montreal: DSR

Phone:	514-923-2102
Modem:	514-281-5601H, 514-466-0592H, 514-738-3664 (Telebit)
E-mail:	info@cam.org

Internex Online Toronto: DRF

Phone:	416-363-8676
Modem:	416-363-3783
	Log in as new
E-mail:	vid@io.org

Australian Providers

apanix.apana.org.au: DSH

Phone:	+08 373-5485
	Log in as guest
E-mail:	adrian@apanix.apana.org.au

connect.com.au pty ltd: DS

Phone:	+61-3-528-2239
E-mail:	connect@connect.com.au

interconnect.com.au: D

Phone:	+008 818 262
E-mail:	info@interconnect.com.au

U.K. Providers

CityScape Internet Services Ltd: S

Phone:	0223 566950
E-mail:	sales@cityscape.co.uk

Demon Internet Systems: DSR

Phone: +44-81-349-0063
Modem: +44-81-343-4848
E-mail: internet@demon.net

The Direct Connection: DSR

Phone: +44-81-317-0100
E-mail: helpdesk@dircon.co.uk

Direct Line: DHR

Modem: +44-81 845 8228
E-mail: sysop@ps.com

UK PC User Group: DR

Phone: +44-81-863-6646
E-mail: info@ibmpcug.co.uk

Other European Providers

Ariadne - Greek Academic and Research Network: D

Phone: +301 65-13-392
E-mail: dialup@leon.nrcps.ariadne-t.gr

EUnet Austria: D

Phone: +43.1 3174969
E-mail: mah@austria.eu.net

EUnet Belgium: D

Phone: +32.16 201015
E-mail: postmaster@.belgiumEU.net

EUnet Bulgaria: D

Phone: +359.52 259135
E-mail: postmaster@bulgaria.EU.net

EUnet Czechia: D

Phone: +42.2 3323242
E-mail: prf@Czechia.EU.net

EUnet Denmark: D

Phone: +45.39 179900
E-mail: netpasser@Denmark.EU.net

EUnet Finland: D

Phone: +358.0 4002605
E-mail: nhelpdesk@Findland.EU.net

EUnet France: D

Phone: +33.1 45210204
E-mail: contact@France.EU.net

EUnet Hungary: D

Phone: +36.1 1497986
E-mail: horvath@Hungary.EU.net

EUnet Iceland: D

Phone: +354.1 694747
E-mail: postmaster@Iceland.EU.net

IEunet Ltd., Ireland's Internet Services Supplier: DS

Phone: 353 1 6790832
Modem: +353 1 6790830, +353 1 6798600
E-mail: info@ieunet.ie, info@Ireland.eu.net

Individual.NET: DS

Phone: +49 2131 64190
Local access: Berlin, Oldenburg, Bremen, Hamburg, Krefeld, Kiel, Duisburg,
               Darmstadt, Dortmund, Hannover, Ruhrgebiet, Bonn, Magdburg,
               Duesseldorf, Essen, Koeln, Frankfurt, Dresden, Ulm, Nuernberg,
               Muenchen and other.
E-mail: in-info@individual.net

EUnet Italy: D

Phone: +39.10 3532747
E-mail: iunet@Italy.EU.net

EUnet Norway: D

Phone: +352 470261 361
E-mail: postmaster@Luxembourg.EU.net

EUnet The Netherlands: D

Phone: +31.20 5924245
E-mail: beheer@Netherlands.EU.net

EUnet Portugal: D

Phone: +351.1 2954464 ext: 2507
E-mail: postmaster@Portugal.EU.net

EUnet Romania: D

Phone: +40.1 3126886
E-mail: postmaster@Romania.EU.net

EUnet Russia: D

Phone: +7.095 1983796
E-mail: postmaster@USSR.EU.net

EUnet Slovakia: D

Phone: +42.7 377434
E-mail: postmaster@Slovakia.EU.net

EUnet Slovenia: D

Phone: +38.64 105183
E-mail: postmaster@Slovenia.EU.net

EUnet Spain: D

Phone: +34.1 4134856
E-mail: postmaster@spain.EU.net

EUnet Switzerland: D

Phone: +41.1.2914580
E-mail: pr@Switzerland.EU.net

Muc.dee.V.: DS

Phone: +49 89 324683-0
E-mail: info@spacenet.de

African Providers

EUnet Algeria: D

Phone: +213.2 369791
E-mail: Algeria@EU.net

EUnet Egypt: D

Phone: +20.2 3557253
E-mail: ow@estinet.uucp

EUnet Tunisia: D

Phone: +216.1 787757
E-mail: mondher@Tunisia.EU.net

The Internetworking Company of Southern Africa (Ticsa)

Phone: (021) 419-2768
E-mail: info@ticsa.com

The Internet Solution (TIS)

E-mail: postmaster@apollo.is.co.za

Stellar Systems, Harare, Zimbabwe

E-mail: postmaster@stellar.zw

It's FREE!

Two years or so ago, a bunch of civic-minded people at a university in Cleveland got together and created what they called a *freenet*. This is a free system that people in the community use to share information and to take advantage of the Internet. It was quite successful (the Cleveland Freenet now consists of three machines, each supporting many users), and freenets have appeared all over the United States and Canada.

Freenets provide lots of local community information and offer limited telnet and FTP, which allows general access to libraries and other public-interest kinds of hosts. It's not full Internet access by any means, but it's interesting in its own right. And, after all, it's *free*. One thing you can do is telnet from one freenet to another, so if you can get to one of them, you can get to all of them.

Freenets really are free, but to get full access, you have to register so that they have some idea of who's using the system. They all allow registration on-line.

Freenets all allow incoming telnet access, so if you have Internet access elsewhere, drop into a freenet and look around.

TIP

Don't touch that dial

When we were writing this book, our local cable company in Cambridge, Massachusetts, announced that it would begin providing high-speed Internet connections by way of cable TV wiring. These connections were much faster than dial-up connections and cost only about $100 per month; a fraction of what any other vendor charges for a comparable service. As of mid-1994, although it had been officially announced for six months, the company had not signed up any paying customers, due apparently to equipment problems. If you want a fast connection, try calling your local cable company and ask when and if it will be getting in on the Internet action.

How can freenets really be free?

Most freenets are run by unpaid volunteers who borrow facilities from a local college or university. Many of them have managed to acquire charitable-foundation money, too, because they're community-based and educational.

Most of them welcome contributions from users, although they aren't pushy about it.

Cleveland Freenet, Cleveland, OH

Modem: 216-368-3888
Log in as `fnguest`
Telnet: `freenet-in-a.cwru.edu`
`freenet-in-b.cwru.edu`
`freenet-in-c.cwru.edu`

Youngstown Freenet, Youngstown, OH

Modem: 216-742-3072
Log in as `visitor`
Telnet: `yfn.ysu.edu`

Heartland Freenet, Peoria, IL

Modem: 309-674-1100
Log in as `bbguest`
Telnet: `heartland.bradley.edu`

Lorain County Freenet, Lorain County, OH

Modem: 216-277-2359 (Lorain)
216-366-9753 (Elyria)
Log in as `guest`

Medina County Freenet, Medina County, OH

Modem: 216-723-6732

Tri-State Online, Cincinnati, OH

Modem: 513-579-1990
Log in as `visitor`
Telnet: `end sidebarcbos.uc.edu`

Denver Freenet: Denver, CO

Modem: 303-270-4865
                Log in as `guest`
Telnet: `freenet.hsc.colorado.edu`

Tallahassee Freenet, Tallahassee, FL

Modem: 904-488-5056, 904-488-6313
                Log in as `visitor`
Telnet: `freenet.fsu.edu`

Victoria Freenet, British Columbia, Canada

Modem: 604-595-2300
Telnet: `freenet.victoria.bc.ca`

National Capital Freenet, Ottawa, Ontario, Canada

Modem: 613-780-3733
                Terminals in Ottawa and Nepean public libraries
                Log in as `guest`
Telnet: `freenet.carleton.ca`

Big Sky Telegraph, Dillon, MT

Modem: 406-683-7680
                Log in as `bbs`

Buffalo Free-Net, Buffalo, NY

Modem: 716-645-6128
                Log in as `freeport`
Telnet: `freenet.buffalo.edu`

Columbia Online Information Network (COIN), Columbia, MS

Modem: 314-884-7000
                Log in as `guest`
Telnet: `bigcat.missouri.edu`

Wellington Citynet, Wellington, New Zealand

Modem: +64-4-801-3060
Telnet: `kosmos.wcc.govt.nz`

Coming Soon

Freenets are under construction or have been proposed in Boston, Washington
D.C., and the Silicon Valley.

Chapter 28

Sources of Internet Software

. . . .

. . . .

What Kind of Nerds Do You Take Us For?

When it comes to installing software, there are two kinds of people: those who dislike doing it and those who just plain won't. We expect that you're probably in the latter category, unless you're a PC or Mac user. If you use a different kind of computer or a workstation, it's somebody else's job to acquire software, negotiate contracts, handle installation and maintenance, and otherwise keep things going smoothly. This is particularly true in an office with a bunch of workstations, all of which are on the Internet as a matter of divine right, except that you have a PC that you want to connect — even if only to avoid running around with floppies.

This chapter gives sources of Internet software for PCs and Macs. This listing isn't exhaustive — particularly for the PC. New vendors of TCP/IP software appear practically every month, and new applications appear weekly.

MS-DOS and Windows TCP/IP Software

All these packages include the underlying network software and a set of the traditional applications, including telnet and FTP. Much of the information in this section is adapted from an on-line list compiled by C. J. Sacksteder, at Pennsylvania State University, and is used with his permission. That list is posted to the Usenet newsgroup `comp.protocols.tcp-ip.ibmpc` whenever it has major changes. You can FTP it from `ftp.cac.psu.edu` in `pub/dos/info/tcpip.packages`.

Table 28-1 lists the names and sources of the TCP/IP packages that are listed. Most are commercial; a few are free or shareware. *Note:* The first column is an abbreviated name that is used in later tables in this chapter. Table 28-2 gives contact information for these sources.

Table 28-1	TCP/IP Packages for DOS and Windows			
ID	*Package*	*Version*	*Publisher or Vendor*	*Phone*
PCTCP	PC/TCP	2.2	FTP Software, Inc.	800-282-4387
Chameleon	Chameleon	3.10	NetManage, Inc.	408-973-7171
Super-TCP	Super-TCP	3.00r	Frontier Technologies	414-241-4555
IBM/DOS	TCP/IP for DOS	2.10	IBM	800-IBM-CALL
BW	BW-TCP DOS	3.0a	Beame & Whiteside Ltd.	416-765-0822
Distinct	Distinct TCP	3.02	Distinct Corp.	408-741-0781
Pathway	Pathway Access	2.0	The Wollongong Group	800-962-8649
PC-NFS	PC-NFS	5.0	SunSelect	508-442-0000
LWPD	LAN Workplace	4.1r8	Novell, Inc.	800-772-UNIX
HP	NS & ARPA Services	2.5	Hewlett-Packard	408-725-8111
NCSATel	NCSA Telnet	2.3.0	National Center for Supercomputing Applications	
CUTCP	CUTCP/CUTE	2.2d	Clarkson University	
QVT/Net	QVT/Net	3.4	QPC Software	716-377-8305 (fax)
Ka9q	Ka9q	2		
WATTCP	WATTCP	Aug. 3, 1993	Werick Engelke	
3Com	3Com TCP w/ DPA	2.0	3Com	800-638-3266
Fusion	Fusion		Pacific Software	800-541-9508
	TCP/2 for DOS		Essex Systems	508-532-5511
ICE/TCP	ICE/TCP		James River Group	612-339-2521
AIR	AIR for Windows		Spry, Inc.	206-286-1412
TTCP	TTCP	1.2r2	Turbosoft Pty Ltd.	+61 2 552 1266

(continued)

ID	Package	Version	Publisher or Vendor	Phone
PC-LINKD	PC-LINK for DOS	?	X LINK Technology	408-263-8201
PC-LINKW	PC-LINK for Windows	?	X LINK Technology	408-263-8203 (fax)
Lanera	TCPOpen/ Standard	2.2	Lanera Corporation	408-956-8344
Piper	Piper/IP		Ipswitch, Inc.	617-942-0621
Lantastic	Lantastic for TCP/IP		Artisoft, Inc.	602-293-6363
Wolvrine	MS TCP/IP-32		WFW beta Microsoft	206-882-8080
Trumpet	Trumpet WinSock	1.0a	Trumpet Software International	
InetConn	Internet-Connect	1	Core Systems	510-943-5765
WinNT	Windows NT	3.1[3]	Microsoft	206-882-8080

[1]The version to which information here applies. There may be a newer version.

[2]Subscribe to mailing list `tcp-group@ucsd.edu` by sending mail to `tcp-group-request@ucsd.edu`.

[3]Although not a separate package, Windows NT includes TCP/IP and some utilities, so it is listed for comparison purposes.

Table 28-2	Contact Information and FTP Addresses	
ID	**Address**	**E-mail Address**
PCTCP	2 High St. North Andover, MA 01845	sales@ftp.com
Chameleon	20823 Stevens Creek Blvd. Cupertino, CA 95014	support@netmanage.com
Super-TCP	10201 N. Port Washington Rd. Mequon, WS 53092	tcp@frontiertech.com
IBM/DOS	Dept. E15 P.O. Box 12195 Research Triangle Park, NC 27709	
BW	P.O. Box 8130 Dundas, Ontario CA L9H 5E7	sales@bws.com
Distinct	P.O. Box 3410 Saratoga, CA 95070-1410	mktg@distinct.com

(continued)

Table 28-2 *(continued)*

ID	Address	E-mail Address
Pathway	1129 San Antonia Rd. Palo Alto, CA 94303	sales@twg.com
PC-NFS	2 Elizabeth Drive Chelmsford, MA 01824	
LWPD	122 East 1700 South Provo, UT 84606	
HP	19420 Homestead Rd. Cupertino, CA 94014	
NCSATel		anon FTP simtel20 or mirrors pub/msdos/ncsaelnet
CUTCP		anon FTP sun.soe.clarkson.edu cutcp@omnigate.clarkson.edu
QVT/Net		anon FTP ftp.cica.indiana.edu or mirrors djp@troi.cc.rochester.edu
Ka9q		anon FTP ucsd.edu pub/ham-radio/packet/tcpoip/ka9q as modified by Ashok Aiyar <ashok@biochemistry .bioc.cwru.edu> is available via gopher and anonymous ftp. Gopher to biochemistry.bioc.cwru.edu.
WATTCP		anon FTP dorm.rutgers.edu pub/msdos/wattcp
ICE/TCP	125 North First St. Minneapolis, MN 55401	jriver@jriver.com
AIR	1319 Dexter Ave. North Seattle, WA 98109	sales@spry.com
TTCP	248 Johnston St. Annandale, NSW Aus. 2038	info@abccomp.oz.au

(continued)

ID	Address	E-mail Address
PC-LINKx	741 Ames Avenue Milpitas, CA 95035	tom@xlink.com
Lanera	516 Valley Way Milpitas, CA 95035	lanera@netcom.com
Piper	580 Main St. Reading, MA 01867	ub@ipswitch.com
Lantastic	691 East River Road Tucson, AZ 85704	
Wolvrine anon FTP		ftp.microsoft.com:/pub/peropsys/ WFW/tcpip/vxdbeta
Trumpet	Trumpet Software International PtyLtd. Lower level, 24 Cambridge Rd Bellerive, TAS 7018, AUSTRALIA	trumpet-info@trumpet.com.au tanon FTP, ftp.cica.indiana.edu or mirrors, win3/winsock/winsock.zip and winapps.zip get beta from petros.psychol.utas.edu.au. InetConn anon FTP, ftp.cica.indiana.edu or mirrors lvuong@cais.com, win3/winsock/ inetcon1.zip (trial version)
WinNT	One Microsoft Way Redmond, WA 95052-6399	

Table 28-3 contains the following codes, and here is what they mean:

- **Y:** Yes, feature included
- **N:** No, feature not included
- **M:** Requires this feature
- **S:** Feature supported via shim that simulates a different software interface

Also, the Stack Provided column indicates whether libraries are provided to support new or third-party applications. Ethernet, Token Ring, and FDDI are kinds of physical network connection. Packet Drivers are a standard way to handle many different brands of Ethernet card. NDIS allows sharing cards with LAN Manager. ODI shares with Novell. SLIP and PPP handle serial (modem) communications.

Table 28-3   Hardware Supported

| ID | Drivers Included | | | | Interfaces Supported | | | | |
	Stack Provided	Ethernet	Token Ring	FDDI	Packet Drivers	NDIS	SLIP	PPP	ODI
PCTCP	Y	Y	Y		Y	Y	Y	Y	Y
Chameleon	Y	Y	Y	Y	N	N	Y	Y	Y
Super-TCP	Y	Y	Y	N	Y	Y	Y	Y	Y
IBM/DOS	Y	Y	Y		S	Y	Y	N	N
BW	Y	Y	Y		Y	Y	Y	N	Y
Distinct	Y	Y	Y	Y	Y	Y	Y	Y	Y
PathWay	Y	Y	Y		Y	Y	Y	Y	Y
PC-NFS	Y	Y	Y	Y	S	Y	Y	N	Y
LWPD	Y	Y	Y		S	S	Y	Y	Y
HP	Y	Y	Y		Y	Y	N	N	S
NCSATel	N	Y	N	Y[5]	Y				
CUTCP	N	N	N	M					
QVT/Net	N	N	N		M		Y		
Ka9q[3]	N	N	N	N	Y	N	Y	Y	N
WATTCP	Y	N	N	N	Y	N	N	N	N
3Com		Y	Y		N	Y			
Fusion		Y			N	Y			
ICE/TCP					Y				
AIR	Y[6]	Y	Y	?	?	S	Y	N	N
TTCP	Y	Y	Y	Y	S	S	S	S	
PC-LINKD		Y		Y	Y	Y		Y	
Lanera	Y	Y	Y	N	Y	Y	Y	N	Y
Piper	Y	Y	Y	?	?	Y	Y	?	Y
Lantastic	Y[4]	S							

(continued)

| ID | Drivers Included | | | | | Interfaces Supported | | | |
	Stack Provided	Ethernet	Token Ring	FDDI	Packet Drivers	NDIS	SLIP	PPP	ODI
Wolvrine	Y S	3	3	N	N	S	Y[2]	N	N
WinNT	Y	Y	Y	Y	N	Y[2]	N[1]	N[1]	
Trumpet	Y	N	N	N	Y	N	Y	N	N
InetConn	Y S	N	N	N	N	Y	S	N	N

Note: Most packages include more drivers than are listed here. Any package that supports packet drivers also supports NDIS and ODI by using compatibility software.

[1] Windows NT 3.5 (Daytona) will have SLIP and PPP.

[2] Supports NDIS 3.0 (others are all 2.0).

[3] Installs on top of Windows for Workgroups 3.11, running NDIS 3.0 (or other versions of NDIS). Ethernet and Token Ring drivers are included with Windows for Workgroups.

[4] Lantastic native interface is LANBIOS.

[5] Version 2.3.03 only.

[6] Ships with several choices of stacks (Novell LAN Workplace and Microsoft LAN Manager, for example).

Table 28-4 contains some abbreviations that require some illuminating:

- **All Apps:** All applications are Windows-based.

- **Some Apps:** Some are Windows; some are DOS or character.

- **Stack in DLL:** Stack is implemented as "100% Windows DLL" code.

- **Stack in VxD:** Stack is implemented as a virtual device driver.

- **WinSock:** Supports Windows Socket API (1.1).

- **Supporting VxD:** Includes a virtual device drive to support functions in some way.

- **Network Driver:** A Windows driver that allows connecting and disconnecting drives and remote printing.

Table 28-4			Microsoft Windows Applications and Support				
ID	*All Apps*	*Some Apps*	*Stack in DLL*	*Stack in VxD*	*WinSock*	*Supporting VxD*	*Ntwk. Driver*
PCTCP	N	Y	N	N	Y	Y	Y
Chameleon	Y	N	Y	N	Y	N	Y
Super-TCP	Y	1	Y[1]	N	Y	Y	Y
IBM/DOS	N	Y	N[2]	N	Y	N	?
BW	N	Y	N	N	Y	Y	Y
Distinct	Y	N	Y	N	Y	N	?
PathWay	N	Y	N	N	Y	N	N
PC-NFS	N	Y	N	N	Y	Y	Y
LWPD	N	Y	N	N	Y	N	N
HP	N	N	N	N	N	N	N
NCSATel	N	N	N	N	N	N	N
CUTCP	N	N	N	N	N	N	N
QVT/Net	Y	N	N	N	N	N	N
Ka9q	N	N	N	N	N	N	N
WATTCP	N	N	N	N	Y	N	N
AIR	Y	N	[5]	[5]	Y	?	[5]
TTCP	N	Y	N	N	Y		
Lanera	N	Y	N	N	Y	N	
Piper	N	N	N	N	Y	?	N
Lantastic	N	N	N	N	Y	N	N
Wolvrine	N	Y	N	Y	Y	N	[3]
WinNT	N[4]	N[4]	N[4]	N	Y		
Trumpet	Y	N	[7]	N	Y	N	N
InetConn	Y	N	Y	N	Y	Y	N

[1] Super-TCP/NFS includes DOS-based applications and an optional TSR.

[2] The stack is protected-mode code that sits entirely in extended memory except for a small interface TSR.

[3] Because this runs over Windows for Workgroups, that network driver is used.

[4] Windows NT doesn't run on top of DOS, and TCP/IP is part of the system. Some of the applications are graphical, and many utitities are character-based.

[5] Depends on which stack ("transport") is chosen.

[6] Next version.

[7] When using the internal SLIP driver, no DOS TSR or drivers are involved. Otherwise, needs packet driver and winpkt TSR.

Table 28-5 contains two codes you should know:

┃ ✔ **D:** DOS or character-based application

┃ ✔ **W:** Windows-based application

Also:

┃ ✔ **SMTP:** Outgoing e-mail

┃ ✔ **POP:** Incoming e-mail

┃ ✔ **NNTP:** Usenet news

┃ ✔ **SNMP:** Network monitoring facility

┃ ✔ **NFS:** Remote disk files

Table 28-5									
ID	**Telnet**	**TN3270**	**FTP Client**	**FTP Server**	**SMTP**	**POP[2]**	**NNTP Client**	**SNMP Agent**	**NFS Client**
PCTCP	DW	D	DW	D	D	$D^2 D^3$	D	Y	DW
Chameleon	W	W	W	W	W	W^2	N	W	X
Super-TCP WX	W	W	W	W	W	$W^2 W^3$	W	W	DX
IBM/DOS	DW	DW	DW	D	DW	D^2	N	Y	X
BW	DW	DW	DW	DW	W	$W^2 W^3$	N	Y	X
Distinct	W	N	W	W					
Pathway	DW	DW	DW	D				D	DW
PC-NFS	DW	X	DW	D	DW	$D^{23} W^{23}$ N		Y	DW
LWPD	DW	DWX	DW	DW	N	N	N	Y	X
HP	D		D						
NCSATel	D	4	D		N	N	N	N	N

(continued)

Table 28-5					Major Applications				
ID	Telnet	TN3270	FTP Client	FTP Server	SMTP	POP[2]	NNTP Client	SNMP Agent	NFS Client
CUTCP	D	D	D	D	N	N	N	N	N
QVT/Net	W	N	W	W	N	W	W	N	N
Ka9q	D	N	D	D	D CS	D[23]	D	N	N
WATTCP	N	N	N	N	N	?	N	N	N
3Com									
Fusion									
MSLanMan	D		D						
AIR	W	W	Y					X	
TTCP v2.0	1		DW						
PC-LINKD	D		D					Y	
PC-LINKW								Y	
Lanera	DW	DW	D	D	N	N	N	N	X
Piper	Y	Y	Y	Y	CS	?	Y	Y	Y
WinNT	W	N	D[3]	5	N	N	N	Y	

[1]Terminal-emulation products sold separately.

[2]POP: 2 is version 2, 3 is version 3 and implies an SMTP client to send mail.

[3]D means character-based.

[4]Get TN3270 (CUTCP) package from Clarkson University.

[5]Server for NT will be in production version.

Windows Network Applications

The following are Internet network applications. Most of them require one of the TCP/IP packages in the preceding tables or, for Windows applications, any package that supports WinSock. This list omits gateways between TCP/IP and other networks such as Novell; see the on-line list (mentioned earlier), which you can FTP from ftp.cac.psu.edu in pub/dos/info/tcpip.packages.

Getting free and shareware programs by FTP

Most of the programs listed in Table 28-6 are available on the net, by FTP (see Chapter 16) or Gopher (see Chapter 20).

Table 28-6	FTP Archive Sites	
Name	*Directory to Use*	*Physical Location*
ftp.cica.indiana.edu	pub/pc/win3/winsock	(Indiana USA)
wuarchive.wustl.edu	mirrors2/win3	(Missouri USA)
grind.isca.uiowa.edu	msdos/win3	(Iowa USA)
gatekeeper.dec.com	/.2/micro/msdos/win3	(California USA)
polecat.law.indiana.edu	/pub/mirror/cica/win3/pc/win3	(Indiana USA)
alpha.cso.uiuc.edu	/pub/Mirror/win3	(Illinois USA)
sunsite.unc.edu	/pub/micro/pc-stuff/ ms-windows/winsock	(North Carolina USA)
vmsa.technion.ac.il		(Israel)
nic.switch.ch		(Switzerland)
ftp.cc.monash.edu.au		(Melbourne, Australia)
nctuccca.edu.tw		(Hsinchu,Taiwan)
src.doc.ic.ac.uk		(London, England)

Gopher users can look on `gopher.cica.indiana.edu`.

Programs in the CICA archive

Table 28-7 is a list of some of the more interesting programs available in the FTP archives just listed. The primary archive points are CICA and Sunsite; most other sites have copies of what CICA has.

Table 28-7	CICA and Sunsite Archive Programs
bsdchat.exe	Berkeley WinSock daemon talk client
cello.zip	Cello WWW Browser Release 1.0 (16 Feb 1994)
col_12b1.zip	NCSA Collage for WinSock [203k]
cooksock.zip	Cookie server for Windows Sockets interface
eudora14.exe	PC Eudora 1.4 WinSockAPI 1.1 POP3/SMTP shareware mail client
ewais200.zip	EINet shareware WAIS client application for WinSock [1.5m]
ewan10.zip	EWAN, a free WinSock 1.1 Telnet
finger31.zip	Windows Sockets finger client
gcp_24.exe	GCP++ TCP/IP Tools for WinSock v2.4.2 [1.06mb]
gophbk11.zip	GopherBook, ToolBook-based Gopher client for WinSock
goslip11.zip	GoSlip: A WinSock SLIP dialer (Visual Basic application)
hgoph24.zip	Hgopher 2.4, a WinSock-compliant Gopher client
inetcon1.zip	Internet-Connect, Version 1 WinSock Internet access
ivc10.zip	Internet VoiceChat, Version 1.0 (uses WinSock)
launcher.zip	Launch a win application by way of URL from Cello/Mosaic WWW client
phwin22.zip	Full and free CCSO ph (phonebook lookup) client using the WinSock 1.1 API
qvtws397.zip	Windows-Sockets compliant version of TCP/IP WinQVT/Net with telnet, ftp, and so on
qws3270.zip	qws3270 WinSock tn3270 emulator 3/25/94 release
serweb03.zip	World Wide Web Server for Windows 3.1 and NT
sticky.zip	Sticky Post-It notes for WinSock
tektel1a.zip	Tektonix (4000) terminal emulation for WinSock
trmptel.zip	Trumpet TELNET (VT100) terminal for WinSock
tsync1_4.zip	WinSock application sets your PC's clock to match a remote host
txtsrv.zip	Text server for WinSock API; speaks finger protocol
vt220.exe	Dart Communications VT220 for workgroup's WinSock
wftpd19c.zip	Windows FTP daemon 1.9c for WinSock 1.1
wgopher.zip	Gopher for Windows Version 2.2
winapps.zip	WinSock applications that were previously bundled with winsock.zip

Table 28-7 *(continued)*

winelm.zip	WinElm e-mail reader for WinSock
winfsp12.zip	FSP download application that uses WINSOCK.DLL
winftp.zip	WinSock FTP program executables for Windows NT
wingp.zip	Green Pages for Window Sockets 1.1 WinSock [951k]
winpanda.zip	Panda:gopher, ftp, e-mail, news clients for WinSock
winsock.zip	Peter Tattam's Trumpet WinSock ver 1.0
wintelb3.zip	NCSA Telnet for Windows (unsupported beta 3)
wlprs40.zip	WLPRSPL v4, a Windows Sockets-based print spooler
wmos20a4.zip	NCSA Mosaic v. 2.0 alpha 4 for Windows
wnvn082s.zip	WinVN, the NNTP newsreader for Windows (winsock)
ws_ftp.zip	Windows Sockets FTP client application Version 94.03.25
ws_ping.zip	Windows Sockets ping client Release 1 Version 93.10.03
wsarchie.zip	March '94 version of WSArchie, Archie client for WinSock
wsatest.zip	WSA test program for WinSock
wschesb1.zip	Multiplayer WinSock chess beta 1
wshost.zip	Windows Sockets host V1.00 (IP number to hostname)
wsirc13a.zip	Windows WinSock Internet Relay Chat client [463k]
wslpd.zip	WinSock line-printer daemon LPD for Windows
wsmtpd16.zip	Windows 3.1 and NT Simple Mail Transport Protocol daemon
wsnwdemo.zip	WinSock echo, ping, finger client applications
wsock1b2.zip	WinSock: Socket-DLLs for NCSA Telnet for Windows
wtalk11.zip	Version 1.1 of WinSock talk client/server
wtwsk10a.zip	Trumpet newsreader NNTP for Windows Sockets API

TCP/IP Software

Nearly every Mac Internet application requrires MacTCP, which is sold by APDA (phone 800-282-2732 or 716-871-6555). You want at least version 2.0.2. Generally, you should have your Macintosh dealer order it from APDA. The order numbers and list prices are as follows:

✔ M8113Z/A   TCP/IP Connection for Macintosh ($59)

   ✔ M8114Z/A   TCP/IP Administration for Macintosh ($199)

Many universities and large corporations have inexpensive site licenses; check before you shell out for your own copy. E-mail to `apda@applelink.apple.com`.

MacSLIP

This is a commercial SLIP (dial-up Internet connections) as a MacTCP extension from TriSoft. E-mail to `info@hydepark.com` or call 800-531-5170.

InterSLIP

This is a SLIP extension to MacTCP from InterCon. It's available as part of the TCP/Connect II package or at no charge by way of FTP from `ftp.intercon.com` in `InterCon/sales`.

Network Applications

MacTCP provides only low-level support and a control panel. If you actually want to do anything, you need applications. Many applications are free or shareware and can be retrieved by FTP. The major Mac FTP archives are shown in this list:

- ✔ `mac.archive.umich.edu` (Also provides files by e-mail. Send a message containing *help* to `mac@mac.archive.umich.edu`.)

- ✔ `ftp.apple.com` (The official Apple archive for free Apple-provided software.)

- ✔ `microlib.cc.utexas.edu`

- ✔ `sumex-aim.stanford.edu` (The best-known archive; hence it's badly overloaded — so try others first.)

- ✔ wuarchive.wustl.edu (Copies of sumex files are in mirrors/infomac, and copies of umich files are in mirrors/archive.umich.edu.)

NCSA Telnet

NCSA Telnet is the oldest and most widely used Mac telnet program. It also provides incoming and outgoing FTP. Available by way of FTP. Unlike every other application listed, it runs with or without MacTCP. While running without MacTCP, it contains its own SLIP (dial-up) package.

Comet (Cornell Macintosh Terminal Emulator)

Features telnet and TN3270. Available by way of FTP from `comet.cit.cornell.edu` in `pub/comet`.

Hytelnet

Hytelnet is a HyperCard version of telnet. E-mail to Charles Burchill at `burchil@ccu.umanitoba.ca`.

Eudora

Eudora is the most widely used mail package: flexible, complete, and the shareware version is free. What more could you ask? FTP from `ftp.cso.uiuc.edu` in `mac/eudora`, or inquire by e-mail to `eudora-info@qualcomm.com`.

LeeMail

This inexpensive shareware mail program is available by FTP or from the author, Lee Fyock, at `<laf@mitre.org>`.

NewsWatcher

NewsWatcher is a free Usenet news program. Available by FTP. Nerds can get the source code by FTP from `ftp.apple.com`.

Nuntius

This is a graphical Usenet reader. Contact the author, Peter Speck, at `speck@dat.ruc.dk`.

TCP/Connect II

This is a full-featured commercial suite (telnet, FTP, news, and more) of Internet applications. Available from InterCon Systems. Phone 703-709-9890 or e-mail to `sales@intercon.com`.

SU-Mac/IP

This suite of network applications (telnet, FTP, remote printing, and more) is from Stanford University. It's available only to "degree-granting institutions of higher education," at little or no cost. Call 415-723-3909 or e-mail `macip@jessica.stanford.edu`.

VersaTerm

VersaTerm is a commercial package from Synergy Software that provides flexible versions of telnet and FTP. SLIP (dial-up) is also available. Call 215-779-0522.

Chapter 29
I Want to Learn More

- -

In This Chapter

▶ On-line resources

▶ Magazines

▶ Organizations

- -

*T*he Internet is growing so fast that no single human can keep up with it all. Here we suggest some resources to help you keep abreast of what's new.

On-line Resources

The net is its own best source of information. Here are a few places to look for what's new:

The Scout Report

InterNIC Information Services publishes a weekly Scout Report listing interesting new sources of information on the net. It has mostly WWW sources, but it always has a few Gopher, telnet, and e-mail resources as well. It's available in just about every possible form on the net:

- ✔ **E-mail:** To get on the e-mail list, send a message to majordomo@is.internic.net that contains this line in the message text:

    subscribe scout-report

    To unsubscribe, repeat this procedure and substitute the word unsubscribe for subscribe.

- ✔ **WWW (Mosaic, and so on):** Point your Web program at http://www.internic.net/infoguide.html.

- ✔ **Gopher:** Look on host is.internic.net and select Information Services/ Scout Report.

Everybody's Guide to the Internet

Everybody's Guide is an introduction to the net written and updated by Adam Gaffin. It's available both on-line and in book form published by MIT Press. There's also a monthly *Everybody's Internet Update,* published by the Electronic Frontier Foundation.

Updates are posted to the usenet group `alt.internet.services`. If you miss one or want to see back issues, they're archived in the same places as the main document.

- ✔ **FTP:** Connect to `ftp.eff.org` and go to directory `pub/Net_info/ EFF_Net_Guide/Updates`. There are different versions for different kinds of computers (PostScript, Windows Help, and so on), but the file `netguide.eff` is the generic text version.

- ✔ **Gopher:** Look on `gopher.eff.org` and select Net Info and then EFF Net Guide. For updates, select Updates.

- ✔ **WWW:** Point your Web program at `http://www.eff.org/pub/ Net_info/EFF_Net_Guide`.

Note: *Everybody's Guide* used to be called the *Big Dummy's Guide to the Internet.* They changed the name to avoid confusion with, er, certain books.

Special Internet Connections

Scott Yanoff at the University of Wisconsin twice a month publishes a list of "Special Internet Connections" to services all over the world. It's posted in the Usenet groups `alt.internet.services`, `comp.misc`, `alt.bbs.internet`, `news.answers`, and `comp.answers`. It's also available in a zillion ways:

- ✔ **FTP:** Connect to `ftp.csd.uwm.edu` and get `/pub/inet.services.txt`.

- ✔ **Gopher:** Connect to `gopher.csd.uwm.edu` and select Remote Information Services.

- ✔ **E-mail:** Send an empty message to `bbslist@aug3.augsburg.edu` and it will automatically mail you the list.

- ✔ **WWW:** Connect to `http://www.uwm.edu/Mirror/ inet.services.html`.

Global Network Navigator

GNN is an on-line magazine published on the World Wide Web by O'Reilly and Associates. There's no charge to use it (it's supported by advertising), but you have to register on-line.

- ✔ **WWW:** Connect to `http://nearnet.gnn.com/` to register and to find the server nearest you.

Cool Site of the Day

The Cool Site of the Day on the World Wide Web highlights a new Cool Site every day. Check it daily! One day it gave us the Frog Page at Yale University with pictures, sounds (digital "ribbit" and such), stories, and much, much, more about our friends the Ranidae.

▌ ✔ **WWW:** http://www.infi.net/cool.html

Publications

Magazines and newsletters abound to track the growth and use of the net. Two of these are available either on paper or in electronic versions over the net.

Internet World

This is a bimonthly, glossy magazine for Internet users. Articles include tips, case histories, interviews with notable Internauts, product and service reviews, and so on. Contact:

Internet World
Meckler Corp.
11 Ferry Lane West
Westport, CT 06880

Phone: 203-226-6967
E-mail: meckler@jvnc.net or 70373.616@compuserve.com

Scott and Gregg's The Internet Novice

This newsletter for Internet novices is published by two brothers. Scott's the DOS guy, and Gregg does Macs. Price is $17.50 per year in the U.S. and $25 per year elsewhere. Contact:

CompuTate, Inc.
Box 3474
Arlington, VA 22203

E-mail: tates@access.digex.net

Inside the Internet

This monthly newsletter has Internet tips and tricks. Price is $69 per year in the U.S. and $89 per year elsewhere. Contact:

Inside the Internet
The Cobb Group, Customer Relations
9420 Bunsen Parkway, Suite 300
Louisville, KY 40220

Phone: 800-223-8720 or 502-493-3300
E-mail: ineteditor@merlin.cobb.ziff.com.

Matrix News

This monthly newsletter is about networks, including but not limited to the Internet. Available on paper or by e-mail. Price is $25 per year delivered on-line, $30 per year on paper, and $10 less for students. Contact:

Matrix Information and Directory Services
1106 Clayton Lane, Suite 500W
Austin, TX 78723

Phone: 512-451-7602
E-mail: mids@tic.com

Internet Business Report

This monthly newsletter tracks business use of and opportunities on the Internet, particularly for larger businesses. Price is $279 per year in the U.S. and $350 elsewhere. Contact:

Kareen Mattadeen-Hall
Internet Business Report
600 Community Drive
Manhasset, NY 11030

Phone: 800-340-6485
E-mail: ibrsub@cmp.com

Internet Business Journal

Covers business issues on the nascent commercial Internet. Case histories, studies, and the like. Available both on-line and on paper. Contact:

Michael Strangelove, Publisher
The Internet/NREN Business Journal
1-60 Springfield Road
Ottawa, Ontario, CANADA, K1M 1C7

Phone: 613-747-0642
Fax: 613-564-6641
E-mail: 441495@acadvm1.uottawa.ca

Internet Business Advantage

A monthly newsletter of tips and advice for business users of the Internet. Price is $99 per year. Contact:

Wentworth Worldwide Media
1866 Colonial Village Lane
P.O. Box 10488
Lancaster, PA 17605-0488

Phone: 800-638-1639

Email: success@wentworth.com (send your paper mailing address for a sample issue)

Organizations

Each of the following organizations also publishes a magazine.

The Internet Society

The Internet Society is dedicated to supporting the growth and evolution of the Internet and to upholding standards to keep the net working as it grows. The society publishes a magazine, holds conferences, and has many on-line resources. Individual and organizational memberships are available. Contact:

Internet Society
Suite 100
1895 Preston White Drive
Reston, VA 22091

Fax: 703-620-0913
E-mail: isoc@isoc.org

The Electronic Frontier Foundation (EFF)

The EFF works at the electronic frontier on issues of free speech, equitable access, and education in a networked context. It offers legal services in cases where users' on-line civil liberties have been violated. It publishes a magazine, has a Usenet group, keeps on-line files, and maintains human resources. Contact:

Electronic Frontier Foundation
1001 G Street, NW
Suite 950 East
Washington, DC 20001

Phone: 202-347-5400
Fax: 202-393-5509
E-mail: eff@eff.org
USENET: comp.org.eff.news and comp.org.eff.talk

The Society for Electronic Access (SEA)

The SEA works to promote civil rights and civilization in the networked digital world, primarily through research and education. Contact:

The Society for Electronic Access
Post Office Box 3131
Church Street Station
New York, NY 10008-3131

E-mail: sea-member@sea.org

Appendix
Internet Geographic Zones

· ·

This list is correct as of July 1994, and will certainly be out of date by the time you read it. But at least the country codes don't change too often.

How to Read This Table

The letters in the *How* field describe what connections the country has to the net. An uppercase *I* means that it's on the Internet. A lowercase *i* means that it has an internet-type network, but it isn't connected to the rest of the world. The other letters refer to other kinds of networks that aren't really part of the Internet but can exchange electronic mail with it. The networks are *B* for *BITNET*, *F* for *FIDONET*, *U* for *UUCP*, and *O* for *OSI*. An uppercase letter means that there are more than five sites of that type; lowercase means one to five.

Table A-1		Two-Letter Zone Names
Zone	**How**	**Country**
——	AF	Afghanistan (Islamic Republic of)
——	AL	Albania (Republic of)
-I—	DZ	Algeria (People's Democratic Republic of)
——	AS	American Samoa
——	AD	Andorra (Principality of)
——	AO	Angola (People's Republic of)
——	AI	Anguilla
-I—	AQ	Antarctica
—u—	AG	Antigua and Barbuda
BIUF-	AR	Argentina (Argentine Republic)
—U—	AM	Armenia
—f-	AW	Aruba
-IUFo	AU	Australia
BIUFO	AT	Austria (Republic of)
b-U—	AZ	Azerbaijan

(continued)

Table A-1 *(continued)*

Zone	How	Country
—u—	BS	Bahamas (Commonwealth of the)
b——	BH	Bahrain (State of)
——	BD	Bangladesh (People's Republic of)
—u—	BB	Barbados
b-UF-	BY	Belarus
BIUFO	BE	Belgium (Kingdom of)
—U—	BZ	Belize
——	BJ	Benin (People's Republic of)
—Uf-	BM	Bermuda
——	BT	Bhutan (Kingdom of)
—Uf-	BO	Bolivia (Republic of)
—u—	BA	Bosnia-Herzegovina
—uf-	BW	Botswana (Republic of)
——	BV	Bouvet Island
BIUFO	BR	Brazil (Federative Republic of)
——	IO	British Indian Ocean Territory
——	BN	Brunei Darussalam
bIUF-	BG	Bulgaria (Republic of)
—U—	BF	Burkina Faso (formerly Upper Volta)
——	BI	Burundi (Republic of)
——	KH	Cambodia
—u—	CM	Cameroon (Republic of)
BIUFO	CA	Canada
——	CV	Cape Verde (Republic of)
——	KY	Cayman Islands
——	CF	Central African Republic
——	TD	Chad (Republic of)
BIUF-	CL	Chile (Republic of)
-lu-O	CN	China (People's Republic of)

Zone	How	Country
——	CX	Christmas Island (Indian Ocean)
——	CC	Cocos (Keeling) Islands
Blu—	CO	Colombia (Republic of)
——	KM	Comoros (Islamic Federal Republic of the)
—u—	CG	Congo (Republic of the)
—u—	CK	Cook Islands
bluf-	CR	Costa Rica (Republic of)
—uf-	CI	Cote d'Ivoire (Republic of)
-luFo	HR	Croatia
—U—	CU	Cuba (Republic of)
bl—	CY	Cyprus (Republic of)
BIUF-	CZ	Czech Republic
BIUFO	DK	Denmark (Kingdom of)
——	DJ	Djibouti (Republic of)
——	DM	Dominica (Commonwealth of)
—Uf-	DO	Dominican Republic
——	TP	East Timor
-lu—	EC	Ecuador (Republic of)
bIU—	EG	Egypt (Arab Republic of)
——	SV	El Salvador (Republic of)
——	GQ	Equatorial Guinea (Republic of)
——	ER	Eritrea
-IUF-	EE	Estonia (Republic of)
—f-	ET	Ethiopia (People's Democratic Republic of)
——	FK	Falkland Islands (Malvinas)
—u—	FO	Faroe Islands
-lu—	FJ	Fiji (Republic of)
BIUFO	FI	Finland (Republic of)
BIUFO	FR	France (French Republic)
—u—	GF	French Guiana

(continued)

Table A-1 *(continued)*

Zone	How	Country
—u—	PF	French Polynesia
——	TF	French Southern Territories
——	GA	Gabon (Gabonese Republic)
——	GM	Gambia (Republic of the)
—UF-	GE	Georgia (Republic of)
BIUFO	DE	Germany (Federal Republic of)
—uF-	GH	Ghana (Republic of)
——	GI	Gibraltar
BIUFO	GR	Greece (Hellenic Republic)
-I-f-	GL	Greenland
—u—	GD	Grenada
b-uf-	GP	Guadeloupe (French Department of)
-I-F-	GU	Guam
—u—	GT	Guatemala (Republic of)
——	GN	Guinea (Republic of)
——	GW	Guinea-Bissau (Republic of)
——	GY	Guyana (Republic of)
——	HT	Haiti (Republic of)
——	HM	Heard and McDonald Islands
——	HN	Honduras (Republic of)
BI-F-	HK	Hong Kong
BIUFo	HU	Hungary (Republic of)
-IUFo	IS	Iceland (Republic of)
bIUfO	IN	India (Republic of)
-IuF-	ID	Indonesia (Republic of)
b——	IR	Iran (Islamic Republic of)
——	IQ	Iraq (Republic of)
BIUFO	IE	Ireland
BIUF-	IL	Israel (State of)

Zone	How	Country
BIUFO	IT	Italy (Italian Republic)
—u—	JM	Jamaica
BIUF-	JP	Japan
——	JO	Jordan (Hashemite Kingdom of)
—UF-	KZ	Kazakhstan
—f-	KE	Kenya (Republic of)
—u—	KI	Kiribati (Republic of)
——	KP	Korea (Democratic People's Republic of)
BIUFO	KR	Korea (Republic of)
-I—	KW	Kuwait (State of)
—U—	KG	Kyrgyz Republic
——	LA	Lao People's Democratic Republic
-IUF-	LV	Latvia (Republic of)
——	LB	Lebanon (Lebanese Republic)
—u—	LS	Lesotho (Kingdom of)
——	LR	Liberia (Republic of)
——	LY	Libyan Arab Jamahiriya
-I-f-	LI	Liechtenstein (Principality of)
-IUFo	LT	Lithuania
bIUFo	LU	Luxembourg (Grand Duchy of)
-I-F-	MO	Macau (Ao-me'n)
—u—	MK	Macedonia (Former Yugoslav Republic of)
—u—	MG	Madagascar (Democratic Republic of)
—f-	MW	Malawi (Republic of)
bIUF-	MY	Malaysia
——	MV	Maldives (Republic of)
—U—	ML	Mali (Republic of)
—u—	MT	Malta (Republic of)
——	MH	Marshall Islands (Republic of the)
——	MQ	Martinique (French Department of)

(continued)

Table A-1 *(continued)*

Zone	How	Country
——	MR	Mauritania (Islamic Republic of)
—uf-	MU	Mauritius
——	YT	Mayotte
BIuF-	MX	Mexico (United Mexican States)
——	FM	Micronesia (Federated States of)
—uF-	MD	Moldova (Republic of)
——	MC	Monaco (Principality of)
——	MN	Mongolia
——	MS	Montserrat
——	MA	Morocco (Kingdom of)
—Uf-	MZ	Mozambique (People's Republic of)
——	MM	Myanmar (Union of)
—Uf-	NA	Namibia (Republic of)
——	NR	Nauru (Republic of)
—u—	NP	Nepal (Kingdom of)
BIUFO	NL	Netherlands (Kingdom of the)
—u—	AN	Netherlands Antilles
——	NT	Neutral Zone (between Saudi Arabia and Iraq)
—U—	NC	New Caledonia
-IUF-	NZ	New Zealand
-Iu—	NI	Nicaragua (Republic of)
—u—	NE	Niger (Republic of the)
—f-	NG	Nigeria (Federal Republic of)
—u—	NU	Niue
——	NF	Norfolk Island
——	MP	Northern Mariana Islands (Commonwealth of the)
BIUFO	NO	Norway (Kingdom of)
——	OM	Oman (Sultanate of)
—U—	PK	Pakistan (Islamic Republic of)

Zone	How	Country
——	PW	Palau (Republic of)
bIuF-	PA	Panama (Republic of)
—u—	PG	Papua New Guinea
—u—	PY	Paraguay (Republic of)
-IUf-	PE	Peru (Republic of)
-IuF-	PH	Philippines (Republic of the)
——	PN	Pitcairn
BIUF-	PL	Poland (Republic of)
bIUFO	PT	Portugal (Portuguese Republic)
bIUF-	PR	Puerto Rico
——	QA	Qatar (State of)
-Iu—	RE	Re'union (French Department of)
BIuf-	RO	Romania
BIUF-	RU	Russian Federation
——	RW	Rwanda (Rwandese Republic)
——	SH	Saint Helena
——	KN	Saint Kitts and Nevis
—u—	LC	Saint Lucia
——	PM	Saint Pierre and Miquelon (French Department of)
——	VC	Saint Vincent and the Grenadines
—u—	WS	Samoa (Independent State of)
——	SM	San Marino (Republic of)
——	ST	Sao Tome and Principe (Democratic Republic of)
B——	SA	Saudi Arabia (Kingdom of)
—Uf-	SN	Senegal (Republic of)
—u—	SC	Seychelles (Republic of)
——	SL	Sierra Leone (Republic of)
BIuF-	SG	Singapore (Republic of)
bIUF-	SK	Slovakia
-IUFO	SI	Slovenia

(continued)

Table A-1 *(continued)*

Zone	How	Country
—u—	SB	Solomon Islands
——	SO	Somalia (Somali Democratic Republic)
-IUFO	ZA	South Africa (Republic of)
BIUFO	ES	Spain (Kingdom of)
—U—	LK	Sri Lanka (Democratic Socialist Republic of)
——	SD	Sudan (Democratic Republic of the)
—u—	SR	Suriname (Republic of)
-I—	SJ	Svalbard and Jan Mayen Islands
—u—	SZ	Swaziland (Kingdom of)
BIUFo	SE	Sweden (Kingdom of)
BIUFO	CH	Switzerland (Swiss Confederation)
——	SY	Syria (Syrian Arab Republic)
BIuF-	TW	Taiwan, Province of China
—u—	TJ	Tajikistan
—f-	TZ	Tanzania (United Republic of)
-IUF-	TH	Thailand (Kingdom of)
—u—	TG	Togo (Togolese Republic)
——	TK	Tokelau
—u—	TO	Tonga (Kingdom of)
—u—	TT	Trinidad and Tobago (Republic of)
bIUfo	TN	Tunisia
BI-F-	TR	Turkey (Republic of)
—u—	TM	Turkmenistan
——	TC	Turks and Caicos Islands
——	TV	Tuvalu
—F-	UG	Uganda (Republic of)
-IUF-	UA	Ukraine
——	AE	United Arab Emirates

Zone	How	Country
bIUFO	GB	United Kingdom (United Kingdom of Great Britain and Northern Ireland)
BIUFO	US	United States (United States of America)
——	UM	United States Minor Outlying Islands
-IUF-	UY	Uruguay (Eastern Republic of)
—UF-	UZ	Uzbekistan
—u—	VU	Vanuatu (Republic of, formerly New Hebrides)
——	VA	Vatican City State (Holy See)
-IU—	VE	Venezuela (Republic of)
—U—	VN	Vietnam (Socialist Republic of)
——	VG	Virgin Islands (British)
—f-	VI	Virgin Islands (U.S.)
——	WF	Wallis and Futuna Islands
——	EH	Western Sahara
——	YE	Yemen (Republic of)
—uf-	YU	Yugoslavia (Socialist Federal Republic of)
——	ZR	Zaire (Republic of)
—f-	ZM	Zambia (Republic of)
—uf-	ZW	Zimbabwe (Republic of)

Copyright © 1994 Lawrence H. Landweber and the Internet Society. Unlimited permission to copy or use is hereby granted subject to inclusion of this copyright notice.

Glossary

. . . .

account

Just like at a bank, computers used by more than one person use accounts to keep track of (and bill) who's doing what on their system. When you sign up with an Internet provider, you get an account name that allows you access.

address

Secret code by which the Internet identifies you so that people can send you mail. It usually looks like username@hostname — where username is your username, or login name, or account number; and hostname is the Internet's name for the computer or Internet provider you use. The hostname can be a few words strung together with periods. The official *Internet For Dummies* address, for example, is internet@dummies.com because its username is internet and it's on a computer named dummies.com. See Chapter 7 for more information about addresses, including yours, and Chapter 9 to learn how to find out other people's addresses.

All-in-1

An office-management software package from DEC that includes electronic mail. Some All-in-1 systems can exchange mail with the Internet, and some can't.

alt

Type of newsgroup that discusses alternative-type topics. The alt groups are not official newsgroups, but lots of people read them anyway. We particularly like alt.folklore.urban and alt.folklore.suburban. See Chapter 12 for lists of interesting newsgroups.

America Online (AOL)

A public Internet provider. If you have an account on America Online, your Internet address is username@aol.com, where username is your account name. See Chapter 7 of *MORE Internet For Dummies* to learn how to use America Online to access the Internet.

anonymous FTP

Using the FTP program to log on to another computer to copy files, even though you don't have an account on the other computer. When you log on, you enter anonymous as the username and your address as the password. This gives you access to publicly available files. See Chapter 16 for more information about FTP-ing in general and anonymous FTP in particular.

ANS

Advanced Network Services, which runs one of the large, high-speed networks on the Internet. Run by Merit, MCI, and IBM.

Archie

A system that helps you find files that are located anywhere on the Internet. After Archie helps you find the file, you can use FTP to get it. Archie is both a program and a system of servers (that is, computers that contain indexes of files). See Chapter 19 for more information.

archive

File that contains a group of files that have been compressed and glommed together for efficient storage. You have to use an archive program to get the original files back out. Commonly used programs include compress, tar, cpio, and zip (on UNIX systems) and PKZIP (on DOS systems). See Chapter 17 to learn how to use them.

ARPANET

The original ancestor of the Internet, funded by the U.S. Department of Defense.

article

A posting to a newsgroup. That is, a message someone sends to the newsgroup to be readable by everyone who reads the newsgroup. See Chapter 11 for general information about newsgroups. See Chapter 12 of *MORE Internet For Dummies* to learn how to use Trumpet to read newsgroups if you use a SLIP connection to the Internet, and Chapter 16 for power newsreading via trn.

AT&T Mail

A commercial mail system that connects to the Internet. If you have an AT&T Mail account, your Internet address is `username@attmail.com`, where `username` is your account name.

AUP

Acceptable Use Policy; a set of rules describing what sorts of activities are permitted on a network. The most restrictive AUP was the one on the NSFNET that prohibited most commercial and non-academic use. The NSFNET AUP is no longer in force anywhere, although many people erroneously believe that it is.

automatic mailing list

A mailing list maintained by a computer program, usually one named LISTSERV or Majordomo. *See also **mailing list***. Chapter 10 provides information about how to use mailing lists.

bang path address

An old-fashioned method of writing network addresses. UUCP, an old, cruddy mail system used to use addresses that contained bangs (that is, exclamation points!) to string together the parts of the address. Forget about them.

BBS

Bulletin board system; a system that lets people read each other's messages and post new ones. The Usenet system of newsgroups is in effect the world's largest distributed BBS.

binary file

File that contains information that does not consist only of text. For example, an archive, a picture, sounds, a spreadsheet, or a word-processing document (which includes formatting codes in addition to characters).

bionet

A type of newsgroup that discusses topics of interest to biologists. If you're not a biologist, don't bother reading them.

bit

The smallest unit of measure for computer data. Bits can be turned on or off and are used in various combinations to represent different kinds of information. Many bits form a byte. Bytes form words. Do you care? Also, a type of newsgroup that is actually a BITNET mailing list in disguise.

BITFTP

The most widely available FTP-by-mail server. *See also* **FTP-by-mail**.

bitmap

Lots of teeny, tiny, little dots put together to make a picture. Screens (and paper) are divided into thousands of little, tiny bits, each of which can be turned on or off. These little bits are combined to create graphical representations. *GIF* files are the most popular kind of bitmap files on the net.

BITNET

A network of mostly IBM mainframes that connects to the Internet. If you have an account on machine `xyzvm3` on the BITNET, and your username is `abc`, your Internet mail address is `abc@xyzvm3.bitnet`, or, if your system isn't well-informed about BITNET, `abc%xyzvm3.bitnet@cunyvm.cuny.edu`. See Chapter 9 for more information about BITNET.

BIX

A commercial system formerly run by *Byte* magazine and now run by Delphi. If you have a BIX account, your Internet address is `username@bix.com`, where `username` is your account name.

biz

A type of newsgroup that discusses business and commercial topics. Most other types of newsgroups stay away from commercial messages.

bps

Bits per second. A measurement used to describe how fast data is transmitted. Usually used to describe modem speed.

bridge

Connects two networks so that they appear to be a single larger network. For the distinction between bridges, routers, and gateways, see Chapter 6.

broadband network

A network that can handle many separate signals at the same time. Broadband networks use different channels to transfer different forms of information, such as data, voice, and video.

bulletin board system

Electronic message system for reading and posting messages. *See also* **BBS**.

byte

A series of bits of a particular length, usually eight. Computer storage is usually measured in bytes.

Cello

Program, written at the Cornell Law School, that enables you to access the World Wide Web from your PC running Windows. It provides a nifty point-and-click graphics interface to WWW. A similar program is called Mosaic.

CERFnet

One of the regional networks originally set up to work with the NSFNET, headquartered in California.

Chameleon

Commercial Windows software that allows you to connect directly to the Internet by way of a SLIP Internet provider.

chat

To talk live to other network users. To do this, you use Internet Relay Chat (IRC), described in Chapter 19 of *MORE Internet For Dummies.*

Cisco

A company that makes bridges and routers.

CIX

The Commercial Internet Exchange, an association of Internet providers who agree to exchange traffic without *AUP*-type restrictions.

ClariNet

Usenet newsgroups that contain various categories of news, including news from the AP newswire, distributed for a modest fee. Not all systems carry the ClariNet newsgroups because they cost money. You can also subscribe to some of them yourself — send mail to info@clarinet.com for information.

click

If you have a mouse, you already know. If you don't have one, don't worry.

client

A computer that uses the services of another computer (such as Usenet or Gopher or FTP or *Archie* or the World Wide Web.) If your computer is a PC or Macintosh and you dial in to another system, your computer becomes a client of the system you dial in to.

client/server model

A division of labor between computers. Computers that provide a service other computers can use are known as servers. Servers provide such services as FTP or *Archie* or the World Wide Web. If you don't have these services on your very own machine, you can connect to these machines and use these services and thereby become a client.

com

When this appears at the last part of an address (in internet@dummies.com, for example), it indicates that the host computer is run by a company rather than by a university or governmental agency. It also means that the host computer is probably in the United States.

command language

Words that tell a computer what to do. Used honorably for years before the invention of Macintoshes, Windows, and other graphics-based systems. Such notables as DOS and UNIX are systems rooted in command-language syntax.

communications program

A program you run on your personal computer that enables you to call up and communicate with other computers. It makes your computer pretend to be a terminal (that's why they are also known as *terminal programs* or *terminal emulators*). The most commonly used communications programs on PCs are Windows Terminal (because it's free with Windows), Crosstalk, and Procomm, though there are lots of others.

comp

A type of newsgroup that discusses topics about computers, such as `comp.lang.c` (which discusses the C programming language) and `comp.society.folklore` (which covers the folklore and culture of computer users). See Chapter 12 for lists of interesting newsgroups.

CompuServe

An on-line information provider that gives you some Internet access. It provides lots of forums, which are like newsgroups, including many that provide excellent technical support for a wide range of PC and Mac software. If your CompuServe account number is `7123,456`, your Internet address is `7123.456@compuserve.com` (notice the period in the account number).

country code

The last part of a geographic address, which indicates which country the host computer is in. An address that ends in *ca* is Canadian, for example, and one that ends in *us* is in the U.S. For a complete list, see Appendix A, which discusses Internet geographic zones.

daemon

Mysterious little programs that run while you're not looking and take care of things you would rather not know about.

DARPA

Defense Advanced Research Projects Agency, the funding agency for the original *ARPANET,* the precursor of today's Internet.

Delphi

An on-line information provider that includes access to lots of Internet services. If you have an account on Delphi, your Internet address is `username@delphi.com`, where `username` is your account name. See Chapter 5 of *MORE Internet For Dummies* to learn how to use Delphi to access the Internet.

digest

A compilation of the messages that have been posted to a mailing list over the last few days. Many people find it more convenient to receive one big message than a bunch of individual ones. See Chapter 10.

directory

A structure, sort of like a file folder (and called a folder in the Macintosh world). A special kind of file used to organize other files. Directories are lists of other files and can contain other directories (known as subdirectories) that contain still more files. UNIX, DOS, and Windows systems all use directory structures. The more stuff you have, the more you need directories in which to organize it. Directories enable you to organize files hierarchically.

domain

The official Internet-ese name of a computer on the net. It's the part of an Internet address that comes after the @. Internet For Dummies Central is `internet@dummies.com`, for example, and its domain name is `dummies.com`.

domain name server

(Or just name server, or abbreviated as DNS). A computer on the Internet that translates between Internet domain names, such as `xuxa.iecc.com`, and Internet numerical addresses, such as `140.186.81.2`.

DOS

Disk Operating System. The original and still popular program that runs on PCs and takes care of the system basics, such as talking to files and printers and screens. Not the operating system of choice for new buyers.

download

To bring software from a remote computer "down" to your computer.

dumb terminal

A screen and a keyboard and not much else. Dumb terminals connect to other computers and use their data and their computing. When you use your computer to dial in to another computer (ignoring SLIP and PPP connections for the moment), your computer generally acts like a dumb terminal and relies on the computer you've dialed in to for processing the requests you make.

dynamic rerouting

A method of addressing information on the Internet so that if one route is blocked or broken, the information can take an alternative route. Pretty darned clever. The U.S. Department of Defense built this method into the design of the Internet for the benefit of the military, to resist enemy attack. Also useful when nonmilitary networks are attacked by errant backhoes.

e-mail

Electronic mail (also called *email* or just *mail*) messages sent by way of the Internet to a particular person. See Chapter 7.

Easylink

An e-mail service formerly run by Western Union and now run by AT&T. If you have an Easylink account, your Internet address is `1234567@eln.attmail.com`, where `1234567` is your account number.

edu

When these letters appear at the last part of an address (in `info@mit.edu`, for example), it indicates that the host computer is run by an educational institution, probably a college or university. It also means that the host computer is probably in the United States.

elm

An easy-to-use UNIX mail reader, which we vastly prefer over mail. Another good one is pine. See Chapter 7.

environment variable

Values that can be set to help automatically get your computer into a state ready for you to use. Environment variables are part of your operating system's machinations and are specific to the operating system you run.

Ethernet

A cable that connects pieces of a local area network in a particular pattern. Developed by Xerox, it is sometimes called IEEE 802.3, which refers to the standard that defines it.

Eudora

A mail-handling program that runs on the Macintosh and under Windows. Originally a shareware program, it is now sold by Qualcomm. See Chapter 7 in this book and Chapter 11 in *MORE Internet For Dummies*.

FAQ

Frequently Asked Questions. This regularly posted Usenet article answers questions that come up regularly in a newsgroup. Before you ask a question in a newsgroup, make sure that you read its FAQ, because it may well contain the answer. People get annoyed if you ask questions that are answered in the newsgroup's FAQ. FAQs are posted regularly, usually once a week or once a month. To read all the regularly posted FAQs for all newsgroups, read the newsgroup `news.answers`.

FAX Modem

Really should be fax/data modems. Modems that enable you to send and receive faxes in addition to ordinary computer-type data. Fax is short for facsimile or exact copy, and fax technology uses ordinary phone lines to send copies of printed material from place to place. If you stick fax technology on to your computer, what you send may never touch paper. It can go from your computer to theirs, or to their fax machine if they don't have a computer.

FIDONET

A worldwide network of bulletin board systems (BBSs). Each individual BBS is called a *node* on FIDONET and has a three- or four-part numeric address in the form *1:2/3* or *1:2/3.4*. To send mail to someone on FIDONET, address it to `firstname.lastname@p4.f3.n2.z1.fidonet.org` (for nodes with four-part names) or `firstname.lastname@f3.n2.z1` (for nodes with three-part names), substituting the addressee's username for `firstname.lastname`.

file

A collection of information (data or a software program, for example) treated as a unit by computers.

file-transfer protocol

A method of transferring one or more files from one computer to another on a network or phone line. The idea of using a protocol is that the sending and receiving programs can check that the information has been received correctly. The most commonly used dial-up protocols are xmodem, ymodem, zmodem, and Kermit. The Internet has its own file-transfer protocol called FTP (clever name, huh?) to transfer files among computers on the net. See Chapter 16.

finger

A program that displays information about someone on the net. On most UNIX systems, the command tells you who is logged on right now. On most Internet hosts, it tells you the actual name and perhaps some other information, based on the person's Internet address and the last time she logged on. See Chapter 9 to learn how to use it.

firewall

A system has a *firewall* around it if it lets only certain kind of messages in and out from the rest of the Internet. If an organization wants to exchange mail with the Internet, for example, but it doesn't want nosy college students telnetting in and reading everyone's files, its connection to the Internet can be set up to prevent incoming telnets or FTPs.

folder

See ***directory***.

freenet

A free on-line system. Wow! The first one, created at the University of Cleveland, is called the Cleveland Freenet, offering local community information and limited access to the Internet. Lots of other freenets have sprung up, and because you can telnet from one to another, if you can access one, you can access them all. For a list of freenets, see Chapter 27.

FTP

File-transfer protocol. This is also the name of a program that uses the protocol to transfer files all over the Internet. See Chapter 16.

FTP-by-mail

A method by which you can send a mail message to a server computer to request that a file be mailed to you by way of e-mail. This is a way to get files over the net, slowly, if you have access only to e-mail. See Chapter 17.

gateway

A computer that connects one network with another, and the two networks use different protocols. The UUNET computer connects the UUCP network with the Internet, allowing messages to move between the two networks. For more information about how gateways work, see Chapter 6 in this book and Chapter 3 of *MORE Internet For Dummies*. Also an older name for what's now called a *router*.

GEnie

An on-line service run by General Electric. If you have a GEnie account and your mail name (not your username!) is `ABC`, your address is `ABC@genie.gies.com`.

GIF

A type of graphics file originally defined by CompuServe and now found all over the net (GIF stands for Graphics Interchange Format). See Chapter 17.

global kill file

A file that tells your newsreader which articles you always want to skip. This file applies to all the newsgroups to which you subscribe. See Chapter 16 of *MORE Internet For Dummies* to learn how to make kill files by using trn.

Gopher

A system that lets you find information by using menus (lots of menus). To use Gopher, you usually telnet to a Gopher server and begin browsing the menus. For the straight dope on Gopher, see Chapter 20. Chapter 18 of *MORE Internet For Dummies* contains more information about using Gopher.

Gopherspace

The world of Gopher menus. As you move from menu to menu in Gopher, you are said to be moving around Gopherspace.

gov

When these letters appear at the last part of an address (in `cu.nih.gov`, for example), it indicates that the host computer is run by some part of a government body, probably the U.S. federal government, rather than by a company or university. Your tax dollars at play! Most `gov` sites are in the U.S.

hardware

The actual, physical computer itself and all its wires and friends, such as the printer, the disk drive, and the modem. Pretty useless without software.

HGopher

A cool Microsoft Windows program that helps you view Gopher information, including seeing graphics right on the screen. It's described briefly in Chapter 20 in this book and in detail in Chapter 13 of *MORE Internet For Dummies.*

host

A computer on the Internet you may be able to log in to by using Telnet, get files from by using FTP, or otherwise make use of.

HTML

Hypertext Markup Language, used in writing pages for the World Wide Web. It lets the text include codes that define fonts, layout, embedded graphics, and hypertext links. Don't worry: You don't have to know anything about it to use the World Wide Web. See Chapter 22.

HTTP

HyperText Transfer Protocol, how World Wide Web pages are transferred over the net. See Chapter 22. Also see Chapter 15 of *MORE Internet For Dummies* for more details about how to read the World Wide Web from a PC with Windows.

hypermedia

See **hypertext**, except think about all kinds of information, such as pictures and sound, not just text.

hypertext

A system of writing and displaying text that enables the text to be linked in multiple ways, available at several levels of detail, and contain links to related documents. Hypermedia can also contain pictures, sounds, video — you name it. The World Wide Web uses hypertext. Both are discussed in Chapter 22.

ICMP

Internet Control Message Protocol, an exceedingly uninteresting low-level protocol that Internet computers use. Used by ping (see Chapter 28).

icon

A little picture intended to represent something bigger, such as a program or a choice of action or object.

Internet

You still don't know what it is, and you're way back here in the glossary! Yikes — we must have done a terrible job of explaining this stuff. It's an inter-connected bunch of networks, including networks in all parts of the world.

Internet Protocol

See **IP**.

Internet Relay Chat (IRC)

A system that enables Internet folks to talk to each other in real time (rather than after a delay, as with e-mail messages). Chapter 13, and also Chapter 19 of *MORE Internet For Dummies,* describe how to get in on the action.

Internet Society

An organization dedicated to supporting the growth and evolution of the Internet. You can contact it at `isoc@isoc.org`.

INTERNIC

The Internet Network Information Center, a repository of information about the Internet itself. It is divided into three parts: Information Services run by General Atomics in California, Directory Services run by AT&T in New Jersey, and Registration Services run by Network Solutions in Virginia, funded primarily, for now at least, by the National Science Foundation. To FTP information from INTERNIC, try `ftp.internic.net`.

interrupt character

A key or combination of keys you can press to stop whatever's happening on your computer. You might find that you have started something and you don't want to wait for it to finish. Common interrupt characters are Ctrl-C and Ctrl-D. Telnet's usual interrupt character is Ctrl-].

IP

Internet Protocol, a scheme that enables information to be routed from one network to another as necessary (you had to ask). Don't worry: You don't have to know about it. For a long and tedious discussion, see Chapter 6. For even more tedium, see Chapter 2 of *MORE Internet For Dummies*.

IRC

See **_Internet Relay Chat_**.

ISO

International Organization for Standardization. (Yes, we know that the name and the letters don't match. No, we don't know why.) A multinational, independent body formed to define international standards for, among other things, network communications. Often a little late in coming to terms with the reality of what's already in place.

Jughead

A program that helps you find information in Gopher by searching Gopher directories for the information you specify. Sort of like *Veronica*.

JvNCnet

One of the regional networks originally set up to work with NSFNET, headquartered in New Jersey. JvN stands for John von Neumann, inventor of the modern computer and host of many a wild party in Princeton, New Jersey.

k12

A type of Usenet newsgroup that contains information for elementary through high school students and teachers.

Kermit

A file-transfer protocol developed at Columbia University and available for a variety of computers, from PCs to mainframes. See Chapter 4 of *MORE Internet For Dummies* for more information about file-transfer protocols.

kill file

A file that tells your newsreader which newsgroup articles you always want to skip. See Chapter 11 in this book and Chapter 16 in *MORE Internet For Dummies* to learn how to make kill files by using trn.

line-at-a-time interface

See **command language**.

link

A connection. Two computers can be linked together. Also can refer to a pointer to a file that exists in another place. For example, rather than have a copy of a particular file reside in many places, some file systems (like the ones in UNIX, for example) enable a filename to point to another file.

link-level protocol

One of the seven layers of protocols defined by ISO. Sometimes referred to as the data link layer. You really, really don't care.

LISTSERV

A family of programs that automatically manage mailing lists, distributing messages posted to the list, adding and deleting members, and so on, without the tedium of someone doing it manually. The names of mailing lists maintained by LISTSERV usually end with -1 (that's an el, not a one). See Chapter 10 for information about how to get on and off LISTSERV mailing lists.

LYNX

A World Wide Web client program that works with plain, old terminals, which means that you can telnet to systems that use it. See Chapter 22.

MacTCP

TCP/IP for the Macintosh. Not very interesting except that you can't put your Mac on the Internet without it.

mail

Pieces of paper stuffed in envelopes with stamps on the outside. This old-fashioned type of mail is known among Internauts as *snail-mail,* casting aspersions on your local letter carrier. Other types of mail include *voice mail,* which you probably already know and hate, and *e-mail* (or electronic mail), which is a powerful service the Internet provides. For an introduction to e-mail, see Chapter 7.

mail server

A computer on the Internet that provides mail services. A mail server usually sends mail out for you (using a system called SMTP) and may also enable you to download your mail to a PC or Mac by using a protocol called POP. See Chapter 11 of *MORE Internet For Dummies* to learn how to use Eudora to grab your mail from a mail server.

Mailing list

A special kind of e-mail address that remails any incoming mail to a list of *subscribers* to the mailing list. Each mailing list has a specific topic, so one subscribes to the ones of Interest. See Chapter 10.

Mainframe

A large computer usually sold complete with all its peripherals and often a closed architecture (meaning not friendly to other vendors' products). Often refers to large IBM machines.

Majordomo

Like LISTSERV, a program that handles mailing lists. See Chapter 20 of *MORE Internet For Dummies.*

MCI Mail

A commercial e-mail system linked to the Internet. If you have an MCI Mail account, you have both a username and a seven-digit user number. Your Internet address is `1234567@mcimail.com` or `username@mcimail.com`, substituting your username or number.

Watch out when you're addressing mail by name on MCI Mail — more than one person may have the same name! Numbers are safer. If a name is ambiguous, MCI Mail returns a message with hints about how to find the user you want.

MERIT

A regional network in Michigan. Affiliated with ANS.

message

A piece of e-mail, or a posting to a newsgroup.

mil

When these letters appear at the last part of an address (in `wsmr-simtel20@army.mil`, for example), it indicates that the host computer is run by some part of the U.S. military rather than by a company or university.

mirror

An FTP server that provides copies of the same files as another server. Some FTP servers are so popular that other servers have been set up to mirror them and spread the FTP load on to more than one site.

misc

A type of newsgroup that discusses topics that don't fit under any of the other newsgroups types, such as `misc.forsale`, `misc.jobs.offered`, and `misc.kids`. See Chapter 12 for lists of interesting newsgroups.

modem

A gizmo that lets your computer talk on the phone. A modem can be internal (a board that lives inside your computer) or external (a box that connects to your computer's serial port). Either way, you need a phone wire to connect the modem to your phone jack. For tons of information about modems and how to use them, get *Modems For Dummies*.

moderated mailing list

A mailing list run by a *moderator* (*q.v.*, or for you non-Latin speakers, go check out the definition of *moderator*).

moderated newsgroup

A newsgroup run by a moderator (go ahead, *see* **moderator**).

moderator

Someone who looks at the messages posted to a mailing list or newsgroup first before releasing them to the public. The moderator can nix messages that are stupid (in his opinion, of course), redundant, or inappropriate for the list or newsgroup (wildly off the topic or offensive, for example). Yes, this is censorship, it's true, but the Internet is getting so big and crowded that nonmoderated discussions can generate an amazing number of uninteresting messages. *See also* **moderated mailing list** and **moderated newsgroup**.

Mosaic

A super-duper all-singing, all-dancing program that lets you read information on the World Wide Web. Comes in Windows, Mac, and UNIX flavors. See Chapter 22 in this book and Chapter 15 in *MORE Internet For Dummies*.

Motif

A graphical user interface for UNIX computers, sort of like Windows for the PC. Ugly. See *UNIX For Dummies* if you really care.

MUD

Multi-User Dungeon; a "dungeons and dragons" type of game that many people at a time can play. These games can get so complex and absorbing that players can disappear into their computers for days and weeks at a time. For information about how to join a MUD, consult the newsgroup `rec.games.mud.announce` or send a request to be added to the mailing list to `mudlist@glia.biostr.washington.edu`.

name server

See **domain name server**.

NDIS

A small program used on DOS and Windows PCs to connect network software to a particular kind of network card. Defined by Microsoft. Similar to *packet driver* or *ODI* driver.

NEARnet

One of the regional networks originally set up to work with the NSFNET, headquartered in New England.

network

Don't get us started. Lots of things are called networks, but for our purposes, we are talking about lots of computers that are connected together. Those in the same or nearby buildings are called *local area networks,* those that are farther away are called *wide area networks,* and when you interconnect a large number of networks all over the world, you get the Internet! For more than you want to know about how networks are connected together into the Internet, see Chapter 6 in this book and Chapters 2 and 3 in *MORE Internet For Dummies.*

network layer protocol

The third layer of the OSI seven-layer protocol scheme. Not something you have to think about.

networking conventions

Standards that everybody, or almost everybody, agrees to so that networks can talk to each other.

news

A type of Usenet newsgroup that contains discussions about newsgroups themselves, such as `news.announce.newusers` (announcements of interest to new users). Also used to refer to Usenet itself.

news server

A computer on the Internet that not only gets Usenet newsgroups but also lets you read them. Programs such as Trumpet and Cello use a news server to get the articles for the newsgroups you request. See Chapter 12 in *MORE Internet For Dummies* to learn how to install Trumpet to read the news.

newsgroup

A distributed bulletin board system about a particular topic. Usenet news (also known as *net news*) is a system that distributes thousands of newsgroups to all parts of the Internet.

See Chapter 11 for a description of how to read newsgroups, and Chapter 12 for lists of interesting newsgroups. While you are at it, check out Chapter 12 of *MORE Internet For Dummies* to learn how to read newsgroups by using Windows programs, and Chapter 16 of that book to learn how to use advanced newsreaders such as trn and nn.

newsgroup kill file

A file that tells your newsreader which articles you always want to skip. This file applies to only a specific newsgroup (*see also **global kill file***). See Chapter 16 of *MORE Internet For Dummies* to learn how to make kill files by using trn.

newsreader

A program that lets you read the messages in Usenet newsgroups and respond if you are absolutely sure that you have something new and interesting to say. See Chapter 12 of *MORE Internet For Dummies* to learn how to use the Trumpet newsreader on your PC, and Chapter 16 to learn how to use two UNIX newsreaders, trn and nn.

NFS

Network File System, defined by Sun Microsystems; allows files on a remote computer to appear as though they're on your computer and vice versa. Notoriously buggy. Based on TCP/IP, so in principle any two computers on the Internet can share files by way of NFS.

NIC

Network Information Center. The address of the one for the U.S. part of the Internet is `rs.internic.net`. An NIC is responsible for coordinating a set of networks so that the names, network numbers, and other technical details are consistent from one network to another.

NIS

Formerly known as the *Yellow Pages,* before some trademark lawyer in the U.K. complained. The Network Information System is a facility used on some TCP/IP networks to administer a group of computers (usually UNIX workstations and PCs) as through they were one big computer. For Internet purposes, who cares? Well, NIS sorts incoming e-mail on some UNIX systems and can cause peculiar-looking mail addresses. See Chapter 4 if you care about this stuff.

NNTP server

See **news server**.

node

A computer on the Internet, also called a *host.* Computers that provide a service, such as FTP sites or places that run Gopher, are also called *servers.*

NSFNET

The National Science Foundation's network, a part of the Internet devoted to research and education and funded by government money. Chronically reported to be going away, to be replaced by pieces of commercial networks.

NYSERnet

One of the regional networks originally set up to work with the NSFNET, headquartered in New York.

OARnet

One of the regional networks originally set up to work with the NSFNET, headquartered in Ohio.

ODI

A small program used on DOS and Windows PCs to connect network software to a particular network card. Defined by Novell. Similar to *NDIS* or *packet driver*.

Open Book Repository

A collection of on-line text, including the text of books, journals, and other reference materials, maintained by the Online Book Initiative at obi.std.com.

operating system

The basic software that runs on a computer and is responsible for all the ordinary things a computer has to keep track of, such as files and disks and printers. Windows, UNIX, VMS, and System 7 are all operating systems. (MS-DOS is thought by some to be an operating system, but after careful examination, we believe that they're mistaken.)

packet

A chunk of information sent over a network. Each packet contains the address it is going to, the address of who sent it, and some other information. For more than you ever wanted to know about how the Internet handles packets, see Chapter 6 of this book and Chapter 2 of *MORE Internet For Dummies*.

packet driver

A small program used on DOS and Windows PCs to connect network software to a particular kind of network card. Similar to *NDIS* or *ODI* driver.

page

A document, or hunk of information, available by way of the World Wide Web. To make information available on WWW, you organize it into one or more pages. Each page can contain text, graphics files, sound files — you name it. Don't worry: You don't have to create WWW pages — you can just read them.

pager

A feature in *Archie* (and other programs) that breaks up the data Archie displays into chunks that fill up only one screen at a time, enabling you to read what's there before it scrolls off the screen.

parameter

A value a computer program needs to know in order to behave correctly.

password

A secret code used to keep things private. Your account on the system that connects you to the Internet is no doubt protected by a password. Be sure to pick a code that is not obvious, preferably combining numbers and letters so as to thwart any untoward activity.

password file

The file in which all the passwords for a system are stored. Most systems are smart enough to keep passwords encoded so that even if someone gains access to this file, it won't be of much value.

pine

A UNIX-based mail program based on elm. (It stands for Pine Is Nearly Elm.) Pine is easy to use, at least for a UNIX program; it's described in Chapter 17 of *MORE Internet For Dummies.*

ping

A program that checks to see whether you can communicate with another computer on the Internet. It sends a short message to which the other computer automatically responds. If you can't "ping" another computer, you probably can't talk to it any other way either. Chapter 9 of *MORE Internet For Dummies* describes how to get and use a program called Pingw for Windows systems connected to the Internet by using SLIP.

Pipeline

An Internet provider in New York City (`pipeline.com` is its address) that works with a special Windows communications program, also called Pipeline. It uses its own protocol to talk to this program, which enables it to display everything in a nice Windows-y way. Several other providers use the program, giving it different names to avoid consistency.

PKZIP

A file-compression program that runs on PCs. PKZIP creates a *ZIP file* that contains compressed versions of one or more files. To restore them to their former size and shape, you use PKUNZIP. *PK,* by the way, stands for Phil Katz, who wrote the program. PKZIP and PKUNZIP are shareware programs available from many FTP sites. If you use the programs, you are honor-bound to send Mr. Katz a donation (the program will tell you the address). If you use a Windows computer, you will probably prefer WinZip, which has nice Windows-y menus and buttons.

POP

Post Office Protocol, a system by which a mail server on the Internet lets you pick up your mail and download it to your PC or Mac. See Chapter 11 of *MORE Internet For Dummies* for how to install and run Eudora, which requires POP.

port number

On a networked computer, an identifying number assigned to each program that is chatting on the Internet. The program that handles incoming telnet sessions uses port 23, for example, and the program that handles some other service has another number. You hardly ever have to know these — the Internet programs work this stuff out among themselves. See Chapter 6.

posting

An article in a newsgroup.

PPP

Point-to-Point Protocol, a scheme for connecting two computers together over a phone line (or a network link that acts like a phone line). Like *SLIP*, only better. See Chapter 2 of *MORE Internet For Dummies*.

Prodigy

A large on-line system run by IBM and Sears. If you have a Prodigy account, your Internet address is `username@prodigy.com`, substituting your username for `username`.

protocol

A system that two computers agree on. When you use a file-transfer protocol, for example, the two computers involved (the sender and the receiver) agree on a set of signals that mean "go ahead" and "got it" and "didn't get it, please resend" and "all done." The Internet involves tons of different protocols as the many different types of computers on the net interact.

pseudoterminal

A fake terminal. On most systems, telnet uses a pseudoterminal to log you in and run your commands.

PSI

Performance Systems International, a large commercial Internet network.

public service provider

A time-sharing or SLIP service that enables you to use the Internet on a paying (by the month or hour) basis. Chapter 27 lists some of them.

RCP

Remote Copy, a UNIX command that lets you copy files from one computer to another. See Chapter 16 for details.

rec

A type of newsgroup that discusses recreational topics, such as `rec.humor.funny` (jokes that are sometimes funny) and `rec.gardens` (guess). See Chapter 12 for lists of interesting newsgroups.

recursive

Sort of like reincarnation, only more technical. Commands that call themselves are called recursive. If you want to list all the files in a hierarchical file structure, for example, the list command you use might first list all the files at the top level and then call itself to list the files in the directories or folders below it. If it finds more subdirectories in these subdirectories, it calls itself again to list the layer below. And so on until a specific end condition is met.

regular expression

Not what one would usually think of as regular. For UNIX hackers and those who love to encode the ordinary into arithmetic representation. Many kinds of conditional searches (meaning, under these conditions, do this) can be represented by using mathematical expressions. If you haven't studied much math or logic, forget about it.

RMS

The file-handling part of a DEC operating system. Only if you know already should you care.

router

No, not a power tool used for finish work on fine cabinetry (that's pronounced "rowter"). This system, pronounced "rooter" in most countries, connects two or more networks together, including networks that use different types of cables and different communication speeds. The networks must use IP (Internet Protocol), though. If they don't, you need a *gateway* — see Chapter 6.

RTFM

Read The, Uh, Friendly Manual. A suggestion made by people who feel that you have wasted their time asking a question you could have found the answer to another way. A well-known and much-used FTP site named `rtfm.mit.edu` contains FAQs for all Usenet newsgroups, by the way. Read the, uh, friendly FAQ.

sci

A type of Usenet newsgroup that discusses scientific topics.

security

In the computer world, means to allow access only to those who should have access. Security includes using passwords to protect your account.

Selectric typewriter

An electric typewriter with a golfball-shaped typing element that was popular before word processing came into fashion.

serial line

A connection between computers using the serial protocol.

serial port

The place on your computer where you can plug in a serial line.

serial protocol

The simplest way to send data over a wire — one bit at a time.

server

A computer that provides a service to other computers on a network. For example, an Archie server lets people on the Internet use Archie.

shareware

Computer programs that are easily available for you to try with the understanding that if you decide that you're keeping the program, you will pay for it and send the requested amount to the shareware provider specified in the program. This is an honor system. A great deal of good stuff is available, and people's voluntary compliance makes it viable.

SIMTEL

A computer that used to contain an amazing archive of programs for MS-DOS in addition to Macintosh and UNIX. It was run by the U.S. Army in New Mexico and was shut down in 1993. Fortunately, its files live on in mirror (duplicate) archives at `oak.oakland.edu` and `wuarchive.wustl.edu`. See Chapter 18 for other top spots for FTP'-able files, as well as Chapters 21 through 23 of *MORE Internet For Dummies.*

SLIP

Short for Serial Line Internet Protocol, a software scheme for connecting a computer to the Internet over a serial line. For example, if you can run SLIP on your personal computer and you call up an Internet provider that does SLIP, your computer is actually *on the Internet;* it's not just a terminal — it's right on it. You can telnet and FTP to other computers, and when you get files, they arrive back on your PC, not on the Internet provider's computer. For instructions about how to run SLIP on your computer, see Chapter 9 of *MORE Internet For Dummies.*

SMTP

Simple Mail Transfer Protocol, the optimistically named method by which Internet mail is delivered from one computer to another.

soc

A type of newsgroup that discusses social topics, covering subjects from `soc.men` to `soc.religion.buddhist` to `soc.culture.canada`. See Chapter 12 for lists of interesting newsgroups.

socket

A logical "port" a program uses to connect to another program running on another computer on the Internet. You might have an FTP program using sockets for its FTP session, for example, while Eudora connects by way of another socket to get your mail.

software

Computer programs that make computers usable as something other than a paperweight. Compare to *hardware*.

Spam

Originally a meat-related sandwich-filling product. The word is now used to refer to the act of posting inappropriate commercial messages to a large number of unrelated, uninterested Usenet newsgroups. See Chapter 23. Also see the section "I don't like Spam!" in Chapter 22 of *MORE Internet For Dummies*.

Sprintlink

One of the large commercial networks in the Internet, run by Sprint (the telephone company).

Sprintmail

An e-mail system provided by Sprintnet and formerly named Telemail. Believe it or not, if you have a Sprintmail account, your Internet address is `/G=firstname/S=lastname/O=company/C=countrycode/A=TELEMAIL/@sprint.com`. Substitute your first name, last name, company name, and country code (`us` for United States folks).

string

A bunch of characters strung together, like "Internet For Dummies." Strings are composed of any characters available in the character set being used, typically all letters, digits, and punctuation.

subdirectory

A directory within a directory.

substring

A piece of a string. *See* **string**.

SURAnet

One of the regional networks originally set up to work with the NSFNET, headquartered in Florida.

System 7

The latest, most feature-laden, Macintosh operating system.

talk

A type of newsgroup that contains endless arguments about a wide range of issues, such as `talk.abortion` and `talk.rumors`. See Chapter 12 for lists of interesting newsgroups.

TCP/IP

The system networks use to communicate with each other on the Internet. It stands for Transmission Control Protocol/Internet Protocol, if you care. See Chapter 6 in this book and Chapters 2 and 3 of *MORE Internet For Dummies* for the gory details.

telnet

A program that lets you log in to other computers on the net. See Chapter 14 to learn how to telnet to another computer (that is, log on to it from afar) and Chapter 15 for a list of interesting computers to telnet to.

terminal

In the olden days, a terminal was a thing consisting of a screen, a keyboard, and a cable that connected it to a computer. These days, not many people (not many people *we* know) use terminals, because personal computers are so cheap. Why have a brainless screen and keyboard when you can have your own computer on your desk? Of course, there are still lots of times when you want to connect to a big computer somewhere. If you have a personal computer, you can run a program that makes it *pretend* to be a brainless screen and keyboard — the program is called a *terminal emulator, terminal program,* or *communications program.*

terminal emulator

See **communications program** and **terminal**.

terminal program

See **communications program** and **terminal**.

text file

A file that contains only textual characters, with no special formatting characters, graphical information, sound clips, video, or what-have-you. Most computers other than some IBM mainframes store their text by using a system of codes named *ASCII,* so these are also known as *ASCII text files.*

third party

Sometimes you buy your computer from one place and your operating software from somewhere else, but you find that you still need other hardware or software pieces to make it all work. The people from whom you buy those other pieces are known as third-party vendors.

Token Ring

A way of connecting computers in a local area network. A competitor of Ethernet.

thread

An article posted to a Usenet newsgroup, together with all the follow-up articles, the follow-ups to follow-ups, and so on. Organizing articles into threads makes it easier to choose which articles in a newsgroup you want to read. See Chapter 11 in this book and Chapter 16 of *MORE Internet For Dummies* for a description of a newsreader that enables you to choose which threads to read.

threaded newsreader

A newsreader that enables you to select articles by thread. See Chapter 11 in this book and Chapter 12 of *MORE Internet For Dummies* for a description of vnews, a threaded newsreader for Windows, and Chapter 16 in that book for trn, a threaded newsreader for UNIX.

Trumpet

A cool newsreader program that runs on computers that run Windows. Chapter 12 of *MORE Internet For Dummies* tells you all about it. Only slightly related (in that it was written by the same guy) to Trumpet *Winsock,* a separate program that provides TCP/IP connections for Windows PCs.

UNIX

An operating system everyone hates. No, an operating system everyone ought to love. No, it's both! It's an operating system that can be confusing to use, but it sure is powerful. Internet users are likely to run into UNIX if they use The World or another shell provider as their Internet provider or when they telnet to UNIX computers. For the truth about UNIX, get a copy of *UNIX For Dummies.*

upload

To put your stuff on somebody else's computer (see Chapter 16).

URL

Uniform Resource Locator, a way of naming network resources, originally for linking pages together in the World Wide Web. Luckily, you don't have to know much about them — only the people who *write* WWW pages really have to fool with them. See Chapter 22.

Usenet

A system of thousands of distributed bulletin boards called *newsgroups.* You read the messages by using a program called a *newsreader.* See Chapters 11 and 12 for an introduction to newsgroups and a list of some interesting ones.

UUCP

An elderly and creaky (but cheap) mail system still used by many UNIX systems. UUCP stands for UNIX-to-UNIX-copy. UUCP uses mail address that contain exclamation points rather than periods between the parts (and they are in reverse order), a method known as *bang path addressing.* Whenever possible, use regular Internet addresses instead.

uuencode/uudecode

Programs that encode files to make them suitable for sending as e-mail. Because e-mail messages must be text, not binary information, *uuencode* can disguise nontext files as text so that you can include them in a mail message. When the message is received, the recipient can run *uudecode* to turn it back into the original file. Pretty clever. For more information, see Chapter 17.

UUNET

A nonprofit organization that, among other things, runs a large Internet site that links the UUCP mail network with the Internet and has a large and useful FTP file archive. See it in addresses that contain uunet.uu.net at the end. It also runs Alternet, one of the larger commercial network providers.

V.32

The code word for a nice, fast modem (one that talks at a speed of 9600 bits per second). Even faster modems (that talk at 14,400 bits per second) are called V.32bis, French for V.32-and-a-half.

VAX/VMS

Digital Equipment's major computer line over the last 15 years is the VAX, and its proprietary operating system is known as VMS.

Veronica

A program that finds things in Gopherspace (see Chapter 20); friend of Archie's.

version creep

A problem that occurs when lots of people are adding features to programs that people are already using. Unless care is taken to keep programs compatible, sooner or later the program you're using won't talk to its "new and improved cousin" until you get the latest and greatest version that should make everybody happy 'til they add more features again.

viewer

A program used by Gopher, WAIS, or World Wide Web client programs to show you files that contain stuff other than text. For example, you might want viewers to display graphics files, play sound files, or display video files.

VT100

The part number of a terminal made about 15 years ago by the Digital Equipment Corporation. Why do you care? Because many computers on the Internet expect to talk to VT-100-type terminals, and many communications programs can pretend to be (emulate) VT-100 terminals. See Chapter 4 for more information about communications programs and terminals. The VT102 was a cheaper version that for most purposes acted exactly the same.

WAIS

Wide Area Information Servers (pronounced "ways," not "wace"), a system that lets you search for documents that contain the information you are looking for. It's not supereasy to use, but it gets there. See Chapter 21 in this book to learn how to use WAIS, and see Chapter 14 of *MORE Internet For Dummies* for even more info about it.

WELL

The WELL (the Whole Earth 'Lectronic Link) is a public Internet provider in Sausalito, California. You can contact it at info@well.sf.ca.us.

whois

A command on some systems that tells you the actual name of someone, based on the person's username. *See also **finger**.* You can use whois by way of the World Wide Web — see Chapter 15 of *MORE Internet For Dummies.*

Windows

An operating system for the PC that includes a graphical user interface; also a religion.

Windows95

The version of Windows after 3.1. Windows95 is supposed to include (we can't say for sure because at the time we wrote this book, the product was nowhere near being released) built-in support for TCP/IP, the Internet's networking scheme, which will probably work by the time they ship Windows 4.12.

WinGopher

A Windows program that lets you see Gopher pages. See Chapter 14 of *MORE Internet For Dummies* to learn how to get, install, and use it.

WinSock

WinSock (short for Windows Sockets) is a standard way for Windows programs to work with TCP/IP. You use it if you directly connect your Windows PC to the Internet, either with a permanent connection or with a modem by using SLIP or PPP. Chapter 28 lists a bunch of WinSock packages and programs that run by using WinSock.

WinWAIS

A Windows-based program that lets you use WAIS to search for information about the Internet. See Chapter 21 in this book and Chapter 14 in *MORE Internet For Dummies* about both WAIS and WinWAIS.

WinZip

A Windows-based program for zipping and unzipping ZIP files in addition to other standard types of archive files. WinZip is shareware, so you can get it form the net. See Chapter 10 of *MORE Internet For Dummies* to learn how to get WinZip and install it.

Workstation

Though this term gets bandied about in a lot of different contexts, we generally mean high-powered microcomputers with big screens, somewhat overkill for the average PC user. We mean things like SPARCstations and other typically single-user but very powerful machines, generally running UNIX.

World

The World is a widely used Internet shell provider, described in Chapter 6 of *MORE Internet For Dummies.* If you have an account on The World, your e-mail address is username@world.std.com.

WWW (World Wide Web)

A hypermedia system that lets you browse through lots of interesting information. See Chapter 22 in this book for an introduction, and then check out Chapter 15 of *MORE Internet For Dummies* for the latest in PC programs that make the WWW even niftier. The best-known WWW client is Mosaic.

X.25

A protocol defining packet switching. You shouldn't care. The thing that TCP/IP is much better than.

X.75

The way you splice X.25 networks together, which shouldn't interest you either.

X Terminal

A terminal that uses the X graphical user interface. This interface enables you to open lots of windows on your screen and do all kinds of things at the same time. Popular in the UNIX world.

xarchie

A version of *Archie* that runs on UNIX under X Windows. If you use a UNIX workstation and Motif (or another windowing system), try typing **xarchie** to see whether you have a copy. If you do, see Chapter 19 to learn how it works.

xgopher

A version of Gopher that runs on UNIX under X Windows. If you use a UNIX workstation and Motif, try running xgopher.

xmodem

A file-transfer protocol developed ages ago (1981?) by Ward Christiansen to check for errors as files are transferred. It has since been superseded by ymodem and zmodem, but many programs (especially Windows Terminal) still use it. See Chapter 4 of *MORE Internet For Dummies* for information about transferring files.

xwais

A version of WAIS that runs on UNIX under X Windows. If you use a UNIX workstation and Motif, try running xwais.

Yellow Pages

See **NIS**.

ymodem

A file-transfer protocol that is faster than xmodem but not as powerful as ZMODEM. See Chapter 4 of *MORE Internet For Dummies.*

ZIP file

A file that has been created by using WinZip, PKZIP, or a compatible program. It contains one or more files that have been compressed and glommed together to save space. To get at the files in a ZIP file, you usually need WinZip, PKUNZIP, or a compatible program. Sometimes you may get a self-extracting file, which is a ZIP file that contains the unzipping program right in it. Just run the file (that is, type the name of the file at the command line), and it will unzip itself. For information about how to get and set up WinZip on a Windows computer, see Chapter 10 of *MORE Internet For Dummies.*

zmodem

A fast file-transfer protocol defined by Chuck Forsberg, used by many programs. With zmodem, you can transfer several files with one command, and the names of the files are sent along with them. Some communications programs (such as Procomm) can detect when a zmodem transfer has begun and automatically begin receiving the files. Nifty. See Chapter 4 of *MORE Internet For Dummies* for more info.

Index

• J •

• K •

• X •

Drowning in the sea of Internet access?
Get to the shore!

North Shore Access

SLIP/PPP
$30/month
$50 set-up fee.

info@shore.net

Shell account
$9/month
No sign-up fee.

A service of Eco Software, Inc.
145 Munroe Street, Suite 405
Lynn, MA 01901
(617) 593-3110

Installation
and Training
Available

No-risk 3 hour trial

All accounts include prompt and friendly customer support, full Internet access,
ClariNews, Commerce Business Daily. Personal FTP, Gopher and Web servers no extra
charge. Sun Microsystems hardware.

Dial (617) 593-4557 (8 bit/no parity/1 stop bit), or telnet shore.net. Login as 'new'.

MV Communications, Inc.   Public Access Internet
_____   _____

PO Box 4963   voice: 603-429-2223
Manchester, NH 03103   modem: 603-424-7428
                                           login as `info`

Email: `info@mv.mv.com` for an autoreply with detailed info;
       `mv-admin@mv.mv.com` to reach a staff person.

Providing:

- SLIP/PPP Internet   - World Wide Web (WWW)
- Online accounts   - Gopher
- UUCP access   - Telnet
- Electronic Mail   - FTP
- Usenet news   - ClariNet news
- NH Statewide access   - Low cost and free trials
- Local calls in many towns   - NH 1-800 access via InfoPath
- UNIX shell   - User-friendly menus
- Corporate accounts   - Personal accounts
- Full commercial access
   (CIX member)
- Domain forwarding

Most accounts have no setup fees, with free trials.
Present this coupon for a $10 credit against usage.
Limit one per customer.

The fun & easy way to learn about computers and more!

11/11/94

Windows 3.1 For Dummies™, 2nd Edition
by Andy Rathbone

ISBN: 1-56884-182-5
$16.95 USA/$22.95 Canada

MORE Windows For Dummies™
by Andy Rathbone

ISBN: 1-56884-048-9
$19.95 USA/$26.95 Canada

DOS For Dummies®, 2nd Edition
by Dan Gookin

ISBN: 1-878058-75-4
$16.95 USA/$21.95 Canada

The Internet For Dummies™ 2nd Edition
by John R. Levine & Carol Baroudi

ISBN: 1-56884-222-8
$19.99 USA/$26.99 Canada

Personal Finance For Dummies™
by Eric Tyson

ISBN: 1-56884-150-7
$16.95 USA/$21.95 Canada

PCs For Dummies™, 2nd Edition
by Dan Gookin & Andy Rathbone

ISBN: 1-56884-078-0
$16.95 USA/$21.95 Canada

Macs For Dummies®, 2nd Edition
by David Pogue

ISBN: 1-56884-051-9
$19.95 USA/$26.95 Canada

Over 12 Million in print!

Here's a complete listing of IDG's ...For Dummies Titles

Title	Author	ISBN	Price
DATABASE			
Access 2 For Dummies™	by Scott Palmer	1-56884-090-X	$19.95 USA/$26.95 Canada
Access Programming For Dummies™	by Rob Krumm	1-56884-091-8	$19.95 USA/$26.95 Canada
Approach 3 For Windows For Dummies™	by Doug Lowe	1-56884-233-3	$19.99 USA/$26.99 Canada
dBASE For DOS For Dummies™	by Scott Palmer & Michael Stabler	1-56884-188-4	$19.95 USA/$26.95 Canada
dBASE For Windows For Dummies™	by Scott Palmer	1-56884-179-5	$19.95 USA/$26.95 Canada
dBASE 5 For Windows Programming For Dummies™	by Ted Coombs & Jason Coombs	1-56884-215-5	$19.99 USA/$26.99 Canada
FoxPro 2.6 For Windows For Dummies™	by John Kaufeld	1-56884-187-6	$19.95 USA/$26.95 Canada
Paradox 5 For Windows For Dummies™	by John Kaufeld	1-56884-185-X	$19.95 USA/$26.95 Canada
DESKTOP PUBLISHING / ILLUSTRATION / GRAPHICS			
CorelDRAW! 5 For Dummies™	by Deke McClelland	1-56884-157-4	$19.95 USA/$26.95 Canada
CorelDRAW! For Dummies™	by Deke McClelland	1-56884-042-X	$19.95 USA/$26.95 Canada
Harvard Graphics 2 For Windows For Dummies™	by Roger C. Parker	1-56884-092-6	$19.95 USA/$26.95 Canada
PageMaker 5 For Macs For Dummies™	by Galen Gruman	1-56884-178-7	$19.95 USA/$26.95 Canada
PageMaker 5 For Windows For Dummies™	by Deke McClelland & Galen Gruman	1-56884-160-4	$19.95 USA/$26.95 Canada
QuarkXPress 3.3 For Dummies™	by Galen Gruman & Barbara Assadi	1-56884-217-1	$19.99 USA/$26.99 Canada
FINANCE / PERSONAL FINANCE / TEST TAKING REFERENCE			
QuickBooks 3 For Dummies™	by Stephen L. Nelson	1-56884-227-9	$19.99 USA/$26.99 Canada
Quicken 8 For DOS For Dummies™, 2nd Edition	by Stephen L. Nelson	1-56884-210-4	$19.95 USA/$26.95 Canada
Quicken 5 For Macs For Dummies™	by Stephen L. Nelson	1-56884-211-2	$19.95 USA/$26.95 Canada
Quicken 4 For Windows For Dummies™, 2nd Edition	by Stephen L. Nelson	1-56884-209-0	$19.95 USA/$26.95 Canada
The SAT I For Dummies™	by Suzee Vlk	1-56884-213-9	$14.99 USA/$20.99 Canada
GROUPWARE / INTEGRATED			
Lotus Notes 3/3.1 For Dummies™	by Paul Freeland & Stephen Londergan	1-56884-212-0	$19.95 USA/$26.95 Canada
Microsoft Office 4 For Windows For Dummies™	by Roger C. Parker	1-56884-183-3	$19.95 USA/$26.95 Canada
Microsoft Works 3 For Windows For Dummies™	by David C. Kay	1-56884-214-7	$19.99 USA/$26.99 Canada

FOR MORE INFORMATION OR TO ORDER, PLEASE CALL ▶ 800 762 2974

For volume discounts & special orders please call
Tony Real, Special Sales, at 415. 312. 0650

Title	Author	ISBN	Price
INTERNET / COMMUNICATIONS / NETWORKING			11/11/94
CompuServe For Dummies™	by Wallace Wang	1-56884-181-7	$19.95 USA/$26.95 Canada
Modems For Dummies™, 2nd Edition	by Tina Rathbone	1-56884-223-6	$19.99 USA/$26.99 Canada
Modems For Dummies™	by Tina Rathbone	1-56884-001-2	$19.95 USA/$26.95 Canada
MORE Internet For Dummies™	by John R. Levine & Margaret Levine Young	1-56884-164-7	$19.95 USA/$26.95 Canada
NetWare For Dummies™	by Ed Tittel & Deni Connor	1-56884-003-9	$19.95 USA/$26.95 Canada
Networking For Dummies™	by Doug Lowe	1-56884-079-9	$19.95 USA/$26.95 Canada
ProComm Plus 2 For Windows For Dummies™	by Wallace Wang	1-56884-219-8	$19.99 USA/$26.99 Canada
The Internet For Dummies™, 2nd Edition	by John R. Levine & Carol Baroudi	1-56884-222-8	$19.99 USA/$26.99 Canada
The Internet For Macs For Dummies™	by Charles Seiter	1-56884-184-1	$19.95 USA/$26.95 Canada
MACINTOSH			
Macs For Dummies®	by David Pogue	1-56884-173-6	$19.95 USA/$26.95 Canada
Macintosh System 7.5 For Dummies™	by Bob LeVitus	1-56884-197-3	$19.95 USA/$26.95 Canada
MORE Macs For Dummies™	by David Pogue	1-56884-087-X	$19.95 USA/$26.95 Canada
PageMaker 5 For Macs For Dummies™	by Galen Gruman	1-56884-178-7	$19.95 USA/$26.95 Canada
QuarkXPress 3.3 For Dummies™	by Galen Gruman & Barbara Assadi	1-56884-217-1	$19.99 USA/$26.99 Canada
Upgrading and Fixing Macs For Dummies™	by Kearney Rietmann & Frank Higgins	1-56884-189-2	$19.95 USA/$26.95 Canada
MULTIMEDIA			
Multimedia & CD-ROMs For Dummies™, Interactive Multimedia Value Pack	by Andy Rathbone	1-56884-225-2	$29.95 USA/$39.95 Canada
Multimedia & CD-ROMs For Dummies™	by Andy Rathbone	1-56884-089-6	$19.95 USA/$26.95 Canada
OPERATING SYSTEMS / DOS			
MORE DOS For Dummies™	by Dan Gookin	1-56884-046-2	$19.95 USA/$26.95 Canada
S.O.S. For DOS™	by Katherine Murray	1-56884-043-8	$12.95 USA/$16.95 Canada
OS/2 For Dummies™	by Andy Rathbone	1-878058-76-2	$19.95 USA/$26.95 Canada
UNIX			
UNIX For Dummies™	by John R. Levine & Margaret Levine Young	1-878058-58-4	$19.95 USA/$26.95 Canada
WINDOWS			
S.O.S. For Windows™	by Katherine Murray	1-56884-045-4	$12.95 USA/$16.95 Canada
MORE Windows 3.1 For Dummies™, 3rd Edition	by Andy Rathbone	1-56884-240-6	$19.99 USA/$26.99 Canada
PCs / HARDWARE			
Illustrated Computer Dictionary For Dummies™	by Dan Gookin, Wally Wang, & Chris Van Buren	1-56884-004-7	$12.95 USA/$16.95 Canada
Upgrading and Fixing PCs For Dummies™	by Andy Rathbone	1-56884-002-0	$19.95 USA/$26.95 Canada
PRESENTATION / AUTOCAD			
AutoCAD For Dummies™	by Bud Smith	1-56884-191-4	$19.95 USA/$26.95 Canada
PowerPoint 4 For Windows For Dummies™	by Doug Lowe	1-56884-161-2	$16.95 USA/$22.95 Canada
PROGRAMMING			
Borland C++ For Dummies™	by Michael Hyman	1-56884-162-0	$19.95 USA/$26.95 Canada
"Borland's New Language Product" For Dummies™	by Neil Rubenking	1-56884-200-7	$19.95 USA/$26.95 Canada
C For Dummies™	by Dan Gookin	1-878058-78-9	$19.95 USA/$26.95 Canada
C++ For Dummies™	by Stephen R. Davis	1-56884-163-9	$19.95 USA/$26.95 Canada
Mac Programming For Dummies™	by Dan Parks Sydow	1-56884-173-6	$19.95 USA/$26.95 Canada
QBasic Programming For Dummies™	by Douglas Hergert	1-56884-093-4	$19.95 USA/$26.95 Canada
Visual Basic "X" For Dummies™, 2nd Edition	by Wallace Wang	1-56884-230-9	$19.99 USA/$26.99 Canada
Visual Basic 3 For Dummies™	by Wallace Wang	1-56884-076-4	$19.95 USA/$26.95 Canada
SPREADSHEET			
1-2-3 For Dummies™	by Greg Harvey	1-878058-60-6	$16.95 USA/$21.95 Canada
1-2-3 For Windows 5 For Dummies™, 2nd Edition	by John Walkenbach	1-56884-216-3	$16.95 USA/$21.95 Canada
1-2-3 For Windows For Dummies™	by John Walkenbach	1-56884-052-7	$16.95 USA/$21.95 Canada
Excel 5 For Macs For Dummies™	by Greg Harvey	1-56884-186-8	$19.95 USA/$26.95 Canada
Excel For Dummies™, 2nd Edition	by Greg Harvey	1-56884-050-0	$16.95 USA/$21.95 Canada
MORE Excel 5 For Windows For Dummies™	by Greg Harvey	1-56884-207-4	$19.95 USA/$26.95 Canada
Quattro Pro 6 For Windows For Dummies™	by John Walkenbach	1-56884-174-4	$19.95 USA/$26.95 Canada
Quattro Pro For DOS For Dummies™	by John Walkenbach	1-56884-023-3	$16.95 USA/$21.95 Canada
UTILITIES / VCRs & CAMCORDERS			
Norton Utilities 8 For Dummies™	by Beth Slick	1-56884-166-3	$19.95 USA/$26.95 Canada
VCRs & Camcorders For Dummies™	by Andy Rathbone & Gordon McComb	1-56884-229-5	$14.99 USA/$20.99 Canada
WORD PROCESSING			
Ami Pro For Dummies™	by Jim Meade	1-56884-049-7	$19.95 USA/$26.95 Canada
MORE Word For Windows 6 For Dummies™	by Doug Lowe	1-56884-165-5	$19.95 USA/$26.95 Canada
MORE WordPerfect 6 For Windows For Dummies™	by Margaret Levine Young & David C. Kay	1-56884-206-6	$19.95 USA/$26.95 Canada
MORE WordPerfect 6 For DOS For Dummies™	by Wallace Wang, edited by Dan Gookin	1-56884-047-0	$19.95 USA/$26.95 Canada
S.O.S. For WordPerfect™	by Katherine Murray	1-56884-053-5	$12.95 USA/$16.95 Canada
Word 6 For Macs For Dummies™	by Dan Gookin	1-56884-190-6	$19.95 USA/$26.95 Canada
Word For Windows 6 For Dummies™	by Dan Gookin	1-56884-075-6	$16.95 USA/$21.95 Canada
Word For Windows For Dummies™	by Dan Gookin	1-878058-86-X	$16.95 USA/$21.95 Canada
WordPerfect 6 For Dummies™	by Dan Gookin	1-878058-77-0	$16.95 USA/$21.95 Canada
WordPerfect For Dummies™	by Dan Gookin	1-878058-52-5	$16.95 USA/$21.95 Canada
WordPerfect For Windows For Dummies™	by Margaret Levine Young & David C. Kay	1-56884-032-2	$16.95 USA/$21.95 Canada

FOR MORE INFORMATION OR TO ORDER, PLEASE CALL ▶ 800 762 2974

For volume discounts & special orders please call
Tony Real, Special Sales, at 415. 312. 0650

Fun, Fast, & Cheap!

NEW!

CorelDRAW! 5 For Dummies™ Quick Reference
by Raymond E. Werner

ISBN: 1-56884-952-4
$9.99 USA/$12.99 Canada

NEW!

Windows "X" For Dummies™ Quick Reference, 3rd Edition
by Greg Harvey

ISBN: 1-56884-964-8
$9.99 USA/$12.99 Canada

SUPER STAR

Word For Windows 6 For Dummies™ Quick Reference
by George Lynch

ISBN: 1-56884-095-0
$8.95 USA/$12.95 Canada

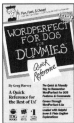

SUPER STAR

WordPerfect For DOS For Dummies™ Quick Reference
by Greg Harvey

ISBN: 1-56884-009-8
$8.95 USA/$11.95 Canada

Title	Author	ISBN	Price
DATABASE			
Access 2 For Dummies™ Quick Reference	by Stuart A. Stuple	1-56884-167-1	$8.95 USA/$11.95 Canada
dBASE 5 For DOS For Dummies™ Quick Reference	by Barry Sosinsky	1-56884-954-0	$9.99 USA/$12.99 Canada
dBASE 5 For Windows For Dummies™ Quick Reference	by Stuart J. Stuple	1-56884-953-2	$9.99 USA/$12.99 Canada
Paradox 5 For Windows For Dummies™ Quick Reference	by Scott Palmer	1-56884-960-5	$9.99 USA/$12.99 Canada
DESKTOP PUBLISHING / ILLUSTRATION/GRAPHICS			
Harvard Graphics 3 For Windows For Dummies™ Quick Reference	by Raymond E. Werner	1-56884-962-1	$9.99 USA/$12.99 Canada
FINANCE / PERSONAL FINANCE			
Quicken 4 For Windows For Dummies™ Quick Reference	by Stephen L. Nelson	1-56884-950-8	$9.95 USA/$12.95 Canada
GROUPWARE / INTEGRATED			
Microsoft Office 4 For Windows For Dummies™ Quick Reference	by Doug Lowe	1-56884-958-3	$9.99 USA/$12.99 Canada
Microsoft Works For Windows 3 For Dummies™ Quick Reference	by Michael Partington	1-56884-959-1	$9.99 USA/$12.99 Canada
INTERNET / COMMUNICATIONS / NETWORKING			
The Internet For Dummies™ Quick Reference	by John R. Levine	1-56884-168-X	$8.95 USA/$11.95 Canada
MACINTOSH			
Macintosh System 7.5 For Dummies™ Quick Reference	by Stuart J. Stuple	1-56884-956-7	$9.99 USA/$12.99 Canada
OPERATING SYSTEMS / DOS			
DOS For Dummies® Quick Reference	by Greg Harvey	1-56884-007-1	$8.95 USA/$11.95 Canada
UNIX			
UNIX For Dummies™ Quick Reference	by Margaret Levine Young & John R. Levine	1-56884-094-2	$8.95 USA/$11.95 Canada
WINDOWS			
Windows 3.1 For Dummies™ Quick Reference, 2nd Edition	by Greg Harvey	1-56884-951-6	$8.95 USA/$11.95 Canada
PRESENTATION / AUTOCAD			
AutoCAD For Dummies™ Quick Reference	by Bud Smith	1-56884-198-1	$9.95 USA/$12.95 Canada
SPREADSHEET			
1-2-3 For Dummies™ Quick Reference	by John Walkenbach	1-56884-027-6	$8.95 USA/$11.95 Canada
1-2-3 For Windows 5 For Dummies™ Quick Reference	by John Walkenbach	1-56884-957-5	$9.95 USA/$12.95 Canada
Excel For Windows For Dummies™ Quick Reference, 2nd Edition	by John Walkenbach	1-56884-096-9	$8.95 USA/$11.95 Canada
Quattro Pro 6 For Windows For Dummies™ Quick Reference	by Stuart A. Stuple	1-56884-172-8	$9.95 USA/$12.95 Canada
WORD PROCESSING			
Word For Windows 6 For Dummies™ Quick Reference	by George Lynch	1-56884-095-0	$8.95 USA/$11.95 Canada
WordPerfect For Windows For Dummies™ Quick Reference	by Greg Harvey	1-56884-039-X	$8.95 USA/$11.95 Canada

11/11/94

"An essential guide for anyone managing Mac networks."

Reese Jones, CEO, Farallon Computing, on Macworld Networking Handbook

Demystify the Mac!

Macworld books are built like your Macintosh

— Powerful, Easy, Fun,

and at a Great Value!

"I sell Macs and will recommend this book to my customers. Best computer book I have ever owned."

John Schultz, McLean, VA, on Macworld Macintosh SECRETS

Macworld System 7.5 Bible, 3rd Edition
by Lon Poole

ISBN: 1-56884-098-5
$29.95 USA/$39.95 Canada

NATIONAL BESTSELLER!

Macworld Mac & Power Mac SECRETS,™ 2nd Edition
by David Pogue & Joseph Schorr

ISBN: 1-56884-175-2
$39.95 USA/$54.95 Canada

Includes 3 disks chock full of software.

Macworld Complete Mac Handbook + Interactive CD, 3rd Edition
by Jim Heid

ISBN: 1-56884-192-2
$39.95 USA/$54.95 Canada

Includes an interactive CD-ROM.

Macworld Ultimate Mac CD-ROM
by Jim Heid

ISBN: 1-56884-477-8
$19.99 USA/$26.99 Canada

CD-ROM includes version 2.0 of QuickTime, and over 65 MB of the best shareware, freeware, fonts, sounds, and more!

Macworld Networking Bible, 2nd Edition
by Dave Kosiur & Joel M. Snyder

ISBN: 1-56884-194-9
$29.95 USA/$39.95 Canada

Macworld Photoshop 3 Bible, 2nd Edition
by Deke McClelland

ISBN: 1-56884-158-2
$39.95 USA/$54.95 Canada

Includes stunning CD-ROM with add-ons, digitized photos, new filters from Kai's Power Tools, and more.

NEW!

Macworld Photoshop 2.5 Bible
by Deke McClelland

ISBN: 1-56884-022-5
$29.95 USA/$39.95 Canada

NATIONAL BESTSELLER!

Macworld FreeHand 4 Bible
by Deke McClelland

ISBN: 1-56884-170-1
$29.95 USA/$39.95 Canada

Macworld Illustrator 5.0/5.5 Bible
by Ted Alspach

ISBN: 1-56884-097-7
$39.95 USA/$54.95 Canada

Includes CD-ROM with QuickTime tutorials.

FOR MORE INFORMATION OR TO ORDER, PLEASE CALL ▶ 800 762 2974

For volume discounts & special orders please call
Tony Real, Special Sales, at 415. 312. 0650

11/11/94

"*Macworld Complete
Mac Handbook Plus
CD* covered everything
I could think of and
more!"

Peter Tsakiris, New York, NY

"**Thanks for the best
computer book I've
ever read —** *Photoshop
2.5 Bible* ▸ **Best $30 I
ever spent. I** *love* **the
detailed index...Yours
blows them all out of
the water. This is a
great book. We must
enlighten the masses!**"

Kevin Lisankie, Chicago, Illinois

"*Macworld Guide to
ClarisWorks 2* is the
easiest computer book
to read that I have
ever found!"

Steven Hanson, Lutz, FL

Macworld
QuarkXPress
3.2/3.3 Bible

*by Barbara Assadi
& Galen Gruman*

ISBN: 1-878058-85-1
$39.95 USA/$52.95 Canada

*Includes disk with
QuarkXPress XTensions
and scripts.*

Macworld
PageMaker 5 Bible

by Craig Danuloff

ISBN: 1-878058-84-3
$39.95 USA/$52.95 Canada

*Includes 2 disks with
Pagemaker utilities, clip art,
and more.*

Macworld FileMaker
Pro 2.0/2.1 Bible

by Steven A. Schwartz

ISBN: 1-56884-201-5
$34.95 USA/$46.95 Canada

*Includes disk with ready-to-run
databases.*

Macworld
Word 6 Companion,
2nd Edition

by Jim Heid

ISBN: 1-56884-082-9
$24.95 USA/$34.95 Canada

Macworld Guide To
Microsoft Word 5/5.1

by Jim Heid

ISBN: 1-878058-39-8
$22.95 USA/$29.95 Canada

Macworld
ClarisWorks 2.0/2.1
Companion,
2nd Edition

by Steven A. Schwartz

ISBN: 1-56884-180-9
$24.95 USA/$34.95 Canada

Macworld Guide To
Microsoft Works 3

by Barrie Sosinsky

ISBN: 1-878058-42-8
$22.95 USA/$29.95 Canada

Macworld
Excel 5 Companion,
2nd Edition

*by Chris Van Buren
& David Maguiness*

ISBN: 1-56884-081-0
$24.95 USA/$34.95 Canada

Macworld Guide To
Microsoft Excel 4

by David Maguiness

ISBN: 1-878058-40-1
$22.95 USA/$29.95 Canada

FOR MORE INFORMATION OR TO ORDER, PLEASE CALL ▸ **800. 762. 2974**

For volume discounts & special orders please call
Tony Real, Special Sales, at 415. 312. 0650

IDG BOOKS

Order Center: **(800) 762-2974** *(8 a.m.–6 p.m., EST, weekdays)*

11/11/94

Quantity	ISBN	Title	Price	Total

Shipping & Handling Charges

	Description	First book	Each additional book	Total
Domestic	Normal	$4.50	$1.50	$
	Two Day Air	$8.50	$2.50	$
	Overnight	$18.00	$3.00	$
International	Surface	$8.00	$8.00	$
	Airmail	$16.00	$16.00	$
	DHL Air	$17.00	$17.00	$

*For large quantities call for shipping & handling charges.
**Prices are subject to change without notice.

Ship to:

Name _____

Company _____

Address _____

City/State/Zip _____

Daytime Phone _____

Payment: ☐ Check to IDG Books (US Funds Only)

☐ VISA   ☐ MasterCard   ☐ American Express

Card # _____ Expires _____

Signature _____

Subtotal _____

CA residents add
applicable sales tax _____

IN, MA, and MD
residents add
5% sales tax _____

IL residents add
6.25% sales tax _____

RI residents add
7% sales tax _____

TX residents add
8.25% sales tax _____

Shipping _____

Total _____

Please send this order form to:

IDG Books Worldwide
7260 Shadeland Station, Suite 100
Indianapolis, IN 46256

Allow up to 3 weeks for delivery.
Thank you!

IDG BOOKS WORLDWIDE REGISTRATION CARD

RETURN THIS
REGISTRATION CARD
FOR FREE CATALOG

Title of this book: The Internet For Dummies, 2E

My overall rating of this book: ❑ Very good [1] ❑ Good [2] ❑ Satisfactory [3] ❑ Fair [4] ❑ Poor [5]

How I first heard about this book:

❑ Found in bookstore; name: [6]

❑ Advertisement: [8]

❑ Word of mouth; heard about book from friend, co-worker, etc.: [10]

❑ Book review: [7]

❑ Catalog: [9]

❑ Other: [11]

What I liked most about this book:

What I would change, add, delete, etc., in future editions of this book:

Other comments:

Number of computer books I purchase in a year: ❑ 1 [12] ❑ 2-5 [13] ❑ 6-10 [14] ❑ More than 10 [15]

I would characterize my computer skills as: ❑ Beginner [16] ❑ Intermediate [17] ❑ Advanced [18] ❑ Professional [19]

I use ❑ DOS [20] ❑ Windows [21] ❑ OS/2 [22] ❑ Unix [23] ❑ Macintosh [24] ❑ Other: [25]_____
(please specify)

I would be interested in new books on the following subjects:
(please check all that apply, and use the spaces provided to identify specific software)

❑ Word processing: [26]

❑ Data bases: [28]

❑ File Utilities: [30]

❑ Networking: [32]

❑ Other: [34]

❑ Spreadsheets: [27]

❑ Desktop publishing: [29]

❑ Money management: [31]

❑ Programming languages: [33]

I use a PC at (please check all that apply): ❑ home [35] ❑ work [36] ❑ school [37] ❑ other: [38] _____

The disks I prefer to use are ❑ 5.25 [39] ❑ 3.5 [40] ❑ other: [41]_____

I have a CD ROM: ❑ yes [42] ❑ no [43]

I plan to buy or upgrade computer hardware this year: ❑ yes [44] ❑ no [45]

I plan to buy or upgrade computer software this year: ❑ yes [46] ❑ no [47]

Name: _____ Business title: [48] _____ Type of Business: [49] _____

Address (❑ home [50] ❑ work [51]/Company name: _____)

Street/Suite# _____

City [52]/State [53]/Zipcode [54]: _____ Country [55] _____

❑ **I liked this book!** You may quote me by name in future
IDG Books Worldwide promotional materials.

My daytime phone number is _____

**IDG
BOOKS**

THE WORLD OF
COMPUTER
KNOWLEDGE

❏ **YES!**
Please keep me informed about IDG's World of Computer Knowledge.
Send me the latest IDG Books catalog.

COMPUTER
BOOK SERIES
FROM IDG

NO POSTAGE
NECESSARY
IF MAILED
IN THE
UNITED STATES

BUSINESS REPLY MAIL
FIRST CLASS MAIL   PERMIT NO. 2605   SAN MATEO, CALIFORNIA

IDG Books Worldwide
155 Bovet Road
San Mateo, CA 94402-9833